RESISTANCE AGAINST THE THIRD REICH

Studies in European History from the
Journal of Modern History

John W. Boyer and Julius Kirshner
Series Editors

RESISTANCE

AGAINST THE

THIRD REICH

1933-1990

T291

EDITED BY

MICHAEL GEYER AND

JOHN W. BOYER

The University of Chicago Press

Chicago and London

Many of the essays in this volume originally appeared in the *Journal of Modern History*. Acknowledgment of the original publication date may be found on the first page of each such essay.

The University of Chicago Press, Chicago, 60637
The University of Chicago Press, Ltd., London
© 1992, 1994 by the University of Chicago
All rights reserved. Published 1994
Printed in the United States of America
ISBN (cl.) 0-226-06958-3
ISBN (pa.) 0-226-06959-1

98 97 96 95 94 5 4 3 2 1

Library of Congress Cataloging-in-Publication Data

Resistance against the Third Reich, 1933-1990 / edited by Michael
    Geyer and John W. Boyer.
          p.   cm.
    Papers from a conference sponsored by Interdisciplinary
Perspectives for the Study of Europe (IPSE) at the University of
Chicago and the Goethe-Institut, Chicago.
    Includes bibliographical references and index.
    ISBN 0-226-06958-3 (cl.) ISBN 0-226-06959-1 (pbk.)
    1. Anti-Nazi movement—Germany—Congresses.   2. Anti-Nazi
movement—Europe—Congresses.   3. Government, Resistance to—
Germany—Congresses.   4. Government, Resistance to—Europe—
Congresses.   5. Germany—Politics and government—1933-1945—
Congresses.   6. Europe—Politics and government—1918-1945—
Congresses.   I. Geyer, Michael.   II. Boyer, John W.   III. Title:
Resistance against the 3rd Reich, 1933-1990.
DD256.3.R38   1994
943.086—dc20   94-28406
                                                                      CIP

The paper used in this publication meets the minimum requirements of
American National Standard for Information Sciences—Permanence of Paper
for Printed Library Materials, ANSI Z39.48-1984. ∞

Contents

Nachholender Widerstand—Resistance after 1945

Acknowledgments

In March 1990 a conference on resistance to National Socialism was held at the University of Chicago which brought together scholars from a number of historical fields and scholarly points of view. The conference was sponsored by a group of social scientists and humanists who are members of a program in European studies at Chicago, Interdisciplinary Perspectives on the Study of Europe. It was funded with support from the Andrew W. Mellon Foundation and was cosponsored by the Goethe-Institut in Chicago.

The present volume is a revised and enlarged version of the supplement published by the *Journal of Modern History* in December 1992 which presented the major essays that constituted the core of the conference. This volume inaugurates a new series of book-length publications, Studies in European History from the *Journal of Modern History*, which will reprint scholarly essays previously published in the *JMH*, presenting them in the context of a specific historical theme or subject.

John W. Boyer
Julius Kirshner

Introduction: Resistance against the Third Reich as Intercultural Knowledge

Michael Geyer and John W. Boyer
University of Chicago

The articles in this volume emerged from a conference sponsored by Interdisciplinary Perspectives for the Study of Europe (IPSE) at the University of Chicago and the Goethe-Institut, Chicago. This event came at the tail end of a veritable boom of national and international conferences on the subject of German resistance in particular and of European resistance against the Nazi regime in general, which was accompanied by a proliferation of articles, monographs, and books.[1] Pivotal among the many activities was the 1984 conference of the Historische Kommission zu Berlin in conjunction with the Gedenkstätte Deutscher Widerstand, which led, more recently, to a permanent exhibition on German resistance against the National Socialist regime.[2] Both the conference and the exhibition were noteworthy for their inclusive quality, encompassing a wide range of resistance activities. Traveling exhibitions on party-political, military, and generational traditions of German resistance such as "Resistance: A Problem between Theory and History," held at the

---

[1] Simultaneously, scholarship also turned to the study of collaboration and identified the latter as the dominant aspect of life under the National Socialist regime. However, studies that aim at integrating both aspects remain rare. One of the most successful examples is Robert Gellately, "Surveillance and Disobedience: Aspects of Political Policing of Nazi Germany," in *Germans against Nazism: Nonconformity, Opposition and Resistance in the Third Reich: Essays in Honour of Peter Hoffmann,* ed. Francis R. Nicosia and Lawrence Stokes (New York and Oxford, 1990), pp. 15–36.

[2] This conference yielded a veritable who's who of resistance research: Jürgen Schmädecke and Peter Steinbach, eds., *Der Widerstand gegen den Nationalsozialismus: Die deutsche Gesellschaft und der Widerstand gegen Hitler* (Munich and Zürich, 1988); on the conception of the permanent exhibition, see Peter Steinbach, "Widerstand gegen den Nationalsozialismus; Zur Konzeption der ständigen Ausstellung 'Widerstand gegen den Nationalsozialismus' in der 'Gedenkstätte Deutscher Widerstand' in Berlin," *Geschichte in Wissenschaft und Unterricht* 37 (1986): 481–97. Among the more prominent anthologies on the topic, see Christoph Klessmann and Falk Pingel, eds., *Gegner des Nationalsozialismus: Wissenschaftler und Widerstandskämpfer auf der Suche nach der historischen Wirklichkeit* (Frankfurt, 1980); Richard Löwenthal and Patrick von zur Mühlen, eds., *Widerstand und Verweigerung in Deutschland 1933 bis 1945* (Berlin and Bonn, 1984); Hermann Graml, ed., *Widerstand im Dritten Reich: Probleme, Ereignisse, Gestalten* (Frankfurt, 1984); Klaus Jürgen Müller, ed., *Der deutsche Widerstand, 1933–1945* (Paderborn, 1986).

This essay originally appeared in the *Journal of Modern History* 64, suppl. (December 1992).

University of Passau, or "Youth Resistance in the Third Reich," held at the Ruhrlandmuseum and the Alte Synagoge in Essen, also reflected this broadening definition of resistance.[3] The whole process was duplicated, and not necessarily with difference validations, in the former German Democratic Republic.[4]

In the United States, this preoccupation by German scholars and by the German public with resistance encountered an academic community that had, in the immediate postwar period, undertaken much of the initial research on resistance and had subsequently retained an orientation emphasizing high political action and a certain monumentalism in representing German resistance heroes. Thus, it can be said with some justification that the intellectual foundations for resistance research were laid in the United States.[5]

But American resistance research remained tied to institutional history and to sacrificial heroes, while the majority of American scholars simultaneously acknowledged more explicitly than their German counterparts the popular affirmation that the National Socialist regime met with in German civil society.[6] And American scholars did not, by and large, face the kind of turbulent reconstruction of their research agendas that their German counterparts went through after 1970, and thus they remained attached to intellectual approaches established more than three decades ago.[7] Moreover, their

---

[3] Peter Steinbach, ed., *Widerstand: Ein Problem zwischen Theorie und Geschichte* (Cologne, 1987); Wilfried Breyvogel, ed., *Piraten, Swings und Junge Garde: Jugendwiderstand im Nationalsozialismus* (Berlin and Bonn, 1991).

[4] Klaus Mammach, *Widerstand, 1939–1945: Geschichte der deutschen antifaschistischen Widerstandsbewegung im Inland und in der Emigration* (Berlin, 1987); and the brief summaries of W. Bramke, "Der antifaschistische Widerstand in der Geschichtsschreibung der DDR in den achziger Jahren: Forschungsstand und Probleme," *Aus Politik und Zeitgeschichte: Beilage zur Wochenzeitschrift das Parlament*, no. 328 (July 8, 1988), pp. 23–36; and of Kurt Finker, "Widerstand und Geschichte des Widerstandes in der Forschung der DDR," in Steinbach, ed., pp. 96–112.

[5] Allen W. Dulles, *Germany's Underground* (New York, 1947); Hans Rothfels, *The German Opposition against Hitler* (Hinsdale, Ill., 1948); George K. Romoser, "The Politics of Uncertainty: The German Resistance Movement," *Social Research* 31 (Spring 1964): 73–93; Klemens von Klemperer, *Mandate for Resistance: The Case of the German Opposition to Hitler*, The Katherine Asher Engels Lecture (Northampton, Mass., 1968); Harold C. Deutsch, *The Conspiracy against Hitler in the Twilight War* (Minneapolis, 1968). See also Leonidas E. Hill, "Towards a New History of German Resistance to Hitler," *Central European History* 14 (1981): 369–99.

[6] Ian Kershaw, *Popular Opinion and Political Dissent in the Third Reich: Bavaria, 1933–1945* (Oxford and New York, 1983); Robert Gellately, *The Gestapo and German Society: Enforcing Racial Policy, 1933–1945* (Oxford, 1990).

[7] Peter Hofmann, *The History of German Resistance, 1933–1945* (Cambridge, Mass., 1988); Michael Balfour, *Withstanding Hitler in Germany: 1933–1945* (London and New York, 1988); Nicholas Reynolds, *Treason Was No Crime: Ludwig Beck, Chief of the German General Staff* (London, 1976).

research had neither the public glamour nor the civic consciousness that shaped, for better or worse, so many of the German endeavors throughout the seventies and eighties.

The self-serving quality of (West) German resistance studies surfaced after 1989. Resistance history and civic commitment had begun to reinforce each other and led to a "national" debate on the German past, but this "nation" was distinctly limited to West Germany. The consequences of this debate go a long way to explain the difficulties of the present. The western *Trauerarbeit* separated the West from the East exactly at a moment at which sporadic resistance began to flare up against yet another unjust regime on German territory. While West Germans launched an acrimonious historical debate on the nature of resistance, some East Germans—very few but a crucial minority for the unfolding events—practiced it. They engaged in a subdued resistance that they would never have acknowledged as such, not the least because it was aimed against the monstrosities of the officially authorized antifascist resistance by the GDR government. However, historians and practitioners did not recognize each other. This lack of recognition on both sides will concern the study of resistance against the Third Reich for some time to come. There is good reason to believe that this mismatch will lead to yet another reappraisal of resistance.

The treacherous nature of any history of resistance that goes beyond 1945 is obvious and has begun to exercise historians of Germany. What, were one to compare the two tyrannical regimes, about the singularity of Nazi crimes? What about the difference in motivations, social origins, patterns of organization and communication, the very culture and politics of resistance between resisters in the 1930s and 1940s and the civic group in the 1980s? What about the sheer fact that the history of the Third Reich had preceded and therefore was implicated in every mobilization in the 1980s? These are some of the unsettled and unsettling questions that engage scholars of Germany and a concerned public everywhere. The dangers of a simplistic equivocation of the Third Reich and the GDR are acute. But it must also be said that the clean separation between historical thought and political action points to a lamentable deficit in the intellectual labors of so much of resistance research. The price to be paid is a deep division that runs through Germany today. If the separation between past and present, due to a truncated *Vergangenheitsbewältigung,* has been the sore spot of German postwar politics and culture, we now must add to it the unresolved issue of two simultaneous but segregated German presences and their incomplete *Gegenwartsbewältigung.*

In all of this, the notion of resistance has retained a public and political quality that has deeply affected the scholarly debate in Germany. The opposite happened in the United States, where resistance studies have moved from their acutely political beginnings in the war against Nazi Germany and in the Cold

War into the realm of academic scholarship. Oddly, this apolitical trajectory has rather gained prominence since 1989, because so much of the "official" national resistance history turned out to be a myth. The critique of the political instrumentalization of the resistance against the Third Reich is now used to plead for a more scholarly recovery of the past. This is the case, even though the new scholarly critique follows hard on the heels of the highly political challenge of these resistance myths by civic movements in Eastern and Western Europe. It is scholarship that forgets the actual act of resistance (in 1989), in order to assert a more truthful rendition of the past.

This divergence in historical agendas is only one of many Atlantic disjunctures that have accumulated over time, creating what has been called, quite infelicitously, the problem of "successor generations" in Germany and the United States.[8] The veritable obsession with this issue in some circles of German officialdom has led to a remarkable expansion of all kinds of cultural exchange activities. The result was and is an efflorescence of transatlantic projects that have enriched, literally and metaphorically, American scholarship. In this particular case, the German agendas of resistance studies spawned a secondary exhibition and conference business that began to reach the American shores at the end of the 1980s. "The German Resistance Movement, 1933–1945," a 1988 conference held at the Goethe House in New York, was one of the flagship events in this context. Obviously, the most immediate impulse for the German export of conferences and exhibitions on resistance against Hitler was to demonstrate that a German resistance movement or, at least, German acts of resistance existed in the first place.

In organizing our conference on acts of resistance against the NS regime we wondered if it would be possible to combine the task of public education about resistance against the Third Reich with recent advances in scholarly knowledge across the European continent, thus doing more than simply providing another venue for existing German research in the United States. This seemed to us important for two reasons. First, we see a growing interest on the part of foreign governments and their cultural institutions to present their countries' scholarship (or, for that matter, culture) in the United States. These interventions are often complemented by what appears to be a new sense of empowerment that leads foreign scholars to present their "master" scholarship as the only real and true knowledge to the "apprentices" abroad. Here both partners—Europeans and Americans—walk a thin line. Obviously, universities and colleges have come to depend on this kind of support to enhance cultural exchange and to strengthen research and teaching. Moreover, scholarship relies inadvertently on the prodigious, national knowledge that cannot easily be reproduced abroad, even if the academic community is as

[8] Stephen F. Szabo, ed., *The Successor Generation: International Perspectives of Postwar Europeans* (London, 1983).

unusually far-flung and strong as it is in the United States. By the same token, our immediate responsibility is to an American audience, however international the final impact of scholarship may be.

Second, foreign funding can all too easily aggravate an already evident misbalance between research and teaching or, more generally, between the scholarly and the public dimension of academic labors. Contrary to specialized European research institutions, American universities and colleges have an important public audience. But the presence of this audience raises a difficult question. How does one reconcile the precision and specialization of advanced scholarship with the broader interests of an educated public? These questions confront the basic issue of how we can mediate between the past and the present—in this case a German past and an American present. This mediation is an inescapable concern of all historians, and we cannot avoid it, either as scholars or as teachers.

In organizing the Chicago conference we were also conscious of the fact that studies of resistance cannot ignore the European legacy of resistance thought, one which is grounded in tumultuous and bitter conflicts between church and state and between strident religious confessions and conflicting moralities in early modern European history. Both German and American scholars of the history of resistance in the National Socialist period have given this legacy insufficient attention. This legacy of European "moral politics" encourages the historian to integrate the specifics of resistance against the Nazi regime into more general reflections on the problem of resistance against unjust rule and inhumanity. We therefore sought to link a discussion of the resistance against the Nazi regime to the wider historical implications of such resistance and to encourage public discussion on the general nature of the possibilities of resistance. The result was a conference that combined public addresses with academic panels that were widely advertised and open to the public; reflections on open political resistance and private acts of altruism and disavowal; eyewitness accounts of Germans and émigrés; video documentaries and films; as well as an exhibition that was introduced by Hans Mommsen.[9] The sessions built on the historical scholarship of the past decades, but they aimed at distilling themes of general and present significance.

---

[9] Marion Countess Dönhoff, *Before the Storm: Memories of My Youth in Old Prussia* (New York, 1990) and Lisa Fittko, *Escape through the Pyrenees* (Evanston, Ill., 1991) provided the two eyewitness accounts. The exploration of silences in the life histories of workers as indication of collusion or collaboration with the Nazi regime has been one of the most successful aspects of oral histories (Lutz Niethammer and Alexander von Plato, eds., *"Wir kriegen jetzt andere Zeiten": Auf der Suche nach der Erfahrung des Volkes in Nachfaschistischen Ländern* [Bonn and Berlin, 1985]). Alfred Frei (in this volume) and Deborah Dwork (in this volume), in turn, have pointed to the fact that these silences also occur in cases of altruism (hiding Jewish children, aid to refugees).

We encountered several limitations, some more important than others. We did not escape a Central European focus, even though we had intended to include considerably more material on occupied countries than was actually presented. In the end this imbalance was less troubling than we had feared. Partly this was due to the fact that the scholarly focus was only occasionally overwhelmed by inbred, national particularities that shape so much of the scholarly debate. The key to this beneficial outcome proved to be less a rush toward mechanical comparisons than a readiness by the participants to move beyond their own specializations and to assume overlapping identities and identifications. Mostly, however, the avoidance of scholarly *querelles* was due to the insistence by members of the audience that the specifics of the case (as, e.g., the political agenda of *Der Widerstand*) should be tied to the general theme of the conference: What is required to resist unjust rule and crimes against humanity? The main concern of the conference, then, became less bilateral comparisons (although a richer and more European agenda would have undoubtedly been useful) than a clarification of common features of resistance against the Third Reich.

This outcome raises a more general question concerning the uses and abuses of comparison in resistance studies. When we initially planned the conference, we thought, as most historians do nowadays, that a more encompassing perspective would be appropriate to revisiting the problem of resistance. This makes sense, because Europe (rather than Germany and Austria alone) is the appropriate frame of reference in explaining the Nazi regime, which was a regime of aggression and occupation, a European nightmare that originated in Germany. While national histories of this period still predominate, they fall short, strictly speaking, of the reality of the Nazi regime. Furthermore, the title of this introduction, "resistance as intercultural knowledge," suggests yet another dimension of a more broadly conceived study of resistance. For resistance against tyrannical regimes in the twentieth century is not primarily a European phenomenon, and it is not commonly associated with Europe. If one were to think of the most eminent representatives of resistance thought and action in this century, one would likely mention Mahatma Gandhi or Martin Luther King. We need not be concerned here with the potential misapplication of such comparisons, of which there are many. The urge to expand the horizon of resistance studies is a consequence of the global nature of resistance in the twentieth century.

Hence, there must be a more expansive and differentiated knowledge on resistances. We also need a debate about the location of European resistance in a world of resistances against unjust rule that implicates European nations as unjust and tyrannical power. In any case, the solution to the problem cannot be piling up instances of resistance across boundaries and centuries, which would result in a flattening out of the very special quality of resistance in each location. The more appropriate strategy consists in building or maintaining a horizon of the intercultural reality of resistance in order to probe more deeply beyond the surface appearance of the various national discourses on resistance—as if one were to explain, quite deliberately, one's research and its conclusions to strangers. Intercultural knowledge entails the necessity to localize one's argument and to recognize the very specific locality of an event (and of its interpretation). This strategy of localization is in many ways the exact opposite of an inflationary comparativism. But what would keep it from being just a newfangled word for the same old parochial history? The test is this: Will other knowledge of resistance reverberate in our particular European or, for that matter, national knowledge so that a fruitful dialogue can emerge? It is well understood that every single one of these knowledges is complex and contradictory. However, the yardstick for sorting out differences, which a parochial history seeks within the limits of its own scholarship, ought to be sought in a transnational, transcultural, or, at least, a consciously transatlantic dialogue that honors the global presence of resistance.

This was not what we had in mind, but this is what happened to a remarkable degree. The outcome of the conference was a dialogue on resistance and a history in a minor key. It was not a history of everyday events of the kind that has led to a now canonical struggle in Germany between those who favor grand political history and those who applaud its opposite—a social history of private or at least unpublic life. Rather, we encountered a fragile history that interwove both individual and collective choices and decisions. The "monumental" dimensions of so much of resistance history gave way to the struggles of individuals and groups to resist the regime, in its isolated parts or as a whole. What emerged was a history of finite and dangerous moral actions, a history that presented the human drama of existential choices, in which individuals, groups, and whole nations had to decide on what kind of social, cultural, and political order they thought appropriate for themselves and for others—not only as grand schemes but also as everyday habitus.

This is moral history as straightforward, matter-of-fact history. Moral choice and moral action is indisputably a most powerful source of resistance anywhere. Yet the very mention of the term "moral history" provokes an uproar among historians. Hence, the suggestion that, indeed, moral history is a proper and, moreover, indispensable subject of history needs some justification. It must begin by recalling the misuses of "morality" in history. For the history of moral action and choices is quite commonly mistaken for either a judgmental and incriminating or a melodramatic history. But judgmental and sentimental histories do not equal moral history. The second equally common mistake in approaching moral history is to think of it as the history of the pursuit of high-minded ideals, as if resisters were immaculate heroes who followed the call of their consciences, as opposed to hard-nosed interests.

Resisters as the innocents of our age—this interpretation is about as far as can be from the reality of the wrenching decisions to challenge the normality of tyrannical regimes. All that can be said about these kinds of histories is that they do not live up to the experience of resisters and to the actual drama of resistance that we can reconstruct as historians.

Bad examples of a moralizing history do not mean that there is no moral choice or moral action and that the discrimination between "good" and "evil" does not matter in recalling the history of resistance. It does not mean that the notion of justice and injustice is irrelevant. Neither does it mean that normative thought and action is derivative—or, as they said in the old days, merely a matter of superstructure. It just means to say that present historiography has no ready approaches to deal with the subject and engages in outlandish arguments to get around it.

Wherever historians may place moral thought and action in the end, it is a subject to be studied. Its exploration may expand into complex philosophical and theological arguments, but in the first instance it is the pragmatic discovery and elucidation of a tangible and very personal reality. A history of resistance as moral history thus seeks to explain, first of all, the individual and collective experience of violation and/or revulsion as a powerful source for action. In crucial ways this is a history of the formation of individual and collective identities of resisters against the imposed normalcy of tyrannical regimes. At the center of this study is the "body" of resisters, both as the endangered identity of individuals and groups and as their very physical reality as men and women. If there were any doubts about this, one would only have to recall the unbridled desire of tyrants to mutilate, torture, and destroy—not some abstract thought but the mental and physical integrity of resisters. Second, a moral history seeks to explain the resisters' vision of human beings and institutions and their role in safeguarding and renewing social bonds. This amounts to exploring their sense of justice and liberty—not some abstract norm of what we may like them to have thought. Visions of order, often personal and restricted, gained a very powerful hold over resisters, and this power of conviction needs detailed exploration. Third, it is a history that takes as its guide the struggle of individuals and groups for the viability of human community and nation. This is not to say that resisters are enlightened humanitarians. Rather, the act of resistance requires choices, on an everyday level as much as in treatises and platforms, over the inclusion or exclusion of men, women, and children.

Above all, moral history engages in a debate on violence. It finds its supreme challenge in an age that is marked by genocidal confrontations. If resistance against the Third Reich has come to mean many, too many things in the past decade, this is mostly due to the fact that the centrality of violence has either faded into the background or become incomprehensible. It is also due to the fact that the scholarly notion of violence has lost its sharp edge of explaining human-made death and destruction. In a world of the subjectless violence of states and their apparatuses, anonymous torturers, and technologies of destruction, a record of violence is difficult to establish. Yet without this reference we lose sight of the key experience of resisters, and the horizon of their action becomes unintelligible. In so many different ways resistance aims at reconstituting civility. A moral history is thus a history that is concerned with what institutions, groups of people, and individuals do in order to safeguard and to renew the social bonds that constitute communities and nations and the integrity of their "body politic." While resisters are not models and their visions of society do not establish norms, they witness distress over the absence of civility "in dark times" (Hannah Arendt). In this way, they are indispensable for any history of the twentieth century.

The extreme situation of the National Socialist regime in Europe, in which virtually everyone faced, at one point or another, profound choices over life and death and over acknowledging or denying the humanity of others, provided the single most powerful example of this drama in the twentieth century. While the conditions of the Nazi regime were unique, this extreme situation with its often irreconcilable challenges seemed to reflect more clearly than anything else the basic problem of constituting social and political order in resistance against unjust rule and inhumanity.

That resistance remained the exception (and not just in Germany) was evident to everyone. At the same time, the fact that many Europeans between 1933 and 1945 were deeply concerned about civility, finding themselves in situations of perplexing moral unease, was one of the most striking findings of our discussions. Other troubling and surprising outcomes were that individual experiences proved to be difficult to translate into civic action and into collective representation and that such a circumstance was not limited to Germany. Ultimately, the proceedings pointed to a deep chasm between a venerable European tradition of opposition against unjust rule and the cultural and social means available in the middle of the twentieth century to guide individuals in situations of extreme moral choice. Thus, the singular situation of the Third Reich shed an oblique light on the moral and human condition of our century.

We have grouped the essays that emerged from these deliberations into three clusters. "Normality, Exceptionalism, Resistance" explores the habitual situations in which ordinary people (nurses, workers, and soldiers among others) faced extraordinary choices by virtue of their specific work, task, or location and the affirmative or insubordinate practices that emerged in these contexts. This exploration, above all, pointed to the weakness of the common characterization of the Nazi regime as "exceptional." Indeed, the reverse is a much more appropriate starting point: only the successful normalization of the exceptional—not just by the Nazis but by almost everyone—makes comprehensible the political and intellectual labor of resisters. Their first challenge consisted in making exceptional what most everyone desperately wanted to be normal.

''Apocalypse, Human Solidarity, and the Restoration of Politics'' looks at the extraordinary difficulties in putting together what had been rent asunder by the Nazi state—conceptions of human solidarity and responsibility, a sense of polity and politics, and the experience of a participatory definition of a common destiny. This civic consciousness was all too easily presumed in the postwar debates on the political orientations of resisters and resistance groups, when, in fact, the difficulties of thinking politics in the first place were and remained the major obstacles. The main challenge consisted in thinking collectively *and* politically in a world in which social ties had given way to the ''violence of linkage.''[10] That is a condition in which the sociability among people was displaced by hostility and the curiosity about strangers gave way to the fear and loathing of otherness.

''*Der nachholende Widerstand*—Resistance after 1945'' studies the postwar monumentalizations of resistance, but it also pays attention to National Socialist practices in the professions, the grounds for collaboration with an inhuman and anti-Christian regime in the churches, or the recovery of a human right to and political theory of resistance. *Nachholender Widerstand,* then, can be two quite contrary things: the appropriation of resistance in order to further the affirmation of the present or the effort to think ''order'' critically as an imperfect and fallible order, to be resisted if and when order negates one's civic obligation to others. This latter notion of resistance implies, on one hand, continuities of the Nazi regime beyond the collapse of the Nazi state and its institutions, and, on the other, a renewal of a European heritage of resistance from working through the Nazi experience. It is in this context of resistance as an ongoing concern that resistance against the National Socialist regime can be linked both back to the European legacy of resistance thought and practice and also forward to resistance in our own time—without destroying respective particularities and unique urgencies.

The history of resistance affords a powerful example of why the present should try to remember a more distant, early modern past. The right to resistance is a powerful European intellectual, political, and theological legacy for our time.[11] This is not a convenient bequest, despite memorializations and

[10] Alexander Kluge and Oskar Negt, *Geschichte und Eigensinn* (Frankfurt, 1981), pp. 777 ff.
[11] See, among others, Franklin Ford, *Political Murder: From Tyrannicide to Terrorism* (Cambridge, 1985); Robert A. Lauer, *Tyrannicide and Drama* (Stuttgart, 1987); Roland Mousnier, *The Assassination of Henry IV: The Tyrannicide Problem and*

aestheticizations. Hesitation about resistance is not merely a result of the ambivalent nature of the resistance act—who is to be counted among the resisters and how is resistance to be distinguished from treason? Nor is it entirely a matter of what folklore knows as the Saint Florian principle—that resistance is for other places and other times, but not for us.[12] Rather, to think about the possibility of resistance seems to challenge order, not necessarily with the intention of overthrowing it, but as a strategy for viewing order as imperfect and fallible. For many, this is an uncomfortable breach. But this breach, provoked by resistance against the Nazi regime and opened up anew by the events of the last four years in Central and Eastern Europe, is again relevant in contemplating our own world.

---

the Consolidation of the French Absolute Monarchy in the Early Seventeenth Century (London, 1973); Pierre Chevallier, *Les régicides: Clément, Ravaillac, Damiens* (Paris, 1989); Yves-Marie Bercé, *Révoltes et révolutions dans l'Europe moderne: XVIe–XVIIIe siècles* (Paris, 1980).

[12] The well-known couplet puts the most common reaction to resistance in a timeless perspective:

> Heiliger Sankt Florian
> Verschon' mein Haus,
> Zünd'andre an.

NORMALITY,
EXCEPTIONALISM,
RESISTANCE

Ethical Dilemmas and Nazi Eugenics: Single-Issue Dissent in Religious Contexts*

Claudia Koonz
Duke University

During the first decades after 1945, scholarship and memoirs about "the Resistance" (*Widerstand*) counterpoised the forces of good against massive evil. In reality, of course, David did not defeat Goliath. It took an even more powerful giant in the form of the Allied forces. But in historical memory, the resisters' heroism and often martyrdom offset the dismal record of collaboration and obedience in nazified Europe. Among liberal scholars, Peter Hofmann's classic study established the benchmark definition of "Resistance" that centered on ideological commitment, clandestine networks, and armed action.[1] In the German Democratic Republic before November 1989, historians eulogized the heroic communist resistance that began the day Hitler became chancellor. In the West, scholars focused on wartime actions: the courage of the Scholls, the July 14 plot, and the Kreisau Circle. Recently, however, the stark image of a monolithic "Resistance" has yielded (among Marxists and liberals) as the historical profession itself has shifted its perspectives. Oral histories, memoirs by victims, and local history projects have blurred sharp contrasts between resistance and collaboration. "Resistance" loses its capital *R*. Nachema Tec, Seymour and Pearl Oliner, Pierre Sauvage, and Detlev Peukert discover heroism in daily life among people without particularly deep political commitments. Resisters' ideological zeal seems less important as a basis for courage than empathy for the victims.

The diversity among the articles in this collection illustrates the collapse of clarity about the divisions between those who opposed and those who supported Nazi policies. However, there are limits beyond which the term "resistance" ought not be stretched. In this article, I explore the actions and motivations of individuals whom I would not consider part of either "the Resistance," or "a resistance," or even *Resistenz.* I introduce a cluster of

---

* This essay is based on the essay entitled "Eugenics, Gender, and Ethics in Nazi Germany: The Debate about Involuntary Sterilization, 1933–1936" by Claudia Koonz which appeared originally in Thomas Childers and Jane Caplan (eds.), *Reevaluating the Third Reich* (New York: Holmes & Meier, 1992). Copyright © 1992 by Holmes & Meier Publishers, Inc. Published by permission.

[1] Peter Hofmann, *The History of the German Resistance: 1933–1945,* trans. Richard Barry (Cambridge, Mass., 1977), p. 15.

issues that incited opposition by individuals who fundamentally approved of Nazi policy and government. In contrast to other studies that examine people who placed themselves at grave risk to rescue victims and thwart Nazi power, the individuals I discuss did not endanger their lives or even risk prison, although they worried realistically that they would lose status and jobs. They did not set themselves against Nazi policies generally, but they did vigorously oppose the particular aspects of the Nazi state's biopolitical project that directly affected their lives. They feared intrusion by the state into decisions that they believed lay in a private and religious realm.

For the most part, these single-issue dissidents were women. In the health care networks the lowest positions were generally held by women, while the higher positions were occupied by men. When it came to matters related to "blood and race," declared the Nazi party chief of racial politics, "the German woman participates more fully than the man, [who is busy] with his state, and his fighting units, ever can."[2] "Aryan" women heard exhortations to bear many children, select "racially fit" mates, indoctrinate their children, and volunteer to help the "racially worthy, deserving poor." More ominously, they were also exhorted to target clients for forced abortion, sterilization, or euthanasia, to report on "suspicious" activities in the neighborhood, to boycott Jewish shops, and to refuse shelter to friends wanted by the police. I will examine the bioethical dilemmas faced by women as mothers and health care professionals in church-affiliated settings. Although I will focus mainly on Catholic women, I will add some brief comparative comments on their Protestant counterparts.

THE NAZI APPEAL TO WOMEN

The tasks assigned to the inferior sex of the master race presented Nazi planners with several intrinsic problems, not the least of which was the difficulty of inspiring sufficient racial arrogance to insure women's cooperation without at the same time inculcating gender pride that might produce anger against Nazi misogyny.[3] On a different level, Romantic idealism, so

---

[2] Walter Groβ, *Nationalsozialistische Rassenpolitik: Eine Rede an die deutschen Frauen* (Berlin, 1933), p. 4. All English translations throughout this article are mine unless otherwise noted.

[3] For a comparative perspective, see Carolyn Wallace, "The Priesthood and Motherhood in the Church of Jesus Christ of Latter Day Saints," in *Gender and Religion: On the Complexity of Symbols*, ed. Carolyn Walker Bynum, Stevan Harrell, and Paula Richman (Boston, 1986), pp. 117–40. Wallace concludes that "men have the priesthood; women have motherhood," complementary but not symmetrical institutions. While the spiritual exaltation of men is widely accepted, "motherhood remains problematic." However, like the Nazi regime, the Latter Day Saints knew how

widespread among bourgeois Germans, enshrined women as the guardians of virtue, "angels in the home," and protectors of life. Racial policies not only required women to enter public life but to violate conventional moral precepts associated with their gender.

The Nazi state launched a comprehensive drive, using laws and propaganda, to popularize its racial mandates. This meant not only encouraging the "worthy" to bear more children but curtailing "unworthy" life as well. As Gisela Bock's research makes clear, "Nazi pronatalism for desirable births and its antinatalism for undesirable ones were tightly connected."[4] A new term made the new morality explicit: "life unworthy of living" (*Lebensunwertes Leben*). The value of a life was not judged in terms of the suffering of the individual in question; on the contrary, standards of "worth" shifted to the community. By this standard, some "defectives" were so unproductive, and even genetically dangerous, that they lost their right to be supported by the "fit."

The mandate for women, as health workers or educators, to target individuals for sterilization or, after 1940, for euthanasia marked a startling departure from a symbolic system that has for centuries separated childbearing and warfare by gender. In Western mythology, as Nancy Huston points out, while virgins or Amazons in unusual circumstances take up arms, mothers cannot take life.[5] Nazi rhetoric, by contrast, explicitly told women that the national future depended on their willingness not only to bear many healthy babies but also to prune "unworthy" members from the "fit" racial stock.

Such a reversal of traditional gender concepts and moral values could not be coerced, even in a police state. Laws against birth control and abortion were stringently enforced. Marriage loans and disincentives for single people improved the marriage rate. Motherhood medals and child bonuses induced women to bear more children. But these incentives confronted Nazi planners with a dilemma: if mercenary rewards did motivate women to bear more children, would the women they influenced make "good mothers"? Even

---

to lavish praise on women in "appropriate" roles. See also Kathleen M. Blee, *Women of the Klan: Racism and Gender in the 1920s* (Berkeley and Los Angeles, 1991), pp. 42–69.

[4] Gisela Bock, "Racism and Sexism in Nazi Germany: Motherhood, Compulsory Sterilization, and the State," in *When Biology Became Destiny: Women in Weimar and Nazi Germany*, ed. Renate Bridenthal, Atina Grossmann, and Marion Kaplan (New York, 1984), pp. 271 ff.

[5] "One of the strongest indications that it is as *mothers* that women are excluded from life-taking activities is the fact that as *virgins* they are not" (Nancy Huston, "The Matrix of War," in *The Female Body in Western Culture: Contemporary Perspectives*, ed. Susan R. Suleiman [Cambridge, Mass., 1986], p. 128). In her concluding paragraphs, Huston comments that the nuclear and demographic explosions have undermined the seemingly timeless paradigm she identified.

more vexing to the framers of Nazi policy were the problems implicit in so-called negative eugenic measures. What could impel nurses, social workers, and teachers, committed to improving the lives of their clients, to fill out the forms reporting their "unworthy" wards to local health boards? Against the propaganda that enshrined motherhood as the fundamental role for all women, how could some women be proscribed from bearing children?

Before Hitler became chancellor, few Nazi leaders gave any thought to the "racial revolution" promised in their program. But soon after political victory (which they called the *Machtergreifung*), they launched a campaign to convert all citizens to a new domestic crusade for racial purity. This amounted to a veritable "seizure of opinion" (*Meinungergreifung*), although they did not use the term. During Weimar election campaigns Nazis had solicited new converts. After January 1933, propaganda incited the "racially fit" to assault the "unworthy."

The major weapon in this racial crusade was the Nazis' genius for manipulating the media to convert people to new social definitions of life and death, duty and choice. Besides addressing general audiences, special propaganda appealed to the people who would administer the battle against the "unworthy": women and health and education professionals. In these appeals, individual conscience fell to the demand of collective duty. The drive against "undesirables" attacked personal freedom in the most intimate matters. Nazi policy aimed to eliminate privacy for everyone—except, as Propaganda Minister Joseph Goebbels once quipped, for the person who was asleep. The confrontation that emerged did not simply pit the virtuous private woman in her home against the ruthless public man in his racist state. Despite sentimental visions of the home as refuge from public life and guarantor of individualism, private life had never been truly private; and women had in reality never stood guard alone at the thresholds of their sacrosanct homes.

Religion had always shaped the experience of "private" family life. Since the nineteenth century, religious institutions had provided women with expanded access to public life by organizing them as charity volunteers, teachers, nurses, mothers, and students—in precisely the areas affected by Nazi racial policies. Except in unusual circumstances (e.g., during World War I and at election time in the Weimar Republic), German political leaders had not mobilized women. Most German women first experienced the impact of Nazi takeover when, in the summer of 1933, they heard the summons to a new Nazi crusade. The tone of the propaganda may have reminded them of Kaiser Wilhelm's appeals in World War I or of the frenzied political rhetoric of Weimar elections. But the "enemy" had shifted. In wartime, the threat came from foreign nations; in political campaigns, opponents were ideological rivals. In the Nazi crusade, an "enemy within" threatened the "racial purity" of the German *Volk*.

When I began work on this topic I naively anticipated that the debate around racial policy would have led to a confrontation between Nazi eugenicists and religious leaders. Religious values mandated giving aid to the neediest, while Nazi law demanded helping the racially "fit." But the issues involved proved to be more complex. A three-way competition pitted secular Nazi eugenicists against Protestant proponents of eugenics and Catholic opponents of eugenics. To further complicate the debate, substantial disagreements evolved within each camp between moderates and fanatics. Women, as participants in the debates, enforcers of the new laws, and the objects of eugenic intervention, played a crucial role. Early eugenics legislation thus shaped thinking about gender, race, and ethics within the crucible of race war.

THE NAZI "TRANSVALUATION OF MORALS"

With unlimited confidence in the "magical power of the spoken word," Hitler aimed at nothing less than a transformation (*Umwertung* in Nietzschean terms) of values regarding human life and the nature of society. Joseph Goebbels, master of public persuasion, wielded extraordinary influence in the new age of mass communications. Years earlier Max Weber had anticipated the techniques of power in the modern age when he defined power as the ability to make people do what you want them to do—whether or not they want to do it.[6] More recently Michel Foucault has reminded us of the pervasive impact of knowledge as power. Hitler applied a similar understanding of power when he made the formation of his followers' weltanschauung the center of his strategy. In 1922 he explained why conversion worked better than coercion: "The construction of a propaganda organization provides the best preparation for future success. Whatever we can win with paper ammunition does not have to be achieved by steel weapons later."[7] Easy triumph over the Weimar government, achieved largely by that "paper ammo," enticed Nazi leaders after 1933 on to a new battlefield.

The major goal of any state, Hitler often proclaimed, was to pull its race of people up to greatness.[8] Admitting no earthly predecessor, he likened himself

[6] H. H. Gerth and C. Wright Mills, eds. and trans., *From Max Weber: Essays in Sociology*, 2d ed. (New York, 1958), p. 180.

[7] "Power is everywhere: not because it embraces everything, but because it comes from everywhere . . . power is not an institution, nor a structure, nor a possession. It is the name we give to a complex strategic situation in a particular society" (Michel Foucault, *The History of Sexuality*, vol. 1, *An Introduction*, trans. Robert Hurley [New York, 1978], p. 93). Eberhard Jäckel, ed., *Hitler: Sämtliche Aufzeichnungen: 1905– 1924* (Stuttgart, 1980), p. 705.

[8] Eberhard Jäckel, *Hitlers Weltanschauung: Entwurf einer Herrschaft*, 2d ed. (Stuttgart, 1972), p. 89.

to another hero. "Two thousand years ago another man was denounced by the same race that today defames and burdens [*verlästert*]."[9] As prophet, messiah, führer, reformer, and revolutionary, Hitler declared racial revolution against "defectives." But what did he want to accomplish? That was not clear, even in 1933. At the 1929 party rally Hitler had suggested that a million "burdensome" lives could be eliminated by racial measures.[10] On the eve of becoming chancellor, Hitler used words like "cleansing and regeneration" (January 1, 1933). But even after initial legislation was drawn up in haste, the "experts" seemed as vague as their leader. In 1934, Frick estimated that as many as 20 percent of all Germans would be prevented from bearing children. A Swiss eugenicist in 1934 concluded that "only" about six million (or 10 percent) of all Germans would be deemed physically or mentally to have less than full value (*nicht vollwert*).[11]

Without a clear prognosis, the racial scientists set to work. Barely six months after the Nazi takeover, new programs encouraged marriage and fertility among those non-Jewish Germans certified by physicians as genetically healthy. To guide couples, the state established genetic counseling centers throughout the nation. In July 1933, legislation removed the ban against involuntary sterilization of "genetically deficient" people. Anticipating Catholic objections, the new laws remained secret until August, a few weeks after the Concordat between the pope and the Nazi state was signed, and were scheduled to go into effect only in January 1934. The new regulations mandated employees in social work, health, and educational institutions to report (*anzeigen*) to local health authorities all clients, pupils, and patients with signs of the following supposedly inherited conditions: feeblemindedness, schizophrenia, manic-depressive syndrome, Huntington's chorea, epilepsy, blindness, speechlessness, severe alcoholism, and marked physical deformities. In only two circumstances did "inferior racial ancestry" justify reporting: the offspring of Polish parents in Silesia and the children of black French soldiers and German women in the Ruhr region. Jewish ancestry did not rank as grounds for eugenic scrutiny. Once reported,

[9] Hitler, speech, "Die 'Hetzer' der Wahrheit," in *Völkische Beobachter*, Munich, April 12, 1922; quoted in Jäckel, ed., doc. 378, p. 642.

[10] Adolf Hitler, *Ballastexistenzen!* in *Nazism, 1919–1945: A Documentary Reader*, ed. Jeremy Noakes and Geoffrey Pridham (Exeter, 1988), 3:1002; quoted in Paul Weindling, *Health, Race and German Politics between National Unification and Nazism: 1870–1945*, Cambridge History of Medicine (Cambridge, 1989), p. 545.

[11] The participants noted that projected rates in the United States reached about one hundred thousand per year—which would have produced 15 million sterilizations by 1980. On the other hand, the author noted that as of 1930, only about eleven thousand Americans in twenty-three states had actually been sterilized ("Ein Wort zum Sterilisationsgesetz," *Basler Nachtrichten* [May 28, 1934]). Lifton attributes the 20 percent estimate to Seigfried Lenz (*The Nazi Doctors: Medical Killing and the Psychology of Nazism* [New York, 1986], p. 26).

a three-member health panel (with at least two physicians) would investigate a case. Consistent with the tradition of the *Rechtsstaat*, the law guaranteed each individual the right of appeal. Over two hundred fifty health tribunals handled individual cases and the Department of Genetic and Racial Care in the Interior Ministry established over one hundred offices to collect genetic data on every citizen. However, in practice, panel decisions were virtually always upheld. Conversely, panels habitually rejected requests from individuals who wished to be sterilized. In November 1933 the category of "dangerous moral criminal" (brutal rapists, e.g.) was added to the list of genetically dangerous characteristics meaning that such individuals could be castrated.[12] The Office to Combat Homosexuality and Abortion launched programs to eliminate the two major causes of "unnatural" infertility. Efforts to combat venereal diseases continued and ultimately brought about 750,000 cases under observation. In 1936 local health authorities were empowered to compel "genetically unfit" pregnant women to have abortions.

In addition to sweeping coercive measures, the Reich Health Office, in coordination with the Office of Racial Policies, launched a campaign to popularize the new programs. Officials realized that without grassroots enthusiasm the laws would remain unenforced and, perhaps worse, occasion hostility to the Reich. Under the direction of Walter Groß, physician and longtime Nazi supporter, indoctrination efforts were directed at all citizens, from schoolchildren through professionals.

After three years of Nazi power, a population that had previously displayed considerable hostility toward eugenic measures was saturated by a propaganda campaign to purify the blood. Having drafted a series of sweeping and compulsory laws, the National Socialist regime needed to popularize them. This meant first of all making their intent credible. In addition, the administrators of these laws had to appear respectable. To accomplish both goals, high-ranking officials from several branches of the government told Germans that race regeneration constituted the central aim of Nazi policy. Hitler advocated the new laws in a major address to the Reichstag (January 30, 1934). Cabinet ministers, party officials, administrators, and racial experts made personal appearances, sponsored conferences, launched programs, drafted laws, addressed special constituencies, spoke on the radio, and wrote scores of books and dozens of guidelines to back up the racial laws proclaimed between 1933 and 1936. A host of "experts" won overnight recognition for

---

[12] Gisela Bock, "Racism and Sexism in Nazi Germany," and *Zwangssterilisation im Nationalsozialismus* (Opladen, 1986); Ernst Klee, *"Euthanasie" im N.S. Staat* (Frankfurt, 1983); Kurt Nowak, *"Euthanasie" und Sterilisierung im "Dritten Reich": Die Konfrontation der evangelischen und katholischen Kirche mit dem "gesetz zur Verhütung erbkranken Nachwuchses," und der "Euthanasie"-Aktion* (Göttingen, 1980); Robert Proctor, *Racial Hygiene: Medicine under the Nazis* (Cambridge, Mass., 1988); and Weindling.

their pioneering eugenic ideas: R. W. Darré, Walter Groβ, Arthur Gütt, Leonardo ("Ludwig" on book covers) Conti, Conrad Wagner, Hermann Althaus, Herbert Linden, Franz Maβseller, Hans F. K. Günther, Ernst Rüdin, and Falk Ruttke.

Documentary films, often shown as "shorts" before feature films, popularized eugenics. The titles suggest their intent: *The Inheritance (Das Erbe* [1935]), *Victim of the Past (Opfer der Vergangenheit* [1937]), *Mother Love (Mutterliebe* [1935?]), *Danger in Friesia (Friesenot* [1937]), and *J'accuse (Ich klage an* [1940]).[13] Dozens of educational "shorts" shown before feature films and traveling exhibits constituted what eugenicists called daily propaganda *(Dauerpropaganda)*. Popular magazines like *New Volk (Neues Volk)* and *Volk and Race (Volk und Rasse)* were published in editions of 400,000. They were flanked by a host of medical publications like *Path and Goal (Weg und Ziel)*. Patients in any medical facility would find pamphlets and charts. A half-million calendars popularizing racial purity were distributed annually. Teenagers memorized the "Ten Commandments for Selecting a Mate":

1. Remember you are a German.
2. If you are genetically healthy, you shall not remain unmarried.
3. Keep your body pure!
4. Keep your soul and mind pure!
5. As a German, select only someone of Nordic blood as a mate.
6. In selecting a mate, inquire into ancestry.
7. Health is a precondition for superficial beauty.
8. Marry only for love.
9. Don't select a playmate. Choose a life partner.
10. Hope for as many children as possible.[14]

Nowhere were the new ethical mandates more evident than in slogans that "adapted" Christian maxims. Racial thinking outlawed mercy and proscribed empathy: "Do unto others as you are ordered" and "Love only thy neighbor who is like thyself." Even the marriage vow was reversed. "What God has rent asunder [i.e., different races], let no person unite."

Throughout the 1930s, the virulent language of *Mein Kampf* stocked Hitler's verbal arsenal with terms like "intervention" *(Eingriff)* and "attack" *(Angriff)*. "The greatest revolution ever experienced by Germany comes with

---

[13] Friedrich Zipfel, *Macht ohne Moral: Eine Dokumentation über Heinrich Himmler und die SS,* sound recording, Ariola, 1962. Hitler throughout his life spoke of the "Zauberkraft des gesprochenen Wortes" (Max Domarus, ed., *Hitler: Reden und Proklamationen* [Munich, 1965], 1:45).

[14] Arthur Gütt and Herbert Linden, *Blutschutz- und Ehegesundheitsgesetz* (Munich, 1937), pp. 12–14.

the beginning of a planned attack [*Angriff*] to improve racial hygiene among the *Volk*. The consequences of . . . racial politics will be decisive for the future of our *Volk* . . . because it creates new people [*Menschen*]."[15] The equation between race and political glory became axiomatic. "A healthy, German blooded people is the basis and precondition for the German Reich."[16] Walter Groß, the director of the Office of Racial Policies, spelled out the new ethic at the 1933 party rally. "This bloodstream must be kept pure and where false pity and false humanity attempt to preserve [*mitschleppen*] sickness, then people sin against the will of the Creator himself: because he created the laws of life that brutally destroy the weak again and again. As soon as the survival of the race is in jeopardy [these laws go into effect] to make way for the healthy and strong, the young, beautiful, and fit for the future that will in distant times bear new buds and precious fruits."[17] Every proclamation prepared its audience for a new collectivist moral standard.

A "revolution of the spirit" would sweep away traditional inhibitions, leading Nazis declared. "We live in a period of upheaval . . . everything breaks apart. New ideas take over."[18] Justice Minister Hans Frank insisted that eugenics formed the basis of Nazi society. "The national [sterilization] law proclaims the national socialist philosophy in stark clarity."[19] Rudolf Hess told a mass meeting of 1934, "National Socialism is nothing but applied biology." A leading eugenicist declared, "Every development of a people is ultimately bound via the blood to its racial essence."[20] The sheer volume (as well as the vehemence) of eugenics propaganda suggests that Nazi leaders, having orchestrated brilliant electoral campaigns before 1933, believed a media campaign could transform Germans' beliefs and behavior regarding both the "inferior" members of the superior race and the members of "inferior" races.

Alongside admonitions to sacrifice, popular literature featured self-interest as a subtext. In *Volk und Rasse,* for example, readers saw photos of pathetic

---

[15] Hitler, speech, September 7, 1937, in Domarus, ed. (1:711). See also his speech to the Deutsche Arbeitsfront on September 7, 1937 (2:717).

[16] Gütt and Linden, pp. 25, 29.

[17] Zipfel, *Macht ohne Moral,* p. 9. For a study of how films deployed the eugenic message, see Karl Ludwig Rost, *Sterilisation und Euthanasie im Film des Dritten Reiches: Nationalsozialistiche Propaganda im ihrer Beziehung zu rassenhygienischen Massnahmen des NS–Staates* (Husum, 1987), pp. 59–77, 121–54.

[18] "Revolution des Geistes," *Neues Volk,* vol. 10, no. 2 (October 1, 1934). For similar themes, see Walter Groß, "Ewige Stimme des Blutes im Strome deutscher Geschichte," *Neues Volk* 1 (August 5, 1933): 2.

[19] Hans Frank, *Nationalsozialistische Rassenpolitik,* in *Hier Sprach das neue Deutschland* (Munich, 1934), 2:815.

[20] Gütt and Linden, p. 31. Lifton coined a special term, "biocracy," to describe the result (n. 11 above), p. 16.

infants or "genetically sick" inmates in an asylum. Not only were these photos paired with pictures of healthy counterparts but they also bore captions such as "This three year old, born deaf, crippled, and completely retarded, costs the city of Berlin 8 Marks a day. The family of five with an unemployed family father receives only 24 Marks a week and spends half of that on rent."[21] Physician Karin Magnussen indignantly reported that of 250,000 mentally ill people in 1925, 60,000 were married and would probably reproduce! Taxpayers spent 1.2 billion Reichsmarks per year just to keep these "burdens to valuable racial stock" alive.[22] A feebleminded child would cost taxpayers RM 26,000, Groß reminded his women readers.

The center of moral gravity shifted from the individual body to the biologized body politic. A new term, "national body" (*Volkskörper*), displaced the traditional term, "national community" (*Volksgemeinschaft*). In the discourse describing the "unfit" and "unworthy," the body in question appeared as nongendered and subhuman. Not only did the eugenics courts order the sterilization of the same numbers of men and women but eugenic writings did not distinguish between male and female "unworthiness for life" (*Lebensunwürdigkeit*) except in the case of sexual offenders. The "discards" had neither gender nor humanity. The secular racial community transcended religious values in decisions about life, death, and human value.

If the victims lost their gendered identities, the perpetrators certainly did not. Generally, "experts" were men and "administrators" were women. But "feminine" traits shifted. Eugenicists and party leaders realized that they had to prepare people to welcome state intrusion into family life. That meant convincing mothers first of all. Wilhelm Frick used a series of books and speeches to prepare his readers. "We reject those critics of racial hygienic measures who object that marriage is a private affair because they rest their

---

[21] "Nicht Länger So!" *Neues Volk* 1, no. 2 (January 1, 1934): 10. Hitler's Reichstag speech of January 30, 1934, stressed the expense to the *Volk* of the millions kept "artificially" alive by modern medicine.

[22] Karin Magnussen (on the staff of the *Rassenpolitischen Amt*), *Rasen- und Bevölkerungs-politische Rüstzeug: Zahlen, Gesetze und Verordnung,* 2d ed. (Munich, 1939). Hitler stressed the economics of sterilization in his Reichstag speech, January 30, 1934, in Domarus, ed. (1:353–55): "Eine weitere schwere Belastung [than political opponents] ist das Heer jener, die aus Erbveranlagung von vornherein auf der negativen Seite des Völkischen Lebens geboren wurden. Hier wird der Staat zu wahrhaft revolutionären Maßnahmen greifen können" (Another worse burden [than political opponents] is the army of those who are born from the very beginning with the negative side of racial/national life. In this area the state can take up truly revolutionary laws). The *Volk* has paid 350 million, he emphasized. Klee cites examples of children's math textbooks that used story problems about money spent on healthy and unhealthy children (pp. 52–53).

opinion on assumptions that ultimately will produce the denial of marriage itself." Frick acknowledged that people might dissent: "Some may object to this law as a powerful legal intrusion [*Eingriff*] in the basic rights and liberties of the individual." But, he responded, only a drastic intrusion could protect the health of the *Volk*. To offset falling birth rates and rising divorce rates, Frick told his audience on Mother's Day, 1934, the state would step in where the father stepped out. All wage-earning wives and mothers who preferred not to work outside their homes should receive state economic assistance.

Frick was not alone in appreciating women's role in the new programs. The party leadership, which until 1933 had overlooked women, suddenly began to solicit women's loyalty. A closer look at the message suggests a reconstruction of the feminine "ideal type" and simultaneously connects that new representation to changes in expectations for physicians, health administrators, and social workers. Intervention into reproductive decisions, Frick and others realized, violated the Hippocratic oath as well as the mandate of motherly love. Because he believed doctors took their vow seriously, Frick called for a new specialist, a "doctor to the Nation [*Volkarzt*]," who would ignore individual patients' interests (and, by implication, even their right to live) in order to improve the life of the *Volk* as a whole. Agnes Bluhm, a respected eugenic researcher at the Kaiser Wilhelm Institute and one of Germany's first women physicians, linked the new vision of the physician to the novel concept of a Mother Nature who protects her creation by killing off the weak. (The connection with Nietzsche's criticism of Darwin is clear here.) The eugenic doctor treats not the individual but the genetic property (*Erbgut*) of the *Volk*. Bluhm called this an "expanded mission . . . that requires a new kind of idealism" and demands a special contribution to "Germanic renewal."[23] She appealed to women to place their "treasure of experience" (*Erfahrungsschatz*) at the service of the *Volk*.

The creation of the *Volkarzt* was complemented by that of the *Volksmutter* who would put the national family above her own children. Frick told women, "We stand now at a turning point! The salvation of Germany depends not only on love for Fatherland, but equally on women's and girls' devotion to the idea of motherhood." Women alone, Frick concluded, could become "the guardians of tradition."[24] What did it mean to "protect" future generations? It meant to attack the weak of the current generation. Bluhm reminded women physicians of their special responsibilities under the new eugenic regime.

---

[23] Agnes Bluhm, *Die rassenhygienischen Aufgaben des weiblichen Arztes,* Schriften zur Erblehre und Rassenhygiene, hrsg. Günther Just (Berlin, 1936), pp. 27, 7; cf. Lifton, p. 32.

[24] Dr. Frick, *Wir bauen das Dritte Reich* (Oldenburg, 1934), p. 55.

"The goal of German renewal is to fill every single member of the racial community with the consciousness that he or she is responsible in the first place to the total *Volk*."[25]

A Hannover eugenicist in 1934 astutely explained how women's thinking could be reoriented. "Women must be politically and racially-politically educated in national demographic politics, so they will not trespass against [the good of] the total People [*Volk*]." In other words, women who did not comply had to feel not that they committed a crime against the law but that they committed a sin against the people.[26] Guilt and fear would reinforce conformity to the new norms. Social worker Ilse Giebel explained the impact of Nazi beliefs on her field. Rather than rescuing "lost" or "endangered" youth, National Socialism would save a modern society that was "drained of blood and disjointed." She called on women to redress alienation by placing "collective need above private greed" ("Gemeinnutz vor Eigennutz!"). Think, she wrote, of "our führer, this unfathomably great gift to the nation!" In conclusion she summarized her message: "Public health has been newly ennobled through the race, because the holy ties to life that were willed by God have been accorded the highest honor." If women felt the task too enormous, she reminded her readers, they could count on help from the "young brown comrades in the Hitler Youth."[27]

Walter Groβ generalized this message for all German women when he ordered them to extinguish egotism from their souls. "You are a link in the chain of life, a little droplet in the great bloodstream of the *Volk* . . . a decisive and little thing [*Stückchen*] in the face of fate's great laws."[28] Gertrud Scholtz-Klink, leader of all Nazi women's organizations, admonished her followers to follow eugenic rules by preserving the family, as the "very source" (others said *Schoβ*, which means both "lap" and "womb") of health, which would promote "genuine mother love, the strongest moral [*sittliche*] power on earth."[29] Hence, "even if the individual suffers, and even fades away, . . . the source [*Quelle*] of the Community will become pure."[30]

---

[25] Bluhm, p. 7.

[26] *Besprechung*, July 30, 1934, Hann 80, II F/460, Niedersächisches Staatsarchiv, Hannover. The programs offering material incentives, the report continued, do not touch the real offenders—women who have the means to act on eugenic considerations but simply lack the conviction.

[27] Ilse Geibel, *Die Umwertung der Wohlfahrtspflege zur den Nationalsozialismus* (Langensalza, 1934) (part of *Fr. Mann's Pädagogisches Magazin*, Caritas Bibliothek 2827/1398). See also Lifton, pp. 12–18, 21–37.

[28] Groβ, *Nationalsozialistische Rassenpolitik* (n. 2 above), pp. 8, 21.

[29] Frick, *Wir bauen das Dritte Reich*, pp. 52–53.

[30] Ibid.

Here we see the true nature of Nazi gender ideals. Beneath the veneer of Gretchen's image quite a different woman emerged: a Brunhilde who would target children for sterilization, refuse shelter for a childhood Jewish friend, or turn her daughter out of the family for dating a boy with communist or Jewish parents. And as German women applied these prescriptions to human society, the Nazi symbolic system reinforced the new ideal by creating a racial Darwinist Mother Nature—who worked for long-term happiness in her kingdom by rejecting the weak who did not deserve to live. Giebel's call for a "propaganda crusade" (*Aufklärungsfeldzug*) epitomized the new values. "Our goal [as women social workers] is to supervise the selection process . . . and liberate the qualified '*Erbgut*' "—a term that has a double meaning: the landed property inherited by offspring and genetic property. Frick told mothers to do their scientific and moral duty. "We must have the courage again to grade our people according to their genetic value."[31] Eugenicist Martin Staemmler, in a book dedicated to his wife, admonished women to follow their "holy duty" as mothers. They must become "hard, without pity, and ruthless. The battle is waged without humanity."[32] Women must live by two principles: fertility and selection. The underlying logic was clear. If you do not produce unhealthy people, you will not have to eliminate them later.

The explicit demand for new ethical principles and revolutionary priorities in thinking about the value and definition of life directly impinged on terrain normally within the purview of religion. Because women, like physicians, had been socialized to preserve the lives of children and people under their care, Nazi racial purity legislation affected them directly. It is not surprising that many Germans took their concerns to the clergy.

CATHOLIC REACTIONS

Catholic bishops traditionally met to work out common responses and policies in the medieval monastery city of Fulda. In the fall of 1933 bishops had pressing matters to discuss. During the previous July the Concordat between Rome and Berlin had acknowledged Catholic rights in Nazi Germany and paved the way for close cooperation between church and state. In many respects, especially regarding gender roles in modern society, Catholic teaching harmonized with Nazi doctrine. For both, the family constituted the "germ cell" of the social order. The Nazi marriage loan scheme and pronatalist policies offered financial support to social goals of which Catholics

[31] Wilhelm Frick, *Ansprache auf der ersten Sitzung des Sachverständigenbeirates für Bevölkerungs- und Rassenpolitik* (Berlin, 1933), 1:8.
[32] Martin Staemmler, *Rassenpflege im völkischen Staat* (Munich, 1934), p. 37.

approved.[33] Further, the aggressive government stance against venereal disease, abortion, birth control, and pornography won the bishops' endorsement.

But eugenic policies created consternation because they signaled state intervention into a sphere that the bishops regarded as purely religious. Meeting at Fulda, the bishops decided to negotiate with health officials rather than to oppose directly the new measures and risk a breakdown of the Concordat. Six months of intense discussion between July, when the sterilization law was written, and January 1934, when it took effect, produced no solution.[34] Lengthy disputes with the Interior Ministry's representative failed. On November 3, 1933, the Catholic representative noted, "No progress. The total state insists on its rights and on the purifying, strengthening effect of the law on the *Volk.*" An official at the Ministry of the Interior scoffed at the Catholics' demand for written agreements. Further, he dishonestly hinted that force would not be used since the law stipulated that clients "may," not "must," be sterilized. Further, even though the obligation to report (*Meldepflicht*) obligated Catholic health professionals, he said Catholics could be released from the obligation to issue a sterilization order (*Antragspflicht*).

In January 1934, when the sterilization measures went into effect, Catholic priests throughout Germany reminded their congregations of *casti connubii* in one of two formulations, the first of which was more unequivocal.

A. It is not permitted to request sterilization for oneself or to submit others to sterilization. This is Catholic teaching.
B. According to the declaration of our Holy Father, a Catholic may not morally request sterilization for himself or order sterilization for others.[35]

---

[33] The marriage loan program offered substantial grants to young couples planning marriage provided they met eugenic requirements, the woman agreed not to work for wages, neither partner was "non-Aryan," and both were of childbearing age. The loans came in the form of coupons for the purchase of household items. For each child born, the total debt was reduced by 25 percent. A new tax on unmarried people financed the scheme.

[34] "Bericht über Verhandlungen in Berlin," Bertram, bishop of Osnabrück (report of meeting on November 21, 1933, at Fulda between Bertram and ministry director Dr. Buttmann. See also notes from November 7, 1934, meeting in Berlin, Erzbischöfliches Archiv Freiburg (hereafter, EAF), Gröber Nachlaß/Nb8/46.

[35] Wilhelm Frick, January 26, 1934, to Fulda bishops, RM d Innern Berlin. Note the slightly different wording here than in Zipfel's only mention of Christian reactions to the sterilization law (Friedrich Zipfel, *Kirchenkampf in Deutschland, 1933–1945: Religionsverfolgung und Selbstbehauptung der Kirchen in der nationalsozialistischen Zeit* [Berlin, 1965], doc. 10, p. 279). According to Zipfel, the statement closed on a

Within a week, Frick threatened reprisals if such statements did not stop, but also added conciliatory hope that "friendly" negotiations would obviate further friction. Nazi officials ridiculed Catholic scruples, noting that popes had for centuries tolerated the castration of choir boys. Catholics responded that such practices had stopped in the early nineteenth century. Recriminations continued. In April Vice Chancellor Papen, having failed to change opinion at high levels, told Cardinal Adolf Bertram, "In my opinion more moderate voices now prevail." On June 27, 1934 (on virtually the eve of the storm troopers' purge), Hitler, Frick, and Bishop Berning discussed eugenics legislation. No compromise appeared.

The acrimony did not abate. Nor did confusion among Catholics diminish. The Fulda bishops, in deciding not to oppose the laws head-on, placed their hopes on winning exemptions, not repeal. A few priests openly endorsed the goals behind eugenic law and criticized only the application; if only sterilization were voluntary, they argued, Catholics could support it without reservation. "The *purpose* of the law to prevent genetically defective offspring is, in itself, praiseworthy from a moral theological standpoint and therefore merits support."[36] Catholics feared that a flat rejection could jeopardize their newly won civic equality. Any appeal for exception status might restigmatize them.

Nazi officials yielded on only one point. Catholic physicians who objected to sterilization (or abortion) were exempted from performing the operation unless they served on public health boards.[37] Prelates warned Health Ministry officials that physicians and health officials (usually not women) ought never to be placed in a terrible situation by the state. Nazi negotiators gave Catholics "no very great hopes," and promised only that residents of sex-segregated facilities would not be sterilized as long as they remained institutionalized at private expense. Perhaps the prelates thought that would settle the matter. It did not. Throughout Catholic Germany nuns, institution directors, social workers, and educators demanded clarity. Bertram (himself a defender of moderate eugenics) noted, "Powerful

---

weak note: "Dankbar anerkennen wir jede Rücksicht auf diesen Grundsatz." Frick's version omitted this weak clause.

[36] Emphasis in the original, twenty-five-page unsigned mimeographed report on the "moral theological implications" of sterilization, n.d. [Spring 1934], EAF, B2/48/20 Sterilization.

[37] Several versions of the wording on this exist, the most common one a statement quoted in the newspapers. Doctors who "innerlich auf dem Boden des Gesetzes stehen" must perform the operation, thereby leaving the way open for others to say no. Only Cardinal Faulhaber acknowledged the insidious moral implications: "Ein furchtbares Wort ist gefallen, 'Gut ist, was dem Volke dient' " (Klee [n. 12 above], p. 53).

agitation for sterilization has unleashed great confusion in Catholic circles."[38]

The bishops, not wanting to lose the gains made in the Concordat, proceeded cautiously. But the laity faced daily inroads into their lives. When, for example, the church opposed Nazi marriage policies and eugenics, officials of the National Socialist Bureau of Welfare (NSV) forbade social workers from discussing reproduction at Catholic marriage counseling centers. Since virtually all couples seeking advice asked questions related to marriage or eugenics or both, this measure encouraged Catholics to look elsewhere for advice.[39] Other worries abounded. "If we fundamentally refuse, we will run the risk that Party leaders will accuse us of not being staunch Nazis. We might not receive any more referrals from welfare agencies."[40] Elisabeth Zillken, national chair of the Board for Catholic Charity for Women, Girls, and Children, feared that NSV social workers would only assign cases deemed hopeless to Catholic welfare institutions if Catholics did not cooperate.[41] While the religious associations expressed a commitment to mercy for the neediest (as opposed to only the racially "fit"), practical considerations entered into the balance as well. The relegation of "hopeless" cases to religious charity would have placed a large burden on the resources of organizations such as Catholic Caritas and Protestant Inner Mission; it would have deprived them of potentially useful members as well.

The Sisters of Mercy begged for guidance from ecclesiastical superiors. "Our sisters hope through prayer, sacrifice, and penance to be guided by the Holy Ghost and the grace of God's leadership in these times when decisions are so difficult." When no assurance arrived, they wrote directly to Interior Minister Frick and received exemption from cooperating with the operation. But their questions persisted. "Our concern now is to give practical guidance in accord with the official [Catholic] position to the sisters who come with questions. Yet we want also to avoid possible disturbances in hospital

[38] *Abschrift* accompanying Bertram's letter to Orsengingo, July 13, 1935, EAF, 48/19. Bertram notes that Frick accused Catholics of creating a hate (*Hetze*) campaign and maintained that the state determines the limits of the Concordat. Bertram commented presciently that if the state always had the last word, then the Concordat had no meaning.

[39] Estimates from 1931 to 1933 showed that 75 percent asked legal and 25 percent asked eugenics-related questions ("Katholische Eheberatung," *Märkische-Volkszeitung*, no. 22 [January 22, 1933]). Further, 60–80 percent of all clients came from "mixed" marriages—i.e., between Protestants and Catholics.

[40] Sr. M. Clementina, St. Franziskusheim, Schwarzach/Bühl, May 25, 1934, EAF, B2/48/19.

[41] Kreutz (but not signed or noted) to Bishop Wilhelm Berning of Osnabrück, June 26, 1934. Here are many questions that Caritas is not qualified to answer. Elisabeth Zillken to Kreutz, March 16, 1935, Dortmund.

administration that would endanger the positions of nurses who are also nuns."[42] It was all very well to exempt physicians, but that actually eliminated only a small part of the team. Nurses and nuns prepared the patient, cooked the food, filled out the initial forms, dressed the wounds, sterilized the instruments. Where, they asked, does one draw the line?

Confronting this problem, Archbishop Gröber, advised by theologians, hit on a compromise that shifted the decision away from the clergy and onto the individuals involved. He distinguished between "formal" and "material" cooperation, and applied it to the difference between filling out the initial papers (*Anzeige*) and signing the final contract (*Antrag*) recommending sterilization. Gröber assured the nuns "that the obligation for hospital and institution directors to file reports on their inmates as laid out by administrative directives of December 5, 1933 for the [sterilization] law . . . in no way contradicts Catholic doctrine. This obligation can be met by the devout Catholic without conflicts of conscience."[43] The obligation to report potential cases (*Anzeigepflicht*), said Gröber, did not constitute cooperation, but authorizing sterilization (*Die Antragsstellung*), by contrast, is not allowed for Catholics. Theologians worked out complex logical formulations to distinguish between "material" and "formal" cooperation.

The director of Catholic Charities insisted upon avoiding any confrontation with the state (which he believed the church would inevitably lose). "In my opinion, we must achieve a *modus vivendi* that on the one hand makes it clear that the secular power can force obedience, but on the other that avoids the unnecessary application of physical force."[44] Refusing to cooperate might result in dismissal, loss of funding, or even the demise of an institution. Full cooperation might well violate the prohibition against intervening in childbearing.

Subtle theological distinctions between "material" and "formal" cooperation may have salved prelates' consciences. But it did little to still the consciences of the people, usually women, who confronted the effects of eugenic laws in their daily lives. Because of occupational gender stratification, the conflicts often pitted women who worked with clients against prelates who thought in theological terms and negotiated with officials from the health bureaucracy. Health care workers and teachers deluged their superiors as well as local health tribunals with requests for guidance. A half-century removed

[42] Barmherzigen Schwestern, to Erzbischöfliches Ordinariat Freiburg, February 5, 1934, EAF, B2/48/19.

[43] "Aussprache" Erzbischöfliches Ordinariat, letter, January 26, 1934. The bishop added, "Die Antragsstellung dagegen ist dem Katholiken nicht erlaubt" (EAF, B2/48/19). Compare also Gröber to Hauer, May 8, 1934, ibid.

[44] Answer from the director of Caritasverbandes, Berlin, June 26, 1934, Deutsche Caritas Verein Archiv, Freiburg (R 567) (hereafter, DCV-A).

from these events, it is difficult to evaluate the letter writers' intent. Did they mean to use stalling techniques to delay decisions? Or did they intend to clog the health care bureaucracy and slow down the rate of success? Given the general hostility to eugenic measures expressed in internal memos within Catholic institutions, I am inclined to see these queries as one kind of bureaucratic defense.

How, many asked, can one gauge the impact of "damaged" genes as against a "damaged" environment in assessing a child's poor performance on tests? What really measures intelligence? These doubts, expressed by individuals who probably knew their Thomas Aquinas, continued. Catholic teachers at a kindergarten in Riegel asked the district leader about their obligations.[45] How can one draw the line between delivering a victim to an operation that contradicted Catholic dogma and accompanying a client in the moment of great spiritual need (*Seelsorge*)? Zillken believed "that at the very first moment when we are asked to accompany clients, we must say that someone else has to fetch the child from our institution, and that we will not accompany her."[46] She and other supervisors continued to request clear directives. None arrived.

The director of a course for health administrators in Dortmund wrote that directors reported "great confusion," and most wanted to declare outright opposition to any kind of cooperation with laws they considered immoral.

The nuns here face difficult conflicts of conscience when they receive orders to deliver the girls to forced sterilization. These girls have been entrusted to the sisters for protection. The sisters see the very mission of their work in taking responsibility for individual girls. But on the other hand we have no judicial custody over the girls. If the Home resists, then eventually the authorities will proceed with force and fetch the girls with the help of a round-up squad [*Überfallkommando*]. If the Home does not object, people will assume we have given our approval. If the girl herself objects [to sterilization] the issues become even more complicated. ... The participants were seriously disquieted ... but finally the opinion coalesced that somehow some form of resistance [*Widerstand*] had to occur.[47]

Luise, duchess of Roeder and Diersburg, the director of a school in Mannheim, reacted more unequivocally. On May 30, 1934, she wrote, "If we fundamentally refuse to cooperate we do not fear any disadvantages. We will stand fast." Confident of her public relations skills and perhaps emboldened

[45] Kinderheim Riegel to Erzbischöfliches Ord. Freiburg January 23, 1934, EAF, B2/48/19.

[46] E. Zillken, May 7, 1934, Dortmund, and June 3, 1935, DCV-A, R218.iv. For a stunning example of the impact of nuns on patients about to be sterilized, see the excerpt in Klee (n. 12 above), p. 49.

[47] Gv. Mann [signature unclear], Caritasverband, Freiburg, July 17, 1933, to Rudolf Geis, Erzbischöfliches Konvikt, EAF, B2/48/20.

by her noble status, she concluded that they would neither encourage nor allow a sister to accompany a patient to hospital.

Other institutions moved toward compliance. Maria Matheis of Karlsruhe said, "We have always assumed that a nun would, like a mother, stand at the side of the girls as they walk along a difficult path. The girls are grateful."[48] And some theologians asserted that filling out an *Antrag* might be justified to preserve communal well-being. "Considerations of the general welfare include, for example, preventing a great evil ... such as dismissal of Catholic personnel from all public offices and positions, etc. etc." Moreover, cooperation would also protect individuals against state reprisals.[49] The passage of time exacerbated the confusion and dampened morale. The spirit of opposition was undercut as theologians rationalized where they might have stood firm.

A circular letter by an anonymous Catholic to the Fulda bishops communicated widespread alarm. Catholics wanted strong guidance and instead they received the same sort of equivocal statements the church gave out on the issue of divorced persons' right to remarry. In this seven-page letter the author described the case of a physician on a local health board who had resigned his post despite assurance from his confessor that such a step was not necessary. People want, the author wrote, "authoritative instructions," not "subtle distinctions."[50] When prelates negotiated, they demonstrated great concern about Catholic (usually male) physicians' consciences; but they virtually never defended nuns' and social workers' concerns. These low-level personnel traditionally had eschewed contacts with the secular world and felt safe, as they said, "behind church walls." When Catholic health workers objected to church reactions to Nazi eugenics, they criticized their religious superiors as well as state policies. While objecting strongly to specific legislation, these Catholics nevertheless defended their loyalty to both church and state.

PROTESTANT RESPONSES

The Nazi regime in early 1933 invited Protestant eugenicists to cooperate in drafting legislation and administering policy. Whereas Catholics (like Hermann Muckermann) lost their research and teaching positions, Protestants (like Hans Harmsen) fared quite well.[51] Centuries of close cooperation

---

[48] Letter to the archbishop of Freiburg, May 26, 1934, EAF, Generalia/B2/48/19.

[49] A report on the "moral theological implications" of sterilization, n.d., EAF, B2/48/20 Sterilization.

[50] "Rundfrage an die hochwürdigsten Herrn Oberhirten," mimeograph, unsigned, Breslau, January 23, 1935, EAF, B2/48/20.

[51] Nevertheless, moderate eugenicists like those in the *Arbeitsgemeinschaft*, which initially strongly supported Hitler and included Gütt as a member, broke with the

between the Lutheran Church and the Prussian state had given Protestants an assurance that Catholics did not feel. In addition, as James Zabel has noted, the Protestant belief system harmonized in key respects with the general Nazi weltanschauung.[52]

Gleichschaltung (nazification) for the Protestants proceeded smoothly for about a year. The Confessing Church broke with the Nazis in 1934 on theological grounds but never doubted eugenic and racial hygiene programs. Within the majoritarian Protestant establishment (Deutsch-Evangelische Kirche, or DEK), social welfare organizations continued to function. In 1936, for example, Interior Minister Frick explicitly encouraged the Protestant Committee on Sexual Ethics to continue its cooperation with the state.[53] Protestant hospitals applied for licenses to conduct eugenic operations. At least some cooperation must have been motivated by opportunism, perhaps the calculation that early compliance with the new Nazi state would produce rewards. But the long tradition of progressive Protestant support for various schemes for racial improvement makes it clear that much collaboration stemmed from genuine enthusiasm: some progressives within the Protestant church, like Hans Harmsen, had supported such schemes since the 1920s.[54]

Protestants charged with implementing sterilization laws reconciled religious faith and patriotic fervor. Most Protestant defenders of eugenics supported the new laws within a Christian framework. This meant that while they perceived medical intervention as a means of improving the social order and carrying out God's commands on earth, they balked at Nazi rhetoric that extolled a racially superior *Volk* as an end in itself.[55] "Our *Land* and *Volk* stand at a turning point of immeasurable meaning. Our *Vaterland* needs not only eugenically superior people, but morally better people. . . . As long as sin exists in the world, we will need the blessings [*Segnungen*] of science to

---

regime. In 1935 Catholics dissented, Harmsen left shortly thereafter, representatives from the government resigned, and the organization (which lost half its membership) added "Christian" to its name. See the correspondence between Kreutz and the organization, 1935–42, DCV-A, 241.4.1 Fasz. in A. Sterilization and 465.4, .065, and .024.

[52] James Zabel, *Nazism and the Pastors* (Missoula, Mont., 1976).

[53] Nora Hartwich, "Aktennotiz aus einer Besprechung am 17.4.1936, Archiv des diakonischen Werkes, Berlin (hereafter, ADW), CA/GF 1419/9 II.

[54] Weindling (n. 10 above), pp. 422–25, 446–48.

[55] An excellent source on these confidential opinions is the Inner Mission file, "Gefärdtenfürsorge," ADW, 1.255. Correspondence between the Central Committee and D. Jeep, H. Harmsen, N. Hartwich, and Frau Marx-Langenberg. For a theological view, see Alfred D. Müller, *Ethik: Der evangelische Weg zur Verwirklichung des Guten* (Berlin, 1937), vol. 4. See also "Durchführung des Gesetzes," ADW, CA/GF 2000/I.6 p. 105.

combat it."[56] Protestants seldom mentioned the secular-scientific Nazi doctrines that praised the superior race. Instead, they spoke of ameliorating suffering in the world and bolstering their faltering attempts to stave off social degeneration. God's will rather than the führer's wish guided their acts and inspired their rationalizations.

A report from March 1935 highlights the contrast between progressive health workers in the Protestant Inner Mission and their Catholic counterparts. It began with an expression of sympathy not for the handicapped clients but for social workers who faced the daily "agony of watching the suffering and misery in hospitals, asylums, and nursing homes." Sterilization would ameliorate their difficulties because the staff could console themselves that after a couple of generations such damaged clients would no longer exist. That must be God's will. "As Christians we take the eugenic laws seriously as God's rules [*Ordnungen*], which place us under an obligation." Children, therefore, the report implied, ought never suffer for the sins of the father. No offspring. No suffering. With no sense of irony (or pathos), the author noted that "it is extremely difficult for our poor, simple minded girls to grasp that despite the propaganda for bearing many children [including support for unmarried motherhood], at the same time sterilization can be desirable for some. A few years ago, when the desire for abortions was widespread, the readiness for sterilization would have probably been more common."[57] The author described the "great upheaval" when children in an institution realized they were being considered for sterilization and deplored "her" girls' tendency to gossip among themselves about the operation. And, too, she noted that depression and sometimes suicide resulted. Nevertheless, she persevered. "We realize that each person lives in the chain of inherited guilt and fate, and that we work with the victims of social guilt, of our collective guilt. We have to make good that guilt and care for the victims." Guilt, while frequently mentioned in this passage, was deflected away from the perpetrators and onto patients' parents.

Even as Protestant reports emphasized that their clients were being "protected, not punished," they admitted that sterilization left patients miserable. "The saddest are those who have no more family left and fall into depression and think of suicide." Gisela Bock quotes similar pleas made to the health officials.[58]

[56] "Die fürsorgerische Betreuung Sterilisierter und zu Sterilisierender," ADW, CA/GF 2000/I.6, p. 108.

[57] Ibid., p. 26. Klee (n. 12 above) brilliantly explores the Protestant response—even among supporters of the Confessing Church.

[58] Bock, *Zwangssterilisation im Nationalsozialismus* (n. 12 above), pp. 278–89. See Klee's excellent discussion of Protestant callousness and the limits of charity, pp. 34–45.

The case of Rosa typified a whole range of young women. She told the local eugenic health administrators: "I do not agree to undergo sterilization. I insist that I can bring healthy children into the world and raise them respectably. If I could not, then I don't know what in the world I would do. I will begin a respectable life, so that later when I marry I can be an energetic and honorable housewife. I await your answer."[59] None came. Rosa, it seemed, had a strong moral sense, but she possessed a weak intellect. When clients expressed reasonable objections to sterilization, their arguments supposedly demonstrated their lack of understanding of the issues involved (i.e., the national genetic property or *Erbgut*). A request for sterilization, by contrast, demonstrated loose morals in the eugenicists' view.

How are we to interpret such stubborn adhesion to a belief system, especially among health care professionals? Part of the answer lies in the tradition from which Protestant social work developed. The Protestant eugenics consensus developed within the Inner Mission among people concerned about moral degeneration. Initially, in the nineteenth century, a few brave Protestants had set out to rescue "endangered" girls from social and economic exploitation by establishing homes for unmarried mothers, employment services, railway station hospitality centers, educational projects, and dormitories. The Depression, however, underscored their failure to eradicate (or even retard) moral decline. Overwhelmed by the task, social workers began to reverse subject and object in their discussions about social danger. Increasingly, they perceived the vulnerable social order as "endangered" by unrepentant women who came to be seen as less than fully "worthy" human beings. Social workers' reports and minutes from Inner Mission meetings are tinged with the Calvinist language of predestination. Protestant eugenicists perceived a world divided between genetic "unregenerates" (characterized by visible signs and spiritual scars) and the "elect." Biological sin placed these unfortunates beyond the reach of this mission in the urban wilderness.

Protestant rhetoric evoked the dread of unseen sources of evil. Fear of hidden "sick" genes that might infect the healthy mounted, and fear of the "unworthy" increased apace. Unseen pollution attacked the genetic inheritance (*Erbgut*), operating secretly. Although the parallel was not made, the descriptions of a hidden genetic threat resonated with descriptions of a Jewish conspiracy. The respectability of eugenic thinking, reinforced with Christian underpinnings, ultimately enhanced the acceptability of a related brand of biological thinking—anti-Semitism. As Ulrich Herbert's work shows, by the

---

[59] "Die fürsorgerische Betreuung," March 26, 1935, ADW, CA/GF 2000/I.6, p. 105.

time war began racial categories had thoroughly established themselves as a part of daily life.[60]

CONCLUSIONS

The reactions of prelates and laity to eugenics legislation suggests that people who generally supported National Socialism retained their critical capacities in areas that concerned their private lives despite a deluge of propaganda and the threat of reprisals. Did such single-issue opposition damage compliance with National Socialist eugenics measures? Specifically, did compliance rates in predominantly Catholic areas differ from other regions? National statistics suggest not. After reading a government report on forced sterilization, Archbishop Gröber noticed that the rates in his home bishopric were the highest in Germany (and far higher than Protestant, liberal Berlin). "These statistics on sterilization put Baden at the head of the national list . . . and demonstrate that only a small percentage of objections (6.3%) are granted by the health tribunals."[61] Over the next decade, during which time about 300,000 people were sterilized, compliance rates showed no particular correlation with religion. This suggests that in practical terms objections to eugenics from ordinary people in Catholic regions had little impact. Letters exchanged among health care workers and educators on the subject of eugenics reveal considerable disagreement; one could speak about a *Kirchenkampf* not merely between church and state but also within religious communities.

One might observe that widespread disaffection about particular issues dampened enthusiasm for specifically National Socialist projects and conclude, as Ian Kershaw has, that Germans accepted Hitler as a leader without subscribing to specifically Nazi ideology.[62] But single-issue opposition does not in itself assume broader dissent. Nor did specific criticisms necessarily incite more profound criticism. It often happened that individuals who

[60] Ulrich Herbert, *A History of Foreign Labor in Germany, 1880–1945* (Ann Arbor, Mich., 1990), pp. 147–50.

[61] Die Auswirkung des Sterilisationsgesetzes in Baden, State Ministry of Health, Ministry of the Interior, June 21, 1934. Gröber threatened to transfer priests who undermined eugenics programs, insisted that sterilized people not be allowed to marry (not even each other), and continued to justify Catholics' support for sterilization, as long as they did not actually perform the operation. In Baden, 3,025 contracts were issued, 997 people were sterilized, and 940 cases were pending; 289 men and 283 women were sterilized. Nationwide, 84,526 orders were issued and 31,002 people were already sterilized in 1934 (Bock, *Zwangssterilisation im Nationalsozialismus*, pp. 230–31).

[62] Ian Kershaw, *The Hitler Myth: Image and Reality* (New York, 1987), and *Hitler* (London, 1991).

criticized one aspect of policy became more compliant in other ways to prevent detection. People, in this case mainly women, who objected to a policy that impinged directly on their daily lives may have felt that they could disagree and fashion their own individual values. A bit of freedom to shape their own vision of nazism may well have given them a sense of independence and lessened the psychological oppression of a total ideological claim. The evidence I have used in this article does not permit sweeping conclusions. I present this case study as a caution to those who conclude that every sign of dissent indicates resistance. To preserve the memory of those Germans who took major risks to rescue a victim or to thwart the Nazi regime, we need to keep the line clear between resistance and more narrowly based dissent.

The Conduct of War: Soldiers and the Barbarization of Warfare

Omer Bartov
Rutgers University

The most conspicuous instance of resistance to the regime in the Third Reich is arguably the July 1944 *Putsch* attempt. This act of rebellion by a number of officers has been the focus of a rich literature concerned with the technical, personal, political, and moral implications of a coup d'état against a criminal regime at a time of grave military crisis.[1] Conversely, one of the most striking features of the Nazi dictatorship is the remarkable loyalty to the regime manifested by the *Wehrmacht*'s rank and file and by the junior officer corps throughout the war.[2] The following pages will attempt to sketch out the boundaries of collaboration and resistance in the German army by exploring three separate but related spheres of the soldiers' existence at the front: the formal sphere of military discipline and martial law; the personal sphere of survival, fear, comradeship, and family; and the ideological sphere, molded by preconscription and army indoctrination.

I

A seemingly obvious and clear-cut boundary to opposition and resistance is military discipline. Under the Third Reich, and increasingly during the war, the *Wehrmacht* resorted to ever harsher punishments, legitimized not least by the politicization of martial law, whereby offenses such as desertion, cowardice, and self-inflicted wounds came to be considered subversion and were consequently often punished by death. During the Second World War at least 15,000 German soldiers were executed by their own army, and many more were shot on the spot while trying to cross over to the enemy, fleeing in panic, or simply failing to carry out orders on the battlefield; these facts testify to the severity with which the *Wehrmacht* enforced

---

[1] See P. Hoffmann, *Widerstand gegen Hitler und das Attentat vom 20. Juli 1944*, 2d ed. (Munich and Zürich, 1984) and sources quoted therein.

[2] See, e.g., I. Kershaw, *The "Hitler Myth": Image and Reality in the Third Reich* (Oxford, 1987), pp. 209, 217–18; M. G. Steinert, *Hitler's War and the Germans,* trans. T. E. S. De Witt (Athens, Ohio, 1977), pp. 196, 264–73, 282–83, 289, 298–302.

This essay originally appeared in the *Journal of Modern History* 64, suppl. (December 1992).

combat discipline.[3] There is little doubt that the fear such disciplinary practices induced in the soldiers played a major role in preventing any large-scale revolts and in keeping the majority of men at the front.

Discipline alone, however, rarely suffices to explain conformity; on the contrary, when administered in disproportionate doses, and especially in conscript armies, it may well cause rather than prevent mutiny.[4] But in the *Wehrmacht,* and especially in the *Ostheer* which constituted the lion's share of the German armed forces throughout most of the war, there were other important aspects to the transformation of martial law which both encouraged compliance with combat discipline and enhanced the troops' sense of a common destiny, purpose, and guilt. As policy combined with unforeseen circumstances, the *Wehrmacht* created a mechanism that allowed the increasingly brutalized soldiers to vent their anger and frustration at targets other than their superiors and then tied them to each other with terror of the enemy's vengeance in case of defeat. Consequently, when we speak of the individual choosing between collaboration and resistance, we must take into account not only the brutal response of his superiors to failure to comply with orders but also the dread of retribution by prospective vanquishers for his own brutalities. This dilemma was very much at the core of the soldiers' existence at the front and remained a central motif in their subsequent rationalizations of the war experience.

If we are to understand indiscipline as a possible indication of resistance, then it is worthwhile to examine its changing manifestations among the troops and the means employed to curb it by the *Wehrmacht.* During the invasion of Poland, German senior officers complained about the high incidence of disciplinary problems, which was especially disturbing considering the swiftness of the campaign and the relatively low number of casualties.[5] This was probably caused both by the lack of enthusiasm with which war was greeted in Germany as a whole, and by the fact that the newly founded *Wehrmacht* still experienced numerous organizational, technical, and disciplinary hitches.[6] Moreover, officers complaining about soldiers' acts of

[3] M. Messerschmidt and F. Wüllner, *Die Wehrmachtjustiz im Dienste des National-sozialismus* (Baden-Baden, 1987), esp. pp. 63–89; and, for examples, see O. Bartov, *Hitler's Army: Soldiers, Nazis, and War in the Third Reich* (New York and Oxford, 1991), pp. 59–105.

[4] See, e.g., G. Pedrocini, *Les mutineries de 1917,* 2d ed. (Paris, 1983); L. V. Smith, "Command Authority in the French Army, 1914–1918: The Case of the 5ᵉ Division d'Infanterie" (Ph.D. diss., Columbia University, 1989).

[5] See, e.g., Bundesarchiv-Militärarchiv, Freiburg im Breisgau (henceforth BA-MA), RH26-12/252, 25.10.39, 20.11.39, 18.12.39; RH26-12/279, 29.9.39; 1.10.39; RH26-12/99, 25.10.40; RH26-12/236, 8.11.39.

[6] W. Wette, "Ideologien, Propanganda und Innenpolitik als Voraussetzungen der Kriegspolitik des Dritten Reiches," in *Ursachen und Voraussetzungen der deutschen*

brutality toward civilians attributed them to the example set by the SS.[7] Thus as early as the Polish campaign the army experienced two distinct though, of course, not unrelated forms of indiscipline: one that might be construed as constituting explicit or implicit, conscious or unconscious resistance to the regime and its policies of expansion and another that actually conformed with the underlying ideological assumptions and goals of the regime.

During the campaign of May and June 1940, the lingering effects of fighting and occupation in Poland could clearly be observed. While combat units recorded an alarming rise in acts of brutality such as rape, armed robbery, and indiscriminate shooting, senior commanders insisted on draconian punishment, including the death penalty, in order to nip such occurrences in the bud.[8] Here was another curious example of the ambivalent relationship between military discipline and ideological penetration. The soldiers behaved as they did because in Poland they had become used to treating the enemy as inferior, a notion they had in fact acquired long before their conscription; in the West, however, due to political and ideological considerations, their superiors refused to tolerate unauthorized brutalities vis-à-vis the occupied population. But in their efforts to enforce discipline, the generals established the practice of executing their own troops on a scale vastly different from that of the *Kaiserheer* of the First World War. In this the senior officer corps manifested the spirit of ruthlessness and contempt for life that characterized the Third Reich.

Unlike previous campaigns, the *Wehrmacht* marched into the Soviet Union equipped with a set of orders that translated Hitler's notion of a war of extermination and subjugation into the practical terminology of the military.[9] Thus martial law as regarded the occupied population and Soviet prisoners of war was curtailed, since it was stipulated that German soldiers could not be tried for offenses against enemy troops and civilians as long as they did not impinge thereby on military discipline. Here the close tie between the two aspects of law and discipline was most clearly revealed. On the one hand, the troops received and dutifully obeyed orders to shoot on the spot captured Red Army commissars, to deliver other politically and "racially" suspect individuals to the death squads of the SS and SD, to punish collectively entire communities for any guerrilla activities in their vicinity, to "purge" whole

---

Kriegspolitik (Stuttgart, 1979), vol. 1 of *Das Deutsche Reich und der Zweite Weltkrieg* (henceforth *DRZW*), pp. 25, 138–42.

[7] E. Klee et al., eds., *"Schöne Zeiten": Judenmord aus der Sicht der Täter und Gaffer* (Frankfurt am Main, 1988), pp. 14–15.

[8] BA-MA, RH26-12/183, 21.5.40; RH26-12/274, 27.6.40; RH26-12/235, 2.10.40, 3.10.40; RH26-12/99, 25.10.40; RH26-12/108, 9.4.41; RH26-12/21, 6.5.41, 7.5.41, 8.5.41.

[9] C. Streit, *Keine Kameraden* (Stuttgart, 1978), pp. 28–61.

areas of alleged partisan but, in reality, often Jewish civilian concentrations, and to support themselves, as well as the rear, by large-scale requisitions of food, livestock, clothes, and labor, thereby rapidly creating conditions of acute famine in widespread parts of occupied Russia. On the other hand, the otherwise rigidly disciplinarian *Wehrmacht* allowed the troops to go unpunished for unauthorized acts of brutality, indiscriminate shootings of prisoners of war and civilians, looting, and wanton destruction, though commanders repeatedly urged the soldiers to desist from such "unsoldierly" conduct.[10] Indeed, it was difficult to punish the men for acts that merely emulated similar and far more destructive official actions; and, considering the almost complete immunity provided by the "Barbarossa" decree, it was exceedingly problematic and politically unwise to press charges even against soldiers who had maltreated the most helpless and obviously innocent civilians.

Curiously, although this situation could have been expected to cause a general disintegration of discipline (as some generals indeed warned), it in fact greatly enhanced military cohesion, which in turn goes some way to explain the almost complete absence of opposition within the lower ranks of the *Wehrmacht*. Soldiers faced with the grim realities of an extraordinarily brutal and costly war, on the one hand, and with the prospects of harsh punishment for any attempt to evade it, on the other, were now given an outlet for their accumulated fear and anger, especially when officers turned a blind eye to ostensibly forbidden actions. As long as they fought well, the soldiers were allowed to "let off steam" both by transgressing accepted civilian norms of behavior and by acting illegally even according to the far from "normal" standards of the front. Legalizing these actions would have deprived them of their value as a unifying element that bound the troops together by creating a keen awareness of their shared responsibility for horrific crimes. Commanders may have neglected to punish their soldiers for unauthorized actions because in Russia they had their hands full just keeping combat discipline intact, were hampered by the "Barbarossa" decree, were reluctant to imprison soldiers in view of the manpower crisis, and were at least in part themselves imbued with the same anti-Bolshevik, anti-Slav, and anti-Semitic sentiments proclaimed by the regime.[11] But by acting as they did, they enhanced the military cohesion of the army by making submission to brutal combat discipline more acceptable in view of the license given to the soldiers to act with similar brutality toward their real and imaginary enemies. They also made the idea of resistance to military superiors (and thereby to the regime)

[10] O. Bartov, *The Eastern Front, 1941–45: German Troops and the Barbarisation of Warfare* (London, 1985), pp. 106–41, and sources quoted therein.

[11] J. Förster, "Das Unternehmen 'Barbarossa' als Eroberungs- und Vernichtungskrieg," in *Der Angriff auf die Sowjetunion*, ed. H. Boog et al. (Stuttgart, 1983), vol. 4 of *DRZW*, pp. 440–47.

extremely difficult to contemplate, particularly on moral grounds, for the vast majority of their soldiers became implicated themselves in precisely the kind of crimes that might have otherwise caused moral revulsion, demoralization, perhaps even revolt.

II

Although draconian disciplinary measures proved effective in preventing mass desertions and disintegration, it is interesting to note that soldiers who did try to dodge the fighting in spite of the tremendous risks involved appear to have rarely been morally, politically, or ideologically motivated.[12] Soviet interrogation files of *Wehrmacht* deserters, for instance, reveal that these soldiers tended to refrain from voicing opposition to the Nazi regime, though they could have expected to reap some benefits from such pronouncements.[13] Nor did *Wehrmacht* courts-martial, trying soldiers for cowardice, desertion, or self-inflicted wounds, normally accuse them of having had any overt ideological or moral motivation.[14] Indeed, most soldiers tried for self-inflicted wounds, for example, seem to have been young, often poorly educated men from the lower classes, who either could not face the prospect of returning from leave to the front, or broke down shortly after rejoining their units.[15] To be sure, martial law defined such offenses a priori as political, thereby legitimizing the severity of the sentences; but even the military judges themselves did not claim that the prosecuted had had any conscious political intentions. Thus the impression one gains is that deserters, cowards, and all other kinds of shirkers were often men who had been unable to integrate socially into their units and to adapt to combat conditions, rather than enemies of the regime; that is, they were psychologically and socially, not ideologically or morally, exceptional.

Comradeship was indeed an extraordinarily important element in the social and military cohesion of the *Wehrmacht*. As long as the rate of casualties permitted the existence of "primary groups" in the army, what kept the units together was to a large extent the carefully fostered social ties between their members. But even when the fighting in the East physically destroyed such socially cohesive groups, the sense of responsibility for one's comrades, even if one no longer knew them so well, remained extremely strong. At the core

[12] See, e.g., BA-MA, RH26-12/131, 25.12.41; RH26-12/45, 5.10.41; RH26-12/139, 4.5.43; RH26-12/131, 24.9.43.

[13] See, e.g., BA-MA, RH26-12/85, 24.10.42.

[14] BA-MA, RH26-12/45, 5.10.41; RH26-12/262, 27.12.41; RH26-12/267, 7.5.42; RH27-18/28, 18.8.41; RH27-18/63, 10.12.41; RH27-18/76, 19.3.42.

[15] F. Seidler, *Prostitution, Homosexualität, Selbstverstümmelung: Probleme der deutsche Sanitätsführung, 1939–45* (Neckargemünd, 1977), pp. 233–317.

of this loyalty to other members of the unit was a sentiment of moral obligation, though of course not unaffected by the expectation that individual altruism would eventually be repaid in kind by the group as a whole or by any one of its constituent members. Thus the cohesiveness of the original "primary group," which had derived its strength from long-term familiarity and shared experience as well as from the premilitary affinities resulting from regional conscription, was replaced by the widespread sense of existential dependence among those who happened to be together on the line at any given moment, seen as the only means to confront that very same danger which had already destroyed the old, more traditional groups.[16] It is interesting that participants and contemporary observers were themselves struck by the outstanding fighting performance and combat cohesion of the troops in the face of not only extremely unfavorable military odds but also of the increasing disintegration of those social ties previously considered essential for morale. The explanation was repeatedly sought in the individual's will to survive as the most important factor in keeping the men together and fighting, and it should come as no surprise to find echoes of the nihilistic social darwinism of National Socialist rhetoric in almost every contemporary account, memoir, or oral reminiscence.[17] Yet once out of the realm of the "primary group," the new sense of existential comradeship extended also far beyond the purely military circle to encompass first the soldier's family and friends in the rear, and ultimately the Reich as a whole, if not, indeed, what the propagandists of the period referred to as "German culture" and "European civilization." Both the worsening situation at the front and the growing impact of the war on the rear convinced increasing numbers of soldiers that they were in fact fighting for the bare existence of everything they knew and cherished.[18] Numerous reports speak of how troops on leave became demoralized by the devastation the Allied strategic bombing offensive had wrought on German cities, and of the rapid revival of their spirits once they could avenge themselves on the

[16] Further in Bartov, *Hitler's Army* (n. 3 above), pp. 29–58, and Omer Bartov, "Daily Life and Motivation in War: The Wehrmacht in the Soviet Union," *Journal of Strategic Studies* 12 (1989): 200–214.

[17] See, e.g., H. Spaeter and W. Ritter von Schramm, *Die Geschichte des Panzerkorps Grossdeutschland* (Bielefeld, 1958), 1:365–66, 2:251–70; L. Niethammer, "Heimat und Front: Versuch, zehn Kriegserinnerungen aus der Arbeiterklasse des Ruhrgebietes zu verstehen," in *"Die Jahre weiss man nicht, wo man die heute hinsetzen soll": Faschismus im Ruhrgebiet,* ed. L. Niethammer (Berlin, 1983), pp. 191–92.

[18] See, e.g., H.-U. Rudel, *Stuka Pilot,* 2d ed. (Maidstone, 1973), p. 189; O. Buchbender and R. Stertz, eds., *Das andere Gesicht des Krieges* (Munich, 1982), pp. 146, 158–59, 161, 167; W. Bähr and H. W. Bähr, eds., *Kriegsbriefe gefallener Studenten, 1939–1945* (Tübingen and Stuttgart, 1952), pp. 403, 410, 421–24, 449–50.

enemy through fighting.[19] By now evasion of action was perceived as betrayal not only of one's comrades but also of one's family, friends and relations, nation and culture. Thus going into action became both a means of protecting the rear and of venting one's frustration at the suffering and destruction in the Reich which one could not directly alleviate.

The other pole of the troops' conformity to combat discipline was their immense dread of the enemy, particularly in the Soviet Union. The soldiers had been exposed quite early in the war to scenes of brutalities by Soviet troops, and these blended well with the images of the enemy provided them by the *Wehrmacht*'s propaganda. From the available evidence it is clear that terror of the enemy in the East was so powerful that it must be seen as a major element in motivating the soldiers to go on fighting until almost the very end.[20] To be sure, such fear alone might have produced the opposite effect by inducing men to escape to the rear, even if it effectively prevented mass desertions to the Soviet enemy up to and including the last weeks of the war, when whole divisions marched rapidly westward in a desperate attempt to be taken prisoner by the "Anglo-Americans" rather than by the "Bolsheviks."[21] But the realities and images of the East also greatly tempered the natural tendency to escape by deserting to the rear. As court-martial reports indicated, the rate of desertion in Russia remained for a long time actually lower than in the West. The reasons were not hard to find: having penetrated so deeply into enemy territory, the *Ostheer* became bogged down with its front turned to an enemy which refused to give up the struggle and its rear exposed to vast stretches of insecure areas, where an increasingly hostile population was willy-nilly coming over to the side of the Soviet partisans. To this was added the prevalent feeling, derived partly from fact and partly from prejudice, that the Russians were much more foreign than any previously occupied peoples in the West.[22] In this sense, the individual soldier was physically and mentally trapped, able neither to advance and conquer nor to run away, totally dependent on his comrades for survival in an alien, harsh, and dangerous country whose language he did not speak, to whose climate, geography, and ways of life he could not adapt, and whose armed forces became more menacing by the month. While crossing over to the enemy presented the prospect of being shot either by one's own comrades (which in fact often

---

[19] See, e.g., BA-MA, RH26-12/89, 26.6.43.

[20] See, e.g., Buchbender and Stertz, eds. (n. 18 above), pp. 71, 78, 85, 112, 117–18, 166–67.

[21] See, e.g., C. Wagner, *Heeresgruppe Süd: Der Kampf im Süden der Ostfront, 1941–1945* (Bad Nauheim, n.d.), pp. 340–41.

[22] See, e.g., BA-MA, RH26-12/131, 25.12.41; RH26-12/139, 4.5.43; RH26-12/151, 24.9.43.

happened) or by the Russians (which contrary to expectations appears to have actually been less common), escaping to the rear involved not only the danger of being caught and sentenced to death by the military authorities but also of falling into Soviet partisan hands, or even simply of losing one's way and perishing in the vast territories between the front and the homeland.[23] The choice made by most soldiers was thus clear and simple: safer to stay and fight than to run and be killed; which happened to be precisely what their commanders repeatedly and successfully urged them to believe.

There is, however, a wholly different dimension to the soldiers' conformity with army discipline. In the case of unauthorized plunder and brutality, officers complained a great deal, though they refrained from taking disciplinary action. But commanders seem to have confronted no such difficulties regarding the army's official policies of exploitation, destruction, and murder, for not only were no charges pressed, one is also hard put to find any other evidence to show that soldiers tried to evade these activities. This is all the more striking because there are indications that even SS and police units occasionally presented their men with the choice of not taking part in murder "operations" they felt unable to withstand.[24] To be sure, while for the SS mass killing of civilians was its raison d'être, the army considered this merely one and not the most important aspect of fighting in the East. Moreover, the *Wehrmacht* authorities themselves objected to shootings of women and children by the troops (though not to executing thousands of male hostages nor to killing suspected partisans and agents of all ages and both sexes), fearing that this would undermine military discipline and demoralize the men. Instead, either the SD was called in, or these "undesirable elements" were ejected from their villages in circumstances that ensured death by starvation and exposure. Nevertheless, it is interesting that, while some SS "professionals" relented from the killings, the army, which had its fair share of gruesome actions, recorded no such instances. It should also be added that those SS and police unit members who chose not to take part in such operations—and were not punished in any obvious way for their choice—stated both at the time and in subsequent postwar interviews that they had simply become physically and mentally incapable of going ahead with the murders; that is to say, at no point did they imply that their choice either had been caused by or had itself influenced their general attitude toward the regime. In other words, they saw

[23] See, e.g., BA-MA, RH26-12/267, 7.5.42; RH26-12/85, 27.5.42.

[24] C. R. Browning, "German Memory, Judicial Interrogation, and Historical Reconstruction: Writing Perpetrator History from Post-War Testimony" in *Probing the Limits of Representation: Nazism and the "Final Solution,"* ed. S. Friedlander (Cambridge, Mass., 1992), pp. 22–36. D. Goldhagen, "The 'Cowardly' Executioner: On Disobedience in the SS," *Patterns of Prejudice* 19 (1985): 19–32; Klee et al., eds. (n. 7 above), pp. 77–86.

themselves as too weak to perform what they fundamentally believed ought to be done rather than strong enough to resist taking part in an atrocity.[25]

The way in which soldiers coped with these criminal aspects of the war adds much to our understanding of the real and perceived parameters of collaboration and resistance. There is little doubt that soldiers felt, indeed were, powerfully motivated by moral outrage during the war, but they appear to have directed it against the enemy rather than against the regime and the army. Their own actions the troops came to view as an essential part of an ideological war that by definition demanded extraordinary measures, just as Nazi propaganda had claimed all along. Moreover, the soldiers, who constantly experienced the practical implications of Hitler's "ideas," went one step further. Their very conviction of the need to act in a manner which they would have considered criminal under any other circumstances depended on the assumption, or rather belief, that the enemy was inherently worse. No matter the scale of the *Wehrmacht*'s atrocities, the enemy's, by definition, were greater. Thus as long as the morality of one's actions was gauged in relation to the enemy's, there could not be any absolute moral limit. Personal moral outrage, instead of tempering one's conduct, rather enhanced it, by being directed at those perceived as the cause of all enormities. This was the mechanism whereby the soldiers came to terms with an unprecedented and, in many ways, unbearable psychological, moral, and physical situation. Indeed, what is the meaning of morally opposing one's own regime when even those who see through its propaganda simultaneously feel that they are fighting against a similarly, if not more, evil political system? This reasoning liberated the individual from responsibility for his own actions, for the root of the evil was to be found on the other side of the hill.[26]

III

The parameters of collaboration and resistance, the tension between what soldiers considered inadmissible and unavoidable, forbidden and necessary, therefore had to do not merely with their rational analysis of the objective situation but at least as much with their perception of reality. In turn, the views and beliefs prevalent among frontline troops reflected the efficacy of Nazi propaganda and indoctrination, which, of course, owed much of its own success to popular prejudices and half-baked ideologies predating the "seizure of

[25] C. R. Browning, *Fateful Months: Essays on the Emergence of the Final Solution* (New York, 1985), pp. 39–56, 68–85; Bartov, *Eastern Front* (n. 10 above), pp. 119–29, and documents cited therein; H. Krausnick and H.-H. Wilhelm, *Die Truppe des Weltanschauungskrieges* (Stuttgart, 1981), pp. 243–49.

[26] For recent arguments along these lines, see A. Hillgruber, *Zweierlei Untergang* (Berlin, 1986); and E. Nolte, "Vergangenheit, die nicht vergehen will," *Frankfurter Allgemeine Zeitung* (June 6, 1986).

power."[27] The unresisting participation of the troops in actions which seem to us obviously criminal was thus not merely the result of harsh discipline but also of the successful dissemination of a dehumanized image of the enemy that excluded him from the norms of behavior and morals.of human society.

This does not mean that a few years of Nazi rule had managed completely to erase the moral sensibilities of the troops. Evidence shows that many were indeed shocked by what they and their comrades were doing and even more so by the mass murders carried out by the *Einsatzgruppen* and witnessed by substantial numbers of soldiers.[28] But as a rule, the soldiers justified themselves by referring to the inhumanity of the victims. Their reaction derives both from the savage fighting which had blunted the troops' emotions, and from the maltreatment of the enemy which physically reduced individuals to such a wretched condition that they appeared very close to the image of the *Untermenschen* propagated by the regime.[29]

When speaking of the moral dilemmas faced by the *Wehrmacht*'s frontline troops, it is useful to keep in mind that these were mostly recently conscripted young men who had spent the formative years of their youth not only in an increasingly Nazified school system but, much more important, in the Hitler Youth (reaching the *Arbeitsdienst* just before conscription), in whose militarized atmosphere they were exposed to relentless National Socialist indoctrination. Many of these youngsters were attracted both to the regime's rhetoric of rebellion against old norms and traditions, on the one hand, and to the heroic image of a conquering, invincible Germany, charged with the mission of cleansing the whole world from the plague of communism and plutocracy, increasingly identified with "world Jewry," on the other. The Hitler Youth insisted on rigid regimentation, "blind" obedience, and unquestioning faith in the supreme value of action, while teaching profound contempt and distrust for any form of contemplation and discussion; it worshiped the united strength of the group and the "iron" will of the individual, and it despised any manifestation of physical or psychological weakness. In many ways the Hitler Youth resembled a youth gang, longing to smash all the symbols and representatives of the existing social order, be they parental and school authority, the church and bourgeois values, or just as much the socialist and communist loyalties of the working class; it was as violent as any gang and just as much centered around an admired, tyrannical leader.[30] But by becoming a vast national organization, and through its intimate association

[27] See, e.g., the recent study by G. L. Mosse, *Fallen Soldiers: Reshaping the Memory of the World Wars* (New York, 1990).
[28] Klee et al., eds. (n. 7 above), pp. 31–51, but see also pp. 103–29, 131–45.
[29] See, e.g., Buchbender and Stertz, eds. (n. 18 above), pp. 78–80, 84–87, 170.
[30] See, e.g., Niethammer (n. 17 above), p. 210.

with and cult of the Führer of the Reich, it simultaneously satisfied the youthful desire for conformity and became the most important forerunner or school for what was rapidly becoming Hitler's army. This powerful combination of total revolt and total submission, of destructiveness and obedience, this fascination with smashing the present in the name of an ideal, ill-defined future somehow linked to a mythical past had far-reaching consequences for the mentality of the *Wehrmacht*'s troops.[31]

To be sure, it did not make them all into committed Nazis; but it provided them with an outlook that profoundly influenced their manner of both physically and mentally coping with and reacting to the realities of the war they were soon to find themselves fighting whether or not they happened to be enamored of the regime. In other words, it drastically narrowed their perceived alternatives for action on the battlefield. Equipped with an apocalyptic view of history, a social darwinian division of humanity into those who must survive and those who must be exterminated, and a vocabulary that celebrated the abolishment of all previous norms of behavior, values, morals, and beliefs, the troops were necessarily left with precious little choice. Having gaily rid themselves of the present, the young soldiers of the Reich had no notion of the kind of future they would like to forge for themselves. Attachment to the nihilistic rhetoric of the regime supplied the best escape from the absence of a positive prospect. The more it became clear that the war would not lead to the promised victory, the more powerful became the faith in the mythical *Endsieg,* whose essence was a belief in the need to keep on destroying the present until eventually the ideal future emerged from the debris.[32]

The Hitler Youth's rebellious conformism played a major role in the profound transformation of the *Wehrmacht,* flooding it with hundreds of thousands of fresh recruits within an extremely short span of time. The generals were quick to note the changing character of the army, both when they claimed (some with satisfaction, others apologetically, and yet others with sorrow) that the lower ranks would not support a *Putsch* against Hitler and when they appealed (some cynically, some with much conviction) to the troops' Nazi loyalties in times of military crisis.[33] Thus the average combat soldier or junior officer, in his profound sense of a complete lack of choice, drilled into him through years of ideological indoctrination and social-organizational pressures, in his inability to conceive of any other alternative to

---

[31] See, e.g., H. Scholtz, *Erziehung und Unterricht unterm Hakenkreuz* (Göttingen, 1985); A. Heck, *A Child of Hitler,* 3d ed. (New York, 1986); R. Schörken, "Jugendalltag im Dritten Reich," in *Geschichte im Alltag—Alltag in der Geschichte,* ed. K. Bergmann and R. Schörken (Düsseldorf, 1982), pp. 236–46.

[32] See, e.g., pep talk by a company commander cited in G. Sajer, *The Forgotten Soldier,* 2d ed. (London, 1977), pp. 263–67.

[33] See, e.g., J. von Herwarth, *Against Two Evils* (London, 1981), p. 255.

the values propagated by the regime, and in his dependence on the polarized images of a deified Führer and a demonized enemy as his motivating engine, was probably closer to the National Socialist model of the fanatic, politically committed *Kämpfer* than generals such as Reichenau and Manstein whose notorious orders of the day have come to symbolize the nazification of the senior officer corps.[34] Not surprisingly, soldiers' diaries, letters, and memoirs are strikingly devoid of references to opposition, be it active or passive.

It is interesting that many of West Germany's more prominent novelists and filmmakers seem to imply the same lack of moral choice under the Nazi regime. In Edgar Reitz's sixteen-hour film *Heimat* the one brief episode concerned with the soldiers exposes them to an incident that might be construed either as a (distasteful but perhaps justified) execution of partisans or as an atrocity, that is, the killing of innocent civilians. The soldiers cannot change that reality; they can only act within it, either shoot, watch, or record it, as one of them, a member of a film crew in a propaganda company, actually does. The director provides his protagonists with no moral choices; they are the victims of a possibly immoral situation that they cannot escape. Similarly, in Helma Sanders-Brahms's *Germany, Pale Mother,* the soldiers go off to war, leaving the women to fend for themselves, and then return years later, drained and brutalized, to the debris of their homes and families. Here everyone is perceived as a victim of some savage, barbaric, yet strangely amorphous and faceless force; the only choices to be made concern one's own physical and mental survival, followed by a struggle for reconstruction. Defeat in these films is usually presented in the form of (often black) American GIs, who descend on the prostrate homeland. In Rainer Werner Fassbinder's *The Marriage of Maria Braun,* which sets out to expose the perversity and hypocrisy of the *Wirtschaftswunder,* the returning soldier is once more a victim of circumstances beyond his control, as is ultimately the woman who had tried to master fate and coolly control the chaos that surrounds her. To survive the occupation while waiting for her husband to return from captivity, she must take a black GI as a lover; but then she kills the lover to defend the husband. To survive the reconstruction while waiting for her husband's return from prison (he takes the murder upon himself) she must take another lover, this time an elderly industrialist and emigrant, who betrays her by paying the husband to stay away; finally she and her husband are blown up in a gas explosion in her modern villa, forever wretched and helpless victims of circumstances dating back to the Nazi regime and the war.[35]

---

[34] Cited in Streit (n. 9 above), pp. 115–16.

[35] A recent excellent analysis of these films can be found in A. Kaes, *From Hitler to Heimat: The Return of History as Film* (Cambridge, Mass., 1989), pp. 73–103, 137–92.

The sense of helplessness and lack of choice is especially evident in many of the literary attempts to deal with the war. In Heinrich Böll's early story, "The Train Was on Time," Andreas returns to the front filled with immense fear of what awaits him, yet he sees no other choice. In Poland he meets a Polish prostitute, who is simultaneously also a pianist and an agent working for the Polish resistance. They fall in love, but there is no way out, no choice but liberation through death, which she finally arranges for the two of them at the hands of the partisans. Thus Andreas, who is one of the "innocents" Olina herself believes she is killing, encounters his own nemesis in a situation filled with the Nazi images of the period. For though unintended by the author, this story reveals the extent to which he had himself become permeated with the regime's presentation of reality during his years of education in the Third Reich and of service in the *Wehrmacht.*[36] For Andreas is ultimately killed by a woman who powerfully displays the qualities of the perfidious enemy agent, attractive, intelligent, yet murderous, using her intellectual talents and physical qualities to emasculate and annihilate him, even if here the act is performed in the name of love and includes her own sacrifice. The soldier is humanized, is indeed "innocent," but is trapped in a situation that leaves him only the choice of collaboration or death.[37] The other alternative, desertion, is similarly portrayed as hopeless, meaningless, and inconsequential, more an inner process than a concrete step, performed by rare and exceptional types (or clowns) as in Günther Grass's *Cat and Mouse,* or as an act both secondary to the novel and of no possible significance to the course of the war as in Siegfried Lenz's *Deutschstunde.*[38]

Insofar as these authors concern themselves with the moral choices of the troops, it is clear that such choices were available only to individuals who were totally different from the vast majority of their contemporaries. The act of resistance, if it appears at all, is due to the personal uniqueness of the individual; if it involves a moral stand (which is not always the case), this too is a private, intimate position not shared by the multitude. Indeed, precisely because the evasion of or resistance to collaboration is reserved in these works to the insanely suicidal acts of extraordinary characters, one gains the impression of a consensus regarding the complete absence of viable avenues of resistance, at least as perceived by contemporaries; though even this consensus is implied by its opposite rather than actually discussed. The more extreme one's uniqueness is, the more one is a complete outsider, an alien, the more one is likely to manifest resistance and refuse to go along with the rest.

---

[36] In spite of resistance to the regime in his youth; see H. Böll, *Was soll aus dem Jungen bloss werden?* (Bornheim, 1981).

[37] H. Böll, *The Train Was on Time* (1949), trans. L. Vennewitz (London, 1973).

[38] G. Grass, *Cat and Mouse* (1961), trans. R. Manheim (Harmondsworth, 1979); S. Lenz, *Deutschstunde* (1968; Munich, 1979).

But this also implies that we are no longer dealing with questions of moral choice but simply with a stroke of (mis)fortune that makes nonconformity inevitable due to pronounced physical and mental deformity, as is most vividly portrayed in Grass's *The Tin Drum* (where the beautiful eternal Aryan child who drums and shrieks his way through the Third Reich significantly turns into a morose dwarf in the new Federal Republic).[39]

To conclude, contemporary personal documentation, postwar memoirs, and fictional treatments of the war all provide one with a stark impression of a grim, determined, and increasingly hopeless commitment to professional and national duty. As the war became ever more painful and disillusioning, these documents reflect a powerful conviction of the necessity to go on fighting for a good cause against a demonic enemy; hence the perceived lack of alternative is in no way merely the function of a ruthless penal system. Moreover, in fighting the devil, the ends must surely justify the means, and nothing can be more immoral than giving in to his camp. Only the conspirators, mostly high-ranking officers, seem to have discussed the moral aspects of their actions at length, some of them indeed reaching such elevation as to doubt the morality of killing even Hitler. For the majority, however, the choice remained between continued collaboration justified by an increasingly irrational faith, and suicidal resistance triggered by hopelessness and dejection. Both alternatives might lead to death, but the former provided one at least with hope, comradeship, trust, and belief. It was this course that most of the *Wehrmacht's* soldiers chose to follow.

[39] G. Grass, *The Tin Drum* (1959), trans. R. Manheim (Harmondsworth, 1978).

The Appeal of Exterminating "Others": German Workers and the Limits of Resistance

Alf Lüdtke
Max-Planck-Institut für Geschichte

I

This article was triggered by the shock of reading through large stacks of letters that German soldiers had sent to their employers during World War II.[1] The authors were blue-collar workers or lower-level clerks in middle- if not large-size machine tool factories located primarily in the Saxon city of Leipzig. What I found particularly striking was how intensely the authors of the letters seemed to identify with both the Nazi policy of utter contempt for "peoples of the East" and the actual killing of "enemies" at the front line or in the *Hinterland*. To be sure, historical reconstruction is bound to reveal the "otherness" of its "objects." At first glance these "others" had shown a rather familiar face. They were single or married males who occupied good jobs in industry. In their letters they gave testimony to the duress and dangers of military life in war times. As I read on, though, this seeming familiarity increasingly became blurred.

Two aspects stand out. Fundamentally, these writers did not define themselves by their industrial work and their relations to other workers. On the contrary, their identity was completely framed by what they encountered as the profile of the military man. These letters dismantle notions both of the homogenous workers' consciousness and of social class as the primary focus of peoples' efforts to place themselves in society and history. Second, these letters raise doubts about the claim that the "masses" in Nazi Germany were completely subdued and thus made victims to the dominant cliques and bureaucracies of state and party. In view of these letters the question arises to what extent the "ordinary people" were involved in or aware of what actually happened at the front.

II

After 1933 most Germans readily accepted the führer, Adolf Hitler, and many actively supported him.[2] In general, the goals of Nazi leaders such as "restoring" the grandeur of the *Reich* and "cleaning out" alleged "aliens" in

---

[1] Staatsarchiv Leipzig (StAL), Rudolf Sack, nos. 353, 356, 358, 371, 397–400; Meier and Weichelt Eisen und Stahlwerke, nos. 322, 323 (esp. 298); Braunkohlenwerk Salzdetfurth AG, nos. 184, 185.

[2] Ian Kershaw, *The Hitler Myth: Image and Reality in the Third Reich* (Oxford, 1987).

This essay originally appeared in the *Journal of Modern History* 64, suppl. (December 1992).

politics and society were widely cheered. Critical comments about, for instance, the demonstrative brutality of the Sturmabteilungen (SA) or the arrogance of party functionaries were only rarely pushed into the public consciousness. This popular mode of coping with demands and incentives from above by no means contested the Nazi mode of domination. The vast majority of industrial workers tried to pursue their immediate interests by obtaining jobs and earning higher wages. Only a very few extended their criticism beyond mismanagement or injustice on the shop floor or, in their respective neighborhoods, to the political regime or the social order as a whole. And after 1939 notions of the Germans at war and their "people's community" tended to absorb the remnants of skepticism that remained. It was no longer the party but the "fatherland" that called most urgently.[3]

Such perspectives on Nazi Germany focus on the "grand total." They do not pay particular attention to the specificity of each single decision, which always involved a moment of uncertainty even, for instance, if the co-workers on the shop floor or the distinctive features of a job have been known quantities for many years. In such broad perspectives the historian perceives individual action or passivity only in summation, that is, only in hindsight. Accordingly, this perspective elides those ambiguities which distinctively mark each moment of action. It underrates, if not totally neglects, the very openness of situations which turns counter to its structured and analytically accurate outcome. For this much is certain: even inside "total institutions" choices were possible. The inmates of concentration camps constantly made decisions which had wide-ranging effects on life and death.[4]

In Nazi Germany, rigorous efforts to control "the masses" were not limited to the institutions of repression and confinement. The Nazi authorities invested enormous energy in regulating the labor markets.[5] Workers, however, still seized space and time to maneuver for choices about job and employer. Closer

---

[3] Ulrich Herbert, "Arbeiterschaft im 'Dritten Reich': Zwischenbilanz und offene Fragen," *Geschichte und Gesellschaft* 15 (1989): 320–60, esp. 349, "Die guten und die schlechten Zeiten: Überlegungen zur diachronen Analyse lebensgeschichtlicher Interviews," in *"Die Jahre weiß man nicht wo man die heute hinsetzen soll": Lebensgeschichte und Sozialkultur im Ruhrgebiet, 1930–1960,* ed. L. Niethammer (Bonn, 1983), pp. 67–96.

[4] See the account by Primo Levi, *Se questo è un uomo?* (Turin, 1986). On efforts to sustain a "way of one's own" and, in particular, to withstand the brutality of the SS, see Otto Dov Kulka, "Ghetto in an Annihilation Camp: Jewish Social History in the Holocaust Period and Its Ultimate Limits," in *The Nazi Concentration Camps: Proceedings of the Fourth Yad Vashem International Historical Conference* (Jerusalem, 1984), pp. 315–30.

[5] Timothy W. Mason, *Arbeiterklasse und Volksgemeinschaft* (Opladen, 1975), passim, and "The Workers' Opposition in Nazi Germany," *History Workshop Journal* 11 (1981): 120–37.

to home, each day each worker decided how to perform his or her task, when or how to turn his or her back on someone. To those who time and again made these decisions this was nothing but routine. Simultaneously, the question of whom to approach and whom to avoid on the shop floor, on the street, or in the pub posed not small but big and intensely political problems: how was one to assert one's needs and interests? We can clarify this point by considering the recollections of three workers. These demonstrate clearly both the room for choice and the implied permanence of decisions.

In 1934 Walter Uhlmann worked as a toolmaker in a middle-sized machine construction company in Berlin. He recalls that most of his co-workers shared anti-Nazi attitudes and that people could trust each other.[6] Before May 1, 1934, which was the first anniversary of the National Socialist Labor Day, they reassured each other that "nobody will force us to participate at this May-Day parade." Thus, they made sure of showing up at the meeting place but then left in another direction. According to this recollection a considerable number of co-workers abstained from the official parade. In other words, they went but simply decided to follow a different route.

During an interview with the operator of a drilling machine, I asked him how he encountered enforced labor during wartime in the big locomotive production and armament construction works of Henschel.[7] He recalled, "Well, there were lads from concentration camps. At work, they were kept in separate cages within the same workshops. However, we just saw them, we didn't have contact, and we were not allowed to [have contact]. When we took our breaks we sat amongst ourselves. I just don't know how it was and who they were. We also had *Fremdarbeiter* from Russia; to them we once in a while passed a piece of bread which was strictly prohibited." The assertion is that there was no choice in the case of the inmates of the concentration camp but that nonobedience/resistance to authority existed in respect to the *Fremdarbeiter.*[8]

The final recollection, from another company, does not question the possibility of choices. Rather, this anonymous former *Fremdarbeiter* from Russia recalled different decisions of the German workers. Not only did he

---

[6] Walter Uhlmann, "Antifaschistische Arbeit," *Aus Politik und Zeitgeschichte* B 18/80 (1980), pp. 7–15, esp. p. 8.

[7] Interview with H. N., Kassel, September 13, 1987.

[8] As to the policies of enforced labor during World War II, see the general account by Ulrich Herbert, *Fremdarbeiter: Politik und Praxis des "Ausländer-Einsatzses" in der Kriegswirtschaft des Dritten Reiches* (Berlin and Bonn, 1985), Herbert, ed., *Europa und der "Reichseinsatz": Ausländische Kriegsgefangene und KZ-Häftlinge in Deutschland, 1939–1945* (Essen, 1991) and, esp., *A History of Foreign Labor in Germany, 1880–1980: Seasonal Workers/Forced Labourers/Guest Workers* (Ann Arbor, Mich., 1990), pp. 131–92.

remember constant clubbing at different workshops—something which had vanished from the memory of the Henschel worker—but he also mentioned that during breaks at Daimler-Benz the German workers sat down to eat their lunch which was a sandwich (*Butterbrot*).[9] The Russians, however, were not allowed to eat anything; they could only get cold water. In his opinion the *Butterbrot* which many Germans pretended or claimed to have passed to Russians or Poles was not worth mentioning.

As in German society on the whole, the range and impact of resisting behavior was limited during the whole period of Nazi rule to a small minority among the working classes. However, until 1935–36 thousands of people from proletarian neighborhoods illegally labored to make audible the voices of non- and anti-Nazi Germans. The Gestapo ruthlessly persecuted most of the people who repeatedly engaged in such action, putting them under tremendous pressure and threatening them. But the impression which these cases convey can be mistaken: the shift from noncompliance to compliance and even to active, if not enthusiastic, support was no linear change. On the contrary, these cases indicate the permanence of different modes of behavior. Individuals did not pursue one straight line. Rather, many zigzagged back and forth; the traces of their practices may be imagined as distinct "patchworks" which do not show a clear-cut profile of either unqualified support or constant resistance. To reconstruct crucial features of this patchwork mode of decision, it is necessary to trace the diverse elements of people's behavior in specific situations. Reconstructing the bricolage of everyday life enables the historian to explain both compliance and noncompliance.

III

Opinions about workers' attitudes and behaviors during Nazism are overwhelmingly based upon a common set of assumptions. According to this view, factory workers tended to resist the demands and incentives of Nazi rule from the very outset. Recently, however, closer investigation of certain industries and specific regional contexts has questioned this long-standing and widespread belief. Gunther Mai and Wolfgang Zollitsch among others have pointed out that in the elections to the newly established Nazi-*Vertrauensräte* (factory councils), in spring 1933, large groups of wage earners showed their support of Nazism. For instance, in the steel mills and the mines of the Ruhr as well as in the public transportation industry in Berlin, the first *Vertrauensrats-*

[9] "'Wir waren ja niemand': Ein ehemaliger Zwangsarbeiter berichtet über die Jahre 1942 bis 1945 in Genshagen-Obrigheim," in *Das Daimler-Benz-Buch: Ein Rüstungskonzern im "Tausendjährigen Reich,"* ed. Hamburger Stiftung für Sozialgeschichte des 20. Jahrhunderts (Nördlingen, 1987), pp. 471–81.

wahlen in April 1933 yielded remarkable results for candidates nominated by the Nationalsozialistische Betriebszellen-Organisation (NSBO).[10] And not all of those who voted nay seem to have rejected Nazism in general. Rather, they expressed their anger over and critique of the incompetence of certain candidates of the NSBO to improve wages, as Martin Rüther convincingly argues for the consumption industries of Cologne.[11]

The range and forms of actual compliance in the "proletarian masses," however, were recognized only when the secret reports on local Social Democracy in Exile (SOPADE) activists to their party's leaders in exile were published in 1980. In these reports the comrades recorded the *Stimmung* (sentiment) of cooperation with Nazism and the support for Hitler in factories and working-class neighborhoods in Germany. If they did not encounter actual enthusiasm for Hitler, these correspondents time and again sensed attitudes that they interpreted as "total passivity" in their co-workers and colleagues.[12] They emphasized that one had to face the fact that people stubbornly shied away from any activity which might even smell of opposition to the National Socialist regime.

The expectation that workers fundamentally would oppose Nazism can be traced back to the fierce political struggles of the Weimar Republic. Before 1933 both social democratic and communist organizations claimed that the proletariat would fight and ultimately conquer fascism. But the Christian workers' associations also demonstratively reassured their clientele that every "true workingman" would rally around the strongholds of faith and good order, the church and its associations. The approaches of these groups differed widely: after 1929 the communists followed the line of the Communist International, accusing the Sozialdemokratische Partei Deutschlands (SPD) of

---

[10] These elections still provided a secret ballot. W. Zollitsch, "Die Vertrauens-ratswahlen von 1934 und 1935: Zum Stellenwert von Abstimmungen im 'Dritten Reich' am Beispiel Krupp," *Geschichte und Gesellschaft* 15 (1989): 361–81, esp. 375; esp. Günther Mai, "Die Nationalsozialistische Betriebszellen-Organisation," *Viertel-jahrshefte für Zeitgeschichte* 31 (1983): 573–613, passim; V. Kratzenberg, *Arbeiter auf dem Weg zu Hitler: Die nationalsozialistische Betriebszellen-Organisation, ihre Entstehung, ihre Programmatik, ihr Scheitern, 1927–1934* (Frankfurt am Main, 1987), pp. 195 ff., 272–73.

[11] Martin Rüther, *Arbeiterschaft in Köln, 1928–1945* (Cologne, 1990), pp. 173 ff.

[12] Deutschland-berichte der Sozialdemokratischen Partei Deutschlands (SOPADE) (Frankfurt, 1980), 4: 1937, p. 1238; for the following quotation, see ibid., p. 777: "One can discern not only widespread toleration of Nazism but also an increase of its positive acceptance since 1934 among the workforces of big companies of the heavy industries in the areas at the Rhine and the river *Ruhr* (*Gutehoffnungshütte*, Ober-hausen, *Bochumer Verein*), in the mining industries at the *Ruhr*, and also at one of the largest companies of the chemical industry (*Bayer* at Leverkusen)." See also Zollitsch, esp. pp. 369 ff., pp. 375 ff.; and E. Wolff, *Nationalsozialismus in Leverkusen* (Leverkusen, 1988), pp. 196 ff.

pursuing "social fascism" while, simultaneously, the social democrats denounced what they perceived as the similarity of Nazi and *Kozi* (the communists).[13] Nevertheless, the leadership and the functionaries of the left mass organizations as well as of the Christian associations remained convinced that National Socialism did not appeal to any "true" worker.

The notion of the "true workingman" who displayed inexhaustible self-reliance had an enormous impact. It reached far beyond the boundaries of social class and political camps. Even the fiercest enemies shared this view, as is reflected by the policies of the Gestapo after 1933. Persecution of "communist/marxist" adversaries outdistanced by far that of other opponents and ranked highest with the Gestapo throughout the whole Nazi period.[14] It was in this vein that Gestapo and communist or social democratic activists alike aimed at tracing every hint of noncompliance among the working masses. Thus, oppressors and victims focused on almost identical images of the true workingman and his presumed resistance. As a result, any sign of protest was picked up and amplified. By 1935–36 most of the resisters from the working classes were arrested by the Gestapo or ordinary police, brought to jail, or detained in concentration camps.

IV

"Proletarians" would tenaciously fight Nazism. At least during the 1920s both the social democratic and the communist party conceived of workers as the implacable enemies of Nazism. Thus, what else could they do but stand up and combat all efforts to draw them into the sphere of the Nazi? This view prevailed among analysts inside and outside Germany even after 1945. Then the stereotype of proletarian resisters fitted even more perfectly into that bipolar model which informed most explanatory approaches to German fascism. Accordingly, only a few people like Hitler or Himmler (aside from bureaucratic apparatuses) "acted"; everyone else became "victims" including the brave but desperately small groups of resisters.

[13] Eike Hennig, "Anmerkungen zur Propaganda der NSDAP gegenüber SPD und KPD in der Endphase der Weimarer Republik," *Tel Aviver Jahrbuch für Deutsche Geschichte* 17 (1988): 209–40, esp. 215 ff.

[14] Detlev J. K. Peukert, "Der deutsche Arbeiterwiderstand, 1933–1945," in *Der deutsche Widerstand, 1933–1945,* ed. K. J. Müller (Paderborn, 1986), pp. 157–81, esp. p. 176 and, more generally, *Die KPD im Widerstand: Verfolgung und Untergrundarbeit an Rhein und Ruhr, 1933–1945* (Wuppertal, 1980); see also Horst Duhnke, *Die KPD von 1933–1945* (Cologne, 1972). So far a comparable study on social democratic resistance activities has not been written. See, however, esp. Herbert Obenaus, "Probleme der Erforschung des Widerstandes in der Hannoverschen Sozialdemokratie 1933 bis 1945," *Niedersächsisches Jahrbuch für Landesgeschichte* 62 (1990): 77–95.

Most of the surviving inmates of prisons and concentration camps shared those views which minimized individual agency. Their experience of suffering surely entitled them to such a reading of history: if anybody had been victims of Nazi domination, they had, whether they were active communists or social democrats or had other backgrounds. Simultaneously, however, even major perpetrators like Albert Speer claimed victimization.[15] And on the political plane the Allied efforts to organize de-Nazification of German society only too quickly turned into what Lutz Niethammer has called the production of *Mitläufer* (fellow travelers).[16]

The term *Mitläufer* was widely used and gained currency almost immediately. "Just to follow along": the emphasis on being only one among millions reverberated with the almost desperate efforts of many Germans not to be reminded of their mode of coping with Nazism. Nobody wanted to deal with the seamless continuity by which sustaining oneself in many instances turned into accepting (if not sustaining) state-organized mass murder. Precedents of exclusion facilitated these attitudes. The labeling of so-called aliens and the "dangerous" (*Gemeinschaftsfremde*) was a commonly accepted and established practice for a long time,[17] one closely linked to the emergence of a modern police state. Continual discrimination by the state may have fostered people's eagerness to forget their multiple ways of not perceiving seemingly minor acts of discrimination, from the boycott of the Jewish stores on April 1, 1933, to the expulsion of Jews from "German" forests, street cars, or benches, to the pogrom of November 9–10, 1938. And how did people encounter the deportations from 1942 until 1944 and even 1945? Of course, there were noises, there was screaming; and people listened to the hammering boots of marching troops as well as to the shuffling feet of hundreds and thousands of desperate people pushed through the streets of towns which had been home to them. But did not every war impose harsh measures? Especially in wartime, many people felt on safe moral ground; they claimed that after 1939 it was not Hitler but the *Vaterland* that called.[18]

---

[15] Albert Speer, *Erinnerungen,* 8th ed. (Frankfurt, 1972), p. 522.

[16] L. Niethammer, *Die Mitläuferfabrik: Die Entnazifizierung am Beispiel Bayerns,* 2d ed. (Berlin and Bonn, 1982); for a general account, esp. Klaus-Dieter Henke and Hans Woller, eds., *Politische Säuberung in Europa: Die Abrechnung mit Faschismus und Kollaboration nach dem Zweiten Weltkrieg* (Munich, 1991), especially the contributions by Henke (pp. 21 ff.) on the western zones, and by Helga A. Welsh, who depicts the developments in the Soviet zone after 1945.

[17] Detlev Peukert, *Volksgenossen und Gemeinschaftsfremde: Anpassung, Ausmerze und Aufbegehren unter dem Nationalsozialismus* (Cologne, 1982), pp. 219 ff.

[18] Gabriele Rosenthal, ed., *"Als der Krieg kam, hatte ich mit Hitler nichts mehr zu tun": Zur Gegenwärtigkeit des "Dritten Reiches" in Biographien* (Opladen, 1990), pp. 223 ff.

V

Against this background the vigorous attack of Hannah Arendt in the early 1960s stood out in sharp contrast. A victim herself, forced into exile in the 1930s, she followed closely the Eichmann trial in 1961. In this context she pointed to the widespread *Mittäterschaft* or complicity of most Germans with Nazism.[19] In her view, the overwhelming majority of Germans condemned the crimes of the Nazis but obviously almost all had been ready to participate. When questioned about their complicity, most people displayed an innocent conscience. Did not every social and political organization rely on obedience? In addition, people commonly argued that their acceptance and participation in the Nazi regime prevented even "worse" evils. People pointed out that they accepted or cooperated in order to rescue Germany from what they perceived as the "red menace."[20]

According to Arendt, the overwhelming majority of Germans were "accomplices" between 1933 and 1945. Arendt's point was made without further specification of particular groups, classes, or strata of German society. However, since the Eichmann trial revealed the "banality of evil" in the inner workings of the Schutzstaffel (SS), Arendt's point particularly pertained to the bureaucracies of state and party as well as to the functional elites of the Third Reich. Of course, the question remains as to whether other segments and layers of society were affected by the same attitude. How did wage-earning women and housewives perceive the situation in the 1930s and 1940s? How did they act when they faced the constraints or attractions of Nazism in power? Moreover, how did male industrial workers—a segment of society treated with enormous respect but also suspicion by the Nazi authorities—interpret Nazi Germany?

---

[19] Hannah Arendt, *Eichmann in Jerusalem: A Report on the Banality of Evil* (London, 1963), esp. p. 134.

[20] The fear of "the menace from the East" concomitantly remained vague and stark. After the Russian revolutions of 1917 and 1918, large segments of German society including the working class had identified revolutionary violence with "Cossack" brutality. Thus, long-standing popular clichés were revitalized and redesigned to cover the presumed "red" or "Bolshevik menace." This view enhanced other notions of the endangered "order of German things." To save the German people if not Europe and its values from the "savage hordes of—Jewish—Bolsheviks" by any means at hand appeared justified. Such views were not confined to some classes or milieus; see similar perceptions among leading social democrats. See Peter Lösche, *Der Bolschewismus im Urteil der deutschen Sozialdemokratie, 1903–1920* (Berlin, 1967); especially the intriguing approach to male attitudes which closely linked abhorred images of "the female" and the "reds" after 1917–18, particularly among volunteers of the paramilitary Freikorps; Klaus Theweleit, *Männerphantasien* (Frankfurt, 1977), vols. 1, 2.

Questions about German complicity with Nazism were ignored for a long time. Only the focus on the practices of the everyday revealed the enormous degree of routine involvement of the many with the execution of both war and holocaust. The very routines of bureaucratic formality or paperwork directly involved many lower-level officials with practices of extermination: those numerous pedantic railway conductors, for instance, searched every passenger; innumerable city clerks kept books carefully registering everyone, including those who had been declared "Jews" by Nazi laws and decrees.[21] These studies began to reveal that the majority of Germans in their daily practices not only accepted but also actively contributed to sustaining Nazism and its terror. Thus, "the masses" can no longer appear as passive objects or as victims of the brutal visions and fatal organizational skills of only a few "dominant" people.

Like the analyses of state and politics, historical studies of labor focused overwhelmingly on the institutions of power or, in this case of protest, the organized labor movements. Parties and trade unions seemed the only important topic of labor history because they seemingly allowed historians to perceive workers as able to contest discrimination and exploitation. Accordingly, studies related the catastrophic collapse of the labor movement in 1933 to a mixture of petrification within the higher echelons of the party and trade union bureaucracies with personal incompetence if not betrayal among leading functionaries. This view also tended to emphasize the difference between rank-and-file members and the elite: ordinary workers, in spite of the bleak outlook, relentlessly strove to set up organizations and activities of resistance.

Since many of these alleged resisters "without a [well-known] name" were communists, historical research followed the pattern of the respective political camps during the Cold War. While they were declared the only heroes in the East, studies in the West almost completely neglected their hardship and suffering—that is, the history of their defeat by the Gestapo in 1935–36. At the same time, adherents of social democracy were rendered faceless and voiceless. In East Germany they were labeled as traitors to the communists, while Westerners did not care too much for differences within the left. Studies on the rank and file of workers' resistance under the Nazis started only in the late 1970s.[22] Then the partial opening to social and, finally, cultural and

---

[21] See the general account by Uwe Dietrich Adam, *Judenpolitik im Dritten Reich* (Düsseldorf, 1972). The actual steps of being labeled are shown in painstaking detail by Hazel Rosenstrauch with photographs by Abraham Pisarek in *Aus Nachbarn wurden Juden* (Berlin, 1988).

[22] The only exception was and remained for a long time Günter Weisenborn, *Der lautlose Aufstand: Bericht über die Widerstandsbewegung des deutschen Volkes, 1933–45* (Frankfurt, 1953). As to more recent research which has expanded the focus

everyday-life studies in West German historiography also began to have an impact on research on National Socialism. It was at the intersection of increasing awareness of the everyday with renewed interest in the consolidation of German fascism that more studies focused on the everyday behavior and politics of workers. Timothy Mason's magisterial book on industrial workers in the 1930s fueled this turn to a large extent as did the publication of the reports of the Social Democracy in Exile (SOPADE).

VI

Mason argued that the dominant Nazi cliques and agencies pursued three parallel policies regarding industrial workers: repression, neutralization, and integration.[23] From the outset, police and the Nazi militia (SA) were allowed to exercise almost unlimited violence in their furious search for active opponents, in particular members of the socialist and communist but also Christian labor organizations, the SPD and Kommunistische Partei Deutschlands (KPD), and Allgemeiner Deutscher Gewerkschaftsbund (ADGB) (and Rote Gewerkschaftsopposition [RGO]) and Catholic Workers' Associations.[24] While particularly intense during the initial years of the Nazi seizure of power, brutal repression remained a constant feature of the Nazi regime. After 1936, the encroachment of the SS on society became not only crucial for the development of the state apparatus but also severely impinged upon the experience of the masses.

Repression was conceived of as the task of the public domain, or of the state.[25] In contrast, tactics of neutralization and integration of workers

---

from resistance onto the realms of practices of resisting, see esp. Martin Broszat, "Resistenz und Widerstand: Eine Zwischenbilanz des Forschungsprojekts," in *Bayern in der NS-Zeit* (Munich and Vienna, 1981), 4:691–709; Peukert, *Volksgenossen und Gemeinschaftsfremde,* chaps. 3, 5–7. Hans Mommsen, "Der Widerstand gegen Hitler und die deutsche Gesellschaft," in *Der Widerstand gegen den Nationalsozialismus,* ed. Jürgen Schmädecke and Peter Steinbach (Munich and Zürich, 1985), pp. 3–23. He underlines that not institutions, organized movements, or even "the masses" "defended Germany against Hitler" but "outcasts," esp. pp. 17–18. Ian Kershaw, "Widerstand ohne Volk? Dissens und Widerstand im Dritten Reich," in Schmädecke and Steinbach, eds., pp. 779–98; Peter Steinbach, "Widerstandsforschung im politischen Spannungsfeld," in *Aus Politik und Zeitgeschichte* B 28/88, pp. 3–21.

[23] Timothy W. Mason, "Die Bändigung der Arbeitklasse in Deutschland: Eine Einleitung," in *Angst, Belohnung, Zucht und Ordnung: Herrschaftsmechanismen im Nationalsozialismus,* ed. C. Sachse et al. (Opladen, 1982), pp. 11–53, esp. pp. 18 ff.

[24] The most comprehensive study focusing on the communist resistance is Peukert, *Die KPD im Widerstand* (n. 14 above).

[25] However, especially large companies from the sector of heavy industry had invoked the legitimacy of state and police when they called for and installed *Werkspolizei,* which meant in practice they paid for the employment of state or communal

primarily worked through the realm and practices of industry. The introduction of *Leistungslohn* and increasing differentiation of wage scales figured prominently among respective managerial strategies. They were designed to promote or, at least, trigger processes of internal segmentation within the factories; individuals could improve not only their incomes but also their ranking among their co-workers by "climbing the ladder."[26] Of course, efforts to increase fissures and differentiations within respective work forces were not invented in the Third Reich. They can be traced to previous stages of industrialization. But throughout the 1930s a new drive for modernization and rationalization intensified the remodeling of both the material bases and the social relations of industrial production.[27]

At the same time, Nazi authorities presented their own goals and simultaneously denounced the alleged "foes of the German people," using a specific rhetoric. To a large extent they borrowed styles and icons of representation from their declared enemies: well-ordered marching columns resonated with

---

policemen rather often within the company's private confines, esp. Ralph Jessen, "Unternehmerherrschaft und staatliches Gewaltmonopol. Hüttenpolizisten und Zechenwehren im Ruhrgebiet (1870–1914)," in *'Sicherheit' und 'Wohlfahrt': Polizei, Gesellschaft und Herrschaft im 19. und 20. Jahrhundert*, ed. Alf Lüdtke (Frankfurt, 1992), pp. 767–86.

[26] Tilla Siegel, *Leistung und Lohn in der nationalsozialistischen "Ordnung der Arbeit"* (Opladen, 1989); esp. Rüdiger Hachtmann, *Industriearbeit im "Dritten Reich": Untersuchungen zu den Lohn- und Arbeitsbedingungen in Deutschland, 1933–1945* (Göttingen, 1989). The latter focuses on the phases of rationalization since 1933 and scrutinizes its disciplinary effects. Both studies emphasize rewards instead of repressive measures. However, they still share the assumption that the majority of workers did not agree with either the goals or politics of Nazism. Thus, the politics of companies as well as of Nazi party or of the state toward labor is still perceived as part of the larger efforts to "tame" the working class. The working class appears as an entity relying on potential rebelliousness as did the *classes dangereuses* in the nineteenth century.

[27] This did not stop at the factory walls. Carola Sachse argues that factory and family politics in the 1930s and 1940s displayed structural identity. In the Siemens company, for example, the notion of family would unite home and workplace. In addition, it conveyed the seeming necessity of unequal work and pay for male and female workers. The hierarchical differences between occupational denominations and differential wages of men and women would directly reflect the different status of men and women within the family and in the public realm. But it was not a traditional image of family which managers and functionaries tried to invoke. Instead, the "modern" family was appraised. Company interests in a large work force of inexpensive female workers and the goal of the Nazi state to promote an industrial boom but also to strengthen the ties of the presumed (nuclear) family worked in the same direction. However, modes of coping and possible "deviations" from the prescribed path of family are not considered here; see Carola Sachse, *Siemens, der Nationalsozialismus und die moderne Familie: Eine Untersuchung zur Rationalisierung in Deutschland im 20. Jahrhundert* (Hamburg, 1990).

the paramilitary units as well as with demonstrations as they were staged by the political right and the left (and, not least, the church); the color red was appropriated from the labor movement.[28] However, the Nazis connected these elements in new ways; in particular, they employed features that would convey feelings of "modernity." Thus, they developed new modes of approaching the proletarian masses. Walter Benjamin interpreted this as an "aestheticization of politics," a previously unknown form of "representation." The Nazis offered the masses attractive opportunities to express themselves but did not give them any chance to assert their rights.[29]

Detailed analyses of concrete settings reveal, however, that the government and in particular the Deutsche Arbeitsfront (DAF) implemented programs that offered both material benefits and satisfaction of representational needs. Pay for second holidays at Easter or Pentecost and expansion of vacation but also spectacular events on the national and local level or the promise of travel, Kraft durch Freude (KdF), the Nazi organization of and for leisure: at least in the opinion of the DAF, these and other measures would tie people to the state and state politics. Entrepreneurs, however, seemed to read integration and *Volksgemeinschaft* primarily as an attempt to bind a core group of workers to their particular company. In this way, activities that had mostly been developed during World War I were renewed or extended. Then, enterprises of all sizes had organized support of workers at home for "their people" at the front. Parcels and letters were sent to show demonstratively the connectedness of the work force at the "home front" with their co-workers "out there" on the "firing line." Simultaneously, this policy reflected the immediate concerns of enterprises and of government to keep workers and soldiers quiet and to sustain their compliance. Thus, state agencies did not interfere with firms that, for instance, openly circumvented the rationing system.[30]

The claim of *Burgfriedenspolitik* or "civic truce" on the level of central government had its spin-offs within the factory workshops themselves. Social relations of production were to be redesigned. "Works community" (*Werksgemeinschaft*) would supersede traditional hierarchical relations at work. The

---

[28] However, this may not exhaust the meaning of flying red banners in late Weimar Germany. Sexual connotations are emphasized by Klaus Theweleit, *Männerphantasien,* vol. 2, *Männerkörper: Zur Psychoanalyse des weißen Terrors,* 2d ed. (Rheinbek, 1980), pp. 281 ff.

[29] Walter Benjamin, "Das Kunstwerk im Zeitalter seiner technischen Reproduzierbarkeit," in his *Gesammelte Schriften* (Frankfurt, 1974) 1, pt. 2:471–508, esp. 506 ff.

[30] For the "home-front" aspects see esp. the painstaking case study of respective developments and administrative attitudes in the Ruhr area by Anne Roerkohl, *Hungerblockade und Heimatfront: Die kommunale Lebensmittelversorgung in Westfalen im Ersten Weltkrieg* (Stuttgart, 1991).

cooperation of workers, instead of their subordination to the factory's owner (*Fabrikherr*), promised constant flow of production and increased returns. This new trend was favored particularly by bigger companies. In fact, the often cited difference between the especially harsh treatment of workers in heavy industry and the "softer" methods in other branches such as machine construction or electrical engineering seemed to be diminished. During the 1920s the notion of "works community" increasingly overcame its initial flavor of mere propaganda. Bigger companies set up support systems for workers' nuclear families that provided child care, medical services, or practical training in good housekeeping.[31]

During the Weimar Republic, industry interfered with government and party politics primarily to foster policies which protected their own sphere. It was in this vein that companies and associations of industrial entrepreneurs or managers supported various authoritarian pressure groups and perspectives even more intensely after 1930, that is, under the impact of the depression and mass unemployment. Thus, industry either approved or even strongly supported the takeover of the Nazis in 1933.[32] Again, industry's first priority was to maintain or restore a realm of its own. However, most companies only reluctantly cooperated with Nazi efforts to develop measures aimed at integrating workers into the *Volksgemeinschaft* that the latter were attempting to recreate. Most managers perceived campaigns for the improvement of the workplace environment (*Schönheit der Arbeit*) and even for adding better

---

[31] Alf Lüdtke, "Deutsche Qualitätsarbeit: 'Spielereien' am Arbeitsplatz und 'Fliehen' aus der Fabrik industrielle Arbeitsprozesse und Arbeiterverhalten in den 1920er Jahren," in *Arbeiterkulturen zwischen Alltag und Politik,* ed. F. Boll (Vienna and Munich, 1986), pp. 155–97, esp. pp. 188 ff. While during most of the 1920s companies eagerly engaged in some form or other of "works community," the majority of workers still were employed by smaller firms. The majority also did not live in the industrial centers of the Rhine and Ruhr or in Saxony, nor did they populate the conglomerates of Berlin, Hamburg, or even Stuttgart. Here "works community" remained a foreign term. Those who represented the majority of workers either experienced old style paternalism, i.e., unregulated arbitrariness of the boss, or they could pursue life trajectories in which household structures allowed for seasonal detachment from industry since they earned incomes from different sources, mostly as peasant-workers; cf. Jean Quataert, "The Politics of Rural Industrialization: Class, Gender, and Collective Protest in the Saxon Oberlausitz of the Late Nineteenth Century," *Central European History* 20 (1987): 91–124, esp. 105 ff.

[32] David Abraham, *The Collapse of the Weimar Republic: Political Economy and Crisis,* 2d ed. (New York and London, 1986); Reinhard Neebe, *Großindustrie, Staat und NSDAP, 1930–1933: Paul Silverberg und der Reichsverband der Deutschen Industrie in der Krise der Weimarer Republik* (Göttingen, 1981); esp., for the mid-1920s, Bernd Weisbrod, *Schwerindustrie in der Weimarer Republik: Industrielle Interessenpolitik zwischen Stabilisierung und Krise* (Wuppertal, 1979).

lighting for the machines and installing new security equipment as interference with their own affairs.[33]

VII

Workers also seemed to remain at a distance regarding DAF and wider appeals of *Volksgemeinschaft* even if they were the ones to benefit the most. However, the illegal reports to the SOPADE also hinted at a widespread fascination among workers for Nazi or DAF incentives and activities. Many workers ridiculed refurbishments of washrooms and toilets—measures that had been imminent anyway. Nevertheless, they were impressed because these activities proved that at least some of the concerns of their everyday lives were taken seriously.

The actual effects of these improvements should not be overestimated. Only a small percentage of workers actually encountered practical results of the Nazi activities. Mostly they had to do the work themselves: news spread from above by means of newsreels and illustrated papers. Rumors played an important role, too. The imagination overwhelmed the reality on the shop floor. Nevertheless, claims by Nazi leaders that only their policies asserted the "honor of labor" could be confirmed in the daily experiences of workers.[34] For the first time issues were taken up such as washrooms which the former unions and other workers' organizations had considered too petty to pursue. In addition, *Schönheit der Arbeit* was only one among other efforts that were experienced as reestablishing order within the community as well as in state and society at large. In the context of the buildup of the armed forces and the *Vierjahresplan*, after 1935–36 employment increased as did wages. For younger people especially the future appeared brighter. They would be able to feed a family or, at least, to buy a motorbike or a radio.[35]

German workers in the 1930s and 1940s did not strictly distinguish between "economic" and "political" interests. Their socioeconomic well-being was

[33] Ch. Friemert, *Produktionsästhetik im Faschismus: Das Amt "Schönheit der Arbeit" von 1933 bis 1939* (Munich, 1980).

[34] In historical research the impact of material and symbolic satisfaction of workers' presumed need for respect is mostly considered to be highly limited. This supposition is, however, rarely tested in studies of particular local or industrial settings. For a different view, see my article "Ehre der Arbeit: Industriearbeiter und Macht der Symbole: Zur Reichweite symbolischer Orientierungen im Nationalsozialismus," in *Arbeiter im 20. Jahrhundert*, ed. K. Tenfelde (Stuttgart, 1991), pp. 343–92. See also the detailed analysis and painstaking documentation of the Saar area in Klaus-Michael Mallmann and Gerhard Paul, eds., *Herrschaft und Alltag: Ein Industrierevier im Dritten Reich* (Bonn, 1991).

[35] See the results provided by intensive interviews that focused on the cycles of people's life experiences; Niethammer, ed. (n. 3 above).

kept separate neither from assertion of needs on the shop floor or in the neighborhood nor from official politics as proclaimed through the media. As the SOPADE correspondent bitterly noted: workers remained "passive," if they did not applaud the regime.[36]

But for the most part, workers did not keep their distance from the cheering masses. They joined them, for instance, at the Nazi May Day of "national labor," or when Hitler's voice was heard on the radio, or in the newsreel celebrating another "great day" in the "nation's history." Distanced curiosity might also turn into fascination when Hitler denounced, for instance, the Treaty of Versailles (1934), or when he officially presented rearmament plans and declared Germany's military sovereignty (1935). It seems that, at least at these moments, workers applauded no less enthusiastically than most other *Volksgenossen.*[37] Moreover—and this is an issue the historian of the everyday can amply buttress—it would be misleading to assume that positive assessments and articulations would only have distorted people's "real" needs and interests. For one thing, many life trajectories of males and male groups provided experiences that intimately connected individual lives with the nation as a whole. To these people, who were either soldiers during the war or who had grown up listening to the stories of their fathers, uncles, and brothers, internationalism and antimilitarism had no appeal. Their attitude of heroic pride did not necessarily call for another war. Nonetheless, in their view of manly conduct the nation and its army figured most prominently.

Attitudes of this kind are not simply products of manipulation. Instead, workers undoubtedly "read" official politics according to their individual preferences and experiences. Thus, they interpreted and reshaped if not "privatized" politics. But this did not happen in isolation. Their everyday life had been reframed and, increasingly, politicized. Home and workplace had been incorporated into networks of supralocal communication, dependency, and control since well before 1933.[38]

---

[36] Deutschland-Berichte, Bd. 4: 1937, p. 1238; for the following, ibid., p. 777. The rather homogenous distance toward Nazism these workers of Bremen dockyards displayed does not represent a "typical" case. See, e.g., the intense support of Nazism which prevailed in aircraft and automobile construction at Bremen, esp. Inge Marβolek and René Ott, *Bremen im Dritten Reich,* p. 152. Also, see n. 12 above.

[37] Gerhard Paul, *"Deutsche Mutter, heim zu Dir!"* (Bonn, 1986). While positive sentiments may be less surprising in matters of "national" or "German" questions, Mallmann and Paul have recently argued that, at least in the Saar area, even workers' dissent remained within the confines of a "loyal antipathy"; see Mallmann and Paul, eds., pp. 327 ff.

[38] For this point see my article, "Cash, Coffee-Breaks, Horseplay: Eigensinn and Politics among Factory Workers in Germany circa 1900," in *Confrontation, Class Consciousness, and the Labor Process,* ed. M. Hanagan and C. Stephenson (New York, 1986), pp. 65–95, esp. pp. 82 ff.; as to the domain of "popular culture," see the

Most important, in the 1920s almost all notions of an alternate order of society directly reflected crucial features of the existing ones, even among fervent adherents of societal change. Socialist and communist, but also Catholic, workers' organizations also clung to the discipline of military units. To all of them, the shine of polished machinery appealed and triggered immediate and almost unlimited approval: the "better future" would look like an efficiently executed blowup enlargement of the present.[39] And personal longings for any kind of private future were intricately woven into aspirations of restored national greatness. Thus, when people referred to "German quality work," the emphasis lay equally on both terms: "German" and "quality," a claim that united not only workers but most Germans against the "others."

VIII

Official and unofficial efforts to (re)construct a "works community" gained momentum with the war in 1939. Many employers developed networks of communication with and support of their previous employees who were drafted into the army. Businesses regularly mailed newsletters conveying the developments within the company, but they also collected parcels (so-called *Liebesgaben*) and distributed them at occasions like birthdays or Christmas. In many cases the blue-collar or clerical workers who received these gifts or newsletters responded by writing long letters home. Several companies from Leipzig whose work force in 1939 consisted of five to six hundred or, in one case, of more than two thousand workers, regularly received such letters from soldiers whose peacetime employment was suspended during the war. Some of the letter writers obviously used this occasion because they did not have a circle of friends or relatives back home who would be open to reading about their life in the military. Others mentioned in their letters that they primarily

---

overview by Adelheid von Saldern, "Arbeiterkulturbewegung in der Zwischen-kriegszeit," in Boll, ed. (n. 31 above), pp. 29–70; or, from another angle, the explorations by Victoria de Grazia, "Mass Culture and Sovereignty: The American Challenge to European Cinemas, 1920–1960," *Journal of Modern History* 61 (1989): 53–87.

[39] On the proneness to military forms and rituals in social democracy, see Gerhard Hauk, "'Armeekorps auf dem Weg zur Sonne': Einige Bemerkungen zur kulturellen Selbstdarstellung der Arbeiterbewegung," in *Fahnen, Fäuste, Körper: Symbolik und Kultur der Arbeiterbewegung,* ed. D. Petzina (Essen, 1986), pp. 69–89; on the Catholic movement, see the hitherto unpublished research on its public appearances by Josef Mooser, esp. his exploratory outline: Josef Mooser, "Arbeiter, Bürger und Priester in den konfessionellen Arbeitervereinen im deutschen Kaiserreich, 1880–1914," in *Arbeiter und Bürger im 19. Jahrhundert,* ed. Jürgen Kocka (Munich, 1986), pp. 79–105.

wrote to their kin and friends. However, most of these former or, as it were, suspended employees obviously developed a sense of commitment to their respective work community.

Field-post letters had to pass the military censor before they were mailed. The writers were accustomed to orders of the German military command that strongly emphasized that "field-post letters are weapons, too, comrades."[40] Military authorities provided further guidance, distributing to the troops time and again specific formulations which should be used when writing field-post letters. The military aimed at turning these letters into "vitamins of the psyche" which would rejuvenate anybody who became tired. The foremost recommendation was "to display a manly attitude and to write in a strong and clear language."

Close reading of dozens of field-post letters that had been sent to former employers gives the impression that the writers did not strictly obey these rules. To be sure, one topic was the similarity between being a soldier and life as a worker at home. For instance, the soldier Emil Caspar wrote on October 31, 1943, that they just had marched three hundred kilometers in nine days. It had been hard, but in fact, "it is as if you are working at home." A hand at a shale mine wrote on October 8, 1943, from Norway that he had quickly adjusted to the military "and if you only show obedience and good will everything is fine."[41] Another soldier from the Braunkohlenwerk, obviously also a blue-collar worker, wrote on December 8, 1943, that "I never felt as good on my job as I do now with the military."[42]

As might be expected, field-post letters to former employers were most explicit and detailed when soldiers gave an account of the foreignness if not the alienness of their present situation. A very limited set of stereotypes regarding foreign countries surfaced time and again. For instance, Walter Feurig wrote on November 24, 1942, from Italy that there was "poverty and filth all over." This was not "home" to him—although he told his audience that he liked the picturesque scenery. And more than a year later, on December 12, 1943 (that is, after Italy had declared a cease-fire under Badoglio in July), he told his Leipzig correspondents that the people in Italy "seem to be nice and display an enormous hospitality, they are always happy and gay, of course, they do not labor as the Germans are used to do, but they

---

[40] O. Buchbender and R. Sterz, eds., *Das andere Gesicht des Krieges: Deutsche Feldpostbriefe, 1939–1945* (Munich, 1982), p. 26.

[41] StAL (n. 1 above), Braunkohlenwerk 184, fols. 33, 37. See also Curzio Malaparte, *Die Wolga entspringt in Europa* (Cologne, 1989), pp. 32, 44; in these reports to Italian newspapers, written in the summer of 1941, he refers to the Russian and German armies as "mobile steel mills" and also sees an identity in both armies regarding the merger of military discipline and of industrial discipline.

[42] StAL, Braunkohlenwerk 184, fol. 115, Gerhard Melzig.

seem to be unpretentious and always make the best of things."[43] This went along with remarks like Rudolf Harmann's abrupt note from August 18, 1944, that "we mop up with Italy."[44]

The picture was different when soldiers wrote from Poland or the Russian territories. The soldier Heinz Dübner noted on November 21, 1939, that "the Poles played havoc while we had to restore order and by doing this we became real men."[45] Almost the same attitude emerges in the letter of Edmund Heinzel who served in November 1940 with the Reichsarbeitsdienst in occupied Poland. He told his readers that houses and streets at his place "are very deficient, that is, houses are built from wood and mud and, to put it in one word, it is really a *polnische Wirtschaft.*"[46]

Stereotypes of the Russians were almost identical. The private O. Müller wrote on August 27, 1941, from northeastern Russia that "one sees only huts and not houses and you had better not step into them because of the 'odor'; you don't find curtains, there is neither electric light nor [running] water."[47] During the war in Russia many of those who survived the first weeks stayed continuously for one or two years with their unit since leave was granted only rarely. As private first class Rolf Goebeler wrote on June 21, 1943, "many folks develop a stubborn doggedness, it grows during the on-going fighting, and they aim at crushing the enemy at any rate. The mates swear but this is good!"[48] The toil of soldiering reemphasized notions of being "thrown" into an alien and hostile environment. Encounters with the natives in the hinterland only too often fostered the image of their total otherness. At the same time, enduring the dangers of battle stimulated emotional fury which, in turn, became intricately connected with the routines of the military. Thus, soldiers increasingly conceived of the enemy as not only the "other" but also the "subhuman."

The "others" of the distant front, however, were also approaching "home": since 1941, foreign labor was increasingly forced to work in German industry. The companies conveyed this information to their employees who had been drafted as soldiers; the soldiers responded to it. One of the main concerns that worried the employees who were far away was the quality of work. The soldier Roland Groß offered a consolation to himself and to his mates when he wrote on August 18, 1941, that "although the best quality workers are drafted I think the foreign helpers will not degrade the quality of the machine

---

[43] Ibid., Sack 397, fols. 21, 18.
[44] Ibid., fol. 111.
[45] Ibid., Villeroy and Boch, Steingutfabrik Torgau, no. 67.
[46] Ibid., Sack 397, fol. 157.
[47] Ibid., Sack 353, fols. 2–3.
[48] Ibid., fols. 44–45.

[tools]" which were the products of this particular factory.[49] In contrast, another displayed furious hatred. Karl Schreiber wrote on July 21, 1942, that "we have too much sympathy with the Russians but they do not have any with us. These foreign workers will not accomplish anything. And if they do not work, the best would be to put up a machine gun and to shoot them all." It appears that this man had been in bitter fights. He referred to the Russian mode of fighting and paid it respect, saying that "the Russian fights to the last man, unlike the Tommy." This stood in sharp contrast to the impressions of a cook who had a job with the military staff somewhere in the hinterland of the Russian front. His letter revealed a more joyful tone. He wrote that he could "imagine lots of trouble at work [at home] with foreign workers. But with good will and sign language one can get along pretty well. At least that is what I do with the Russians here."[50]

These few examples indicate a range of opinions, observations, and reactions. Yet it is noteworthy that the letter writers frequently employed notions and images that had been launched or, more commonly, reshaped by the agencies of propaganda. It is unlikely that they employed these formulas only because a censor or some other public eye might look at their writing. In addition, it should be granted that the audience which they addressed was different from family, relatives, or friends at home. These letters had to impress workmates while at the same time playing to their supervisors. Thus, there is a certain public quality to these letters that shaped their style. Most writers seem to have aimed at striking the pose of experience and success. In stark contrast to this jovial moderation is the intensity with which most writers engaged in accounts of their hatred, bitterness, and condescension toward the enemy. Yet the two topics reveal a remarkable similarity between public rhetoric and private perception. This conjunction both reflects support of Nazism and simultaneously triggers an alignment with Nazi ideas.

There was, for instance, Herbert Habermalz, a sergeant who had been employed as a clerk with the sales department of the company of Rudolf Sack. This machine construction factory produced farm equipment, in particular plows. Habermalz was a member of a flight crew in the air force and was stationed in southern Poland, mostly in Cracow. In a letter of August 7, 1943, he gave a detailed account of the detection of a mass grave by German authorities. "The people who had been buried were, in his words, victims of the GPU [the soviet secret police]. This grave was in the middle of a 'Volkspark,' only ten meters next to a swing. . . . Of course, I was eager to see the graves. You really can say that the GPU did a very good job—which we,

---

[49] Ibid., Sack 397, fol. 193.
[50] Ibid., Sack 399, fols. 167–68.

of course, cannot grasp at all. One could see rather well kept corpses of males, but also of females. All of them with their hands on the backs. . . . Next to the site a group of physicians was at work. The smell was not the best as you may imagine. In addition, there were those many many people who cried and looked for their people among the corpses and the physical remains."[51] Just a few days earlier he had written a letter in which he described painstakingly the environment of the air base. Accordingly, it was "very nice, the Wisla is really close. . . . It is only a pity that this quiet scenery is occasionally disturbed by 'Iwan' with his artillery. Apart from that one can believe to be in a spa."[52]

In early July of 1943 the firm of Rudolf Sack received a letter from a colleague of Habermalz, Gerd Sauer. He had also been stationed in Poland and for some time in Warsaw. There he encountered "real metropolitan life," as he put it. He felt quite happy and relaxed, especially since he had found a large group of people to mix with, most of them SS and *Volksdeutsche:* "The *Volksdeutsche,* mostly ladies, are very nice, friendly and intelligent and also very well-educated." In June 1943, Habermalz had sent a letter to the Sack firm in which he described a flight from Cracow to Warsaw. "We flew several circles above the city. And with great satisfaction we could recognize the complete extermination of the Jewish Ghetto. There our folks did really a fantastic job. There is no house which has not been totally destroyed. This we saw the day before yesterday. And yesterday we took off for Odessa. We received special food, extra cookies, additional milk and butter, and, above all, a very big bar of bittersweet chocolate."[53]

IX

These letters, to be sure, also reflect perceptions of "being turned into" objects of those who occupy the "heights of command" of policy, economy, and society. However, an interpretation of workers as victims and leaders as the sole agents, comforting as it might be, is not sufficient. The very texture of these letters indicates that the authors did not encounter military draft and participation in war as totally "alien" situations. The intense descriptions of various situations and encounters which these letters contain reflect efforts to "ban" the permanent uncertainties and the dangers to one's own life. At the same time, though, the letters indicate that anxieties were transformed into an intensified loyalty to military superiors. Even more, the experience of being part of the war machinery itself enhanced attachment to the goals the Nazi

[51] Ibid., Sack 353, fol. 31.
[52] Ibid., Sack 352, fol. 32.
[53] Ibid., fol. 46.

leadership proclaimed time and again. These soldiers tried to "get by" under enormous hardship and suffering. Thus, they tried to cope with and appropriate the given situation; but in this very practice of "coping and appropriating" the authors turned into actors. This is true even for those privates who wrote angry or artificial letters home. They all documented how they became both victims and accomplices of Nazism.

The letter writers were trained in (or, at least, socialized to) factory life in large German cities. Their self-images, however, permitted them to easily connect the experiences of civilian work and military life, to accept the dangers as well as the attractions of war. The humiliating rituals of military drill during basic training were very frightening to most people. To be able to "stand it" and, in the end, to master the situation provided an enormous boost to the person's self-esteem.[54] No direct line connected military life under peacetime conditions with the dangers and opportunities of war. But given that the war had begun, it was not merely traveling and "touring hitherto unknown" places that seemed to justify any toil and danger at the front or in the hinterland. To be a soldier did not only mean to be linked to an enormous organization and to modern weaponry. Those at the front or with the units behind actually used their guns; they time and again employed the capabilities of the machinery of war to kill. War was work.

These letters reveal that many individuals perceived their masculinity in military terms and images. To these people, their original claim to perform a "clean" job at home increasingly became linked to the efficient killing

---

[54] Workers who had been claimed by "their" companies as indispensable for sustaining armament production were those who continued to work "at home." They encountered relative though different experiences of confrontation with "the others." After 1940–41 they increasingly encountered *Fremdarbeiter, Ostarbeiter,* prisoners of war, and inmates of concentration camps within their workshops. Of course, industrial and political authorities suspiciously watched and strictly forbade any contact between Germans and these foreigners. Instances of Gestapo intervention show that even handing over a small sandwich or a few grams of tobacco was treated as a serious crime. Violators were sent to prison if not to work camps, and usually they had to serve between one and six months. After they had served their sentences, in a number of cases inmates were also transferred to concentration camps; see Herbert, *Fremdarbeiter* (n. 8 above), passim. The point is, however, that the registered cases of "prohibited contact" and their sharp increase from 1941 to 1942 (see Herbert, p. 123) cannot be interpreted as disobedience not to mention resistance. The same figures rather indicate those persons who had given the information to the authorities. They might have longed for a premium or aspired to other benefits; but did not many share the presumption that only harsh treatment would protect *Führer und Reich?* On aspects of closing the gaps between classes at the German "homefront" as a response to "total war" efforts and Allied air raids after 1943, see Mark Roseman, "World War II and Social Change in Germany," in *Total War and Social Change,* ed. Arthur Marwick (Houndsmill and London, 1988), pp. 58–78, esp. pp. 68 ff.

operations of the army.[55] In the end, participation in the extermination of "others" might appear to many as the ultimate fulfillment of those cherished notions of "German quality work."

[55] On the invasion of the Soviet Union and the aspects of extermination on the level of political military planning and leadership, see esp. *Das Deutsche Reich und der Zweite Weltkrieg,* ed. Militärgeschichtliches Forschungsamt (Stuttgart, 1983), 4:18 ff., 413 ff. For the military occupation army in the East, see the excellent account by Theo Schulte, *The German Army and Nazi Policies in Occupied Russia* (Oxford, 1989). In my opinion, only historical reconstruction of everyday life provides the opportunity to explain the (relative) attractiveness of the military not only in peace but also in war. This perspective reveals the relationships between and ambivalences of ideology and the daily experiences of people. See Lutz Niethammer, "Heimat und Front: Versuch, zehn Kriegserinnerungen aus der Arbeiterklasse zu verstehen," in *"Die Jahre weiß man nicht"* (n. 3 above), pp. 163–232. See also the critique of this assumed connectedness in Omer Bartov, "The Missing Years: German Workers, German Soldiers," *German History* 8 (1990): 46–65.

"In the End I Just Said O.K.": Political and Moral Dimensions of Escape Aid at the Swiss Border*

Alfred G. Frei
Kulturamt der Stadt Singen

"I helped simply out of compassion," says Josef Höfler. The eighty-some-year-old sits in the living room of his small house in Gottmadingen, an industrial village located about two miles from the Swiss border. In the years 1943 and 1944, Höfler showed sixteen Jews the way over into Switzerland in order to save them from certain death in the gas chambers of Nazi Germany. Josef Höfler was a refugee helper. He was not the only one to risk his life to assist the large numbers of persecuted people who poured into the region between the southern German industrial city of Singen am Hohentwiel and Schaffhausen, Switzerland; but there were only a few who tried to help the refugees, and most have been forgotten, their traces now difficult to find. In this essay, I will outline the importance of the Singen border region for escape attempts from Nazi Germany and present three different ways in which escape aid (*Fluchthilfe*) was provided. At the close, I will examine the question of sources and suggest how to interpret the political and moral dimensions of resistance and refugee help in this period.

ESCAPING THE HORROR ON FOOT

In the years between 1940 and 1945, Switzerland was the only country neighboring Germany that was able to negotiate a certain amount of independence. More than 90 percent of the Swiss-German border is determined by Lake Constance and the Rhine, and neither the lake nor the strong currents of the Rhine could be crossed without local knowledge and help. The border police easily controlled the river, but two sections of the Schaffhausen canton extend north of the Rhine and can be reached from Germany by foot. The "green border" of the Schaffhausen canton runs past the cities of Schaffhausen and Stein am Rhein in an erratic course through fields and forests (see fig. 1). Anyone trying to flee Germany needed the help of someone familiar with the confusing features of this border; at the same time, the terrain made escape attempts more difficult to detect.

In his study of escape methods used by RAF airmen during the Second World War, Aidan Crawley writes, "For most pedestrians in the early days of

* Translated from the German by Jillian Warmund and Carol Scherer.

This essay originally appeared in the *Journal of Modern History* 64, suppl. (December 1992).

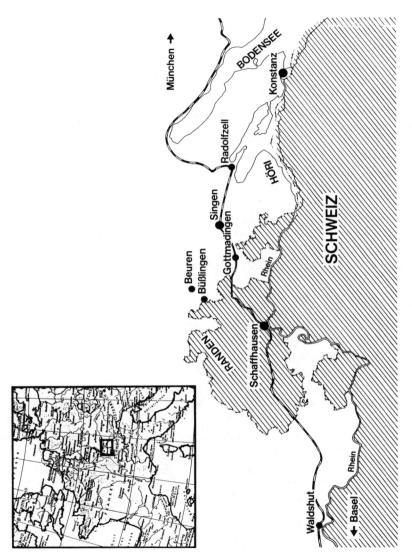

Fig. 1

the war, Switzerland was the usual goal. It was the nearest neutral country and mountain climbers and skiing enthusiasts had a detailed knowledge of some parts of the frontier. In addition, many thousands of Frenchmen, Poles and a few members of the British Army had crossed this frontier in 1940 and 1941 and certain stretches of it, such as the Schaffhausen Salient or the eastern end of Lake Constance, had been carefully mapped."[1] But the geography of the border was not the only reason why so many people sought out the region between Singen and Schaffhausen to escape from Germany: there were at least five other reasons, and these provide points of inquiry into the more particular motivations of local residents who tried to help the refugees.

First of all, in Catholic southern Baden, the National Socialists never succeeded in gaining a clear majority. In the Reichstag elections of March 1933, the Nazis received only 34.7 percent of the vote from Singen's twenty thousand inhabitants, almost ten percentage points less than their 43.9 percent national average. In the November 1932 election, the difference had been as high as 12 percent.[2] In addition, proximity to the border seemed to provide a sense of hope and relative security. A great number of banned artists, for example, among them Otto Dix and Max Ackermann, withdrew from the cities to the Höri peninsula on Lake Constance between Singen and Radolfzell with its view of Switzerland.[3] Similarly, Rosa and Irma Thälmann, the wife and daughter of Ernst Thälmann, the leader of the Kommunistische Partei Deutschlands (KPD) who was arrested in 1933 and murdered ten years later, spent almost the entire Nazi period with their comrades in Singen's working-class district.[4]

In the second place, Singen was home to the factories of three large Swiss firms, Maggi, Georg Fischer AG, and Aluminium Walzwerke, and it had the highest proportion of industrial factory workers in all of Baden. The Singen factory workers remained firmly rooted in their agricultural and Catholic background,[5] however, and they lacked the handcraft traditions from which the workers' movement in other cities drew its strength and identity. While the socialist workers' parties in Singen seldom garnered more than 40 percent of

---

[1] Aidan Crawley, *Escape from Germany: The Methods of Escape Used by RAF Airmen during the Second World War* (London, 1985), p. 56.

[2] Ingrid Pickel, *Die Machtergreifung der Nationalsozialisten in Singen: Eine Dokumentation* (Singen, 1983), pp. 6–7.

[3] Andrea Hoffmann, *Künstler auf der Höri: Zuflucht am Bodensee in der ersten Hälfte des zwanzigsten Jahrhunderts* (Konstanz, 1989).

[4] Käte Weick, *Widerstand und Verfolgung in Singen* (Stuttgart and Singen, n.d.), pp. 224–29.

[5] Alfred Georg Frei and Gert Zang, "Die importierte Arbeiterbewegung: Arbeiter in Singen bis zum Ende des Kaiserreichs," in *Singen: Dorf und Herrschaft*, ed. Herbert Berner, Singener Stadtgeschichte, vol. 2 (Konstanz, 1990), pp. 574–96.

the vote, Singen was by far the "reddest" city in the region. In the November 1932 Reichstag election, for example, the Communists won 23.8 percent and the Social Democrats 14.7 percent of the vote.[6] Across the border, the inhabitants of Schaffhausen voted in a Communist town government for most of the period from 1933 to 1945. The workers from the industrial quarters of the historically bourgeois Schaffhausen repeatedly elected Walter Bringolf, a member of the Kommunistische Partei Opposition (KPO), as mayor. Bringolf openly defied Swiss law which, until 1943, refused to accept refugees except in unusual cases.[7]

Third, the higher wages in Switzerland drew many people from Singen and the surrounding area across the border every day to work. These "border commuters" further strengthened the already close relationships among the socialist parties and labor unions on both sides of the border. The state police precinct of Karlsruhe in its report of January 5, 1938, for example, attributed the "communist activity on the Singen border" to the fact that "many people travel almost daily to Switzerland and read Marxist literature there." German workers were "doubtlessly infected" through contact with Swiss colleagues.[8] In particular, the local German branches of the international cultural organization "Friends of Nature" (Naturfreunde) worked closely with their counterparts in the Schaffhausen area. Hiking, canoeing, and other recreational activities of the Naturfreunde produced the knowledge and practical experience that would prove indispensable to those who helped the refugees.

Fourth, since the end of the nineteenth century, Singen was a hub of the railway system. The railroad lines between Zurich and Stuttgart, Constance and Offenburg, and Basel and Munich, along with two other nearby lines, all crossed in Singen. Singen thus attracted the attention of Swiss businesses, which quickly and heavily industrialized what earlier had been a farming village.[9] For refugees of the Nazi period, the railroad provided a fast exit, at least as far as the border. Especially crucial was Singen's rail connection to Munich, which at that time served as the gateway to both Berlin and central Germany.

[6] Pickel, pp. 6–7.

[7] Walther Bringolf, *Mein Leben: Weg und Umweg eines Schweizer Sozialdemokraten* (Bern, 1965).

[8] Jörg Schadt, comp., *Verfolgung und Widerstand unter dem Nationalsozialismus in Baden: Die Lageberichte der Gestapo und des Generalstaatsanwalts Karlsruhe, 1933–1940,* Veröffentlichungen des Stadtarchivs Mannheim, no. 3 (Stuttgart, 1976), p. 196.

[9] Alfred Georg Frei, ed., *Habermus und Suppenwürze: Singens Weg vom Bauerndorf zur Industriestadt* (Konstanz, 1987).

A final important point was that a short train ride from Singen could bring a refugee into the relative safety of Switzerland. This escape route was to prove especially important during the first years of Nazi rule.

POLITICAL AND MORAL DIMENSIONS OF AID GIVEN TO REFUGEES

"I come from the BMW plants." With this password, many antifascists, especially Communists, gained entrance into the Harlander family's small house in a residential section of Singen. Until 1933, the Harlanders did not belong to any political party. Their twenty-five-year-old son Xaver was a mason by trade and traveled every day to work in Schaffhausen. Because he first joined the Communist Party in 1933, Xaver was not on the list of political suspects under surveillance by the Gestapo.

Xaver Harlander maintained contact with the "Schaffhausen Red Help" (Rote Hilfe). In the first years of Nazi rule, help for refugees was relatively easy. A member of the Schaffhausen Red Help, such as the textile worker Marie Furrer-Grimm, could buy a round-trip train ticket to Singen from Schaffhausen, conveniently forgetting her passport in order to receive a day pass from the border police—a valid, extra border document good for that day. In the Harlander house in Singen, the refugee was given the train ticket to Schaffhausen along with the extra border papers from the forgetful Marie Furrer-Grimm. She then purchased another train ticket to Schaffhausen in Singen, producing at the border her own passport, which of course she had with her the entire time.[10]

Born in 1906, Marie Furrer-Grimm is proud of her Communist identity. In an autobiographical account she notes, "To my satisfaction, I grew up in a working-class family; that is, I was raised with a sense of class consciousness. We were also introduced to nature and taught an appreciation of life, as well as its deficiencies in the existing order." When the enemies of the workers' movement came to power in Germany in 1933, she did not hesitate to help or to resist. In a border region, resistance meant bringing fleeing comrades and other threatened people to safety. In the Swiss countryside, the helpers collected money and found people willing to shelter the escapees—if the Swiss government had not already imprisoned them.[11]

Compared to other political groups, the Communists were relatively well prepared for the German dictator's seizure of power, having founded Red Help as early as 1924. From the beginning the organization was international

---

[10] Weick, pp. 109–26.

[11] Marie Furrer, unpublished account in Schaffhausen, August 23, 1986, Archiv Fritz Besnecker, Singen.

in scope, resting on the close cooperation of its different national sections. Their comparatively overt and constant political engagement would demand much sacrifice. At least half of the estimated three hundred thousand KPD members in 1933 were imprisoned at least once by the National Socialists. An estimated twenty thousand Communists were murdered.[12]

In the years between 1933 and 1939, the National Socialists refined their apparatus of surveillance and repression. Their illusory economic successes led to greater support in the populace, a shift that significantly raised the stakes of refugee help. Tighter border controls circumvented escape attempts by rail and by foot. For their part, until 1943 the Swiss police returned almost every refugee they caught near the border. The fear that Germany would invade its small neighbor, combined with the mounting strength of the pro-Nazi movement, turned Switzerland into a leak-ridden lifeboat. Even in the years between 1942 and 1945, when the Swiss knew the extent of the Nazi terror, the government sent back almost ten thousand people to the National Socialist regime—and these are only the cases that are officially documented and acknowledged by the Swiss government.[13]

The escalating dangers to refugees and refugee helpers also threatened Marie Furrer-Grimm. In the summer of 1935, as she returned to the Harlander house to see if new refugees had arrived, she spotted the Gestapo. She spun around just in the nick of time. The Harlanders and the other German helpers were arrested and incarcerated for years in concentration camps. Marie Furrer-Grimm then took up other contacts in refugee aid. In early 1937, unable to obtain the day off from work, she handed her passport to an associate to pick up a female émigré. He was arrested, and the Gestapo found her passport on him. Marie Furrer-Grimm was ordered to report to the Swiss canton police, and the "wanted" list sent by the central Gestapo office of Baden to the southern border agencies on May 25, 1937, carried her name. From that point on she could no longer cross the border into Germany, and this form of help to refugees ended.

Richard Jäckle, another refugee helper, was born in 1912 into a family with a strong social democratic tradition. His grandfather had lost his job for distributing social democratic pamphlets in the Black Forest. The Jäckles moved to Singen in the hopes of finding work in the new factories. In the 1920s Richard Jäckle's father worked as a party secretary. Richard Jäckle himself became a typesetter at the social democratic daily paper *Volkswille,* and when the National Socialists banned the paper in 1933 he was out of work

---

[12] Horst Duhnke, *Die KPD von 1873 bis 1945* (Cologne, 1972).

[13] Helmut F. Pfanner, "The Role of Switzerland for the Refugees," in *The Muses Flee Hitler: Cultural Transfer and Adaptation, 1930–1945*, ed. Jarrel C. Jackman and Carla Borden (Washington, D.C., 1983), p. 237.

until he found employment at another print shop in Wiesbaden. The Jäckles continued their political work for the Social Democrats into the Nazi period. They smuggled social democratic newspapers and propaganda over the border, and Jäckle's father reported on the situation in the Singen plants for the German Reports of the Social Democratic Party (the SOPADE Reports). During the 1930s, however, the National Socialists succeeded in repressing this form of political work as well.

In contrast to the Communists, the Social Democrats had not developed any functioning and trained resistance networks that could have offered organized help to refugees. All the same, the Nazi machine was not able to alter their inner moral convictions, which had been shaped by the social democratic, working-class milieu of the 1920s. This was also true of Richard Jäckle. When the young typesetter discovered that a business partner in the Wiesbaden firm had to leave Germany with his Jewish wife, he immediately offered his help. Jäckle first brought the woman, who was in particular danger, to stay with his father in Singen; six weeks later he brought her husband. In 1943 he returned to his hometown to lead the couple over the border. From the Gottmadingen cemetery, they studied the terrain for a possible escape route. His father had thought up a good story in case they were interrogated by the border police: they would say they had heard that fabric, a scarce commodity worth any trip, was to be had in a nearby village. The flight of the couple was successful. Even today, Richard Jäckle sees his help to refugees as a moral obligation.[14]

The escape help undertaken by Josef Höfler, mentioned earlier, was not prompted by the same kind of political considerations and identification that inspired Marie Furrer-Grimm and Richard Jäckle. Höfler was born in 1911 in the border town of Bietingen. His parents were poor farmers. He could not inherit the farm, nor could his parents afford to provide him with an apprenticeship. After leaving grammar school he became an unskilled worker in Fahr, a large agricultural equipment factory in Gottmadingen. But Josef Höfler did not resign himself to this fate, and at twenty he apprenticed himself to a blacksmith in the Swiss village of Ramsen. After his apprenticeship and a short stint as a journeyman in the Black Forest, he returned to Fahr as a skilled worker and found a position manufacturing harvesters on the assembly line. In 1943 he was conscripted to work for the war effort in the Singen plant of Aluminium Walzwerke.

Josef Höfler was not politically active and was also very careful. However, it was known that he did not support National Socialism, and another conscript at Aluminium Walzwerke approached him about helping endangered people escape into Switzerland. They spoke several times. Then Luise Meyer,

---

[14] Richard Jäckle, interview by Manfred Bosch on July 11, 1981, in Singen, Archiv Manfred Bosch, Rheinfelden.

who directed an escape organization for German Jews in Berlin, visited Höfler in Gottmadingen to enlist him and his excellent knowledge of the border in escape efforts. He thought about it for a long time. In contrast to Marie Furrer-Grimm or Richard Jäckle, helping was no foregone conclusion for him. He had married in 1935, and a year later his in-laws had helped the pair build a small house in Gottmadingen. He and his wife had a son and felt comfortable, even within their modest financial circumstances. They had taken in a lodger to help make ends meet. The lodger turned out to be an extreme National Socialist who repeatedly told his landlord that he would have all enemies of the regime imprisoned in concentration camps.

Should Josef Höfler risk his family's happiness under such conditions? Asked why he finally did help, he modestly shrugged, "Out of compassion." He had carefully followed the development of the Nazi regime. The day after the synagogue in nearby Randegg had been destroyed in November 1938, he rode his bicycle over to take a look for himself. Had he dared, he would have taken one of the Torah scrolls with him. Höfler watched the expulsion of the Jews from the village and discovered that Wagner, the especially fanatical Gauleiter of Baden, had ordered that all the remaining Jews of the area be transported to the French concentration camp Gurs on October 20, 1940. Höfler knew that the National Socialists wanted to destroy the Jews. It was the last straw; Luise Meyer and Höfler's antifascist colleague were finally able to persuade him to help. "They begged and pleaded for so long that, in the end, I finally said O.K., I would do it once." He brought a married Jewish couple over the border. Although Höfler became a staunch Social Democrat after the war, today he candidly admits that he probably would not have helped Social Democrats or Communists. He wanted to be certain that the people whom he brought over the border were in immediate danger of losing their lives. On that point, he could be certain only about the Jews. He had seen their plight in villages throughout the Höri peninsula.

Höfler's promise to help one time was soon renewed. The oppression of the German Jews escalated, while the possibilities of escape diminished rapidly. In 1943 Switzerland finally liberalized its refugee policy. If a refugee could make it across the border, which the Swiss continued to patrol as tightly as the Germans, he or she had a chance to stay. The reward for success made the work of refugee helpers like Josef Höfler even more crucial.

Höfler let himself be persuaded again and again. He forgot his fear. Despite his dangerous lodger, he even sheltered the refugees arriving in the night from Berlin in his home. From there, he guided them across the border by Gottmadingen, where Richard Jäckle had smuggled out the married couple from Wiesbaden. Höfler, who five years before had been afraid to pick up the Torah scrolls from the Randegg synagogue, then convinced two friends—one of them a customs official—to be humane and help. They brought eight more Jews across the border. During 1944 they generally chose the path over the "green border" in the secluded and thinly populated hills of the Randen, about twenty miles west of the sharply guarded area around Singen.

Despite the grave danger, Höfler and his friends continued to work with the refugees, who often were unwilling to follow the advice of their helpers. The point of contention was usually baggage: was it not possible to save the fewest bits of belongings, prized possessions, something to preserve history as well as life in the new country? These were problems not only on the Rhine and Lake Constance: the refugees whom Hans and Lisa Fittko led along the perilous path over the Pyrenees into Spain during these years regularly begged to take just one trunk. As Lisa Fittko wrote in her gripping book, many refugees remained stubborn on this point and refused to heed the warnings.[15]

For Josef Höfler and his helpers the question of luggage finally proved their undoing. As Luise Meyer detailed in her account for the Wiener Library, she had sent a woman accompanied by a fourteen-year-old girl to Höfler in May 1944. They insisted on taking along bulky baggage. When the customs official in Höfler's group saw the two with their luggage waiting at the rendezvous point, he became anxious and returned home. For the entire night the two women attempted in vain to find the way over the border. In the morning they took the early train back to Singen. A worker in the train noticed their muddy shoes and probably their luggage as well. He denounced them to the police. At her interrogation the woman named names, and the Gestapo arrested the entire refugee help group. Höfler awaited his trial in jail until he was liberated by the French. An unexpected twist of war saved him from the notorious Berlin Volksgerichtshof and, most likely, death: a bombing raid on Berlin destroyed his files and that circumvented the proceedings that had already been prepared.[16]

In the last years of the Third Reich, many people who previously had been indifferent or even sympathetic to National Socialism decided on religious and moral grounds to aid the refugees. The Singen priest August Ruf paid with his life for his decision to help. An imprudent note of thanks fell into the hands of the Gestapo, who incarcerated Ruf and two other priests for bringing Jews over the border. Ruf died as a result of that prison term.

Whereas feelings of altruism motivated the dangerous work of refugee helpers in the Catholic and socialist camps, in a few cases refugee helpers

---

[15] Lisa Fittko, *Mein Weg über die Pyrenäen* (Munich, 1985).
[16] Josef Höfler, " 'Ich habe mich immer wieder überreden lassen': 16 Juden unter Lebensgefahr den Weg über die Grenze gewiesen," *Südkurier* (September 2, 1986), Luise Meyer, November 22, 1957, Berlin, Wiener Library P. III f (Berlin), No. 193/02/188.

received some form of payment for their services. The Jewish teacher Jizchak Schwersenz, brought over the "green border" by Josef Höfler's two friends in February 1944, reported that the people who helped him received RM 4,000 worth of clothing from Berlin. Another escapee disparagingly labeled the Höfler group "smugglers" because they demanded his bicycle, which he had had sent by rail, as a "premium." Had he hoped to be able to take his bicycle with him? He and his friend—Herbert A. Strauss, the director of the Berlin Center for Research on Anti-Semitism—also gave the helpers a camera.[17] This flight occurred in July 1943, when Josef Höfler was still guiding refugees over the border near Gottmadingen.

Against all odds, there seem to have been quite a few successful escapes. According to a report sent by the Constance county commissioner to the border police, "lately . . . a considerable number of people have successfully crossed the green border into Switzerland." He demanded that "broader circles of the population be mobilized in support" of the fight against refugees and that "the successful cooperation of the population be recognized through praise and rewards."[18]

FORCED LABORERS AND PRISONERS OF WAR

Toward the end of the war, one of every six Singen inhabitants, or about three thousand people, had been unwillingly transported to Singen as forced laborers, among them many prisoners of war. Almost every European nationality was represented, with the majority of people coming from the Ukraine, Poland, or Russia. Most were employed in the three large factories. In keeping with the racist policies of the Nazis, the Eastern Europeans were treated with particular brutality. Work and living conditions depended on the factory. The situation in the Maggi food factory was so poor that the forced laborers went on strike in the summer of 1943. The strikers were physically beaten, and the six Eastern Europeans who had organized the strike were placed in concentration camps. Only three returned.

According to official records, about 15 percent of the forced laborers attempted to escape. It is difficult to determine their chances of success because many of the documents are either unavailable or inaccessible. Capture meant certain incarceration in the *Straflager*, which were even worse than the

---

[17] Ernst Ludwig Ehrlich, September 1959, London, Wiener Library P III d (Berlin), No. 1141/Yad Vashem 02/1067.
[18] Manfred Bosch, " 'Der Abschied von Singen fiel uns nicht schwer . . .': Die Hohentwielstadt als letzte deutsche Station auf der Flucht verfolgter Juden," in *Singener Jahrbuch* (Singen, 1983), pp. 40–48.

concentration camps. The traces of many forced laborers who sought freedom in Switzerland ended up instead in the *Straflager* of Nazi Germany.[19]

In a memo dated June 2, 1943, the Singen commissariat of the border police for the Gestapo detailed the favorite escape routes for the police in Singen and the surrounding areas. Apparently the forced laborers sought out paths to freedom throughout the border area around Singen. Many attempted to swim across the Rhine. According to Swiss reports, the corpses of escaped foreign laborers or prisoners of war washed up daily along the banks of Lake Constance or the Rhine. The reports also mention that the Swiss authorities returned the corpse of a Russian shot during his escape attempt to the Germans, who displayed it in a labor camp on the border in order to intimidate the Eastern European workers.[20]

There were mass escape attempts in the days just before liberation. On April 15, 1945, one hundred people crossed the border, mostly in the Randen region. The escaped prisoners, from France, Russia, Poland, Croatia, Africa, and Indonesia, filled the border area. Fleeing Russian prisoners stood out among the refugee groups. The denigrating label "SU" they were forced to wear in large letters on their backs made them an object of particularly brutal "special treatment" by the Germans.[21] On the morning of April 16, 1945, one week before the French liberation of Singen, a group of sixty Polish men and women, forced laborers from the countryside, appeared at a border station in the Randen hills. They had organized an escape attempt and even managed to obtain weapons. The two German customs officials stationed at the border wanted at first to prevent the group from leaving but quickly reconsidered their decision and joined forces with the Poles. They marched together with the forced laborers into Switzerland and were put up in the gymnasium of the border town of Schleitheim. Similar cases occurred at other border stations in the region.

Walter Bringolf, the mayor of Schaffhausen, recalled in his memoirs the thousands of freed prisoners who passed daily through the small city. From April 21 to April 25, 1945, approximately 5,500 people were accommodated in Schaffhausen, a canton with around fifty-five thousand inhabitants. According to estimates, by the end of April more than five thousand prisoners of war stopped in the Singen border region, so that altogether there were over ten

[19] Wilhelm J. Waibel, "Zwischen Dämonie und Hoffnung: Zwangsarbeiter und Kriegsgefangene in Singen," in *Erinnern, Bedenken, Lernen: Das Schicksal von Juden, Zwangsarbeitern und Kriegsgefangenen zwischen Hochrhein und Bodensee in den Jahren 1933 bis 1945,* ed. Alfred G. Frei and Jens Runge (Sigmaringen, 1990), pp. 725–57.

[20] Bosch, *Als die Freiheit unterging,* pp. 257 ff.

[21] Kurt Bächtold, "Die Ereignisse im April 1945," *Schaffhauser Magazin,* no. 1 (1985), pp. 9–11.

thousand additional people in a comparatively small space. The Swiss set up emergency camps by the border and later collected the refugees into an indoor stadium near Zurich in Oerlikon. Approximately five thousand displaced persons passed through this stadium on their way back to their home countries.[22]

Forced laborers were not the only ones who attempted to cross the green border. From the entire southern half of Germany, many prisoners of war, especially the French and British, made their way toward Switzerland. Many of them were seized and incarcerated in *Straflager.* Very seldom do we know the details. However, the British Defense Ministry did document the escape attempts and routes of RAF members. These prisoners, usually the crews from downed bombers or fighter planes, had been trained in possible methods of escape. They were equipped with maps disguised as silk handkerchiefs which detailed the region between Schaffhausen and Singen.[23]

The concentration camp inmates who tried to escape ran an especially high risk. In fact, only one successful escape from the camp near Überlingen is known. In the years 1944–45, approximately seven hundred prisoners were sent from Dachau to Überlingen, on Lake Constance, in order to construct bomb-proof factories for the armaments industry in the city of Friedrichshafen, the center of zeppelin production. Escape attempts were punishable by death. Inmates reported that captured refugees were ripped to shreds by the dogs of the SS. Nonetheless, on March 26, 1945, the Austrian communist and Spanish Civil War veteran Adam Puntschart along with a Russian prisoner escaped over the "green border" in the Randen.[24]

THE UNMASTERABLE PAST OF ESCAPE HELP: SUPPRESSION AND PROBLEMS WITH SOURCES

In July 1941 the Singen farmer Hermann Denzel helped two French prisoners of war escape over the border. The two Frenchmen reached their Swiss haven, but Hermann Denzel was denounced and arrested by the Nazis. After six months in jail, he was sent as part of a penal company to the eastern front and ended up as a French prisoner of war. After the war, his wife was forced to turn to the authorities in Singen for help because she could not manage the farm and raise her six children without her husband. Only recently did the children of the now deceased farmer learn from a Singen "grass roots" historian that their father had saved the lives of two young Frenchmen. That subject had

---

[22] Girijan Mookerjee, *Labyrinth Europa* (Düsseldorf, 1956), p. 203.

[23] Crawley (n. 1 above), 1985.

[24] Adam Puntschart, *Die Heimat ist weit: Erlebnisse im Spanischen Bürgerkrieg, im KZ, auf der Flucht,* ed. Oswald Burger (Weingarten, 1983).

become a family taboo, probably because their father's jail sentence could have jeopardized the family's reputation in the 1950s.[25]

The refugee helper Josef Höfler received a total of DM 1,710 from the German government as compensation for the year he was imprisoned. Höfler had to give most of the money to the lawyer whom he had hired to get the "compensation" in the first place, and he received nothing for his personal possessions confiscated by the Gestapo after his arrest in 1944. In the political climate of the 1950s and 1960s, both refugee helpers and émigrés had to reckon with the peculiar morality of the people who had remained in Nazi Germany. As Peter Steinbach has elaborated, "The émigrés were seen as having taken the easier way out," and escaping Germany was the first step on this path.[26] Like deserters, the refugee helpers must fight even today for social recognition and acceptance of their bravery under the Nazi regime.

In the political climate of the cold war hardly any refugee helpers were encouraged to tell their stories. Even in Singen, the crucial role that the border region had played during the Third Reich was forgotten and suppressed. No one chose to remember that on November 26, 1942, a Jewish couple from Berlin committed suicide by overdosing on sleeping pills in the Singen train station because they saw no other way out, or that on February 15, 1943, a Jewish domestic servant, also from Berlin, hanged herself in the Singen jail after falling into the hands of the Gestapo.[27]

A fundamental crisis of sources pervades the topic of refugee help. This is especially true for successful escapes because escapes were successful only if they were not found out and documented. Even in Switzerland, files were opened only if the refugees had a difficult fate—that is, if they had been arrested or detained. Files also exist when the Swiss sent the refugees back to Germany. Almost all of these files end in the death registers of concentration camps or *Straflager*.

In order to create some documentation of a successful escape, the *Kulturamt* (Office of Culture) in Singen enlisted the help of Jizchak Schwersenz, the Jewish teacher discussed earlier, to reconstruct his escape route over the "green border." We also recorded the reconstruction on videotape, and it is shown in many German states as part of their political education program. Rather than confine his history to classrooms and lecture halls, Jizchak Schwersenz was willing to reenact his escape from Nazi

[25] Wilhelm J. Waibel, conversation with Alfred G. Frei, Singen, 1990.

[26] Peter Steinbach, "Widerstandsforschung im politischen Spannungsfeld," *Aus Politik und Zeitgeschichte,* suppl. to *Das Parlament* (July 8, 1988), p. 10.

[27] Reinhild Kappes, "Singener Juden im Nationalsozialismus," in Frei and Runge, eds. (n. 18 above), pp. 47–71, and . . . *und in Singen gab es keine Juden? Eine Dokumentation* (Sigmaringen, 1991).

Germany. We had prepared the groundwork for his personal contribution by compiling railway schedules and maps, along with other documents of the period, in order to determine the specifics of his escape. The interaction of scientific research with Jizchak Schwersenz's own memory of the experience resulted in a kind of historical project that can suggest to both participants and viewers some of the consequences of political persecution.[28]

REFUGEE HELP: COLLECTIVE OR INDIVIDUAL DECISION?

In conclusion, I would suggest that escape aid and resistance fell into two phases, each distinct in the motivations and moral considerations of those involved, which can be explained by the political and social changes wrought by the Nazi regime.

In the first period, lasting until the mid-1930s, those willing to run the risks involved in refugee help were most often already collectively organized through their political orientation; that is, individual moral considerations were an integral part of a larger political awareness. The refugee help undertaken by members of the Red Help in Schaffhausen and Singen exemplified this trend.

In the second phase, this collective and political organization of refugee help gave way to individual acts of assistance and resistance. The decisions of Josef Höfler and his friends, or of the three Singen priests, to help German Jews over the border were motivated by individual moral conviction. This change in refugee help was the consequence of the destruction of the resistance and refugee help networks organized by the left. However, that was not the only or even the most important reason for the change. The constriction in refugee help to instances of individual morality can also be understood as the result of the social modernization which the National Socialists set into motion. As early as 1936, Franz Vogt, a former leader of the miners' union, identified what he termed an "atomization" of society, capable of fragmenting the milieu of the workers' movement and bringing about a pattern of behavior that was more strongly determined by the concerns of isolated individuals.[29] I would argue that this atomization became the guiding principle of social and political life in the Bundesrepublik.

---

[28] Alfred G. Frei and Hilde Storz-Schumm, "Der Zeitzeuge verläit das Klassenzimmer: Die Rekonstruktion einer Flucht," *Geschichtswerkstatt* 15 (May 1988): 339–50; Dieter Bähre, "Von Singen in das schwankende 'Rettungsboot': Eine Flucht aus dem '3. Reich' wird rekonstruiert," in *Singener Jahrbuch* (Singen, 1986), pp. 31–36; Jizchak Schwersenz, *Die versteckte Gruppe: Ein jüdischer Lehrer erinnert sich an Deutschland* (Berlin, 1988).

[29] Detlev J. K. Peukert and Frank Bajohr, *Spuren des Widerstands: Die Bergarbeiterbewegung im Dritten Reich und im Exil* (Munich, 1987), p. 142.

Lamed-Vovniks of Twentieth-Century Europe: Participants in Jewish Child Rescue*

Debórah Dwork
Yale University

When Catherina Blussé van oud Alblas was a young mother in Amsterdam during the war she remained loyal to her Jewish friend, who also had a child. Catherina had two little boys with curly brown hair at the time; her friend's son had curly blond hair. Several times a week Mrs. Blussé van oud Alblas went with her pram to fetch her friend's little boy from their hiding address. She took him on walks with her own children and fed him, changed him, cared for him. In the afternoon, Mrs. Blussé van oud Alblas returned the child to his mother. One day Mrs. Blussé van oud Alblas went to collect the child and he and his mother were gone. They had been betrayed. She returned home with an empty pram.[1]

There are no written or pictorial records of this event: no letters or diary, no photograph of the child in the pram. Neither the child nor his mother survived.

---

* For the convenience of the reader, all books that have been translated into English will be cited in the English version. The original language edition will be noted if it was used. N.B. Quality of translation varies greatly. All other translations (of texts, interviews, and archive documents) have been done by the author. The names of the child survivors as they appear in the text are as they were at the time, with the insertion of women's married names, if used. The corresponding names in the notes are those in current use. Thus, for example, Jooske Koppen-de Neve was born Jooske de Neve. Koppen is her married name. Please note that page numbers have been given for the interview transcripts, although neither the tapes nor texts are held in a public repository. It is my hope that eventually they will be made available, and I have provided specific citations with that end in mind.

[1] Catherina Blussé van oud Alblas is now suffering from Alzheimer's disease. She related these events not to her own three sons (two of whom participated as children), but to her daughter-in-law, Dr. Madelon de Keizer, a historian at the Netherlands State Institute for War Documentation. De Keizer recounted this episode in her mother-in-law's life within the context of a discussion about gender, memory, and resistance work. It is significant, I think, that Mrs. Blussé van oud Alblas's activities have not become part of the oral tradition of her own family: they have not been incorporated into the history the sons tell about the family during the war nor have they become the basis for homey legends told to grandchildren about their grandmother. This is not unusual. Perhaps another example will help to elucidate both the extent to which clandestine activities remain secret and the degree to which the resistance work of women is unrecognized even by those intimately involved. The philosopher, Solidarity activist, and former resister Klemens Szaniawski was a fellow at the Woodrow Wilson Center for International Scholars in 1984. It was my good fortune also to be a fellow at that time, and I took advantage of this chance contact to record Professor (later

No one would know of it at all if Catherina Blussé van oud Alblas had lost her memory before she related the event.

Our goal is to understand the profound significance of a gentile woman pushing a Jewish child in a pram in the midst of the genocide of the Jews. This was the very heart, the stuff and substance of resistance. A woman with a child in a stroller is the most innocuous and ordinary scene imaginable, but that woman with that child at that time was so improbable and so unimaginable that the Germans did not imagine it, and she was never stopped when out with the child. Catherina Blussé van oud Alblas was a *lamed-vovnik,* one of the righteous souls of Jewish tradition for whose sake God permits the world to continue to exist. According to this time-honored myth, their number was limited to thirty-six (*lamed-vov,* in Hebrew), and when one died another came into the world at the same instant. During the Shoah another legend was born: because human torment was so great, and each year, month, and day so long with pain and trouble, thousands of lamed-vovniks sprang up spontaneously throughout Europe to combat the evil they witnessed. Butchers, bakers, and candlestick makers, laundresses, seamstresses, and housekeepers, these outwardly unremarkable, seemingly normal people became resisters: they held fast to an earlier ethic and morality. Catherina Blussé van oud Alblas was such a resister. She did the improbable and unimaginable and it was, she said, not so very difficult: her sons had brown curls, her friend's son had blond curls, the boys blended together. It was, she maintained, the most ordinary thing in the world to have done. But this was a time when what had been unthinkable now occurred every day, and so what had been ordinary was now extraordinary. To take a Jewish friend's child out with one's own children, and, conversely, to allow a gentile friend to take out one's own child—in short, what had been indeed "not so very difficult"—was now a tremendous undertaking. It required faith and determination.

It is in our recovery, analysis, and understanding of the Jewish mother who gave up her child each day and the gentile friend who took the little boy, that we realize the historical significance of personal resistance to the Third Reich and recognize the fundamental importance of the private realm in history. This poses a problem, however, because it is easier to research and to write about the history of institutions or organizations, even if they were informally established and loosely coordinated, than it is to research and write about the

---

Rektor) Szaniawski's oral history. Only when questioned specifically about his mother's daily life did Szaniawski recall that she had hidden, for varying periods of time, so many Jews (children and adult men and women) in their home that the flat was practically a hotel. Madelon de Keizer, conversation with author, Amsterdam, November 1992, and by telephone, New Haven–Amsterdam, November 1993; Klemens Szaniawski, interview with author, Washington, D.C., April 4, 1989, transcript pp. 16, 22–24, 28–33, 47–48.

history of private relations. But while writing such history is difficult, it is not impossible, and it certainly is necessary. The history of private relations is of singular importance to our understanding of the Nazi era. In the Nazi state, there were no walls, no boundaries, no limits to the public realm. The German bureaucracy and terror apparatus penetrated the private realm in an unprecedented manner. We need only think of the way in which the Nuremburg Laws codified the personal as well as professional relations between Jews and gentiles, or the use of children as informants against their own parents, or the indoctrination of young women to encourage them to bear children for the Fatherland, to understand that the personal was under attack, was besieged, by this regime. Just as the dominant public has fascinated us for the past three decades, the assaulted private realm now emerges as a compelling area of study that poses new and different historical questions. Unfortunately, it is precisely the history of the private arena that we are least trained to research and write, and for which we have the least material. For while we have begun to ask new questions, traditional archives do not have much of the material we need for our research, and we have not yet, as a discipline, developed and accepted conventions for such work. And so we have begun to create new archives, or to add new collections to established institutions.

This is not so straightforward as one might think. An archive, in the traditional sense, preserves the records of institutions and the people connected to those establishments. There are well-accepted guidelines, standard conventions, as to which documents are to be kept, what will and will not become part of the public domain, and after how many years. In contrast, my own collection of hundreds of taped oral histories of child survivors and the adults who helped them, or an archive like the Fortunoff Video Archive for Holocaust Testimonies, a new department of Yale University's Sterling Library, *creates* as well as preserves a record. That record is about a public event, but the document itself is personal testimony. It comes from the private domain, from the realm of memory, and here the rules are not well worked out. The essential problem is the relationship between memory and history, how memory informs history, and how history corrects memory. Memory is dynamic, and while history as a discipline also is dynamic, each historical study is static. Memory is the existential substructure, history the conventional superstructure. Our historical work depends on the underpinning of archival documents. And here is the difficulty: what happens when those archival documents are testimonies or oral histories, when we write history using memory?[2] Can we write a comprehensive history which conforms to the

---

[2] There is a large literature on oral history, including a number of extremely helpful general studies and several journals which reflect the continuing development in the field. See E. Culpepper Clark et al., "Communicating in the Oral History Interview:

conventions, rigors, and standards of the discipline based on the particular and existential memories of individuals? Do the living speak for the dead? What do we know about the accuracy and reliability of memory?

In traditional archives of written documents, papers are selected for preservation on the basis of certain criteria: they must be typical or representative of, or revelatory about, a public event or person. As only a third of the Jewish population in Nazi Europe alive at the beginning of the war survived to its conclusion, can their testimonies be considered as typical or representative? I, as a historian of Jewish youth in and from Nazi Europe, do not discriminate: I record the oral history of any European Jew who was sixteen years old or younger when Nazism or anti-Semitic fascism first affected his or her life, and I record the histories of gentiles and Jews who helped these young people. However, the very fact that those now-adult children whose histories are recorded survived at all makes them exceptions to the general rule of death.[3] Is it justifiable to use their accounts to speak for the dead also?

Investigating Problems of Interpreting Oral Data," *International Journal of Oral History* 1 (February 1980): 28–40; George Ewart Evans, *Where Beards Wag All: The Relevance of the Oral Tradition* (London, 1970); David Henige, *Oral Historiography* (New York, 1982); Paul Thompson, *The Voice of the Past* (Oxford, 1978); Jan Vansina, *Oral Tradition* (Chicago, 1965), originally published as *De la tradition orale,* in *Annales du Musée Royal de L'Afrique Centrale,* Sciences Humaines no. 36 (Tervuren, Belgium, 1961). Suggested journals for further reading: *International Journal of Oral History, Oral History, Oral History Review.* Articles about oral history projects in other communities, but which deal with problems apposite to this study include Sherna Gluck, "What's So Special about Women: Women's Oral History," pp. 221–37; and Tamara Hareven, "The Search for Generational Memory," pp. 248–63, both in *Oral History: An Interdisciplinary Anthology* (Nashville, 1984); Kenneth Kann, "Reconstructing the History of a Community," *International Journal of Oral History* 2 (February 1981): 4–12.

[3] The percentage of Jewish children alive at the beginning of the war who survived to its conclusion—generally estimated at 11 percent—is much lower than the comparable figure for the Jewish population in general. See Centre de Documentation Juive Contemporaine (hereafter CDJC) Document XCIV-2: Jacques Bloch, "Jewish Child-Care, its Organisation and Problems," report presented at the Geneva Council of the International Save the Children Union, in *When Winter Comes . . . Special Issue of the Information Bulletin of the OSE Union* (Geneva, 1946), p. 12. The precise figures adduced by Bloch were: prewar population of 1.6 million Jews under sixteen years old living in what became the theater of war; postwar population of 175,000; "This figure includes 30,000 children repatriated from the Soviet Union to Poland and Romania." CDJC Document XCIV-3: Z. H. Wachsman, *The Rehabilitation of Jewish Children by the "OSE"* (New York, 1947), p. 3. According to Wachsman, at the time of liberation in 1945, only 6–7 percent of the original number of Jewish children had survived the war. Later, with repatriates from the Soviet Union, the numbers increased to an estimated prewar child population of 1.5 million and a postwar figure of 170,000. The percentage of child survivors was not uniform across Europe, of course. According to Lucjan Dobroszycki, there were close to a million Polish Jewish children aged fourteen

The answer is yes. While ultimate survival was an exception, it does not follow that the survivor's life was itself atypical. There is no evidence to indicate that survival was due to anything more—or less—than luck and fortuitous circumstances. The notion that longevity was due to some "survival strategy" or a special "will to live" is not only nonsense but a pernicious construct. The logical conclusion of such a supposition is to blame the victims in a subtle but vicious way. It suggests failure or stupidity on the part of those murdered. If those who survived did so because they were determined, staunch, and firm in their endeavor, the implication is that those who did not survive were undetermined, weak-willed, and irresolute; in short, inadequate to so great a task. Similarly, the neo-Darwinian proposal that those who survived did so because they employed a strategy to that end suggests that they, the survivors, were clever, fit, and adaptable, while their dead cohorts were foolish, deficient, and incompetent; in a word, inferior.

Let us be very clear: the purpose of such proposals is to divert attention from the enormity of the crimes committed against the victims to a scrutiny of the ability or inability of those victims to resist the system of murder in which they were trapped. The reason to repudiate these propositions, however, is because they are wrong. There is no evidence to support them. People survived who tried to commit suicide, while others were killed or died of disease or starvation who desperately wished to live. Then too, people made choices which happened to work out well for them, whilst others made the very same decisions, and their course ended in death. The historical sociologist Ewa Morawska has suggested that we need to study the historicity of chance, and she is correct.[4] The daily lives of those whose existence ultimately would be extinguished and those who would have the good luck to survive were the same. The testimonies of survivors are, therefore, legitimate documents for a history of the victims in general and not of survivors alone. They may justifiably bear witness for the others—until the last moments of life in the death camps. It is obvious, but perhaps bears repeating that those who experienced Auschwitz in

---

or under in 1939. After the war there were approximately five thousand, or half a percent of the 1939 number. This figure does not include children who survived in the Soviet Union and were repatriated later, nor, N.B., those aged fifteen and sixteen. Nevertheless, it is clear that the survival rate for children in Poland was lower than elsewhere, as was the survival rate (10 percent) for Polish Jews in general (Lucjan Dobroszycki, "Redemption of the Children," in *An Inventory to the Rescue of Children, Inc. Collection, 1946–1985,* ed. Alizah Zinberg, Barbara Martin, and Roger Kohn [New York, 1986], p. 6). Kiryl Sosnowski has adduced the same figure of five thousand children in his book, *The Tragedy of Children under Nazi Rule* (Poznan, 1962), p. 73.

[4] Suggestion made by Ewa Morawska in the discussion following a seminar I gave on "Flight from the Reich: The Historical and Historiographical Problems of Rupture and Dislocation" to the History Department of the University of Pennsylvania, February 24, 1992.

all its horror are dead. The living can tell us nothing about those final three hundred meters from the selection point to the gas chambers.

Another issue raised by the use of recorded memories to write history is the problems the survivors have describing their experiences. "If I utter words, they are just words," one woman exclaimed in despair. "And when I say them, I remember myself there, but we are here."[5] Because many survivors have not articulated their histories before, and because these experiences were so outside the realm of life as we know it, language, our medium of communication, fails us. This does not have to do with the command of language but with the possibility of expressing the ineffable. How, as one survivor queried, with a mere combination of letters, and then of words, to explain what even the imagination cannot comprehend? For the survivors, their histories were a numinous experience that cannot be captured within the conventional rules of discourse. For historians, however, the events described are part of history; they are and must be subject to theoretical analysis and logical interpretation. No period of history, no events of our past, can be relegated to the realm of enigma, the recondite, or the metaphysical. They cannot be so easily dismissed or so conveniently ignored.

Given the fundamental, existential nature of these particular experiences, the discrepancy between contemporary participant and post facto analyst raises the question of how events are coded in memory and how the historian is to interpret what is told. There is a tension—and sometimes a confusion—between the "objective" historical past (what "really" happened, the sort of facts one expects to find in a traditional archive), the "subjective" psychological experience (that which the survivor believes to have occurred, the existential experience captured in the oral account), and those fictional elements which are part of the retelling of any event (the way in which human beings consciously or unconsciously use literary conventions to structure the stories, or histories, they recount). In other words, in memory, historical truth, psychological truth, and narrative truth are not always separate and distinct entities. For example, many women who were in camps after the age of menarche have expressed their conviction that the Germans added a chemical to their food to prevent them from menstruating.[6] This is not a conjecture, but a conviction. "Do you think a chemical was added to your food, or do you think that perhaps, because your nutrition level was so low, and your intake of calories so small, your body ceased to menstruate?" I asked. While some

[5] Sara Grossman-Weil, interview with author, Malverne, N.Y., April 29–30, 1987, conversation preceding taped recording.

[6] Not surprisingly, this belief is often mentioned in the survivor memoir literature written by women. See, e.g., Livia E. Bitten Jackson, *Elli: Coming of Age in the Holocaust* (New York, 1983), p. 95.

women refused to accept this, others remembered that yes, after the war they had heard that this was the reason for their premature menopause. By the next day, however, they once again had forgotten this explanation.

This lapse led to a different question in an attempt to reach the truth behind the objective falsehood. "Why do you think the Germans would add such a chemical to your food?" I asked. Their answers were precise and unequivocal. Even if the Germans were to lose the war, I was told, and even if these women survived, the poison they had eaten would prevent them from ever conceiving children and the Jewish people would die out sooner or later. This construct provided a conventional—accepted historical—context for their experiences. The Germans wanted to annihilate the Jews, and everything they did conduced to that end. Thus, many women who ceased to menstruate understood this phenomenon within that context; that was the truth. While this truth, this memory, does not tell us about the components of the concentration camp diet, it illustrates a fragment of the mental conditions of the women in camps. Such an incident helps us to understand their fears and anxieties, the psychological circumstances of their daily lives.

Survivors' oral histories also relate the historical (or objective) "facts" of their lives. This is well within the realm of traditional methods, and to use them for this purpose the historian corroborates the oral history as one does any other source: against, for example, the calendar, public record office documents, photographs, or the site itself.

The problems of narrative truth are perhaps the most subtle. What is remembered? How does anyone reduce the experiences of several years to one or two dozen hours of recorded oral interview, and how is that account structured? Unfortunately, we do not know. We do not know everything that happened to each individual, and so we cannot note what was remembered and what forgotten, what told, and what left unsaid. But we should be aware of the problem, and we should take note of the attention in recent years (from Hayden White, among others) to the idea of explanation by emplotment.[7] Just as the historian structures her account of the past in conventional ways, so do

---

[7] The issue of narrative structure usually has been discussed from the perspective of the professional historian, but obviously it is applicable to the history recounted by what I call the "participant/historian," i.e., child survivor or adult resistance worker. See Lionel Gossman, "History and Literature," pp. 3–40; Louis O. Mink, "Narrative Form as a Cognitive Instrument," pp. 129–50; and Hayden White, "The Historical Text as Literary Artifact," pp. 41–62, all in *The Writing of History: Literary Form and Historical Understanding,* ed. Robert H. Canary and Henry Kozicki (Madison, Wis., 1978). See also the first three chapters in Hayden White, *The Content of Form* (Baltimore, 1987), pp. 1–82. David Faris has applied some of White's ideas to oral history (David Faris, "Narrative Form and Oral History: Some Problems and Possibilities," *International Journal of Oral History* 1 [November 1980]: 159–80).

people who recount their personal histories, albeit unconsciously. Recognizing these story forms and realizing that, by employing one or another of them, the survivor has explained, or given meaning to, her life in a specific way provides the historian with a tool to investigate that particular oral history.

The relationship between the chaos of memory and the structure of narrative is equally complex. In *Moments of Reprieve* (1981), the writer and survivor Primo Levi addressed the issue of memory—his own memory. "It has been observed by psychologists that the survivors of traumatic events are divided into two well-defined groups: those who repress their past *en bloc,* and those whose memory of the offense persists, as though carved in stone, prevailing over all previous or subsequent experiences. Now, not by choice but by nature, I belong to the second group. Of my two years of life outside the law I have not forgotten a single thing. Without any deliberate effort, memory continues to restore to me events, faces, words, sensations, as if at that time my mind had gone through a period of exalted receptivity, during which not a detail was lost."[8] Levi returned to this theme five years later in *The Drowned and the Saved,* and by then he viewed the problem rather differently. "Human memory is a marvelous but fallacious instrument. . . . The memories which lie within us are not carved in stone; not only do they tend to become erased as the years go by, but often they change, or even grow, by incorporating extraneous features. . . . Certainly practice (in this case, frequent re-evocation) keeps memories fresh and alive in the same manner in which a muscle often used remains efficient, but it is also true that a memory evoked too often, and expressed in the form of a story, tends to become fixed in a stereotype, in a form tested by experience, crystallized, perfected, adorned, installing itself in the place of the raw memory and growing at its expense."[9]

Undoubtedly, Levi was right. He had begun to forget because bringing his private past into the public realm had robbed him of his own experience: he had given it up, or given it over. And he had begun to forget precisely because he had set himself the task of translating what he had seen and experienced into written words. The process of writing crystallizes and objectifies. It diminishes, or reduces, the entire universe of a moment into one particular rendition of it. To achieve clarity, the minutiae of which memory is composed are lost. The experience is fixed. It is so fixed for the participant that details which do not quite fit, or would enrich, the public rendition recede into oblivion. And it is so fixed for the reader that it becomes history. The

---

[8] Primo Levi, *Moments of Reprieve* (New York, 1986), pp. 10–11, originally published as *Lilit e altri racconti* (Turin, 1981).

[9] Primo Levi, *The Drowned and the Saved* (New York, 1988), p. 23, originally published as *I sommersi e i salvati* (Turin, 1986).

characters and the events remain as described on the printed page, static and unchanging.

A final point to consider with regard to the use of memory to write history is that of reliability and accuracy or, as some historians have called it, validity. According to the oral historian Alice Hoffman, "reliability can be defined as the consistency with which an individual will tell the same story about the same events on a number of different occasions. Validity refers to the degree of conformity between the reports of the event, and the event itself as recorded by other primary source material such as documents, photographs, diaries, and letters."[10] My own research, as well as that of numerous other historians who use oral history as documentary material, reveals an astonishing degree of both reliability and validity. By and large, the events survivors recall and the way in which they articulate their memories validate Primo Levi's observation that the "memory of the offense persists, as though carved in stone, prevailing over all previous or subsequent experiences," perhaps precisely because they, unlike he, have not transmuted the memory into written prose.

We have elaborated some of the problems in the use of oral histories. Our own education is based on and grounded in traditional sources, however. We learned to ask a conventional set of questions about—and of—such material. We know about provenance, dating, paper, ink, letterheads, and margin notes. And we presume such sources will answer the questions with which the discipline traditionally has concerned itself. But there are different questions to be asked about, and of, oral accounts. The purpose of the recorded oral histories and the video archives is to help us answer key historical questions which, formerly, we did not consider. Now we have collections of these new documents, and it has become clear that they pose their own methodological problems.

Let us conclude this discussion with a few remarks about the narrative modes we employ to communicate our historical analyses of the personal realm. Until very recently, historians have concerned themselves with the public, and novelists with the private. The plethora of evidence about public events was subjected to the rigors of historical analysis and a disciplinary convention of restraint in narrative. In literature, by contrast, much is made of little. By using his rich imagination and astonishing narrative skills, Tolstoy created the tale of Anna Karenina from a small notice in the newspaper. While historical novels (such as those by Lion Feuchtwanger) enjoy the advantages and strengths of both history and literature, a history of the private is

---

[10] Alice Hoffman, "Reliability and Validity in Oral History," in *Oral History,* ed. David K. Dunaway and Willa K. Baum (Nashville, 1984), p. 69. See also Trevor Lummis, "Structure and Validity in Oral Evidence," *International Journal of Oral History* 2 (June 1981): 109–20.

impoverished indeed. And so those who are interested in such questions have been compelled to reevaluate and reassess the disciplinary conventions of narrative. This does not mean that historians can adopt the imaginative license of the novelist. But in our reconstructions of the personal realm, we have much to learn from the novelist's skill in the construction of a fictional world. And for the communication, the articulation of our analyses, we can profit from the literary conventions of fiction.

* * *

These techniques and methodologies allow us to investigate, analyze, and relate to others the extraordinary nature of what passed for ordinary events, in this case, the history of participants in Jewish child rescue. What do sentences like "I was hidden" or "Of course I transported Jewish children to safety" suggest and signify? What kinds of networks arose spontaneously to save and protect Jewish children? Who volunteered to do this kind of work and how did they carry out their projects? What sorts of families took in the young people, and why?

In the context of the Shoah, the single most important genre of resistance work was the task of hiding Jews or transporting them over national borders to safe havens. Arrangements for hiding children were made in one of two ways: informally through a network of family and friends, or with the help of some type of organization. In other words, the problem of an individual child was resolved through a personalized solution, while those who were concerned with the plight of all Jewish children tried to devise a generalized or universally applicable solution. The most common situation was that of informal contacts. Thus, for example, Margaret Ascher-Frydman, who came from a prominent and assimilated family, was helped through her parents' acquaintances. In the summer of 1942 she, her mother, and younger sister were living in the Warsaw ghetto. Frydman's mother sought a refuge for her daughters, then aged twelve and six. "My mother learned that there were some children in [the Family of Mary] convent, and asked a woman, a friend, a wife of a lawyer whom my father knew and who was very religious, whether she could ask the sisters to take me. And they took us [the two girls] on the ninth of September. . . . We came to the convent, the sisters were there, and the Sister Superior said yes; she accepted us."[11] In Rome, eighteen-year-old Roberto Milano and his friends were helped in very much the same way; that

[11] Margaret Ascher-Frydman, interview with author, Paris, June 5, 1987, transcript p. 2. The Congregation of Franciscan Sisters of the Family of Mary was specially committed to helping Jewish children. According to Władyslaw Bartoszewski, the Family of Mary "concealed several hundred Jewish children in their homes throughout the country [Poland]" (Bartoszewski, "On Both Sides of the Wall," in *Righteous among Nations: How the Poles Helped the Jews, 1939–1945,* ed. Władyslaw

is, through his father's gentile business associates. On September 8, 1943, the Italian government asked the Allies for an armistice and it became clear that Germany would occupy Italy. The situation for Italy's Jews, who until then had been spared the worst, became urgent. A few of Milano's friends' fathers met in his parents' home to discuss the state of affairs, and they decided that the boys had to hide. The following day Milano and three of his companions went into the Abruzzi mountains. "We went to this area because it was the birth place of a delivery man for my father's stores. He was a trustworthy person who had worked for my father for thirty years, and he himself suggested that we be sent to that tiny village where there were not even streets, and which could be reached only by climbing through the woods and up the mountains."[12] The physical circumstances of Milano and Frydman could not have been farther removed, but both were menaced by the threat of deportation, and in both cases arrangements for their flight to safety were made informally, through the family's own network of contacts.

"Informal" contacts meant that the parents would ask a friend, or a friend of a friend, or the relative of a gentile relative-by-marriage whether she would hide, or help to hide, their family. Families usually separated when they went into hiding (unlike the well-known example of Anne Frank's household). Some did so to reduce the risk of total annihilation. Most, however, found that for purely logistical reasons it was impossible to remain together as a single

---

Bartoszewski and Zofia Lewin [London, 1969], pp. lxxxii–iii). See also the testimonies of Irena Sendler and Władysław Smolski, in ibid., pp. 51 and 347–52. Philip Friedman mentions the Franciscan Sisters in *Their Brothers' Keepers* (New York, 1978), p. 124. In Ewa Kurek-Lesik's study of "The Conditions of Admittance and the Social Background of Jewish Children Saved by Women's Religious Orders in Poland from 1939–1945," *Polin* 3 (1988): 244–75, she found that "two-thirds of the 74 female religious communities in Poland took part in helping Jewish children and adults" (p. 246), the Family of Mary among them. Kurek-Lesik has estimated that at least 1,500 children were saved in this way. According to Kurek-Lesik, the sisters of the Family of Mary and the sisters of the Grey Ursulines were encouraged to participate in such rescue activities by their superiors. In other orders, the decision to help was taken on a local basis by each individual convent. Kurek-Lesik's research on the social background of the children who came to the convent and the means by which the contact was made coincides with my own. She has found that although the children who were taken in were, by and large, from professional and educated families, finances were by no means the determining factor: "a decided majority of Jewish children were taken in with no provision for their keep" (p. 268). Rather, it was a question of contacts with the gentile world, access to the community outside the ghetto, fluency in the national language, and chance. "The condition governing the admission of the Jewish child into the house of a female religious community in Poland during 1939–1945 was its fortuitous arrival at the convent gates," Kurek-Lesik has concluded (p. 272).

[12] Roberto Milano, interview with author, Rome, June 6, 1985, transcript p. 3.

unit. To hide one person was an enormous undertaking; it required space and food as well as constant vigilance and luck. The more people hidden in one place, the greater the risk and the more onerous the task. Furthermore, families separated because there were more opportunities for children to be hidden than for their parents. It was easier to hide a child; if they were young enough they did not need papers, and even older children simply were not the subject of official curiosity. Often they could be passed off as relatives who had come to stay or war orphans from a bombed city or evacuated area. The net result of these practical and sensible considerations was that the child found herself alone, separated from her family.

Margaret Frydman's and Roberto Milano's parents' contacts were through their personal acquaintances. In other instances, however, people turned to organizations set up to hide children. The term "organization" may be misleading. Within the context of the war and the resistance work of hiding children, all it means is the creation of a network or system to save children. Such an organization could have been started by just one person, or by a family like the Boogaards, who developed their own network and hid hundreds of Jews (as well as others) on their farm and their neighbors' farms in the Haarlemmermeer area of Holland.[13] It could have been a group formed by a number of disparate people whose common cause was their concern about the Jews, like Żegota (the Council for Aid to Jews) in Warsaw, or the Naamloze Vennootschap (or N.V., the Dutch equivalent to Ltd., i.e., limited company) in the Netherlands. And finally, extant institutions, such as the Protestant and Catholic churches, self-help associations like the Oeuvre de Secours aux Enfants (OSE), youth groups from the scouts to university student clubs, and the apparatus of political parties, undertook to hide children as part of their resistance work.

For all three organizational arrangements (a person or family, a group of disparate people, extant organizations), the pertinent questions are the same: How was contact made between those who needed help and those willing to offer it, how did the system function, and why had it evolved at all? Antoinette Sara Spier, a fifteen-year-old girl living in Arnhem in 1942, remembered that "a brother of my mother was living quite near the Haarlemmermeer, and it was his idea that we had to hide there. He thought it would be safe and he had the address of the farmer Boogaard, that famous farmer who always came to save the Jewish people."[14]

[13] Maurits Cohen, interview with author, Den Haag, Netherlands, June 9, 1986, transcript p. 3. Cohen claims the Boogaard family organization helped to save 324 people.
[14] Antoinette Sara Spier, interview with author, Amsterdam, June 27, 1986, transcript pp. 1–2. Also interview of June 1984, transcript pp. 3–5.

The Boogaard family had come to hide Jewish children more or less by happenstance. The elderly farmer, Johannis Boogaard, his adult daughter Aagje and four sons, Antheunis, Willem, Hannis, and Piet, their cousin Metje, and their families were known anti-Nazis in Nieuw Vennep. During the first two years of the German occupation the Boogaards manifested their political sentiments through individual acts of economic sabotage. Then, early in 1942, they took in Jan de Beer, a young gentile man who had been called up for forced labor service in Germany and had refused to go. Among the labor conscripts who subsequently took refuge on the Boogaards' farm was a Jewish fellow. When he asked whether his parents also could hide on the farm as they too were in danger, the Boogaards saw a need to be met and a responsibility to accept. From then on, Hannis Boogaard traveled throughout the country to find Jews, especially children, and bring them to the Haarlemmermeer. As in the case of Sara Spier, contact usually was made through family connections between the Boogaards and those who wished to hide.[15]

The Boogaards also found a way to help children who did not have the advantage of familial networks to make either informal or organizational arrangements. Aided by two women collaborators in Amsterdam, Truus de Swaan-Willems and Lies de Jong, Hannis Boogaard had children abducted from the Jewish orphanage in Amsterdam and brought to his farm. Lies de Jong had been a resident of the orphanage in her youth; she knew the habits of the institution and its personnel. It was her task to pick up children as they walked in a queue to school and on outings. She passed them on to de Swaan-Willems who, in turn, handed them over to Hannis Boogaard. It was in this way that Maurits Cohen came to the Boogaard family. In 1942 Cohen was eight years old and living in a Jewish children's home in Amsterdam. "On a certain day, we small children walked along the streets in Amsterdam. The underground came and took me out of the line of children into a urinal and they cut off the star—back on the street—and I was sent to [the] farmer [Boogaard]. I was not told in advance; it just happened."[16] Maurits Cohen and Sara Spier did not remain on the Boogaard farm long. It was their point of departure for the next three years of hiding; it was their access to the network that evolved out of the Boogaard's initial efforts.

---

[15] There is very little published literature on the Boogaard family. See Cor van Stam, *Wacht Binnen de Dijken* (Haarlem, Netherlands, 1986), pp. 67–95; and the article by the investigative reporters Anita van Ommeren and Ageeth Scherphuis, "De Onderduikers in de Haarlemmermeer," *Vrij Nederland* (March 16, 1985), pp. 1–25, and a follow-up in the letters section of *Vrij Nederland* (March 30, 1985). See also Debórah Dwork, *Children with a Star: Jewish Youth in Nazi Europe* (New Haven, Conn., 1991), chap. 2, "Into Hiding," pp. 31–65.

[16] Cohen, interview, transcript pp. 1–2.

The Boogaard family took on the work of hiding Jews and other people who had to disappear out of a deep religious conviction and strong anti-German sentiment. (Indeed, when Hannis Boogaard went to collect a child, he wore his Sunday church clothes: he was doing the Lord's work.) Their network began with a familial nucleus. As their operations became increasingly complex, more people joined them in their efforts. Other groups did not begin with such an organic core. People who were unrelated to each other, and indeed shared nothing except their common cause, came together to establish organizations to accomplish the same ends. Their motivations varied. Animated by political ideology, humanitarian beliefs, and religious principles, they formed alliances to assist Jews through the Nazi years.[17] Thus, for example, in Poland in late September 1942, people as different as Zofia Kossak-Szczucka, a well-known novelist and a founder as well as president of the conservative Catholic social organization, the Front for Reborn Poland, and the democrat Wanda Krahelska-Filipowiczowa worked together to found the clandestine Temporary Committee to Help Jews. The committee's activities were centered in Warsaw, but branches were opened and contacts maintained in Krakow and Lvov also. In the first two months of operation the committee aided 180 Jews, primarily children. At the same time, the committee submitted a proposal to establish a permanent and national version of itself to the Delegatura (the representative on Polish soil of the government-in-exile in London). The Delegatura accepted the proposal in November, and early the next month they established the Council for Aid to Jews (Rada Pomocy Żydom [RPŻ]), which was known by the cryptonym Żegota. Representatives of all the political parties of the Delegatura participated in this work.

The purpose of Żegota was to help Jews by securing hiding places for them, and by providing financial assistance and false documents to those leading a clandestine existence. Like its predecessor, Żegota's activities were concentrated in Warsaw, but it too functioned to some degree in a number of areas in Poland (Krakow, Lvov, Radom, Kielce, and Piotrkow, among others). Furthermore, saving and caring for children remained a central focus of the council's efforts: in July 1943 a Children's Bureau was established under the direction of Irena Sendlerowa. She was well chosen for the task. When the Germans invaded Poland in 1939, Sendlerowa was working in the Social Welfare Department of the Municipal Administration of Warsaw. From the beginning, she used her position to create a network to provide financial and

---

[17] The issue of the motivation to help is a fascinating topic, and there is a developing psychological and sociological literature that focuses on this question. See, for example, Eva Fogelman and V. L. Wiener, "The Few, the Brave, and the Noble," *Psychology Today* 19, no. 8 (August 1985): 60–65; Samuel P. Oliner and Pearl M. Oliner, *The Altruistic Personality* (New York, 1988); Nechama Tec, *When Light Pierced the Darkness* (New York, 1986).

material assistance to Jews, and she continued these activities even after the ghetto was instituted. By that time, Sendlerowa and her collaborators "had about 3,000 people in our care, of which 90% found themselves behind the ghetto walls from the very first day. With the setting up of the ghetto our whole system of assistance, built up with such great effort, was destroyed. The situation became even more complicated when the gates of the ghetto were closed. We then had to solve the problem of how to legally get into the ghetto." Sendlerowa obtained documents for herself and her close colleague Irena Schultz, which allowed them to enter the ghetto legally, and she established contact with Eva Rechtman who, on the other side of the wall, organized a secret network of women employed by the Jewish charitable organization CENTOS. In this way, Sendlerowa and Schultz were able to bring money, food, medicine, and clothing (which they obtained by presenting false documentation to the Social Welfare Department) into the ghetto, where it was distributed by Rechtman and her associates.[18]

Mass expulsions of the Jews from Warsaw had begun in 1942, and Sendler and Schultz were determined to smuggle children out of the ghetto to hide them on the "Aryan" side. They had addresses of families in the city who were willing to take the children; their problem was to spirit them out of the ghetto. According to Irena Sendlerowa, Schultz specialized in this. In her account of their activities she explained that "the children were usually brought out of the ghetto through the underground corridors of the public courts building and through the tram depot in Muranow district." The children were placed with families or in orphanages and convents; the former received a maximum of five hundred złotys a month from the council, in addition to clothing, food parcels, and milk coupons as needed. By the end of 1943, in addition to those in private homes, the Children's Bureau had found berths for six hundred youngsters in public and ecclesiastical (over five hundred fifty children), and relief organization (at least twenty-two young people) institutions. In total, some 2,500 children were registered by the Warsaw branch of the council.[19]

----

[18] Irena Sendler, "People Who Helped Jews," in Bartoszewski and Lewin, eds., pp. 41–42.

[19] Bartoszewski; and Sendler (see also the section, "Under the Wings of 'Zegota,'" pp. 41–108); Friedman, pp. 118–21; Yisrael Gutman and Shmuel Krakowski, *Unequal Victims: Poles and Jews during World War II* (New York, 1986), pp. 252–99; Yisrael Gutman, "The Attitude of the Poles to the Mass Deportations of Jews from the Warsaw Ghetto in the Summer of 1942," pp. 413–14; and Joseph Kermish, "The Activities of the Council for the Aid to Jews ('Żegota') in Occupied Poland," pp. 367–98, both in *Rescue Attempts During the Holocaust,* ed. Yisrael Gutman and Efraim Zuroff. Proceedings of the Second Yad Vashem International Historical Conference (Jerusalem, 1977) (see also the debate, pp. 451–63); Kazimierz Iranek-

The Council for Aid to Jews was one branch of Poland's official underground work. Other underground groups equally devoted to saving Jews, and Jewish children in particular, were organized far less formally. Unaffiliated with any established association or political party, they were formed by people who, very simply, felt the need to act. It is important to note that many of these groups, which were organized specifically to protect human lives, received neither honor nor attention after the war. Indeed, while much is known about the armed resistance, the history of the organizations that helped children only recently has become part of the legitimate public past. There are a number of reasons for this: practical, political, and social. First, as the majority of these underground networks (like the N.V. or Piet Meerburg Group) did not apply for or receive financial assistance from their respective national central councils of resistance organizations, their work was never on public record. But there were also ideological reasons for the marginalization of underground activity dedicated to the rescue and relief of children. For many years after the war, each country's "Resistance Movement" was defined in terms of those groups that undertook activities of a more public nature: armed defiance, underground newspapers, lightning attacks to destroy records or steal documents, tactical maneuvers, sabotage. These more "heroic" operations were clearly patriotic and nationalistic, and they became part of the history of the honor of each country. Saving children was, by contrast, neither a public deed at the time nor the stuff of glory afterward. In short, celebrating or commemorating such work did little to foster the ideology of the suffering of the nation under Occupation, and of the illustrious deeds which were undertaken to throw off the yoke of oppression. Less obviously nationalistic and manifestly humanitarian, the business of saving lives during the war was not politically useful in reconstructing a national consciousness and patriotic pride when the hostilities ended.

Finally, the majority of the resistance workers who undertook to save and sustain life were women, and the people for whom they cared were children—Jewish children. In other words, the disparity between this and other resistance work is the difference between the nursery and the battlefield; one is private, the other public. The former is seen as personal, family history, while the latter is national in scope and character, the realm of women and children in contrast to the domain of men. These divisions were enhanced by the fact that the perceptions of the rescuers as to the work they had done, their

Osmecki, *He Who Saves One Life* (New York, 1971), pp. 139–51, 224–26, 234–37, 315–16; Teresa Prekerowa, "The Relief Council for Jews in Poland, 1942–1945," in *The Jews in Poland,* ed. Chimen Abramsky, Maciej Jachimczyk, and Antony Polonsky (London, 1986), pp. 161–76; *Saving Jews in War-torn Poland* (Melbourne, 1969), pp. 22–23, 40–41.

view of their achievements, was rather different from that of the militant resisters. After the war these women underground workers disappeared from public life. They did not seek publicity and they left few records. Unlike the men who had joined the official resistance and who assemble each year at the national monuments of remembrance to mourn their fallen comrades, these women to this day speak unceremoniously of their activities as just another job that had to be done, and they insist that they are not remarkable for having undertaken it. As Rebecca van Delft, one of the couriers of the Dutch N.V. group, put it, the question was, "would I be ready to accompany Jewish children by train from Amsterdam to Heerlen (in the province of Limburg, in the south of Holland) where better could be found homes for them to hide, in order to save them out of the hands of the Germans. Of course I was willing to do such a thing: it was just a natural thing to do." Van Delft was eighteen years old at the time.[20] Jooske Koppen-de Neve, who was brought into the N.V. network both by Rebecca van Delft and through her friendship with the first people the group hid, the Braun family, echoed van Delft's assessment of her role in the operation. "To praise [me] would be the worst thing that ever could be for me. Everything I did during those days was just normal. Any other person in my place would have taken that on, I'm sure of that. . . . When it comes so real to you in person, in a living person then, yes, you get involved. You can't get on with your ordinary things."[21]

Let us return to the question of how informally established underground groups which were organized to save Jewish children functioned. How were they created, how did they operate, and how were contacts made between them and those they wished to help? The history of the N.V. group is essentially typical of the development and operation of the marvelous, but tragically too few, underground networks which sprang up spontaneously throughout Europe to rescue Jewish children from Nazi persecution. The organization which became the N.V. began with an encounter between two young men, Gerard and Jacob Musch, who refused to accept the German invaders' deprivation of human liberty, and Marianne Marco-Braun and her family, who were in danger. The Brauns had come to Amsterdam from Vienna in 1938. Marianne was then fifteen years old. In Amsterdam, the family took the unusual step of conversion to the Dutch Reformed Church. "There we made new friends," Braun explained. "So when things, after the invasion, got worse as they did slowly and gradually, there was a lot of concern for us in the church where every Sunday we used to go for service." In May 1942, "we had

[20] Rebecca van Delft, written testimony to author, Graft-de Rijp, Netherlands, June 16, 1986, pp. 5–6.

[21] Jooske Koppen-de Neve, interview with author, Amerongen, Netherlands, August 7, 1987, transcript pp. 24, 4.

to wear the star," she recalled. "And with the star, of course, on Sundays we went to church. So then [the situation] was even more obvious, and people used to come and commiserate and think how terrible it was." Soon thereafter, Marianne and her brother Leo "were called up to go to Germany for work. . . . This is when the brothers Jacob and Gerard Musch came to us. We knew them, but not all that well. They came up one day and they said to us, 'Are you going? What's happening?' I said, 'Well, what can we do?' They said, 'We could possibly find you some addresses to hide.' "[22]

Jacob (or Jaap) and Gerard Musch, the original two central figures of the organization that eventually was known as the N.V., came to create an underground network to save Jewish children's lives more or less by happenstance. In the spring of 1942 they had no such formed concept. Like so many others who became involved in this work, they did not have numerous Jewish friends. But when they realized that the Brauns were in danger and needed help, they were ready to organize that assistance. Gerard Musch co-opted his friend Dick Groenewegen van Wijk, and, after resolving the immediate problem of placing the Braun family, the three young men began to plan a way to rescue Jewish children from the Germans. They concentrated their energies on children because they themselves were young and they felt they would not be able to deal so effectively or authoritatively with older people, and also because they believed they would have greater success hiding children. They faced two major practical problems: finding homes for the children and establishing contacts with those who needed to be hidden. They did not have an easy start. They went to the northern province of Friesland in the hope of securing addresses but, perhaps because they did not have sufficient connections or the right introductions, they were unsuccessful. Undaunted by their failure, they decided to try the southern province of Limburg. There, in the rather large mining town of Heerlen, they made contact with a Protestant minister named Gerard Pontier. As the population of Limburg was overwhelmingly Catholic, the Protestant community was tightly knit. Domine Pontier knew his congregants personally, and the church members were well acquainted with each other and each other's business. It was through this chain of contact that the Musches and Groenewegen came to the Vermeer family in nearby Brunssum, which became the secure core of the network in the area. Truus Grootendorst-Vermeer still remembers when Jaap Musch came to the door to speak with her parents. And suddenly half her family was involved—her mother and father, her brother Piet, and very soon Truus herself, who gave up her job to do this work full-time. "My parents couldn't afford to do without my salary then. (I gave them everything and got

[22] Marianne Marco-Braun, interview with author, London, May 9, 1987, transcript pp. 8, 10–12.

pocket money!) So for them and for me it was a big step. . . . I thought, here these bloody Germans are doing something against innocent people, and that put my back up. . . . Yes, I liked my office job, but I liked the people more."[23]

Leaving the Vermeer family to identify potential hiding addresses, Jaap and Gerard Musch and Dick Groenewegen returned to Amsterdam to get children. By the summer of 1942 the situation for the Jews in the Netherlands had become desperate. During the first half of 1942 the Germans had forced the Jewish population to leave their homes throughout the Netherlands and relocate in Amsterdam. As they were permitted to lodge only in Jewish quarters or to live with Jewish families, a ghetto without walls was created. This physical concentration of Jews facilitated the process of wholesale deportation, which began in July 1942. Initially, Jews (like Marianne Braun and her family) were sent letters commanding them to report for "labor service," but by the late summer the Germans decided that too few were complying with these written orders. The *razzias* (dragnet operations) began. Arrested Jews were marched or driven to a central deportation point, a theater called the Hollandsche Schouwburg.

The Germans interned enormous crowds in the theater; often more than 1,500 people plus their allowed luggage were packed into the building. The noise was unbearable, even for the jailers. To reduce their own discomfort, the Germans decided to send children under the age of twelve across the street to a child-care center. This crèche had been a well-established neighborhood institution used by working-class families. In 1942 it was taken over as an annex to the Schouwburg. The director, Henriette Rodriquez-Pimentel, and the young Jewish women who assisted her had no illusions as to the fate awaiting the children. They were determined to smuggle the children out of the crèche and pass them on to others who would take them to safe addresses. As every person, adult or child, who entered the Schouwburg was registered by an employee of the Jewish Council (which was controlled by the Germans, of course), Pimentel needed help from an insider to destroy the children's records. This task was undertaken by Walter Sueskind and Felix Halverstad. Their positions with the Council did not give them access to the registration cards, but they too were resolute and concocted all sorts of ruses to rifle the records. Thus a number of children disappeared from the files of the bureaucracy, and this meant that neither their parents nor the crèche personnel would be held responsible for them. Officially they did not exist. It was now

---

[23] Ida Groenewegen van Wyck-Roose, Cor Grootendorst, and Truus Grootendorst-Vermeer, interview with author, Nieuw Vennep, Netherlands, July 1, 1986, transcript p. 3. Ida Groenewegen was a member of the N.V.; she and Dick married after the war. Cor Grootendorst was a friend of Truus Vermeer. She asked him to come to Limburg to help soon after her family got involved. They too got married.

up to Pimentel and her assistants to get the children out of the crèche and to pass them to resistance workers to be hidden.[24]

Jaap and Gerard Musch and Dick Groenewegen knew about the crèche but not about its underground traffic, and they had no connections with Jews who had not yet been arrested. Probably through Piet Meerburg, a leader of an Amsterdam student operation devoted to the same cause, they were given the name of Joop Woortman, alias Theo de Bruin.[25] De Bruin was the sort of person who knew almost everybody in the city ("a real Amsterdammer"), and he was a serious and dedicated resister. Because of his huge social network, which included many Amsterdam Jews, de Bruin had been approached early in the occupation for help in obtaining false identity cards, ration coupons, and, finally, hiding places. By the time he met the Musch brothers he and his wife Semmy were constantly involved with it.

Semmy Woortman-Glasoog's recollection of the initial meeting was that "the boys came to our house. We had a meeting, we talked, but the boys didn't know too much because they were very young. But Jaap was a serious man and Theo was, on this point, also very serious. And we talked about what we could do and how it would take shape. I listened and I told them 'You have to realize that if you are going to do what you are talking about, then your life after this is a gift. If you don't want that, you shouldn't go on.' And they all said, yes, they wanted to do it. I think the younger boys didn't realize exactly what they did. But Jaap, he knew what he did, he knew; and Theo knew very well, and I knew."[26]

In the plan they evolved, Theo de Bruin and Semmy made the connections with the crèche and with the Jewish families who had not yet been taken to the

[24] Anonymous, interview with author, Amsterdam, June 19, 1986, transcript pp. 1–2; Anita van Ommeren and Ageeth Scherphuis, "De Creche, 1942–1943," *Vrij Nederland* (January 18, 1986), pp. 2–21; Jacob Presser, *The Destruction of the Dutch Jews* (New York, 1969), originally published as *Ondergang* (Den Haag, Netherlands, 1965), pp. 281–82.

[25] Groenewegen, Grootendorst, and Grootendorst, interview, transcript p. 8; Semmy Riekerk-Glasoog, interview with author, Amsterdam, July 4, 1986, transcript p. 19.

[26] Riekerk-Glasoog, interview, transcript p. 20. Of the five people at that original meeting, only Semmy Riekerk-Glasoog is still living. Jaap Musch was caught by the Germans on September 7, 1944, and shot for his underground activities. Theo Woortman was arrested on July 19, 1944, in Amsterdam and sent to Amersfoort. On September 4 he was deported to Bergen-Belsen where he died on March 12, 1945. Gerard Musch and Dick Groenewegen were arrested in Amsterdam's central railway station on May 9, 1944. Both were deported, Dick to Burscheid (via Amersfoort) and Gerard to Sachsenhausen (via Vught). Both survived and died of natural causes much later (Musch in 1979 and Groenewegen in 1985). For a history of the N.V., see journalist Max Arian's personal and historical account, "Het grote kinderspel," *De Groene Amsterdammer* (May 4, 1983), pp. 5–7, 9; and his interview with Semmy Riekerk in the same issue, pp. 10–12. See also Bert-Jan Flim, "De NV en Haar Kinderen, 1942–1945 (Master's thesis, Gronigen University, 1987; and a series of articles by Jan van Lieshout in the *Limburgs Dagblad*: "Joop Woortman: 'Breng ze

Schouwburg. According to Rebecca van Delft, who had worked with him, de Bruin was a man of "almost improbable courage and boldness" who did things others considered impossible, including "simply picking up [children] during a razzia in the street."[27] Sometimes he sent one of the younger men to collect crèche children from the agreed delivery point, or he gave them the address of a Jewish family with a child to be hidden. But in general it was he who undertook that part of the rescue work. Gerard, Jaap, and Dick got the children from Theo and Semmy and, with the young women like Rebecca van Delft and Jooske Koppen-de Neve who had joined the organization, brought them to Limburg. Marianne Braun had been the connecting link between the original women couriers, Rebecca van Delft and Jooske Koppen-de Neve, and the Musch brothers because she was friends with all of them. When Braun and her family went into hiding, Marianne told the Musches that she thought van Delft and de Neve would help.

By midsummer 1942, Theo de Bruin found children who were then passed to Gerard, Jaap, Dick, Rebecca, and Jooske. The women traveled alone with the children, or in the company of one of the men, passing as a married couple. They were brought to foster homes in Heerlen, which had been arranged for them by the Vermeer family. In the autumn, de Bruin began to get children from the crèche as well. With the permission of the parents, Sueskind and Halverstad destroyed the children's registration records, and Pimentel and her assistants smuggled the youths out of the child-care center. There were two nearly impossible aspects of this system. The first was practical: how to get the children out of the crèche? After all, they may not have existed on paper, but they were real children and the crèche was guarded by the Germans. Many stratagems were devised to elude their control. For instance, as the young women who worked in the crèche were not under arrest, they were free to go in and out of the building. They took advantage of this mobility and, in their backpacks, carried out infants with pacifiers or bottles in their mouths, praying that the babies would not start to cry. Articles commonly in use in the crèche and therefore not likely to arouse suspicion were used for the same purpose: potato sacks, food crates, valises. Older children had to be smuggled out in other ways. Accompanied by one or two of the staff, toddlers and older children were allowed to go on walks. Sometimes on such occasions a few of the unregistered children were included in the outing and, at a previously specified point, whisked away from the rest of the group by an underground worker. Finally, Pimentel obtained the cooperation of a neighboring institution.

---

maar naar Limburg'" (May 25, 1977), "De ongehuwde vaders en moeders van Brunssum" (May 26, 1977), "Elke dreumes was een drama" (May 27, 1977), "De vliegende non van het pompstation" (May 28, 1977). See also Dwork (n. 15 above), pp. 31–65.

[27] Statement by van Delft, p. 7.

At one side of the crèche was a small teachers' training college, the Hervormde Kweekschool. Seen from the street the two buildings were not connected, as there was an alley between them. Contrary to appearances, however, their back gardens were adjoined. "The head of the school, Professor van Hulst, saw in the garden that there were a lot of Jewish children and, well, he was good (we call it good or not good) so he tried to help. . . . We could bring the children from the garden of the crèche to the garden of the kweekschool and the students and other 'illegal' people came to the kweekschool and took them out [by the two side streets,] the Plantage Parklaan and the Plantage Kerklaan."[28] As the entrances to the college were not guarded, the controls could be avoided completely.

The first of the two almost insuperable problems—smuggling the children out of the crèche—was practical. The second was emotional: to obtain the parents' permission to hide their child. Who would be willing to give up a child? Who could imagine that life in the "labor camps" was not life but death? The parents did not know the young men and women who asked to hide their children; they were total strangers. They had no reason to trust them. Surely it was better to remain together as a family than to give up one's child to an unknown young person.

This conscious act of separation of parents and children was so painful that many of the resistance workers who were involved with rescuing children came to believe as they grew older that they were able to do this work precisely because they themselves did not have children. At that time they simply did not understand or comprehend the intensity of the parent-child relationship. "We were still very young," one resister reflected. "We were all aged between twenty and twenty-five. Now as parents and grandparents you start thinking. What would your reaction be if a youngster, twenty years old, comes and knocks on your door? Would you so willingly trust them enough to give your child away?"[29] Piet Meerburg, another Dutch student devoted to saving Jewish children during the Nazi occupation, has given this problem some thought over the past half-century.

There must be a reason why most of the people working with the children were so young. My explanation is that we were not fathers ourselves, we were not mothers ourselves. . . . As a boy of twenty-one you don't realize what it means. You think it's very unpleasant; you can cry about it, but you don't realize. And I think that's good; that's why we could do it. And that's the reason so many young people did it and not older people. For older people I think it was very difficult to do that; they realized much more clearly what it did to the parents. . . .

I now realize I understood only half of it. It's a very difficult decision the parents had to make. It took very much courage—and you know how Jewish mothers are. For a

[28] Anonymous, interview, transcript pp. 2–3.
[29] Groenewegen, Grootendorst, and Grootendorst, interview, transcript p. 9.

Jewish mother to give away her son or her daughter to a strange goy, that's something. It took a lot of courage in my opinion, and foresight.[30]

Nevertheless, parents driven to desperation were willing to give away their children to a "strange goy [gentile]"; the N.V. had 252 young people under its care and Piet Meerburg's group between three and four hundred.[31]

One of the interesting and unexpected problems the underground workers faced was that the foster parents had preferences as to the age and gender of the child they wished to have, and that the vast majority of requests was for "a girl of four years old. For a girl of four or five years old you could get as many places as you wanted."[32] Fortunately, this was not a fundamental problem for the foster parents: preferences were largely irrelevant and they took whatever child the organizations could smuggle out of Amsterdam.[33]

Monetary considerations were not a factor in the decision to take a child. Despite the financial strain of supporting an extra person on their family budgets, few of the foster families would accept money from the resistance organizations. Indeed, both networks were run on very little money. Train travel cards for the workers and ration coupons for the children were supplied

[30] Piet Meerburg, interview with author, Amsterdam, June 27, 1986, transcript pp. 5, 13.

[31] Interviews with Groenewegen, Grootendorst, and Grootendorst, transcript p. 12; and Meerburg, transcript pp. 6, 12. Nico Dohmen worked with Piet Meerburg; he and Hanna van der Voort were responsible for the local activities in Limburg. See also Nico Dohmen, interview with author, Baarn, Netherlands, June 30, 1986, transcript p. 23. There is, if anything, even less printed material on the Meerburg group than on the N.V. See the series of short articles by Jan van Lieshout in the *Limburgs Dagblad:* "Het grote gezin van 'Tante Hanna' en 'Oom Nico' " (May 4, 1977), "Het verraad van Tienray" (May 5, 1977), "Duitser verleid: Hanna bevrijd" (May 6, 1977), "Rietje het vergeet—mij—nietje" (May 10, 1977); and Paul J. M. Dolfsma, "Uit de illegaliteit naar de studie: De ontstaansgeschiedenis van de stichting onderlinge studenten steun en haar bioscoop Kriterion," (Master's thesis, Amsterdam, 1985), chap. 3, "Verzet van studenten," pp. 50–84. See also Dwork, pp. 31–65.

[32] Interviews with Meerburg, transcript p. 17; Dohmen, transcript p. 8; and Groenewegen, Grootendorst, and Grootendorst, transcript pp. 4–5. This prejudice in favor of girls may have been due to the fact that Jewish boys were circumcised while the rest of the Dutch male population was not, but resistance workers such as Nico Dohmen and Ida Groenewegen (whose task it was to find homes and to resolve problems that arose in these "foster family" arrangements) believed it had more to do with the foster parents' ideas about boys and girls. Groenewegen thought it was because "a lot of mothers loved little girls. They could make nice little dresses and play with them like a doll." Dohmen's analysis was that it had more to do with the behavioral concomitants of being "a little doll" rather than the dressing up itself. The foster parents, he explained, felt "more confident to have a girl; boys were a bit more strange for them. . . . Boys are more naughty and not as easy to handle as girls." Interviews with Groenewegen, Grootendorst, and Grootendorst, transcript p. 5; and Dohmen, transcript p. 8.

[33] Dohmen, interview, transcript p. 15.

by other underground groups. Clothes were pooled and handed around. Shoes were the biggest problem—as they were for everyone in the Netherlands—and many children learned to wear wooden clogs.[34]

The great question was, Who would take a child? The N.V. was centered in a mining district and one branch of the Meerburg group in a farming community. In addition to the (working-class) miners and farmers, the two communities also had their share of middle-class people. The resistance workers were not selective with regard to income or education level as to whom they approached. Those who were recommended, who were considered safe, were asked whether they would be willing to take in a child. Both networks found that "people with more money and better positions felt more exposed. They were more afraid, more attached to their possessions and status." In other words, they felt "they had more to lose."[35] The miners and small farmers were, by contrast, far more willing to open their homes. The underground workers had a number of explanations for this disparity. Their experience was that the poorer people were "closer to needs and suffering; . . . they were used to helping each other more than perhaps the wealthier people [were]."[36] Thus, those who agreed to be foster parents focused on the fact that "the child had no parents" and they were concerned with "the difficulties of getting food in the big cities in Holland." They were not so interested in the Jewish identity of the children. Living so far from the major cities, and especially from Amsterdam, they did not "one hundred percent realize the danger they had in hiding such a child."[37] Many had never known a Jew before; none of their neighbors was radically afflicted by the German regime; they did not see the *razzias*. Just two hundred kilometers away from the street scenes of Nazi violence and murder, people could not imagine it; it was so totally foreign to their daily lives, so removed from the social order they knew. Their self-help systems, community structures, and strict adherence to religious tenets were not destroyed by the German invasion.[38] In other words, their very isolation made them less fearful and, less blinded by fear, they were better able to see the child in need as a human being to be helped.

[34] Ibid.; also interviews with Meerburg, transcript pp. 4, 6; and Marco-Braun (n. 22 above), transcript p. 18.

[35] Groenewegen, Grootendorst, and Grootendorst, interview (n. 23 above), transcript p. 15.

[36] Ibid.; also Meerburg, interview, transcript p. 16. The comparative willingness of poorer people to open their homes to Jews in contrast to the hesitancy of those who were financially better off was well recognized at the time. It is not clear whether this was a popular (and perhaps populist) myth, but a common saying was, "The poor offer you shelter, the rich someone else's address." My own research tends to support this contention.

[37] Dohmen, interview, transcript pp. 7, 23–24.

[38] Meerburg, interview, transcript pp. 10, 25–26.

We have considered how children came to be hidden through informal family and friend contacts, and with the help of two types of organizational networks: family groups like that begun by the Boogaards in the Haarlem-mermeer, and groups that were run by a disparate group of people who came together because of a common dedication to saving children. Some of these were formally structured, like Żegota; others like the N.V. and Piet Meerburg networks were far less so. The third organizational arrangement involved the transformation of an extant structure from legal to illegal work.

One example of such an organization was the Jewish charitable preventive health care organization, the Oeuvre de Secours aux Enfants (OSE).[39] When the war began in 1939, OSE was supporting three hundred refugee children, primarily from Germany and Austria, in special homes created for the purpose (*maisons d'enfants*). With the fall of France in June 1940 and the subsequent division of the country into the northern "occupied" zone and the southern "free" zone under the collaborationist government of Marshal Pétain in Vichy, the organizational apparatus split along geographic lines.[40]

While OSE-Sud worked to protect children by legal means, OSE-Nord, operating under the conditions of occupation, engaged in clandestine activities from the moment the Germans marched into Paris. Initially, OSE-Nord concentrated on the secret transfer to the south of refugee children. After the ferocious manhunt in Paris of July 16–17, 1942 (the roundup of the Velodrôme d'Hiver, or Vel d'Hiv, as it was known), OSE-Nord engaged in a plethora of underground activities. Ordered by the Germans but conducted

[39] There is a fair amount of published literature on OSE and a wealth of archival documentation. See first, inter alia, *The American OSE Review;* Centre de Documentation Juive Contemporaine (CDJC), *L'activité des organisations juives en France sous l'occupation* (1947; Paris, 1983), pp. 117–79; Dwork (n. 15 above), pp. 31–65 and 113–53; Hillel J. Kieval, "Legality and Resistance in Vichy France: The Rescue of Jewish Children," *Proceedings of the American Philosophical Society* 124, no. 5 (October 1980): 339–66; Serge Klarsfeld, *The Children of Izieu* (New York, 1985), originally published as *Les enfants d'Izieu: Une Tragedie Juive* (Paris, 1984); Anny Latour, *The Jewish Resistance in France* (New York, 1981), originally published as *La résistance juive en France* (Paris, 1970); Lucien Lazare, *La résistance juive en France* (Paris, 1987); Ernst Papanek and Edward Linn, *Out of the Fire* (New York, 1975), esp. pp. 34–35; Zosa Szakowski, *Analytical Franco-Jewish Gazetteer, 1939–1945* (New York, 1966), pp. 73–75 and passim. See also Jacques Adler, *The Jews of Paris and the Final Solution* (New York, 1987), pp. 167, 226–27, originally published as *Face à la Persecution: les organisations juives à Paris de 1940 à 1944* (Paris, 1985); Yehuda Bauer, *A History of the Holocaust* (New York, 1982), pp. 291–93; David Diamant, *Les Juifs dans la Résistance Française, 1940–44* (Paris, 1971), pp. 56–59; Dorothy Macardle, *The Children of Europe* (London, 1949), pp. 184–88; Sabine Zeitoun, *Ces enfants qu'il fallait sauver* (Paris, 1989), pp. 145–70. The major archival collections are in the Centre de Documentation Juive Contemporaine and the OSE institution itself in Paris and in the YIVO in New York.

[40] CDJC, *L'activité des organisations juives,* pp. 118–22.

entirely by French police and their auxiliaries, the *razzia* trapped 12,884 people in two days.[41] For OSE-Nord there could be no more delusions about the ultimate fate of Jews caught in the occupied zone, and their main objective was to hide as many people as possible. Six OSE workers remaining in Paris (Eugène Minkovski, Hélène Matorine, Simone Kahn, Jeanine Lévy, Céline Vallée, and Madame Averbouh) organized a child camouflage service. Using a youth club as a cover for their activities, they passed Jewish children to gentile families who hid them. The OSE workers maintained contact with the foster families throughout the war to ensure that the children were well treated and to provide maintenance funds, ration coupons, and false identity papers as needed. This network helped seven hundred children to survive the German occupation in the north.[42]

Clandestine activities to save Jewish children were undertaken later in the south than in the north. In the wake of the August 1942 dragnets that ravaged several cities in the south, OSE-Sud began underground operations. The legal structure of children's homes and health-care centers remained intact, but they also served as a screen for the organization of secret border crossings, for laboratories to produce false identity papers, and to hide those in imminent danger of arrest. The German occupation of the free zone in November 1942 meant that fewer resources could be wasted on legal work; more energy had to be channeled toward clandestine activities. The young people in the OSE residences had become too obvious and too vulnerable a target. They had to be hidden.[43]

---

[41] Diamant, pp. 119–20; Claude Lévy and Paul Tillard, *Betrayal at the Vel d'Hiv* (New York, 1969), originally published as *La Grande Rafle du Vel d'Hiv* (Paris, 1967); Marrus and Paxton, *Vichy France and the Jews* (New York, 1983), pp. 250–52; Georges Wellers, *L'Étoile jaune à l'heure de Vichy* (Paris, 1973), pp. 83–85; CDJC Document CCXIV-74, "Situation au 25 Aout 1942," pp. 1–3.

[42] CDJC, *L'activité des organisations juives,* pp. 141–42; CDJC Documents CCXVII-12a, "Exposé sur le circuit Garel," p. 2, CCXVIII-104, "Travail clandestin de l'OSE: Temoignage de M. Georges Garel," pp. 8–9, CCLXVI-13, CCLXVI-16, "La situation actuelle du judaisme en France, July 1941," p. 25. According to this report, one thousand to 1,200 children were evacuated by OSE-Nord from the occupied zone to the south.

[43] CDJC Document CCXVII-12a, p. 1. Possibly the most important facet of OSE's legal work was the aid given to Jews (children and adults) in the transit camps. OSE was one of the organizations that sent *assistantes sociale,* or social workers, to live as voluntary *internes* in the French internment or concentration camps *(camps d'internement,* or *camps de concentration).* Their role was "to share the daily life of the internees, to know their real needs, to provide whatever assistance was possible, and to defend their meager rights"; or, as Vivette Samuel-Hermann, an *interne voluntaire* put it, "to be present." Samuel-Hermann was correct: it was precisely because OSE and other philanthropic organizations were present in the camps that they were able to fight for the liberation of children, whom they then passed into the rescue

The OSE leadership asked Georges Garel to "organize a clandestine network in the southern zone of France for children of trapped Jewish families," he recalled.[44] Garel was well chosen for the job. He was not an official leader of any Jewish organization and therefore was unknown to the authorities; he was involved in resistance activities and thus had useful contacts; and he was dedicated.[45]

---

networks. In a September 1941 report on their activities they stressed "the liberation of children. As always that question is the essence of our main preoccupation. We must strive to free as many as possible." While OSE pressed the interests of individual adults who had reason to be administratively exempt according to the particulars of each case, it presented the problem of child internees to the government as an issue of general principle. Following prolonged and intensive negotiations, Vichy for a short time allowed young people under the age of fifteen to leave the camps—on certain conditions. In this way, more than a thousand children were freed from the camps in the south. There are many documents in the archives which describe the activities undertaken by OSE. With regard to their work in the cities, see, e.g., CDJC Document CCCLXVI-11, "Rapport sur l'activité de l'Union OSE pour les mois Juin, Juillet, et Août 1941." This report noted that 1,201 children were under their sole care, which was about one hundred more than in the previous trimester. "The series of tragic cases encountered during the last trimester continues and often we are obliged to admit immediately to our homes children who, in the majority of cases, have nearly been picked up [by the police]; they remain alone in the world without support and it is impossible for us not to take them" (p. 4). With regard to the work of OSE in the camps and in the liberation of the children from the camps, see, inter alia, CDJC, *L'activité des organisations juives,* p. 129; Vivette Samuel-Hermann, interview with author, Paris, June 3, 1987, transcript p. 8; CDJC Document CCCLXVI-11, p. 9; Klarsfeld, pp. 18–19; CDJC Document CCLXVI-13, "OSE"; and Dwork, pp. 56–58, 129–30, 137–41, 148–52.

[44] CDJC Document CCXVIII-104, p. 3.

[45] Georges Garel had gained the respect of the OSE leadership through his efforts to free the children caught in the brutal rafle in Lyon. Late in August 1942, some 1200 Jews were arrested in a sudden dragnet operation in Lyon and sent to the Venissieux internment camp. Shortly thereafter Garel, who was a resistant but not a member of OSE, managed to enter Venissieux in an official capacity to help liberate the children who were legally entitled to their freedom, as well as a number who were decreed prey: 108 in all. Garel, Charles Lederman, Elisabeth Hirsch, and Hélène Levy from OSE; the director of the interconfessional philanthropic group les Amitiés Chretiennes, l'Abbé Glasberg; Madeleine Barot, the general secretary of the Protestant Comité Inter-Mouvements Auprés des Évacués (CIMADE); the Jesuit priest Pierre Chaillet, and others worked furiously to free children under sixteen years of age who were not technically under arrest. Within a few days the policy with regard to the children had been changed, but by that time they had "disappeared." See, inter alia, Bauer, p. 292; Diamant, p. 58; Dwork, pp. 150–51; Lazare, pp. 208–11; Rene Nodot, *Les enfants ne partiront pas!* (Lyon, 1970); Weill, *Camps d'internement dans l'anti-France,* pp. 206–9; CDJC Document CCXVIII-104, pp. 1–3. Lily Garel-Taget, interview with author, Paris, June 19, 1987, transcript pp. 4–6; and Elisabeth Hirsch, interview with author, Neuilly-sur-Seine, France, June 25, 1987, transcript pp. 22, 24.

Garel and his associates developed two extensive networks to move, screen, and save children entrusted to their care. "Circuit B" was run by Andrée Salomon. Her goal was to smuggle Jewish children who, for cultural, religious, or linguistic reasons, could not "pass" as gentiles over the French border, primarily into Switzerland but also into Spain. Some one thousand children traveled through the reseau she created.[46] Elisabeth (Böszi) Hirsch was one of her couriers. Hirsch had come to Paris from her native Romania in 1929, when she was sixteen years old. She became a social worker and, when the war erupted, she dedicated herself to saving the lives of Jewish young people. In 1943, she was recruited to escort children to safety. She feared, she recalled, "the milice, not the Germans. I had very good papers, at the end, the papers of a French social worker who had given me her papers, and we had taken off her photo and attached mine instead. I was afraid because of my accent. And with the French that was more difficult, but with the Germans the accent did not count for anything." Jewish, Romanian, and speaking accented French, Hirsch guided children to the Swiss border several times in 1943 and in 1944 accompanied a convoy of youngsters over the Pyrenees into Spain. The terrain was difficult, and despite their sweaters and scarves the glacial temperatures gnawed at the children. Yet they persevered and crossed with the entire group intact.[47]

The children remaining in France were cared for by Garel's network. With more than fifteen hundred children to look after by the summer of 1943, the network had become so extensive that Garel divided it into four separate geographic sections with a regional director to run each area.[48] Madeleine Dreyfus was in charge of the Lyon-based section of the Garel network. "I was specially responsible for the area of Chambon-sur-Lignon," she recalled. "The first contact obviously was with the Pastor Trocmé and his wife. . . . It was in this way that I came to make the acquaintance of Madame Deléage (she was widowed) and her daughter Eva. [Mme. Deléage] was our devoted friend, she herself contacted those families most likely to help us, to help us hide those little Jewish children hunted by the Gestapo, very aware of what she risked, she herself hiding numerous children at her place and insisting that the small farmers with whom she took contact accepted those children 'from Lyon and St. Étienne so poorly fed and who needed to build themselves up in the

---

[46] CDJC Document CCXVII-12a, pp. 1–2. According to a statement by the American Joint Distribution Committee, OSE was responsible for smuggling two thousand children into Switzerland. CDJC Document CCCLXVI-14, "American Joint Distribution Committee," p. 5. Bruno-Georges Loinger, interview with author, Paris, June 25, 1987, transcript pp. 1–10.

[47] Hirsch, interview, pp. 9, 11; Zeitoun, pp. 280–81.

[48] CDJC, *L'activité des organisations juives,* pp. 157–60; CDJC Documents CCXVIII-104, pp. 3–8, and CCXVII-12a, pp. 1–2.

fresh air of the Haute Loire.' Those people knew very well what sort of children these were, but everyone pretended 'as if' one believed that tale."

The usual procedure was for Dreyfus to be met at the station in Chambon by Eva Deléage. They deposited the ten or twelve children Dreyfus had in tow each time she made the trip (several times a month) at the Hotel May and then made the rounds of farmers whom the Deléages thought might take a child. "In general these small farmers 'prepared' by their pastor and Madame Deléage responded to our demands rather quickly," Dreyfus explained. "If it was a question of boys over twelve years old it was rather difficult, however. 'They talk back,' we were told. I remember one day when a 'case' of two fourteen-year-old boys remained—a difficult task. I went from farm to farm throughout the whole area surrounding Chambon. . . . No one wanted my two boys. Finally I arrived at the house of an older couple, the Courtials, and I recited my tale to them: these were children from the city who were hungry, of course they had their ration coupons, and the air of Chambon, etc. . . . etc. . . . The Courtials answered amiably but firmly that it really was not possible for them to take the two. Then I played all to win all and I told them the truth: 'These were two Jewish boys whose parents had been arrested and whom the Germans pursued so as to imprison them along with their parents.' Not a single hesitation remained: 'But you should have said so sooner, certainly you must bring your two boys to us.' "[49]

* * *

We have discussed the networks that protected and saved Jewish children at such great length that a word of caution may be helpful. Commenting on the situation of Jews in France and Belgium, the historian Lucien Steinberg rightfully observed that "the majority of Jews who survived either did not need the help of the Jewish and non-Jewish rescue organizations, or turned to them very infrequently. It is obvious that these organizations could not save the entire Jewish population. Most of the Jews who survived did so thanks to their own initiative. The majority supported themselves illegally, but on an individual level, they received help from the local population."[50] Although precise figures are not available, the picture that emerges indicates that this pattern prevailed throughout Europe. By and large, the better part of Jewish children were not helped by organized networks but through personal, familial contacts. This point often is obscured because, as I said earlier, it is easier to write the history of institutions or organizations, even if they were informally established and loosely coordinated, than of private relations, the dull gray of everyday that at that time was neither dull nor everyday, but both momentous

[49] Madeleine Dreyfus, unpublished statement, in possession of author, pp. 2–3.

[50] Lucien Steinberg, "Jewish Rescue Activities in Belgium and France," in Gutman and Zuroff, eds. (n. 19 above), pp. 608–9.

and essential. Indeed, first and foremost, the children were saved by their parents. The act of giving up one's child, of surrending one's own daughter or son, of recognizing that one no longer could protect and shelter that small person to whom one had given life, was the first and most radical step in the chain of rescue. It was a paradox: to save one's child, one had to accept that one was unable to protect and defend the child.[51] Whether one relinquished that son or daughter to a personal friend or to a stranger, a resister, that initial act of abdication was the fundamental beginning. The work of the organizations that dedicated themselves to safeguarding Jewish children and the devotion of the great majority of families who took them in should not be underestimated. The women and men who undertook this task for the most part were steadfast and loyal. They did what they believed to be correct and, half a century later, still do not feel that it is extraordinary that they behaved as they did or that they should be specially honored for their actions. In fact, of course, their stance was exceptional. Their wonderful deeds and remarkable feats should be admired, and their probity and rectitude are to be esteemed. Nevertheless, it would be a mistake to say that these people alone, however estimable, just, kind, considerate, or accommodating they may have been, saved the children. It was the parents who took the first and most terrifying step of all.

---

[51] In his book, *Le Comité de defense des Juifs en Belgique, 1942–1944* (Brussels, 1973), Lucien Steinberg has argued that Jewish mothers gave up their children to be saved by strangers out of an instinctual sense of "collective preservation, we can say even an instinctual sense of national preservation." He has argued further that "the Jewish mothers felt that the preservation of the Jewish people would occur through their separation from their children. . . . One could not contend that there was never any hesitation. To the contrary, they often hesitated, sometimes for a long time. But the fact that they did accept, en masse, to entrust their children is the proof, in our view, of the intervention of an instinct of collective preservation that is aroused when the group is threatened" (p. 88). My own research flatly contradicts Steinberg's hypothesis. Parents, mothers and fathers, gave up their children because they came to accept, or believe, that they themselves could not protect their youngsters, that the risks and dangers of the Nazi system were too great and that they, as parents, had neither power nor control. This decision was in no way structured within the context of collective or national preservation. The sole goal, or in any case the overwhelmingly urgent goal, was to protect their children precisely and specifically because those young people were *their children.* For an informative discussion of the networks involved in saving children in Belgium (note the role of women in that work), see Steinberg, pp. 89–109; and Shlomo Kless, "The Rescue of Jewish Children in Belgium during the Holocaust," *Holocaust and Genocide Studies* 3, no. 3 (1988): 275–87.

Between Normality and Resistance:
Catastrophic Gradualism in Nazi Germany

Frank Trommler
University of Pennsylvania

Sovereign is he who decides on the exception, Carl Schmitt has said in his *Political Theology.*[1] Schmitt's interest in the state of exception (*Ausnahmezustand*) has reasserted the importance of the definition of normality (*Normalität*), especially in the case of the National Socialists' legal and political manipulation of German society. According to Schmitt's correlation of norms and exceptions as the basis of sovereignty, the Nazi regime's creation of states of exception is intrinsically related to its obsession with normality, its manifold strategies for normalizing the exceptional.

While the historians' debate about a normalization of the Nazi period within German history has yielded predictable results,[2] the debate concerning the Nazi's own strategies for normalization seems to have been sidestepped in the wake of the criticism against everyday history (*Alltagsgeschichte*) and its inherent loss of an overall perspective on the Nazi regime. As long as these strategies are merely subsumed under a general concept of manipulation, however, the particularities of the drive toward normalcy will remain obfuscated, especially the intricate interplay between official and individual ventures to create *Normalität*. This interplay has assumed a crucial role in the political psychology of the Germans in the twentieth century, undergoing several alterations between authoritarian and democratic structures since the Wilhelmine Reich. It was reinvigorated after every major upheaval since World War I, after the inflation and the Depression as well as after World War II, and has again been reinstated as a key to German politics after the unification of 1990. Under the title "A Normal Germany," with the description, "A powerful yearning is being fulfilled," the *New York Times* summed up the German quest for normalcy after the election of December 1990, quoting Chancellor Helmut Kohl's greatest ambition: "that we become a wholly normal country."[3]

---

[1] Carl Schmitt, *Political Theology* (Cambridge, Mass., 1985), p. 5.

[2] *Reworking the Past: Hitler, the Holocaust, and the Historians' Debate,* ed. Peter Baldwin (Boston, 1990).

[3] Serge Schmemann, "A Normal Germany," *New York Times* (December 4, 1990), p. A20.

This essay originally appeared in the *Journal of Modern History* 64, suppl. (December 1992).

Kohl's concern about the right strategies for normalizing Germany's domestic and foreign situation can be understood as an antidote to previous attempts at normalization that ended in disaster. Schmitt's shadow looms large in the definition of normalcy, and even larger in the avoidance of the exceptional. There can be little doubt that the notion of the exceptional that has shaped the historical approach to National Socialism inside and outside of Germany has itself become a useful reference of German post-Nazi politics. In contrast, this article sets out to reorient the perspective toward the concept of normalcy in Nazi politics. It attempts to explore the interplay of official and individual interests in the process of normalizing the exceptional. This agenda leads into the pragmatics of opportunism as well as into the modes of adjusting to catastrophe and throws some light on the precarious state of the resistance—any resistance.

THE QUEST FOR NORMALITY

The oral-history projects of recent *Alltagsgeschichte* have provided many insights into the strong belief of Germans in normality as an important criterion to which private and public history can be related. The narratives of blue- and white-collar workers of the Ruhr area in the 1980s concur, as Ulrich Herbert has shown in his interviews for the project "Lebensgeschichte und Sozialkultur im Ruhrgebiet zwischen 1930 and 1960" in the characterization of the National Socialist period as a time of secure work, family life, and a new use of leisure time, particularly through the offerings of *Kraft durch Freude* (Strength through joy). Herbert asserts:

Even opponents of the Nazis can look back quite positively on the "Strength-through-Joy" journeys. The basis for this is the splitting of life into distinct, separate realms. Partial dissent *vis-à-vis* Nazi politics is quite compatible with consent in other areas. It is thus quite possible even for political opponents of the Nazi regime to describe the pre-war years as "quiet" or "normal" times. This stress on normality is also a reaction to what are assumed to be the expectations of the interviewer. But the central point is that the period can be described as one of peaceful private advance because "politics" has been banished to areas beyond the individual awareness—in order to live as well as to survive.[4]

---

[4] Ulrich Herbert, "Good Times, Bad Times," *History Today* 36 (February 1986): 47. This is an abbreviated English version of his "Die guten und die schlechten Zeiten," in *"Die Jahre weiß man nicht, wo man die heute hinsetzen soll." Faschismus-Erfahrungen im Ruhrgebiet: Lebensgeschichte und Sozialkultur im Ruhrgebiet 1930 bis 1960,* ed. Lutz Niethammer, 3 vols. (Berlin und Bonn, 1983), 1:67–96. See also Victoria de Grazia, *The Culture of Consent: Mass Organization of Leisure in Fascist Italy* (Cambridge, 1981).

The organization *Kraft durch Freude* was only the most visible component of a policy that engendered the feeling of social comfort through a mixture of privatization of traditional life-styles and public participation in modern leisure-time activities. Its main ingredients, especially steady employment, the promise of a car, and unprecedented travel opportunities, again formed the basis for the broad endorsement of Adenauer's reconstruction policy in the 1950s. In both cases the Germans rewarded the leadership for its ability to steer out of chaos and desperation—first out of the economic depression of 1929–33 and, twenty years later, out of the devastation of World War II. Obviously, the politics through which Adenauer's democracy brought about the return to normalcy were sharply different from those of Hitler's dictatorship. While Hitler's exclamation of 1935, "What security and what calm prevail in today's Germany!" (Welche Sicherheit und welche Ruhe beherrscht unser heutiges Deutschland!),[5] seems to foreshadow Adenauer's promise of security in 1957, "No experiments!" (Keine Experimente!), Hitler's statement is incomplete without adding: at the expense of thousands of lives and thousands in concentration camps.

The adjustment of a majority of the population to the political situation rested on a comparable juxtaposition of "normal" and "abnormal" conditions that allowed the individual to articulate his or her historical experience in a rather apolitical way. This dichotomy generally did not reflect the consequences of the exclusion from normalcy, especially the persecution of the Jews. In this context any form of exceptionality seems to have disturbing elements—disturbing to the reestablished order at home and at work—which explains the distance from and fascination with the much-conjured mass excitement of the 1930s. Hannah Arendt, though, was not to be misled by the exceptionalism of the Nazi rule. Unlike Susan Sontag, who called for the study of Leni Riefenstahl's "fascinating fascism" in order to demystify Hitler, Arendt kept the focus on the ordinariness of the regime's machinations, on the "banality of evil." In her analysis of Eichmann's attitude Arendt articulated a classic treatise on the Nazi normalization of the monstrous although she never fully subsumed the evil under the banal. She remained aware of the power of the exceptional and unpredictable.

Studies such as the one on everyday history in the Ruhr area help to focus on the ways the Nazis used the adjustment of different social groups to ordinary life for a general affirmation of their regime. The decisive factor was not their ability to control everyday life and work (which was, at best,

---

[5] Quoted in *Deutschland-Berichte der Sozialdemokratischen Partei Deutschlands (Sopade), 1934–1940,* ed. Klaus Behnken, 7 vols. (Frankfurt, 1980), vol. 2 (August 1935), pp. 917–18.

questionable) but, rather, the realization that Germans, after the devastations of war, inflation, depression, and unemployment, were ready and, indeed, eager to collaborate in the good conduct of everyday life and work. For many Germans the state of exception had already become reality in war and postwar turmoil; this fact gave the Nazis the opportunity to portray Hitler as the savior from chaos. The "Aufruf der Reichsregierung an das Deutsche Volk!" of February 1, 1933, was framed as a proclamation of a general restoration of German identity and unity, accompanied by popular images of a traditional normality of unalienated life and work.[6]

Obvious is a perceived reciprocity between the individual's yearning for a secure existence and the official guarantees against the return to chaos. As a consequence of the extended unemployment during the depression years, workers also learned to pursue the search for normality as a reconfirmation of individual identity at work and at home. In turn, the new regime nurtured the individual worker's sense of a personally secure life, while at the same time dismantling the collective organizations of the working class. In the case of civil servants, the regime legislated their submission to the new state in 1933, expressing the need for a return to normalcy in the very title of the law itself, "Gesetz zur Wiederherstellung des Berufsbeamtentums." The law intended anything but the restitution of a former state of affairs, yet its nomenclature corresponded to deep-seated anxieties of an important social group whose collaboration was sought. Vis-à-vis the Catholic church and organizations, which had been rather critical of the National Socialists, the new leadership succeeded in reaching its objectives through a similar tactic. With the conclusion of the *Reichskonkordat* they fulfilled an old dream of political Catholicism but saw to it through the *Gleichschaltung* that the exercise of tradition did not infringe upon the new political order.

As early as 1932 Theodor Geiger showed how the Nazis lured segments of the middle classes to their side by infusing the mentality of economic materialism (*wirtschaftsmaterialistische Mentalität*) with a new *völkisch*-like idealism.[7] Geiger's analysis of the much propagated corporate ideal (stän-disches Wunschbild) of employers and employees united in common cause reads like a script for the restitution of normality through entitlements facilitated by the National Socialists.[8] This feeling took hold among peasants and artisans as well as the *Berufsstände* (corporate estates) in general;[9] the vigorous pursuit

[6] See the representative volume by Friedrich Heiss, *Deutschland zwischen Nacht und Tag* (Berlin, 1934), pp. 83–84.

[7] Theodor Geiger, *Die soziale Schichtung des deutschen Volkes: Soziographischer Versuch auf statistischer Grundlage* (Stuttgart, 1932), p. 118.

[8] Ibid., p. 120.

[9] Adelheid von Saldern, *Mittelstand im "Dritten Reich:" Handwerker— Einzelhändler—Bauern* (Frankfurt and New York, 1979), pp. 214–33.

of a *Sonderbewusstsein,* the conception of being a special in-group, shows the reciprocity between the group's instrumentalizing of given circumstances and being instrumentalized by the reigning system. The study of the controversy between the Deutsche Arbeitsfront and the Reichsstand des Deutschen Handwerks exemplifies how the enhancement of segmental allegiances helped the government to keep control of organized workers and craftsmen.[10]

The most disturbing manifestation of how National Socialism was instrumentalized for individual purposes occurred in the realm that seems to defy the label of normality most strongly: that of political control through terror and surveillance. In his study of Gestapo files Robert Gellately shows to what an inordinate degree the German population succumbed to the system of terror that enabled a relatively small force of thirty to forty thousand Gestapo members, together with the cooperating police, to terrorize a society of over seventy million.[11] In view of the fact that "the widespread appearance of political denunciation" "normalized" the everyday life of Germans, Gellately concludes: "It turned out that while the Gestapo did indeed represent the regime's most important enforcer of policy and was the key element in the system of terror whose very reputation served to reinforce observance of Nazi doctrines and the laws of the German state, what had been generally overlooked by historians—but certainly not by contemporaries—was that denunciations represented an essential contribution to the political policing process."[12]

Gellately's findings confirm the necessity of not divorcing the "normal" daily concerns of the German population from its indifference to inhumanity, not even from its active support of the policy of racial persecution or, as Ian Kershaw put it, from "the political-ideological-moral framework which focuses upon the genocidal criminality of the Nazi regime."[13] At the same time, these findings illuminate the problems of the juxtaposition of compliance and resistance as the two distinguishable attitudes of the population toward the Nazi state. This juxtaposition received renewed attention when the various expressions of everyday discontent were collected, discussed, and categorized under the heading of "Resistenz."[14] From this viewpoint local and regional history has been rewritten, featuring new heroes and activities.

---

[10] Andreas Kuntz, "Anmerkungen zum Handwerk im Nationalsozialismus," *Zeitschrift für Volkskunde* 78 (1982): 187–99.

[11] Robert Gellately, "The Gestapo and German Society: Political Denunciation in the Gestapo Case Files," *Journal of Modern History* 60 (1988): 659.

[12] Ibid., p. 693.

[13] Ian Kershaw, *The Nazi Dictatorship: Problems and Perspectives of Interpretation,* 2d ed. (New York, 1989), p. 167.

[14] Martin Broszat, "Resistenz und Widerstand: Eine Zwischenbilanz des Forschungsprojekts," in *Bayern in the NS-Zeit,* ed. M. Broszat et al., 4 vols. (Munich and Vienna,

From it historiography gained in status as a venture of broad social and educational appeal. The fact that the concept of *Resistenz* emerged relatively successfully is therefore not due just to its obvious potential for exonerating millions of Germans but also to the exigencies of the historical profession itself. In contrast to such notions as normality and normalization, the focus on moral attitudes provides for a lively presentation of historical material. The application of the compliance-or-resistance scheme extends the narrative into a moral operation and leads to closure, something that the historical discipline, bound by the maxims of objectivity and *Wissenschaftlichkeit,* constantly needs for its redefinition and reassertion. Consequently, the lack of studies on those attitudes in Nazi Germany that do not fit this model is hardly surprising. Historians such as Detlev Peukert, Heide Gerstenberger, and Ian Kershaw have pointed to the necessity of exploring those forms and have provided significant clues for new assessments.[15]

Yet the most important reason why historians have adhered to a relatively schematic use of the compliance-and-resistance model seems to be the failure of German sociology after 1945 to provide a comprehensive analysis of life under National Socialism and, more particularly, a deeper understanding of the conceptions and rituals of the individual *Alltag* both before and after World War II.[16] Little sociological research exists concerning the emergence and active pursuits of *Normalitätsbewusstsein* in its linkage to the individual's own experience of everyday life. A precise definition and historical contextualization of the concept of *Normalitätsbewusstsein* with its narrower, yet politically more volatile, base than *Alltagsbewusstsein* remains a desideratum. While sociologists have been strongly interested in *Alltag*-phenomena,[17] they have tended to study everyday life with an eye toward generalizations about the nature of modernization rather than as an element in constructing historical reality.[18] Norbert Elias has traced the tendency toward *"philosophoide*

1981), 4:691–709, and "Zur Sozialgeschichte des deutschen Widerstands," *Vierteljahrshefte für Zeitgeschichte* 34 (1986): 300–304.

[15] Detlev J. K. Peukert, *Inside Nazi Germany: Conformity, Opposition, and Racism in Everyday Life* (New Haven, Conn., 1987); *Normalität oder Normalisierung? Geschichtswerkstätten und Faschismusanalyse,* ed. Heide Gerstenberger and Dorothea Schmidt (Münster, 1987); Ian Kershaw, *Popular Opinion and Political Dissent in the Third Reich: Bavaria, 1933–1945* (Oxford, 1983).

[16] Thomas Herz, "Nur ein Historikerstreit? Die Soziologen und der Nationalsozialismus," *Kölner Zeitschrift für Soziologie und Sozialpsychologie* 39 (1987): 560–70.

[17] *Materialien zur Soziologie des Alltags, Kölner Zeitschrift für Soziologie und Sozialpsychologie,* Sonderheft 20, ed. Kurt Hammerich and Michael Klein (Opladen, 1978); Thomas Leithäuser, *Formen des Alltagsbewußtseins,* 2d ed. (Frankfurt and New York, 1979).

[18] Peter L. Berger and Thomas Luckmann, *The Social Construction of Reality: A Treatise in the Sociology of Knowledge* (New York, 1967), pp. 19 ff.

Reflexionen" about the *Alltag* to the idiosyncratic machinations of the academic discipline. His warning against *Alltag* as a "speculation" that has been elevated to a universal category addresses the need for empirical studies.[19] The search is still on for a better understanding of what was considered normal in everyday life and what was the historical reference for normality in a given period—beyond such unfocused terms as "*die gute alte Zeit*" (the good old days) after 1918 and "*im Frieden*" (in peacetime) after World War II.

Without a specific distinction between *Alltagsbewusstsein* (with its ritual-izations of modern private life and interests)[20] and the explicit rejection of public matters as a political statement, historians tend to enhance the individual's search for normalcy in work and family life as resistance (or "*Resistenz*"). Although comparisons with "normal" behavior in other con-frontational situations remain highly problematic, a view that goes beyond the conditions under National Socialism is necessary, as the critics of Tim Mason's studies of workers' opposition rightly asserted.[21] As important as the exploration of the regionally and socially diverse gray areas of restiveness under the Nazi regime is, it remains equally important to clarify the role of this particularity in the functioning of everyday affairs in Germany.

In this connection, Alexander Mitscherlich's insight into the reciprocity between the instrumentalization *by* the given circumstances and the instrumentalization *of* those circumstances provides a particularly useful point of departure. Any social situation engenders mechanisms that are based on what Mitscherlich calls the "older forms of expression of our instinctual nature" and through which we define the "external reality." Any adaptation forces us to rearrange our own resources. Mitscherlich explains: "We call it active adaptation since we also adapt the outside object to *us*."[22] This intentionalism is the situational focus of individuals and groups, constantly framing and reordering reality—any reality. That framing results from the tension among numerous factors claiming the attention of the group or individual; the political constellation is but one of many factors. Although strongly affected by political and social demands for compliance in daily affairs, this intentionalism, prompted by such diverse emotions as anxiety, pride, personal ambition, and group solidarity, carries the characteristics of a

[19] Norbert Elias, "Zum Begriff des Alltags," in *Materialien zum Soziologie des Alltags*, p. 29.

[20] Anthony Giddens, *The Constitution of Society: Outline of the Theory of Structuration* (Cambridge, 1984), p. 111 and passim.

[21] Günter Morsch, "Streik im 'Dritten Reich,'" *Vierteljahrshefte für Zeitgeschichte* 36 (1988): 657 ff.

[22] Alexander Mitscherlich, *Gesammelte Schriften V: Sozialpsychologie 3*, ed. Helga Haase (Frankfurt, 1983), p. 238.

definable mode of mastering life for which compliance or resistance are considered secondary.

The mode of constructing reality raised here is a mixture of wishful thinking and the need for orderliness—the sense of how things have to be.[23] While the mixture can assume different forms, each version reflects a fear of chaos and turbulence. In his quest for power, Hitler incessantly played upon this fear of chaos from which the longing for normality, including the suggested resumption of traditions that never had fully become reality, gained its momentum.[24] Based on the conviction that chaos had interfered with the mastery of life in Germany, the brutal side of National Socialism gave promise of the much-desired coalescence of group interests and individual pursuits. More often than not, the authoritarianism of the Nazi regime was but a paradigm for the newly found stabilization of life amid the perceived storms of history.

THE MANIPULATION OF TIME

The Nazi strategies of normalization corresponded to individual strategies of instrumentalizing the Nazi regime. While this complicity differed in the various sectors of German society, it appeared to be largely unilateral to those who were excluded from its notion of normalcy. "For those victims," Dan Diner asserts, "who were chosen for extermination, the Nazi period represents the exact opposite, an absolutely exceptional state of affairs, one distinguished from everyday normalcy and continuity precisely by its incisive and cata-strophic character."[25] In view of this exclusion, Diner finds "a truly synthesizing approach" to the reality of everyday life and that of "existential exceptionalism" no longer possible.

Indeed, any definition of everyday history during that period in Germany has to consider itself conditional within this framework. Nevertheless, if one attempts to avoid the trivialization of the moral categories of good and evil, dread and ignorance, proceeding instead from the actual individual experience to the broader parameters of social behavior under National Socialism, certain psychological patterns of response and endurance become manifest that transcend the insider-outsider paradigm. One of the most visible patterns is the

---

[23] Compare Charles Helm, "The German Concept of Order: The Social and Physical Setting," *Journal of Popular Culture* 13 (1979/80): 67–80.

[24] Compare the first comprehensive studies of this phenomenon by Joachim Schumacher, *Die Angst vor dem Chaos: Über die falsche Apokalypse des Bürgertums* (Paris, 1937; reprint, Frankfurt, 1972); Erich Fromm, *Escape from Freedom* (New York, 1941).

[25] Dan Diner, "Between Aporia and Apology: On the Limits of Historicizing National Socialism," in *Reworking the Past* (n. 2 above), p. 139.

dread of chaos that tends to predetermine the reaction to disturbances of normality as one of delay and persistence. The immediate reaction to such a disturbance is rarely resistance but, rather, an attitude of protecting the familiar and the personal, or "the retention of a structured field," as it was labeled in a psychological study of 1941 that tried to assess the effects of National Socialism on the life of Jews in Germany.[26] This retention translates into "families to defend, children to educate, business to foster, friends to help—in short, the conservation of personality structure and all the major values of life [that] call for tenacity." Pointing to "the dynamic character of the familiar" as an "inadequately developed chapter in psychology," the study suggested that the mobilization of individual consistency and the resistance against change have to be understood as the premier tools for survival before they can be criticized as an illusory response to the threats of persecution. In answer to the question of why they postponed emigration to a point where it became almost impossible, the Jewish respondents to the study confirmed that the reorientation of their *Normalitätsbewusstsein* (which ultimately had to be painfully abandoned) was a decisive strategy for their psychological survival.

Only when it is threatened does everyday normality receive any kind of attention. This fact alone accounts for a whole array of strategies of avoidance, postponement, and selective consciousness on the part of people who feel threatened. While the majority of Germans did not experience such exposure, a sizable minority did. In the most impressive and successful novel about Germany under National Socialism, *The Seventh Cross* (1942), Anna Seghers turned the disintegration of ordinary life ("das gewöhnliche Leben") into a leitmotif. The numerous episodes are connected by the flight of the protagonist, Georg Heisler, from the concentration camp Westhofen near Mainz. When Heisler, in a last attempt at securing shelter in Frankfurt, decides to visit an old political friend, Paul Röder, who now has turned from politics to private family life, he hesitates. Suddenly the ordinary life that the friend has centered on his family appears extremely fragile. "How could he enter here," Heisler thinks, "where they would welcome him innocently without any suspicion? Could not a single pressure on this bell disperse the family inside like a chaff before the wind? Bring in its wake imprisonment, torment, and death?"[27] Despite the comfort of family life, Röder decides to help Georg once informed of his situation. However, the normality of everyday work and family life now appears as a mirage for Röder too.

---

[26] G. W. Allport, J. S. Bruner, and E. M. Jandorf, "Personality under Social Catastrophe: Ninety Life-Histories of the Nazi Revolution," in *Personality in Nature, Society and Culture* (New York, 1950), p. 353.

[27] Anna Seghers, *The Seventh Cross* (Boston, 1942), p. 199.

Anna Seghers's optimism in 1938—that Germans would be able to respond in Röder's manner when such a challenge arose—was rarely reflected in reality. Nevertheless, her focus on ordinary life is illuminating as it demonstrates its political ambiguity. While Heisler, the personification of resistance, longingly pursues "das gewöhnliche Leben" on his escape trail through the small Rhine villages, through Mainz and Frankfurt, and while other characters tend to define the Nazis as spoilers of the ordinary life, Seghers also indicates how the pursuit of normalcy is a part of the Nazis' control efforts. She portrays the willingness of normal citizens to suspend their political and moral commitments in order to preserve undisturbed their roles as workers, citizens, and neighbors. She shows how the suspension of moral commitment leads to a dehistorization of time. When Dr. Kress and his wife realize at the end of the novel that the moment has come to risk their bourgeois existence to save Georg, they feel that they are returning to reality, reentering history. They become aware how the Nazi regime has manipulated their desire to dwell in the present.

Contemporary diaries, autobiographies, memoirs, and letters underscore the reality of Seghers's fictive account. Critical of the official rhetoric about the present as a grand historical era, they confirm the importance of the awareness of time itself as part of the Nazi experience. While the projection of a new kind of political eternity, the Thousand-Year Reich, usually provoked sarcastic comments, Hitler's constant invocation of the *Geschichtlichkeit* (historicity) of his actions tended to stymie a sober assessment of Germany's political and historical constraints. Travelers to Germany noticed the increasing isolation of the population within a self-constructed world of facts and beliefs that, when challenged by the visitors, often was defended with the contention that if this order failed, chaos would break out.[28]

A good account of an outsider's observations within Berlin's upper middle class can be found in Christabel Bielenberg's memoir, *Ride out the Dark,* published in England as *The Past Is Myself* in 1968. Christabel Bielenberg, a niece of Lord Northcliffe, became a German citizen in 1934 when she married Peter Bielenberg and lived in Germany until after the war. Her husband, a good friend of Adam von Trott, participated in the July 20 plot to kill Hitler and was imprisoned in a concentration camp shortly thereafter. In her characterization of life among the Germans the question of resistance transcends mere political considerations. Bielenberg calls attention to the difficulties of breaking out of the bubble of normalcy, as in her description of a night in Berlin in 1941:

Peter and I did not feel like going straight home after our dinner party with our neighbours. The roads were dark and deserted and we could walk alone and talk

---

[28] For a telling example, see *Deutschland-Berichte der Sozialdemokratischen Partei Deutschlands (Sopade)* (n. 5 above), vol. 7 (March 7, 1940), p. 161.

alone—or could we? It seemed strange that after so many years of living with it, I was still unable to gauge the force of evil behind the outward form of National Socialism. In spite of all, life, as it had to be lived, could appear comparatively normal—people could fall in love, the dinner had to be cooked, the children—and then for a moment or two that evening the veil had been lifted on what lay behind, the faceless iniquitous core, man's stark craving to dominate, to wield arbitrary power over his fellow men. The thought left me rather breathless, and feeling young and inexperienced; inadequately armed with nothing much more than a conscience with which to fight such wickedness.[29]

Bielenberg's description leaves no doubts about the urge to extend the limits of "normal" life as much as possible. More than once emphasizing how difficult it was to think of the future and plan ahead, she corroborates Seghers's narrative assessment of the loss of "Zeitgefühl."[30]

To what extent this reaction was a calculated part of the Nazis' strategy of normalization has been demonstrated by Milton Mayer in his interviews with Germans, entitled *They Thought They Were Free.* Mayer's focus is on the "gradual habituation" of the German population to the twists and turns of the regime, "little by little," as one of the Germans put it, "to being governed by surprise; to receiving decisions deliberated in secret; to believing that the situation was so complicated that the government had to act on information which the people could not understand, or so dangerous that, even if people could understand it, it could not be released because of national security."[31] What made this gradual habituation so dangerous is that each step was noticed, yet appeared not so threatening as to provoke resistance, or in the words of Martin Niemöller, pastor of the Confessing Church, who turned from a conservative nationalist into a symbol of resistance, "that, when the Nazis attacked the Communists, he was a little uneasy, but, after all, he was not a Communist, and so he did nothing; and then they attacked the Socialists, and he was a little uneasier, but, still, he was not a Socialist, and he did nothing; and then the schools, the press, the Jews, and so on, and he was always uneasier, but he still did nothing. And then they attacked the Church, and he was a Churchman, and he did something—but then it was too late."[32]

Niemöller's confessional accounting of this gradualism poignantly reveals the irresistible attraction to a perceived normalcy with its reassuring sense of historical continuity. As one contemporary put it: "Each act, each occasion, is

---

[29] Christabel Bielenberg, *Ride out the Dark* (Boston, 1984), p. 88.

[30] For other literary accounts of the "Zeitverlust," see Hans Dieter Schäfer, "Bücherverbrennung, staatsfreie Sphäre und Scheinkultur," in *"Das war ein Vorspiel nur . . ." Berliner Colloquium zur Literaturpolitik im "Dritten Reich,"* ed. Horst Denkler and Eberhard Lämmert (Berlin, 1985), p. 121.

[31] Milton Mayer, *They Thought They Were Free: The Germans 1933–45* (Chicago and London, 1955), p. 166.

[32] Ibid., p. 169.

worse than the last, but only a little worse. You wait for the next and the next. You wait for one great shocking occasion, thinking that others, when such a shock comes, will join you in resisting somehow."[33] And then it is too late. Or is it?

Resistance in this predicament presupposes a reconnecting with history as part of the existential decision concerning life and death. This was the case in the workers' resistance that evolved from the socialist movement but also in the case of the groups that prepared the coup of July 20, 1944. These groups seemed disproportionately concerned with history, German history, and how this history might be perceived in the future. The disproportionate concern was itself a reflection of the isolation with which military officers and certain aristocratic circles hoped to maintain their normalcy in the categories of national honor. Hans Mommsen has assessed the difficulty of breaking through this "bubble" that the Nazis facilitated with skill and brutality: "Many of the problems discussed at that time never reached foreign ears, for they were blanketed off by the Nazi regime; conversely, the opposition was increasingly cut off from outside influences, a psychological factor which led to some degree of introversion in political and social thinking even among those who succeeded in maintaining contacts."[34] In this predicament, the obligation to make German history honorable again in the eyes of the world could at times take precedence over the necessity to save Germany for a democratic postwar order. Henning von Tresckow explicitly expressed the intention to risk the coup against Hitler regardless of the outcome, in order to demonstrate to the world that in Germany a resistance movement existed, not just total submission to the Nazi rule.[35] In his comment on Tresckow, Hans Rothfeld characteristically invoked the fight against chaos, this time, no doubt, as a realization on the part of the resistance that Hitler himself represented the chaos from which he claimed to save the Germans.[36] How much the population still identified with this savior became obvious on July 20, 1944, when most Germans turned their backs on the plot, despite their longing for an end to the war.

There was, of course, growing impatience, a yearning to be rid of the constant bombardments, of shock and fire, danger and dying. A feeling of being imprisoned in the all-too-slow pace of the battle for Germany gained ascendancy. Millions thought they could not survive if the war lasted much

[33] Ibid.

[34] Hans Mommsen, "Social Views and Constitutional Plans of the Resistance," in *The German Resistance to Hitler,* ed. Hermann Graml et al. (Berkeley and Los Angeles, 1970), p. 143.

[35] Hans Rothfels, *Die deutsche Opposition gegen Hitler: Eine Würdigung* (Frankfurt, 1958), p. 88.

[36] Ibid.

longer. Yet the striving for some kind of normalcy established certain parameters within the uncertainty; it projected a closed future and nurtured a desire to continue without history.[37] For this reaction the Nazis had prepared the terrain well. Their most effective tactic had been to coerce the population into a treadmill of work, war, and political organization that did not allow time to reflect upon events or come to grips with the overall political situation. The main goal was to establish a "uniformly stereotypical rhythm" in Germany for which the small and big rituals—from the *Heil Hitler* salute to the parades, rallies, and *Reichsparteitage*—had provided the basis.[38] And indeed, as this rhythm engendered a sense of normalcy amid the controlled excitement, the population collaborated willingly, immersing itself in the present. In the later phases of the war, the preoccupation with the present turned into apathy and fatalism despite the hectic pace of events, as people waited for the great miracle that would change everything at one stroke.[39] Though it assured the regime's control of time—one of the least-researched aspects of power[40]—this collaboration was double-edged as it inadvertently created its own rhythm of activities, insulating the individual in his or her very own treadmill of work. Within this "Arbeitsexistentialismus"[41] increasingly less room was available for ideological demonstrations.

A similar ambivalence characterizes the other manifestation of presentism under the Nazi regime that emerged as part of the rattled *Bildungsdenken* of the middle classes. This thinking expounded the longing for the redeeming aspects of time while rejecting the immersion in concrete political events and activities. In its metahistorical aspirations it corresponded to the official projections of the eternal dimensions of the present order, best symbolized in

---

[37] This is the tenor of numerous reports between 1943 and 1945 in *Meldungen aus dem Reich: Die geheimen Lageberichte des Sicherheitsdienstes der SS, 1938–1945,* ed. Heinz Boberach (Herrsching, 1984). See, e.g., "Meldungen über die Entwicklung in der öffentlichen Meinungsbildung," 16:6498–6501 (April 20, 1944).

[38] Astrid Grenkowitz, Helga Loest, and Rainer Zoll, "Die Zwanghaftigkeit von Zeitstrukturen im Alltag, in der Zwangsneurose und im Faschismus," in *Zerstörung und Wiederaneignung von Zeit,* ed. Rainer Zoll (Frankfurt, 1988), p. 432.

[39] Marlis G. Steinert, *Hitler's War and the Germans: Public Mood and Attitude during the Second World War* (Athens, Ohio, 1977), p. 239.

[40] Compare Klaus Heinemann and Peter Ludes, "Zeitbewußtsein und Kontrolle der Zeit," in *Materialien zur Soziologie des Alltags* (n. 17 above), pp. 220–43; Gerhard Schmied, *Soziale Zeit: Umfang, "Geschwindigkeit" und Evolution* (Berlin, 1985); Thomas Luckmann, "Remarks on Personal Identity: Inner, Social, and Historical Time," in *Identity: Personal and Socio-Cultural,* ed. Antia Jacobson-Widding (Uppsala, 1984), pp. 67–91.

[41] Frank Trommler, "'Deutschlands Sieg oder Untergang': Perspektiven aus dem Dritten Reich auf die Nachkriegsentwicklung," in *Deutschland nach Hitler: Zukunftspläne im Exil und aus der Besatzungszeit, 1939–1949,* ed. Thomas Koebner et al. (Opladen, 1987), pp. 214–28.

the classicist architecture of the Thousand-Year Reich. It elevated the notion of historicity (*Geschichtlichkeit*) beyond the encounter with a mere assemblage of historical happenings.[42] Much of this concept is indebted to a general intellectual history of the period, galvanized by the sense of a passing era that pervaded assessments of European culture following World War I. Its most prominent articulation can be found in Heidegger's disdainful innuendo against "mere" history and his existential self-elevation to the status of *Geschichtlichkeit*.[43] The concept presupposes a utopia of timelessness with which the machinations of historical change would be overcome; it was instrumentalized with considerable success in Hitler's and Stalin's totalitarian rule. The fact that a detailed illumination of this phenomenon in its political ramifications is still outstanding may have to do, as Boris Groys has argued in the case of Stalinism, with the deep involvement of artists and intellectuals in this kind of history thrashing.[44]

A closer look at Goebbels's propaganda tactics reveals how much both forms of presentism augmented each other in the gradual habituation documented by Milton Mayer. Goebbels displayed an exorbitant skill in creating ever-new stages for presentism: "situations," as they were called, in which the individual had to (and wanted to) adjust in a constantly renewable effort to ward off historic reality, that is, imminent chaos, death, catastrophe.[45] In a retrospective of 1946, an astute observer called it the "temporal insulation" of an ever-renewable present: "Even in a period of the most devastating defeats [the Nazi propaganda] was able to suggest to the masses new perspectives for every new situation and thereby to let the old situation (i.e., the fact of the defeat) disappear—from the dominance over Europe back to the Rhine line and, finally, Berlin where it at last gave up its business together with its existence."[46]

The pragmatics of adjusting to catastrophe, with its various combinations of extending normalcy and retarding time, is an integrating element in the political process of Nazi Germany. The notion of the "retention of a structured field" in the aforementioned study on Jews in Germany is applicable in this

---

[42] Henryk Olszewski, "Das Geschichtsbild—ein Bestandteil der NS-Ideologie," *Tradition und Neubeginn: Internationale Forschungen zur deutschen Geschichte im 20. Jahrhundert,* ed. Joachim Hütter et al. (Cologne, 1975), pp. 299–316.

[43] Gerhard Bauer, *"Geschichtlichkeit": Wege und Irrwege eines Begriffs* (Berlin, 1963), pp. 119–28; Peter Hartocollis, *Time and Timelessness; or, The Varieties of Temporal Experience (A Psychoanalytic Inquiry)* (New York, 1983), pp. 23–25.

[44] Boris Groys, *Gesamtkunstwerk Stalin: Die gespaltene Kultur in der Sowjetunion* (Munich, 1988).

[45] Trommler, pp. 218–19.

[46] Hugo Kuhn, "Die verfälschte Wirklichkeit," in his *Text und Theorie* (Stuttgart, 1969), p. 326.

connection, especially in light of the fact that the Nazi policy toward the Jews itself went through a pattern of stages that prompted various delay mechanisms on the part of the victims. The policy of genocide developed, in the words of Berel Lang, "at the levels both of idea and of practice, by a succession of steps, each opening onto further historical possibilities and only later, by this cumulative progression, affirming the intention for genocide." Lang lists as steps the establishment of concentration camps in Germany in 1933; the implementation of the Nuremberg Laws in 1935 by which the Jews were denied certain features of civil protection; the invasion of Poland in 1939 and the concurrent establishment there of Jewish ghettos; the invasion of the Soviet Union in 1941 and the accompanying "Commissar" order to violate the conventions of war in the treatment of prisoners; the starting of the death camps at the end of 1941 and the explicit formulation of the Final Solution at the Wannsee Conference in January 1942. Lang's conclusion: "The sequence here is cumulative and (it shall be argued) intentional—but it also represents a series of individual steps each of which causally influences the one following it."[47]

The conflict among Jews in Germany after 1933 was one between "the positive valence exerted by a familiar, though frustrating, environment and the disagreeable uncertainties awaiting them in an unknown land."[48] In their use of terror against Jews the Nazi leaders utilized this conflict for their politics of gradualism. After imposing restrictive laws and creating terrifying impositions on the lives of Jews, the Nazis seemed to abstain for a while from a strong enforcement of these inhibitions. As a consequence hopes were raised among Jews that the return to some form of normality was not beyond reach. In the succession of anti-Jewish legislation, the concept of normality was increasingly distorted in the adjustment to catastrophe. No time is more cherished than borrowed time, and, indeed, the hope to keep the present as a bulwark against chaos was seen as characteristic of Jewish life in Germany—until the organized pogrom of November 1938.[49] Although it was not until October 1941 that the emigration of German Jews from Germany was formally prohibited, the systematic brutalization and degradation became intolerable in 1938. Thereafter, generalizations about the pragmatics of adjustment to catastrophe lose their explanatory power. The chasm between confronting catastrophe, as in the case of German civilians in World War II, and confronting the absolute evil of genocide, as in the case of the European Jews, is unbridgeable.

---

[47] Berel Lang, *Act and Idea in the Nazi Genocide* (Chicago and London, 1990), p. 9.
[48] Allport et al. (n. 26 above), p. 352.
[49] Jacob Boas, "The Shrinking World of German Jewry, 1933–1938," *Leo Baeck Institute: Year Book XXXI* (1986): 241–66.

Yet in his study "Suppression of the Truth about Hitler's 'Final Solution' " in *The Terrible Secret,* Walter Laqueur has demonstrated that even after November 1938, when the last bit of adjusted normality seemed to have been crushed in the destruction of the shops and synagogues, the pattern of gradual application of terror continued, prompting subsequent adjustments. Laqueur is at great pain to show that one has to first realize the immense emotional and intellectual energies that went into the fight for human integrity in the face of terror before one can discuss the possibility of resistance. Laqueur quotes Louis de Jong's summarizing reflections from "The Netherlands and Auschwitz": "We should commit an immense historical error were we to dismiss the main defense mechanisms employed by the victims—not constantly mind you, but by way of intermittent distress signals—as mere symptoms of blindness or foolishness; rather did these defense mechanisms spring from deep and inherent qualities shared by all mankind—a love for life, a fear of death, and an understandable inability to grasp the reality of the greatest crime in the history of mankind."[50]

THE DELAYED RESISTANCE

George Orwell's concept of "catastrophic gradualism" offers by far the most incisive paradigm of the normalization of the exceptional that was practiced under the dictatorships of the 1930s and 1940s. In the article "Catastrophic Gradualism" of November 1945, Orwell based his theory on Stalinism, yet the focus was on the broader phenomenon that came to be called totalitarianism. "There is a theory," his article begins,

which has not yet been accurately formulated or given a name, but which is very widely accepted and is brought forward whenever it is necessary to justify some action which conflicts with the sense of decency of the average human being. It might be called, until some better name is found, the Theory of Catastrophic Gradualism. According to this theory, nothing is ever achieved without bloodshed, lies, tyranny and injustice, but on the other hand no considerable change for the better is to be expected as the result of even the greatest upheaval. History necessarily proceeds by calamities, but each succeeding age will be as bad, or nearly as bad as the last. One must not protest against purges, deportations, secret police forces and so forth, because these are the price that has to be paid for progress: but on the other hand "human nature" will always see to it that progress is slow or even imperceptible.[51]

As "totalitarianism," Orwell's expanded definition includes fascism and National Socialism (although these political systems did not justify their

[50] Walter Laqueur, *The Terrible Secret: Suppression of the Truth about Hitler's "Final Solution"* (Harmondsworth, 1982), p. 156.

[51] George Orwell, "Catastrophic Gradualism," in *The Collected Essays, Journalism and Letters,* ed. Sonia Orwell and Ian Angus (New York, 1968), 4:15–16.

strategies with the socialist idea of progress that made the Russian Revolution of 1917 such a momentous event). In Germany much of the regime's brutality was condoned (even encouraged) in direct correlation to both the resurgence of nationalism and the "struggle against chaos," while the traditional idea of progress had given way to Nietzschean perspectivism as the ultimate form of modernity.

In order to assess the impact of catastrophic gradualism on twentieth-century history, one certainly needs to distinguish between the various systems and their roots in national traditions. But it is at least as important also to look at the legacy of this phenomenon that is still with us today, although it is often not recognized as such. It comes into view whenever one analyzes the powerful yearning for normality that accompanied the period of economic and social recovery in the West following World War II and which figures prominently in the post–Cold War initiatives in the East. That legacy has also contributed to a tendency within opposition groups, the cultured elite, and ultimately the younger generation to project a resistance that had not materialized during the terror regimes themselves.

This legacy extends from the dramatic reactions to the genocide against the Jews (which led to the founding of the state of Israel in 1948) to the painful reorientation of the Soviet Union to the history of Russia when the Cold War ended in the late 1980s. This legacy, on the one hand, has shaped individual attempts at coming to terms with a sense of guilt and a need for forgiveness and, on the other hand, has inspired a broadly based commitment to civil society that stood in sharp contrast to Orwell's projection of an all-encompassing system of brainwashing and physical terror, presented in the novel *1984*. The legacy was still manifest in the early 1980s when the NATO decision to station new medium-range nuclear missiles in Central Europe caused harsh political confrontations, especially in West Germany, in which the governments were accused of reenacting a Cold War scenario. Speaking for the German left intelligentsia, Günter Grass was applauded when he called the decade "Orwells Jahrzehnt" in order to denounce the pro-missile politics as totalitarian.[52] Grass defined his opposition to the NATO decision as resistance with the explicit reference to the failure of the Germans to resist Hitler's accession to power in 1933. A nation, Grass said in 1983, that still had to bear the consequences of not having resisted fifty years earlier should have learned to recognize different yet comparable dangers at the right time in order "to draw from this insight the right of resistance as a democratic demand."[53]

---

[52] Compare Günter Grass's two speeches of 1980 and 1983, "Orwells Jahrzehnt I" and "Orwells Jahrzehnt II," in his *Werkausgabe in zehn Bänden,* ed. Volker Neuhaus (Darmstadt and Neuwied, 1987), 9:775–88; 844–52.

[53] Günter Grass, "Vom Recht auf Widerstand," in his *Werkausgabe in zehn Bänden,* 9:842.

Grass's reasoning shows the extent to which the West German intellectual opposition drew legitimacy from formulating a response to the failure of the intelligentsia to resist National Socialism. What Grass articulated in the 1980s had already been used by writers and public figures throughout the 1950s, though not by the opposition party itself, the Social Democrats, which pronounced its opposition as part of the democratic process in parliament. One of the most prominent opponents of Adenauer's rearmament policy in the 1950s was Martin Niemöller, who invoked the lack of resistance under Hitler that he himself had characterized so well. Unlike Niemöller, however, who had resisted, many intellectual opponents enacted resistance as if they were still living in a dictatorial system.[54]

When writers of the Group 47 such as Günter Eich, Alfred Andersch, and Hans Magnus Enzensberger articulated their critique of Germany's moral bankruptcy behind the economic miracle, they tended to see the insulation, anxiety, and self-deception of citizens of the Federal Republic as part of an unbroken continuum reaching back to pre-1945 society. Considering the fact that Adenauer kept former Nazis such as Hans Globke and Theodor Oberländer in high government positions, the continuity seemed obvious, as the much abused line "Sind wir schon wieder so weit?" (Are we at that point again?) attested in the 1950s. Under the protective shield of the Cold War confrontation with communism, a new political presentism was allowed to evolve that sheltered German society from the moral acceptance of its very own history. (A similar phenomenon occurred in East Germany despite a more stringent policy of denazification.) While West Germans nurtured the feeling that they were actually succeeding in their efforts to normalize their history, writers demonstrated their opposition by invoking that very history as still current and by reenacting resistance within the predicament caused by it. "We have no time anymore to say Yes," Günter Eich, the most successful author of radio plays in the 1950s and a witness to the corruptive gradualism of the Nazi system, said in accepting the Büchner Prize in 1959. "If our work cannot be understood as criticism, as adversity and resistance, as an uncomfortable question and a challenge to the powers, then we write in vain, then we are positive and decorate the slaughter-house with geraniums."[55] In his poem "Ins Lesebuch für die Oberstufe," Hans Magnus Enzensberger projected a Nazi-style persecution into the everyday reality of 1957, asking the students to prepare for resistance.[56]

---

[54] Heinrich Oberreuter, "Widerstandsrecht als Aspekt politischer Kultur," in *Widerstand: Ein Problem zwischen Theorie und Geschichte,* ed. Peter Steinbach (Cologne, 1987), pp. 293–310.

[55] *Über Günter Eich,* ed. Susanne Müller-Hanpft (Frankfurt, 1970), p. 37.

[56] Hans Magnus Enzensberger, *Gedichte, 1955–1970* (Frankfurt, 1971), p. 13. For a more detailed analysis see my "Die nachgeholte Résistance: Politik und Gruppenethos im historischen Zusammenhang," in *Die Gruppe 47 in der Geschichte der*

Much of the intellectual opposition in the Federal Republic has manifested itself as a delayed resistance (a *nachgeholter Widerstand*). The frequent reference to Sartre's definition of *résistance* is hardly surprising: elevating the re-creation of the self from the active encounter with death and defeat as the core of *résistance*, as Sartre did in 1944, represents a conceptualization ex post facto; indeed, Sartre distilled his successful brand of existentialist resistance *after* the liberation from the Nazis.[57] It can be surmised that the broad appeal of Sartre's language of resistance resulted largely from its ex post facto formulation, something that finds confirmation in the success that Peter Weiss's novel *The Aesthetics of Resistance* had among the German intellectual left in the 1970s and 1980s. In this trilogy the émigré writer Weiss reconstructed the left resistance against Hitler as a vital experience and a source of a new aesthetics. While Sartre enabled his contemporaries to reenact resistance as an existential construction of the self against death and oblivion, Weiss rehabilitated the resistance as an authentic event in the form of an autobiographical novel. The *nachholender Widerstand,* the notion of recouping resistance, constituted a new source of political legitimacy after 1945; in 1968, the year of the student rebellion, this was confirmed when the right of resistance was inserted into article 20, paragraph 4, of the Basic Law of the Federal Republic.[58] After dramatic public confrontations, this right was made part of the constitution to balance the restrictive effects of the Emergency Laws. The confrontations resulted in a strong extraparliamentary opposition in Germany.

Many more legacies of the habituation to terror in everyday life are discernible. One of the more distinctive is the ambiguous ring of the search for normality that has preoccupied and will continue to preoccupy Germans in political and private life. Enzensberger even distinguished between different strategies for normality when he asserted that *Normalität* for the social sciences still appears "as a dark continent," "as an impenetrable black body which swallows the light of curiosity, of criticism, and of the ruling rationality."[59]

To be sure, the historical sciences are aware of the phenomenon of delayed resistance, yet in a rather narrow way. Before attention shifted to the disturbing attempts of conservative German historians to "normalize" the Nazi past, much of the work of liberal scholars such as Ralf Dahrendorf and

---

Bundesrepublik, ed. Justus Fetscher, Eberhard Lämmert, and Jürgen Schutte (Würzburg, 1991), pp. 9–22.

[57] Lothar Baier, "Die Résistance, ein Papiertiger?" in his *Französische Zustände: Berichte und Essays* (Frankfurt, 1985), pp. 124–51; *Resistance and Revolution in Mediterranean Europe, 1939–1948,* ed. Tony Judt (London and New York, 1989).

[58] Werner Hill, "Widerstandsrecht im Rechtsstaat," *Merkur* 37 (1983): 714–19.

[59] Hans Magnus Enzensberger, "Zur Verteidigung der Normalität," in his *Der Fliegende Robert: Gedichte, Szenen, Essays* (Frankfurt, 1989), p. 191.

Hans Ulrich Wehler amounted to an extended search for normality for which the modernized Anglo-Saxon societies served as the model and Germany the exception. As this historical phase draws to a close with the unification of Germany, a new search for normality seems unavoidable. What will the basis for the construction of a new German *Normalität* within Europe be? Which paradigm will the Germans choose: pre-1914 Germany with its preference for the exceptional, or the pre-1945 Germany with its penchant for normalizing the exceptional?

APOCALYPSE,

HUMAN SOLIDARITY,

AND THE

RESTORATION

OF POLITICS

"What Is the Law That Lies behind These Words?" Antigone's Question and the German Resistance against Hitler*

Klemens von Klemperer
Smith College

Sophocles' Antigone needs no introduction as the patron saint of resistance against established authority. Her insistence upon her duty and right to bury her brother Polyneices, even against the orders of Creon, king of Thebes, we have learned to understand as an assertion of "the gods' unwritten and unfailing law" and as superseding the ephemeral "state's decree." A close reading of the drama, however, yields no self-evident case for Antigone. She had to explain not only to the king but also to herself why she had to pay final service to her brother's corpse. Antigone prefaces her explanation with a question: "What is the law that lies behind these words?" It is this question that I should like to call attention to here, for it pertains to all manifestations of resistance and especially to that of Germany during the Third Reich.

Now, in the last decade of this century, we are at last emerging from the landscape of totalitarianism which, by virtue of its almost unprecedented oppression, generated its own antidote: resistance to oppression. As we move away from those terrible times, we are all too easily tempted to see a manichaean pattern of oppression here and resistance there, and to assume a postulate for resistance as if entering into resistance were a matter of decision on the part of all decent and right-minded people. But things were not then and have never been that simple and clear-cut. Much of the literature on the European Resistance against the Nazi tyranny has succumbed to the resistance mystique. In the German case it argued either that the *Widerstand* acted out of unquestionably noble motives or that it should have done so. The positions of the older historians like Hans Rothfels and Gerhard Ritter are, after all, not far removed from those of the so-called revisionists like Hans Mommsen and Klaus-Jürgen Müller. This position (and I deliberately say "this position" rather than "these positions") deserves reexamination. In his 1990 New Year's address, the Czechoslovak poet-president Václav Havel had the recent incidences of resistance against totalitarian oppression in Central and Eastern Europe in mind when he referred to the "contaminated moral environment"

*An earlier version of this article appeared in *Contending with Hitler: Varieties of German Resistance in the Third Reich,* ed. David Clay Large (Cambridge: Cambridge University Press, 1991). Portions © 1991 Cambridge University Press reprinted with permission.

This essay originally appeared in the *Journal of Modern History* 64, suppl. (December 1992).

which made everyone, including Havel himself, accustomed to the totalitarian regime, accepting it as an "unalterable fact." "None of us," Havel said, "is merely a victim of it, because all of us helped to create it together," and the "line of conflict" did not run between the people and the state but rather through the middle of each person: "for everyone in his or her own way is both a victim and a supporter of the system." His observations may be pertinent to our study of Nazi Germany as well.

There is, then, I propose, great wisdom in the question mark behind Antigone's attempt to identify the law that made her act: "What is the law that lies behind these words?" Resistance, which she chose as a course of action, we should understand as an extraordinary response to an extreme constraint. There are no set guidelines for resistance. Wherever and whenever it occurs, it marks a departure from established canons of law and ethics and a plunge into a realm of the uncertain and unknown.

In ordinary life not all actions call for principled decisions on our part, and it may be just as well that our actions and reactions are usually of a pragmatic nature, allowing us to go on putting one foot in front of the other. Such actions, though, are more often than not based on tradition and law. As Kierkegaard would have it, ethics in these cases is reduced to "police ordinances." Tradition and law often relieve us of making decisions of a fundamental nature and thus spare us the moral equivalent of having to reinvent the wheel.

It goes without saying that tradition is not always ethical, and neither is law always tantamount to justice. Our own laws, and certainly yesterday's laws, often conflict with what we have come to perceive as being ethical and just. We tend to obey the laws, if necessary amending them by due process in order to bring them closer to our sense of what is right and wrong and just. We tend also to avoid raising the question of ethics too often and to coast along with tradition and law in a business-as-usual fashion. It stands to reason that in normal times pragmatism rules supreme—pragmatism or, if you wish, callousness.

But all this is bound to change in times that are not "normal," in extreme situations when tradition is being perverted and the law itself is issued to enforce injustice, and when, as a consequence, the business-as-usual approach can no longer do. Antigone had to stand up for her brother and defy her king, who was courting the gods' wrath. The path that she chose, however, was unpaved and the laws that she invoked were unwritten. It was the Chorus that had the last word in the dialogue with Antigone: "Your self-sufficiency has brought you down." Antigone was, after all, a tragic figure.

The extreme situation of constraint and oppression certainly gave legitimacy to all manifestations of resistance in the era of the Third Reich. In every country under the Nazi yoke there were men and women who took the law into their own hands in order to make an end to the regime. In the resistance on both sides of the trenches, so to speak, the challenge of the Third Reich elicited a leap into the unknown and a vision of standing at the threshold of a new age. But let me turn here to a special scrutiny of the German *Widerstand.* I should like to argue that it was the German Resistance in particular that stood under the sign of Antigone's question.

In Germany above all, the "line of conflict" about which Havel wrote was not clearly drawn; the evil of nazism was not as manifest as it was in the occupied territories. The resistance movements in France, in Holland, and in Norway, whatever their indecisions and divisions, it must be remembered, were directed against occupation and oppression by a foreign power. Their struggle for liberation was a clear and unquestioned assertion of national interests as well as of human rights. But the German Resistance against Hitler had no such clear mandate. There was terror, of course, but also something even more bedeviling than terror, namely, the Nazi regime's semblance of legality, respectability, and cleanliness. Dietrich Bonhoeffer remarked on this in a moving and perceptive passage in his minute, "After Ten Years," written for his friends at Christmastime 1942: "The great masquerade of evil has played havoc with all our ethical concepts. For evil to appear as light, charity, historical necessity, or social justice is quite bewildering to anyone brought up on our traditional ethical concepts, while for the Christian who bases his life on the Bible it merely confirms the fundamental wickedness of evil."[1]

This passage was written at a time when the evil of nazism should have been manifest. Bonhoeffer had clearly in mind the spell that nazism exercised in Germany into the war years and, thus, made resistance so difficult. The promise of national rebirth, the freeing from the chains of Versailles, the overcoming of economic crisis and unemployment, and the hopes for a *Volksgemeinschaft* rising above haggling party interests and competing classes had made National Socialism in Germany an enormous "temptation."[2] By its very nature the plot against the regime was out of step with the immediate national effort, indeed the waging of the war, and was subversive of what appeared to be the national interest. The success of the plot after all would have meant defeat for the fatherland. The heroism of the plotters bordered on treason; resistance bordered on defeatism. What a stigma!

Backed up by terror, the masquerade of evil and widespread consensus largely account for the fact that resistance in Germany was scattered. The identification of the Nazi regime with the national cause before, and even more so after the outbreak of the war, discouraged the formation of a resistance movement. It blurred the line of conflict and also blinded the

---

[1] Dietrich Bonhoeffer, "After Ten Years," in *Letters and Papers from Prison,* ed. Eberhard Bethge, enlarged ed. (New York, 1972), p. 4.

[2] Fritz Stern, "National Socialism as Temptation," in his *Dreams and Delusions* (New York, 1987), pp. 147–91.

political judgment of large sectors of the middle and upper classes, including many of those who themselves later moved into the Resistance. It was largely responsible for what Pater Max Pribilla called the "weakness of the beginning" of the German Resistance.[3] There was, moreover, no widespread "social support"[4] for resistance work at home such as was available, at least latently, to the resistance movements elsewhere. Even there, we are told, joining the Resistance was frequently a matter of whim or accident; but the French Fifis and the Yugoslav Chetniks or Partisans were tangible, even if secret, units. But in the Reich there was no resistance movement as such, and the resisters were, as they have been called, " 'strangers' among their own people."[5] Not even the word *Widerstand* was in currency. "We did not consider ourselves as belonging to a *Widerstand,*" attested one of the few survivors of the German Resistance; "we merely wanted to survive in decency."[6]

The point I am trying to make here is that, lacking a clear and undisputed mandate as well as an overall organization, the German Resistance was altogether left to its own devices. I should add here that in Germany in particular, where the doctrine of natural law never really had found a home, there has always prevailed a presumption in favor of obedience. Bonhoeffer addressed himself to this proposition also in the minute for his friends to which I alluded earlier. In his chapter on "civil courage" he pointed to the fact that in their history the Germans had learned the need for and the strength of obedience, but in so doing they had come to misjudge the world. They did not realize that their submissiveness and self-sacrifice could be exploited for evil ends. Only now, Bonhoeffer concluded, were the Germans beginning to discover the meaning of what he called "free and responsible action."[7] In the German case, therefore, the road to resistance was altogether uncharted. Its lack of obvious mandate, identity, and tradition conferred upon it the quality of what Eberhard Bethge, Bonhoeffer's friend, called an "independent risk."[8] The need of the immediate situation propelled the Germans of the Resistance.

---

[3] Europäische Publikationen e.V., ed., *Vollmacht des Gewissens* (Frankfurt am Main and Berlin, 1960), 1:21–22.

[4] Barrington Moore, Jr., *Injustice: The Social Bases of Obedience and Revolt* (London, 1978), p. 97.

[5] Hans-Adolf Jacobsen, "Deutscher Widerstand gegen das nationalsozialistische Regime, 1933–1945," in *"Spiegelbild einer Verschwörung,"* ed. Hans-Adolf Jacobsen (Stuttgart, 1984), p. xxiii.

[6] Mrs. Marie-Luise Sarre, interview with author, March 8, 1978.

[7] Bonhoeffer, p. 6.

[8] Eberhard Bethge, "Adam von Trott und der deutsche Widerstand," *Vierteljahrshefte für Zeitgeschichte* 11 (July 1963): 217.

To the horrors perpetrated in their own country theirs was a truly extraordinary response, "exceptional" and unprecedented.[9] At the same time they in particular were indeed "self-sufficient" in Sophocles' sense. Choosing to follow laws that were unwritten, they overstepped tradition and the written law. But were these laws unfailing? For the moment at least we have reason to suggest that Antigone's question is of paramount significance for our study of the German Resistance.

Recently my attention has been directed to the incidence of the "solitary witnesses" on the scene of German resistance. I am thinking of Johann Georg Elser, Kurt Gerstein, Michael Lerpscher, Franz Jägerstätter, John Rittmeister, Fritz Kolbe (alias George Wood), Eduard Schulte. Johann Georg Elser is well known, of course, in connection with his attempt to blow up Hitler in Munich in November 1939, as is Kurt Gerstein, the "spy of God," who all by himself set out to expose Hitler's euthanasia program. Michael Lerpscher, son of a peasant from the Allgäu, and Franz Jägerstätter, a peasant from Upper Austria, both deeply religious, went to their deaths as conscientious objectors, Lerpscher in 1940 and Jägerstätter in 1943. John Rittmeister, a psychiatrist from Hamburg, charted his course "away from beaten paths,"[10] as he himself put it, helping the oppressed and seeking connections with other dissenters, including Harro Schultze-Boysen of the communist "Red Orchestra," until the Nazi bloodhounds caught up with him in mid-1942. Fritz Kolbe, a courier for the German Foreign Office, carried vital diplomatic and military intelligence across the Swiss border to President Roosevelt's Special Representative, Allen W. Dulles. Generaldirektor Eduard Schulte of the Giesche-Werke in Upper Silesia, a not particularly politically minded man who belonged neither to a persecuted group nor to any of the oppositional circles, took abroad information concerning the Final Solution as well as German military plans. And there were many more of this kind. "Wir waren Einzelkämpfer," reminisced Chaplain Carl Klinkhammer who was repeatedly sentenced by the Nazis to jail. His bishop was all too eager to disavow him: "I have nothing to do with this."[11]

My purpose here, however, is not to present you with some marginal figures who also should be given a place in the studies on the German Resistance. It is precisely these "solitary witnesses" or *Einzelkämpfer,* I should like to argue,

[9] Ibid.
[10] Quoted in Walter Bräutigam, *John Rittmeister—Leben und Sterben* (Ebenhausen nr. Munich, 1987), p. 12.
[11] "Bericht von Kaplan Carl Klinkhammer," in *Gegner des Nationalsozialismus: Wissenschaftler und Widerstandskämpfer auf der Suche nach historischer Wirklichkeit,* ed. Christoph Kleβmann and Falk Pingel (Frankfurt am Main and New York, 1980), p. 261.

who were at the very heart of the German Resistance experience. "And you are not ashamed to think alone?" Creon asked Antigone; and she answered: "No, I am not ashamed." All the German resisters thought alone and were not ashamed of doing so. In the last analysis all were solitary witnesses: an Ewald von Kleist-Schmenzin, a Trott, a Moltke. Entering into resistance entailed for each of them an existential leap, like Antigone's, into self-sufficiency and loneliness. Karl Dietrich Bracher picked up on this theme, writing about the "terrible loneliness" that the move into resistance entailed, "the terrible loneliness in the midst of a mass society,"[12] a loneliness that might be shared with a friend or at most with a group of friends but not with a larger group or institution.

I have moved the solitary witnesses into the center stage of resistance studies, a proposition that seems to fly in the face of the direction such studies have taken during the last three decades. Resistance—in our case the *Widerstand*—has become the object of "historization" whose primary thrust has been to demythologize and to "demonumentalize" resistance and to identify its societal, supraindividual preconditions. The general debate, especially among West German historians, as to whether National Socialism can be identified in terms of the policies of the Nazi elite, or whether it must be seen in the structural context of German history and society, has naturally had reverberations in the field of resistance studies. In the course of this argument, too, motives were downgraded, and in turn the connections (especially of the conservative Resistance) with the infrastructure of history and society were stressed. Thus the ethical impulses of the *Widerstand,* while never wholly questioned, were brought down to earth and coupled with attitudes and positions that were rooted in traditionalist but not really liberal-democratic notions.

The studies of the Munich Institute have also furthered our grasp of resistance by identifying the halfway concept of *Resistenz*[13]—to which Richard Löwenthal, for good reasons, prefers the term "refusal" *(Verweigerung)*[14]—a restricted resistance that was a matter not primarily of principle but of less spectacular forms of nonconformity. Alongside the widespread incidence of individual *Resistenz,* institutional *Resistenz* or refusal was generally offered by the traditional establishments with the aim of

[12] Karl Dietrich Bracher, "Anfänge der deutschen Widerstandsbewegung," in his *Deutschland zwischen Demokratie und Diktatur* (Bern, Munich, and Vienna, 1964), p. 263.

[13] Martin Broszat, "Resistenz und Widerstand," in Martin Broszat et al., *Bayern in der NS-Zeit* (Munich, 1981), 4:691–709.

[14] *Gesellschaftliche Verweigerung:* Richard Löwenthal, "Widerstand im totalen Staat," in *Widerstand und Verweigerung in Deutschland, 1933–1945,* ed. Richard Löwenthal and Patrick von zur Mühlen (Berlin and Bonn, 1982), pp. 14, 18 ff.

preserving their special interests, that is, their autonomy vis-à-vis the regime and the process of "coordination" *(Gleichschaltung)*. *Resistenz* was value-free resistance of sorts, and institutional *Resistenz* in particular had a tendency to obviate the need for outright resistance.

Historizing resistance, however necessary, should not stop short of the dimension of the individual and the lonely conscience of the individual. Large groups as such did not and could not offer resistance. The assumption that resistance can be expected en bloc from industrialists, officers, and churchmen is altogether fallacious. If anything, such groups are disposed to conform, if not actually to collaborate. At best they practiced *Resistenz*. But the latter, we must realize, was a weed of sorts that may look to us historians like the real stuff—like resistance—but is not. And we should not allow the weed to take over and to smother, as it always has a tendency to do, that precious plant in our garden, resistance to tyranny.

What Peter Hüttenberger called the *Repräsentationstheorie* of *Widerstand* (the predominantly sociological approach to resistance)[15] tends to stop short of the existential dimension of resistance as I see it, the autonomous decision of the individual acting in solitude and following the commands of his or her own conscience. A caveat, then, to resistance historians against an all too pervasive reliance on group or class action. Resistance in Germany remained above all the preserve of individuals and of small groups. Of course it can and must be argued that for their behavior there are certain historical and sociological determinants at play; but these mostly point in the direction of conformity or *Resistenz*. All the more does the move into resistance constitute an "exceptional" leap into a situation that defies historical and social stereotypes. In resistance the "solitary witness" emerges supreme.

"Opposition to Hitler," wrote Fabian von Schlabrendorff (and he meant resistance), "began . . . not as an organized political movement, but as the reaction of individuals with religious and moral convictions to the theories, and later to the practices, of National Socialism."[16] Indeed, Axel von dem Bussche explicitly cautioned historians against sociologizing resistance stud-ies, against connecting resistance—and undoubtedly he had the *Widerstand* in mind—with group action. In the occupied countries, where the immediate national interest cemented a bond between the individuals, this may have been a different matter. But in accounting for his own experiences, von dem Bussche wrote that it was a matter of individual decision on the grounds of

---

[15] Peter Hüttenberger, "Vorüberlegungen zum 'Widerstandsbegriff,' " in *Theorien in der Praxis des Historikers,* ed. Jürgen Kocka (Göttingen, 1977), p. 118.
[16] Fabian von Schlabrendorff, *The Secret War against Hitler* (New York, Toronto, and London), p. 34.

"experiences and motivation."[17] In his own case and in that of General Helmuth Stieff, motivation was derived from experiences in Poland.

Eventually, some of these individuals came together in small groups, drawn from their friends, their social circle, their regiment. In the case of von dem Bussche as well as Henning von Tresckow and Fritz-Dietlof von der Schulenburg, it was the renowned IR 9 regiment from Potsdam. But the small group necessarily remains the nucleus of resistance. It was Helmuth James von Moltke who so insistently made reference to the solitude of the German resister in his communications to his English friend Lionel Curtis. In November 1937 he recounted the "absolute loneliness in major questions" that "harassed" him,[18] and in the letter of March 1943, which did not reach its destination before July, he lamented the lack of unity, the lack of men, and finally the lack of communication that plagued the German Resistance, citing in particular the inability to use the telephone, the post, to send a messenger, or even to speak with those with whom you are completely *d'accord*.[19] Solitude, we might summarize, was a major problem for the German Resistance, but it in turn lent it the strength of conviction. Moltke and his friends were not ashamed to "think alone."

So far I have emphasized a particular aspect of the story of the German Resistance that the evolving discussions on the *Widerstand* should not lose sight of. The historization of the Resistance should not stop short of the individual; it must penetrate to the singularity of the act of resistance. If anything, conformity, collaboration, and *Resistenz* are of one and the same order; they do not cross the "state's decree"; not even *Resistenz* does. Resistance is of a unique and "exceptional" order. While I stand ready to endorse wholeheartedly the historization of resistance, I see the need of voicing a caveat against excessive sociologization of resistance. Sociological analysis comes, in a subsidiary way, in the course of any examination of programs, war and peace aims, and like matters. With respect to the question of motivation, however, we cannot settle on a simple equation between any group—occupational, social, economic, religious—and resistance. The solitary witness emerges as the prototype of the resister.

And yet we are still left with Antigone's question: "What is the law the lies behind these words?" She went to "the furthest verge of daring"—and so did the German resisters. Their furthest verge of daring was tyrannicide, the risk of treason and defeat. Tyrannicide was certainly a matter of conscience for

---

[17] "Bericht von Axel von dem Bussche," in Kleβmann and Pingel, eds., pp. 272–75.

[18] Letter from Helmuth James von Moltke to Lionel Curtis, Berlin, November 11, 1937, Curtis Papers Box 28, Bodleian Library, Oxford University.

[19] Letter from Moltke to Curtis, Stockholm, March 25, 1943, in Michael Balfour and Julian Frisby, *Helmuth von Moltke: A Leader against Hitler* (London, 1972), p. 217.

each of the plotters. Although Goerdeler and Moltke held on to their misgivings concerning assassination, for the core of the conspirators, including of course Stauffenberg himself, it constituted without question the lesser evil.

Treason was the risk that all the conspirators knowingly incurred. I name here only Ewald von Kleist-Schmenzin, Hans Oster, Goerdeler, Stauffenberg. All resistance of course borders on treason. By itself treason is not an honorable deed as it connotes betrayal of trust and, in the public domain, an offense against the interests of one's own country. The context of resistance, however, tends to lend dignity to treason and thus to redeem it. Political resistance in itself is an extreme act in an extreme situation in which citizens are denied recourse to legal procedure or to open political opposition. In such a setting treason becomes an extreme manifestation of resistance. Stauffenberg as much as conceded that anyone who had the courage to do what he planned to do "must do so in the knowledge that he will go down in German history as a traitor." And, he added, if he did not do it, he would be a "traitor to his own conscience."[20] The German criminal law of course makes a distinction between *Hochverrat* (high treason) and *Landesverrat* (betrayal of the country), which lent a certain grudging respectability to the former but in turn marked the latter with a singular stigma. To the end Goerdeler maintained that he had committed *Hochverrat* though not *Landesverrat*. But certainly all those, including Goerdeler himself, who in time of war entered into a dialogue with the enemy, were hovering on the threshold of the graver form of treason. They all risked the defeat of their own country. "The shortest way to defeat," Kleist-Schmenzin said sometime before the outbreak of the war to British journalist Ian Colvin, "will be the most merciful."[21] We must try to understand the degree of despair it must have taken a German patriot like this Pomeranian nobleman to think this way, to say this and to act accordingly. And if Dietrich Bonhoeffer really said, at the height of the German war effort in September 1941, that he prayed for the defeat of his country, he did so not lightheartedly. This was the only way, so he argued, to pay for the suffering that Germany had caused to the world. He and his coconspirators were caught in a painful conflict between their love of country and their distaste for the criminal Nazi regime.

It remains for us, then, to probe into the texture of the self-sufficiency of the German resisters. They clearly overstepped the written laws and tradition and chose to follow the laws that were unwritten. They clearly went to "the

[20] Quoted in Joachim Kramarz, *Stauffenberg: The Architect of the Famous July 20th Conspiracy to Assassinate Hitler* (New York, 1967), p. 185.

[21] Quoted in Ian Colvin, *Master Spy* (New York, London, and Toronto, 1952), p. 125.

furthest verge of daring." It should be remembered, however, that German legal practice has specified that the graver form of treason, *Landesverrat,* depends on the criterion of "general motivation." Assuming that the latter was to prevent even greater damage to the Reich than would have been caused by the treasonous act, the charge of *Landesverrat* would not apply. Hitler and Ribbentrop, so Theo Kordt argued, were the ones who committed treason "against the highest interests of the German people."[22] He and his friends had established contact with the British government "not to serve the interests of British policies but to save Germany and the West from a catastrophe."[23] The self-sufficiency of the *Widerstand* was anything but self-serving; instead it was a leap into the service of a higher good.

Antigone's self-sufficiency and daring were finally redeemed, and the question, "What is the law that lies behind these words?" found an answer in terms of her appeal to "the gods' unwritten and unfailing laws." The deeds of the German resisters were similarly directed to a higher purpose. The solitary witness established an identification with a higher sense of community. Franz Jägerstätter, to come back to this stubborn and saintly peasant, was confident that he was, as he wrote to his wife, putting the future into "the hands of God": "He will direct everything for our good. We are called upon after all to fear God more than men." Adam von Trott, who had made it his part in the Resistance to build bridges to the outside world, in his somewhat awkward English wrote to a Swedish friend of the necessity of a "movement springing from solidaric and representative minds in the whole of Christian Europe."[24] And when the dying Stauffenberg invoked the "holy Germany," he gave expression to the same dimension. For some, resisting was a religious obligation; for others it was a matter of identification with a Christian Europe, with a newly found Germany, or with basic human rights. For themselves as well as for posterity all these "solitary witnesses" answered the question asked by Antigone.

---

[22] Theo Kordt, "Wir wollten den Frieden retten," *Stuttgarter Rundschau* 8 (1948): 13.
[23] Ibid.
[24] Letter from Adam von Trott zu Solz to Dr. Harry Johansson, Hälsingborg, September 26, 1942, Archive of the Nordiska Ekumeniska Institutet, Sigtuna: Svensk Korrespondens, E:I:2, även "Hemlig."

The German Resistance against Hitler and the Restoration of Politics*

Hans Mommsen
Ruhr-Universität Bochum

In the first years after the war, contemporary historical research often turned its attention to the German resistance to Hitler. By emphasizing the "Other Germany" researchers sought to combat the belief that Germans as a whole had been responsible for the National Socialist dictatorship and its crimes, and that the dictatorship was a logical consequence of German history.[1] In addition to this apologetic tendency, an attempt emerged early on to see in the history of the German resistance a secondary legitimation for the existence of the two German states. What resulted were two portrayals of the resistance—one in the Federal Republic, the other in the German Democratic Republic (GDR)—that were essentially mirror images of one another. Only in the 1970s did this antithesis begin to subside. In West Germany, working-class resistance and the activities of the illegal German Communist Party (KPD) above all drew increased attention. At the same time, historians in the GDR gradually indicated their readiness to exempt the bourgeois resistance from the verdict of "imperialism" and to accept the resisters, at least in part, due to their advocacy for peace. They were in no way willing to give up the claim that the KPD had played the leading role in the resistance.[2]

In the light of the current situation, these arguments have lost their rationale. Instead, the collapse of the German Socialist Unity Party (SED) regime raises the question of why the Protestant and Catholic churches became, at least in part, places of refuge for the opposition under the communist system, while the church hierarchies, with few exceptions, engaged in no political resistance during the period of the Third Reich. They confined their efforts to defending their own position, although there were specific differences between the comparatively unified stance of the Catholic clergy, on the one hand, and the sharp conflicts between the Nazi-influenced Deutschekirche and the representatives of the Confessing

* Translated for the *Journal of Modern History* by Stephen Duffy.

[1] See the brief overview by Klaus-Jürgen Müller and Hans Mommsen, "Der deutsche Widerstand gegen das NS-Regime: Zur Historiographie des Widerstands," in *Der deutsche Widerstand, 1933–1945,* ed. Klaus-Jürgen Müller, 2d ed. (Paderborn, 1990), pp. 13–21, and the more specialized literature listed there.

[2] See ibid., pp. 14 ff.; and Hans Mommsen, "Der 20. Juli 1944 in der historiographischen Sicht des geteilten Deutschland," *Politik und Kultur* 11 (1984): 9–20.

This essay originally appeared in the *Journal of Modern History* 64, suppl. (December 1992).

Church, on the other. But even the resistance of the latter did not extend beyond the ecclesiastical realm.[3] With the end of the East-West conflict, the influence of anticommunist ideas on the evaluation of the political wings of the German resistance has diminished, although there is still considerable reluctance in the West German public to recognize Soviet collaborationist groups like the Rote Kapelle, the Nationalkomitee Freies Deutschland, and the Bund Deutscher Offiziere as a legitimate part of the opposition to Hitler.[4]

Since the social-liberal coalition and in connection with a changing attitude in historical research, a readiness to view the resistance in all its forms as the expression of an antifascist consensus has emerged. Martin Broszat saw in this "one of the irrefutable elements of the political culture of the Federal Republic."[5] At the same time, a critically distanced perspective on the history of the resistance has developed that has been able to focus more clearly on its political ambivalence. As a result, the previously dominant dualistic approach, which had been tied to a theory of totalitarianism and to the assumption of an inner unity in the National Socialist system of domination, was overcome.[6] The earlier one-sided emphasis on the July 20 movement, whose representatives had been viewed primarily in aesthetic and/or moral categories, also gradually disappeared. In contrast, the new perspective sought to analyze the entire spectrum of oppositional activities, and directed its inquiries toward the degree of penetration of the National Socialist regime into society and toward the extent of dissent and resistance.[7]

In the treatment of the many facets of the German resistance to Hitler, reflections on what chance of success the various and changing constellations may have had has receded in importance. There is widespread agreement that

[3] On this issue, see Heinz Hürten, "Selbstbehauptung und Widerstand der katholischen Kirche," in Müller, ed., pp. 155 ff. Hürten is interested primarily in ideological resistance. See also Günter van Norden, "Widerstand in der Kirche," in *Widerstand und Verweigerung in Deutschland 1933 bis 1945,* ed. Richard Löwenthal and Patrick von zur Mühlen, 2d ed. (Berlin, 1986), pp. 11–128; and Kurt Meier, *Der evangelische Kirchenkampf* (Göttingen, 1984), pp. 587 ff.

[4] See Alexander Fischer, "Die Bewegung 'Freies Deutschland' in der Sowjetunion: Widerstand hinter Stacheldraht," in *Der Widerstand gegen den Nationalsozialismus: Die deutsche Gesellschaft und der Widerstand gegen Hitler,* ed. Peter Steinbach and Jürgen Schmädeke (Munich, 1985), pp. 954 ff.

[5] Martin Broszat, *Nach Hitler: Der schwierige Umgang mit unserer Geschichte* (Munich, 1988), p. 317.

[6] See Hans Mommsen, "Die Geschichte des deutschen Widerstands im Lichte der neueren Forschung," *Aus Politik und Zeitgeschichte* B50 (1986): 3–18.

[7] The basic reference is Martin Broszat, "Resistenz und Widerstand: Eine Zwischenbilanz des Forschungsprojekts 'Widerstand und Verfolgung in Bayern, 1933–1945,'" in his *Nach Hitler,* pp. 136 ff. See also Ian Kershaw, *Popular Opinion and Political Dissent in the Third Reich: Bavaria, 1933–1945* (Oxford, 1983).

even a successful assassination would scarcely have led to a realization of the political plans that had been developed by the conspirators; it might not even have led to the formation of a new government prior to the impending military defeat. On the other hand, greater weight has been placed on questions concerning the conditions that produced, or made possible, opposition and resistance. Such inquiries throw new light on the inner structure of the regime and on the attitude of the population as a whole.[8] The following discussion aims to elaborate the anthropological dimension of resistance activity, without disguising its specifically political character.

The German resistance to Hitler encompassed very different political and social groups. It did not constitute, in any strict sense, a unified movement. Even the Social Democrats and the Communists were never able to overcome their conflicts over political directions. Typologically, one can distinguish two phases of resistance. The first was associated with the political organizations of the Weimar Republic and included, above all, the political left. The Social Democratic groups that had resolved upon conspiratorial activity, such as the "New Beginning," the Revolutionary Socialists, and the German Popular Front, stood in some contrast to SOPADE, the exile organization of the German Social Democratic Party (SPD). The latter sought, by means of the Border Offices, to establish contact with resistance groups forming at the local level.[9]

Parallel to these activities, the illegal organization of the KPD tried, under the influence of the Comintern, to maintain an organizational network that could serve as the backbone for a mass party in a revolutionary situation. Against these efforts the Gestapo waged a ceaseless battle. Although the KPD succeeded in winning over a significant portion of its earlier membership for illegal activity, its strategy was doomed in the long run to failure, since the Gestapo kept such close watch on and, indeed, controlled the illegal organization. Whenever the conspiratorial apparatus grew large enough to establish contacts with potential sympathizers and to agitate for communist ideas, the Gestapo attacked. Hence, despite its declared intention to do so, the KPD never succeeded in mobilizing for its cause significant numbers of sympathizers outside its original membership.[10]

In contrast to the socialist, communist, and diverse Catholic opposition groups, the second stage of resistance was characterized by the absence of any organization in the traditional sense. The July 20, 1944, movement consisted of groups of individuals loosely connected to one another and arose on the basis

---

[8] Broszat has noted: "Research into the resistance has expanded into the study of the social history of political conduct in Germany" (*Nach Hitler*, p. 234).

[9] See the overview by Detlev J. K. Peukert, "Der deutsche Arbeiterwiderstand," in Müller, ed., pp. 163 ff.

[10] See ibid., pp. 165 ff.; and Hermann Weber, "Die KPD in der Illegalität," in Löwenthal and von zur Mühlen, eds., pp. 83–102.

of personal acquaintance in the few social niches that had not been fully destroyed by the National Socialists. Such was the case for the contacts which Carl Goerdeler, who retired as mayor of Leipzig in 1936, sought to establish with generally conservative-minded dignitaries and with the Leadership Circle of the United Trade Unions (Führerkreis der Vereinigten Gewerkschaften), Jakob Kaiser and Wilhelm Leuschner. Goerdeler's coalition with the union leaders was undertaken in order to obtain support among the population for the emerging bourgeois-military opposition. Wilhelm Leuschner's contact with Goerdeler was based on the latter's status as a civilian representative of the military opposition. This link was intended to safeguard the interests of the former trade unions in the event of a return to political conditions such as had existed under the chancellorship of von Schleicher. At that stage Leuschner rejected an active role for labor in the overthrow of the regime.[11]

Goerdeler maintained close contacts with former Chief of the General Staff Ludwig Beck, initially with the ambassador Ulrich von Hassell, and with the Prussian finance minister Johannes Popitz. He also had numerous personal relationships with highly placed individuals in the government and in the army. The informal character of these relationships has made it impossible, even today, to distinguish with certainty between sympathizers and cocon-spirators among Goerdeler's many contacts. There were, to be sure, initiatives toward common planning in the period after the campaign in France. Von Hassell and Popitz as well as the economist Jens Jessen were involved in them. Apart from the trade union group, whose Catholic representatives did have a point of support in the Ketteler House in Cologne and in the Walberberg Monastery, there were virtually no formal discussions among the individuals who stood in contact with Goerdeler. The decisive political plans, which found expression in numerous memoranda by Goerdeler, were as a rule fashioned by him alone. Only to a secondary degree were they influenced by the ideas of third parties. One exception to this was the plan concerning the German Trade Union, which was composed at Leuschner's behest. But it coincided with Goerdeler's scheme to transfer to the trade unions large segments of the social security system, in particular the unemployment insurance system.[12]

The Kreisau circle rejected all institutionalized cooperation but placed great value upon joint discussions. It emerged from the friendship between

[11] Hans Mommsen, "Wilhelm Leuschner und die Widerstandsbewegung des 20. Juli 1944," in *Das Unrechtsregime: Internationale Forschung über den National-sozialismus,* ed. Ursula Büttner (Hamburg, 1986), 1:116 ff.

[12] See Gerhard Ritter, *Carl Goerdeler und die deutsche Widerstandsbewegung* (Munich, 1964), pp. 304 ff.; and Goerdeler's memorandum, "Das Ziel," in *Beck und Goerdeler: Gemeinschaftsdokumente für den Frieden, 1941–44,* ed. Wilhelm Ritter von Schramm (Munich, 1965), pp. 116 ff.

Helmuth James von Moltke and Peter Graf Yorck von Wartenburg that had begun prior to 1933. Because early participants were primarily members of the high nobility it became known as the "Grafenkreis." The three Kreisau meetings that put forward common position papers were attended by only a handful of individuals with similar political convictions, and their composition varied according to the issue under discussion.[13] Around a small circle of individuals sharing common ethical values there ranged a broader group of experts and representatives of various social groups who prepared memoranda on particular issues or who were drawn upon as consultants. The group took on a particular political coloration insofar as Moltke was concerned to attract representatives of the Christian churches and of labor and to win them over to his ideas.[14]

In this latter attempt he had limited success. The socialist members of the Kreisau circle were mainly intellectuals who had been active primarily on the right wing of the SPD. Despite his academic background, Julius Leber, whom Moltke sought to attract after Carlo Mierendorff's death in December 1943, stood far closer to the workers by virtue of his activity as a Social Democratic journalist and as leader of the party in Lübeck.[15] Moltke sensed that there was an unbridgeable distance between himself and Leber. In contrast to Moltke, the former labor leader expected a certain continuity in the various political platforms, which the Nazi domination only concealed.[16] Moltke exerted his efforts toward establishing common basic principles and a common program for the inner circle. Until his arrest, he spent an enormous amount of energy trying to bring about the necessary compromises and agreements. He overestimated the degree of intellectual agreement among his followers, as can be seen clearly on closer examination of the Kreisau documents.[17]

[13] See Ger van Roon, *German Resistance to Hitler: Count von Moltke and the Kreisau Circle* (London, 1971), pp. 110 ff., 140 ff.; Wilhelm Ernst Winterhager, *Der Kreisauer Kreis: Porträt einer Widerstandsgruppe* (Berlin, 1985), pp. 83 ff.; Roman Bleistein, ed., *Dossier Kreisauer Kreis: Dokumente aus dem Widerstand gegen den Nationalsozialismus* (Frankfurt, 1987), pp. 33 ff. and passim.

[14] See Winterhager, pp. 10 ff.

[15] See van Roon, *German Resistance to Hitler*, pp. 122 ff.; Freya von Moltke, *Helmuth James von Moltke, 1907–1945: Anwalt der Zukunft* (Stuttgart, 1975; trans. of Michael Balfour and Julian Frisby, *Helmuth von Moltke: A Leader against Hitler* [London, 1972]), pp. 180, 232; and Hans Mommsen, *Der 20. Juli und die deutsche Arbeiterbewegung*, Gedenkstätte deutscher Widerstand: Beiträge zum Widerstand, 1933–45 (Berlin, 1985), 48:17 ff.

[16] See Hans-Adolf Jacobsen, ed., *Spiegelbild einer Verschwörung: Die Kaltenbrunner-Berichte an Bormann und Hitler über das Attentat des 20. Juli 1944*, 2 vols. (Stuttgart, 1984), p. 497. See also Dorothea Beck, *Julius Leber: Sozialdemokrat zwischen Reform und Widerstand* (Berlin, 1983), pp. 183 ff.

[17] See Helmuth James von Moltke, *Briefe an Freya, 1939–1945*, ed. Beate Ruhm von Oppen (Munich, 1988), esp. letters of July 8, 13, 14, and 15, 1942 (pp. 390 ff. and passim).

For Goerdeler, as for the Kreisau group, the renunciation of all forms of conspiratorial organization was in no way a result of tactical considerations. As dignitaries and high officials, occupying leading positions in administration and diplomatic affairs, they saw no need to create, even in a rudimentary form, a political organization in the traditional sense. It was only after the German attack upon the Soviet Union that the representatives of the national conservative resistance had to face the problem of making their political legitimacy credible. Goerdeler's search for support among representatives of the former Christian and free trade unions constituted a first step in this direction.[18] But it was not until the latter half of 1943 that the idea of seeking stronger organizational ties to the general populace took shape. Characteristically, the suggestion to create a nonpartisan popular movement came from the socialist Carlo Mierendorff.[19] It is understandable that differences in political orientation, which to this point had seemed secondary, now broke out in full force, and that a consensus proved impossible to attain prior to the assassination attempt by Claus Schenk von Stauffenberg.[20]

The fact that the movement of July 20 was so largely composed of high officials contributed in no small way to the movement's remaining essentially undiscovered prior to the assassination attempt. By contrast, all forms of organized resistance had fallen victim to Gestapo terror. But the Gestapo proved unable to distinguish between the general dissatisfaction that was then emerging and a serious opposition movement. In fact, the boundary between the two was a shifting one, and the circle of conspirators changed with time. The new edition of Ulrich von Hassell's diaries demonstrates how tenuous the lines of communication were even among the inner circle of conspirators.[21] External factors such as the effects of the aerial bombardment played a role here, too.

With these limitations in mind, one can still question what the positive points of agreement were among those elements on this "second stage" of resistance that came together in the assassination attempt of July 20, 1944. In the early phases, from 1938 until 1940, an implicit consensus existed among

---

[18] Hans Mommsen, "Gesellschaftsbild und Verfassungspläne des deutschen Widerstands," in *Widerstand im Dritten Reich: Probleme, Ereignisse, Gestalten,* ed. Hermann Graml (Frankfurt, 1984), p. 69; English version in *From Weimar to Auschwitz* (Princeton, N.J., 1991).

[19] Most recently, Christoph Klessmann, "Das Problem der 'Volksbewegung' im deutschen Widerstand," in Steinbach and Schmädeke, eds. (n. 4 above), pp. 828 ff.

[20] Mommsen, "Gesellschaftsbild und Verfassungspläne des deutschen Widerstands," pp. 79 ff.

[21] Friedrich Freiherr Hiller von Gaertringen, ed., *Die Hassel-Tagebücher, 1938–1944: Ulrich von Hassell: Aufzeichnungen vom Andern Deutschland,* rev. ed. (Berlin, 1988).

the conspirators on the chief features of the changes they were seeking. For them the late presidential system under von Papen and von Schleicher was the model, though there were differences over details. Their program included assent in principle to a restoration of the Hohenzollern monarchy, something that Goerdeler actively pursued, though this was to fail owing to the opposition of the crown prince Louis Ferdinand and to the veto from Doorn, the residence of the exiled emperor in Holland.[22] For the early military opposition, such solutions, which Ludwig Beck had pondered as early as 1934, were obvious. In some respects what the national conservatives wanted was to carry forward under an authoritarian, corporative banner the "national regeneration" that had taken a wrong turn with Hitler in 1933.[23]

This constellation changed fundamentally after 1941. While the military opposition was first reshaped under the leadership of Henning von Tresckow, chief of staff of the Army Group Center and later colonel at the Armed Forces High Command, the Bendlerstrasse, and, subsequently, under his successor, Claus Schenk von Stauffenberg, the civilian resistance groups began to develop comprehensive reform plans for a post–National Socialist government. To a certain extent, this already signaled a departure by opposition figures from their earlier belief that they could function as born leaders of the nation. Still, for foreign observers it must have remained a strange spectacle, how much time and energy the two wings of the national conservative opposition, the Goerdeler group and the Kreisau circle, devoted to the elaboration of constitutional and social-political principles as well as to manifold reform plans, instead of concentrating their efforts pragmatically on the overthrow of the system.[24]

This can be explained in part by the fact that, for the overwhelming majority of people at that time, a return to the Weimar constitution seemed out of the question. The conspirators, who came from the conservative camp or who stood under the influence of neoconservative ideas, regarded Hitler and the National Socialist mass movement as consequences of the "over-democratization" of Weimar.[25] There was, moreover, a general rejection of the principle of parliamentarianism in continental Europe, with the exception of

[22] For the restoration plans, see Ritter (n. 12 above), pp. 309 ff.

[23] See Hans Mommsen, "Verfassungs- und Verwaltungsreformpläne der Widerstandsgruppen des 20. Juli 1944," in Steinbach and Schmädeke, eds., pp. 571 ff.

[24] See Goerdeler's memorandum "Das Ziel" in Schramm, ed. (n. 12 above), p. 117; and Moltke's letter to Lionel Curtis of April 18, 1942, in Moltke et al. (n. 15 above), pp. 212 ff.

[25] See Hans Mommsen, "Der lange Schatten der untergehenden Republik: Zur Kontinuität politischer Denkhaltungen von der späten Weimarer zur frühen Bundesrepublik," in *Die Weimarer Republik, 1918–1933: Politik, Wirtschaft, Gesellschaft*, ed. K. D. Bracher, M. Funke, and H. A. Jacobsen (Düsseldorf, 1987), p. 570.

the Benelux and Scandinavian countries. There were virtually no representatives from the liberal camp in the resistance. To a certain extent this was the result of the progressive erosion, after 1918, of the liberal parties of the middle, a phenomenon that was by no means confined to Germany.[26] The erosion of the liberal parliamentary tradition was so extensive that even representatives of the emigration, who maintained close ties to Western political opinion, remained skeptical about the principle of parliamentarianism.[27]

As far as the ideas entertained by the national conservative opposition are concerned, they sought to include and combine a variety of those political ideas that, at this point, did not yet seem historically obsolete. The common denominator of all the various reform plans, whether it was Goerdeler's repeated call for a return to some authoritarian version of Bismarck's imperial constitution, or the Kreisau notion of a fundamental political and social federation of autonomous bodies based on regional and ethnic factors, was simply this: a fundamentally new social order was necessary. The motivations for the concepts developed in this context were various. For Goerdeler, it was a matter of conforming to the "order of justice" established by God and of respecting "His commandments, freedom, and human dignity."[28] He saw the only alternative in a "second November 9, 1918"; according to this scenario, continuation of the National Socialist dictatorship would end with an inner and outer Bolshevization.[29]

In the case of Fritz-Dietlof von der Schulenburg, who stood in contact with the Kreisau group and later became part of the inner circle of conspirators around Stauffenberg, the decision to embark on resistance to the system arose from his conviction that only its violent overthrow could prevent the danger of a social revolution from below.[30] The mood of imminent catastrophe, deriving from the military and the domestic situation, was associated with the memory of the November revolution, whose recurrence had to be prevented. In Kreisau, too, there were ideas in this direction. Claus Schenk von Stauffenberg expressed the view that the army must not sacrifice its connec-

---

[26] See Larry E. Jones, *German Liberalism and the Dissolution of the Weimar Party System, 1918–1933* (Chapel Hill, N.C., 1988), pp. 448, 460 ff.; and Hans Mommsen, "Die Krise der parlamentarischen Demokratie und die Durchsetzung autoritärer und faschistischer Systeme in der Zwischenkriegszeit," in *Geschichte Europas für den Unterricht der Europäer,* ed. K.-E. Jeismann and R. Reimenschneider, Studien zur internationalen Schulbuchforschung (Brunswick, 1980), 27:144–65.

[27] See Ernst Portner, "Koch-Wesers Verfassungsentwurf," *VfZ* 14 (1966): 280–98.

[28] Schramm, p. 245.

[29] Ibid., p. 248.

[30] See Ulrich Heinemann, *Ein konservativer Rebell: Fritz-Dietlof Graf von der Schulenburg und der 20. Juli* (Berlin, 1990), pp. 92 ff.

tion to the people, as it had in 1918.[31] He also had in mind, as did Julius Leber, the German uprising of 1813, that is, a national revolutionary crisis, while the representatives of the conservative wing in the opposition, on the other hand, were more oriented toward the Prussian reform. Therein lay concealed an opposition between representatives of the old and of the new generations, an opposition that was to break out in the weeks leading up to the attempt on Hitler.

Moltke expressly attacked the merely evolutionary character of Goerdeler's program and demanded a revolutionary transformation, a demand that left the politics of notables that had been involved with the earlier reform plans far behind.[32] His demand was connected to the philosophy of history that prevailed at Kreisau. The belief that one stood on the threshold of an epoch-making transformation corresponded to the hope that had been raised earlier, before Hitler's seizure of power, primarily in the neoconservative camp: the hope for a "national renewal" that would overcome class struggle, petty party politics, and pluralism in favor of a social *Volksgemeinschaft*. Neoconservative authors propagated the idea, often reviving the "Ideas of 1914," and sought a general social and intellectual transformation. With this idea went the illusion that the "young generation," which would free itself from the ballast of the Western bourgeois tradition and return to the immediacy and wholeness of human existence, would be capable of bringing about such a transformation.[33]

In fact, throughout the Weimar period the latent belief existed that a fundamental break with the contemporary order was necessary. The dream of a "national resurgence," under the direction of a still unknown "leader" who would rule by plebiscite, fascinated neoconservative intellectuals like Hans Zehrer, influential publisher of *Die Tat*.[34] Basically he took up the idea of a regeneration of the German nation out of the spirit of inwardness as a direct answer to the outward defeat of 1918. The idea had initially found strong resonance among the Freikorps and then in the paramilitary units of the right. They were carried over into the stabilization phase of Weimar (1924–29) by the Jungdeutscher Orden. Arthur Moeller van den Bruck and the authors of

---

[31] See Jacobsen, ed. (n. 16 above), p. 373.

[32] See Moltke to Lionel Curtis on March 25, 1943: "The most important sociological reason for the failure [of the military action] is that we need a revolution, not a coup" (Moltke et al. [n. 15 above], p. 276); and Moltke (n. 17 above), pp. 450, 519.

[33] See Mommsen, "Der lange Schatten der untergehenden Republik" (n. 25 above), pp. 557 ff.

[34] See Klaus Fritsche, *Politische Romantik und Gegenrevolution: Fluchtwege in der Krise der bürgerlichen Gesellschaft: Das Beispiel des Tat-Kreises* (Frankfurt, 1976), pp. 157 ff., 249–50. See also Ebbo Demand, *Von Schleicher zu Springer: Hanz Zehrer als politischer Publizist* (Mainz, 1971), pp. 37–38.

the June Club provided the ideological underpinnings for these ideas. They promised that the Germans "would be able to draw from the national rupture (Selbsterschütterung) of their lives the political basis for their realization."[35]

The programmatic goals of the "Gray Wolves," an esoteric splinter group of the German Youth of November 11, were especially characteristic of the revival of fin-de-siècle ideas, all of which envisioned a long-overdue reckoning with bourgeois civilization.[36] A mixture of progressive ideas and reminiscences of Italian fascism, they put forward a program for a "comprehensive cultural revolution," by means of which nineteenth-century thought would be overcome in favor of a new, creative unity of mind and soul, body and intellect, nation and state. Allied with this was a vague notion that the decline into an increasingly bureaucratized and anonymous social order, dominated exclusively by material and commercial values, could be halted by the "younger generation," which would free itself from the compulsions and conventions of bourgeois existence.[37] It is well known that Goebbels exploited expectations of this sort, which were widespread in bourgeois circles, in order to portray the National Socialist seizure of power as a "national revolution" and so assure the allegiance of the conservative elites.

The myth of a "national regeneration" represented a formative experience for those who later were to belong to the younger generation of the resistance. This can be shown clearly in the cases of Fritz-Dietlof von der Schulenburg and the Stauffenbergs. The starting point for Schulenburg's opposition lay in the conviction that he had to defend National Socialist ideals against their perversion and destruction through National Socialist practice.[38] Berthold Schenk von Stauffenberg shared the same conviction, as he was to tell the Gestapo in 1944.[39] It is possible that the social-romantic background of the Stefan George circle, to which both brothers belonged, had a significant influence here. Schulenburg, by contrast, was most strongly influenced by Oswald Spengler's programmatic book *Preussentum und Sozialismus*.[40] His appeal to the Prussian tradition was linked to a marked social paternalism,

---

[35] Arthur Moeller van den Bruck, *Das Dritte Reich,* 2d ed. (Hamburg, 1931), p. 1; and see Gerhard Schulz, *Aufstieg des Nationalsozialismus: Krise und Revolution in Deutschland* (Frankfurt, 1975), pp. 306 ff.

[36] See Alfred Schmidt, *Erfüllte Zeit: Schriften zur Jugendbewegung* (Altdorf, 1975); and Wilhelm Wald, *Inseln der Unantastbarkeit: Erinnerungen an Alfred Schmidt und das Graue Korps* (Heidenheim, 1980).

[37] See J. Gotz v. Olenhusen, "Die Krise der jungen Generation und der Aufstieg des Nationalsozialismus," *Jahrbuch des Archivs der deutschen Jugendbewegung* 12 (1980).

[38] See Heinemann, pp. 140–41; and H. Mommsen, "Fritz-Dietlof Graf von der Schulenburg und die preussische Tradition," *VfZ* 32 (1984): 223 ff.

[39] Jacobsen, ed., pp. 447–48.

[40] Oswald Spengler, *Preussentum und Sozialismus* (Munich, 1920).

something that set him apart fundamentally from the Kreisau perspective. However, he agreed with Moltke's demand for a radical new beginning. It was precisely his disappointment over the "national revolution" that he had expected after 1933 that played the leading role in his decision to place himself fully in the service of the schemes for an overthrow of the regime.

Just how obligatory an element neoconservative ideas of reform were for the national conservative resistance can also be seen from the fact that the plans for constitutional reform that Hans Zehrer and his coterie propagated in 1932 in the periodical *Die Tat* closely resemble those later proposed at Kreisau and by Goerdeler.[41] Similarly, doctrinal resemblances can be found between the Kreisau ideas and the doctrines of the Jungdeutscher Orden, as well as the thoughts of Edgar Julius Jung.[42] In our context it is of particular interest that the conspirators' plans for a new order were tied to the conception that a fundamental spiritual, political change would lead not only to the end of the Hitler dictatorship but also to the moral regeneration of the nation. In contrast, Ulrich von Hassell, Johannes Popitz, and, in some respects, Goerdeler, too, evinced a much more skeptical attitude and clung to concepts from the Bismarck era. A consequence of this skepticism was that they increasingly had to surrender their leadership claims in the national conservative resistance to the narrower circle of conspirators around Stauffenberg.

The belief that one stood on the threshold of a critical secular turning point was strongest in the Kreisau group. In their view, National Socialism was the culmination of an erroneous line of development in Western history, one that had begun since the time of the Reformation and that involved the loss of personal attachments, the decay of the Christian and natural law bases of society, and a trend toward atomization and mass society. At first, this perspective worked counter to an immediate attack upon the regime, since the regime would meet its inevitable end on "Day X," the day of transition to a new society based on new principles. The utopian character of these views is unmistakable. But they also furnished the necessary prerequisite for a clear-sighted assessment of the exclusively destructive character of National Socialist politics. As a result, the inner circle at Kreisau, unlike traditional conservatives in the resistance, did not have to go through years of torment

---

[41] Hans Zehrer, "Der Sum der Krise," *Die Tat* 23, no. 2 (1932): 937–57.

[42] This relates to the emphasis on the principle of neighborhood in Artur Mahraun, *Das Jungdeutsche Manifest* (Berlin, 1927), pp. 95 ff. See also Jones, *German Liberalism* (n. 26 above), pp. 229 ff.; and James M. Diehl, *Parliamentary Politics in Weimar Germany* (Bloomington, Ind., 1977), pp. 222 ff. For Jung, see also Larry E. Jones, "Edgar Julius Jung: The Conservative Revolution in Theory and Practice," *Central European History* 21 (1990): 142–74; and Bernhard Jenschke, *Zur Kritik der konservativrevolutionären Ideologie in der Weimarer Republik bei Edgar Julius Jung* (Munich, 1971), pp. 132 ff.

before coming to the conclusion that partial measures were not enough and that in order to destroy the criminal features of the system a thoroughgoing destruction of its foundation was required.[43]

The anthropological element on which the Kreisau conception was based coincided to a marked degree with the sharp antiliberal cultural and social criticism of the 1920s. The latter had focused its attack on the effects of industrialization and urbanization, drawing idealized portraits of preindustrial social structures to contrast with contemporary industrial society and reflecting contemporary agrarian romanticism and hostility to urban existence.[44] In spite of these problematic features, there exists even today an undeniable fascination with the social-political reform program put forth at Kreisau. Moltke envisioned "small communities," emerging spontaneously, each characterized by a strong sense of social responsibility. A radically decentered, regionalized and federated state structure, with marked resemblances to an elitist council system, would be based on these communities through a subsidiary principle. With this vision of an overcoming nation state, the Kreisau circle contemplated the division of Europe on a regional basis, albeit with centralized committees for economic coordination and guidance.[45]

In recent times, the source material available for studying the Kreisau positions has been significantly augmented. Roman Bleistein's publication of the papers of Lothar König, a close associate of Pater Alfred Delp, allows us to follow the course of Kreisau discussions more closely.[46] In our context, an unsigned memorandum from the summer of 1942 describing the Kreisau "principles" is of great importance. It was composed before the second Kreisau conference of October 1942. For the most part it seems to reflect Moltke's own conceptions, though the more emphatic nationalist sections suggest another author as well. In light of the date of composition, the decisiveness with which a military defeat of the Third Reich is equated with "the spiritual and moral end of Germany and of Europe" is noteworthy.[47] At the same time, the memorandum voices the concern that the loss of moral, spiritual, and physical substance that a military defeat would entail for the German people would represent a serious problem for later movements

---

[43] See Hans Mommsen, "Kreisauer Vorstellungen als Antwort auf die Herausforderung des Nationalsozialismus," in *Bevölkerung, Wirtschaft, Gesellschaft seit der Industrialisierung,* ed. D. Petzina and J. Reuelcke (Dortmund, 1990), pp. 389–98.

[44] See Klaus Bergmann, *Agrarromantik und Grossstadtfeindschaft* (Meisenheim, 1970), pp. 277 ff.

[45] See the summary in Winterhager (n. 13 above), pp. 122 ff.; van Roon, *German Resistance to Hitler* (n. 13 above), pp. 265 ff.; and Klemens von Klemperer, *Die Aussenpolitik des deutschen Widerstands* (Berlin, 1992).

[46] Bleistein, ed. (n. 13 above), pp. 33 ff.

[47] Ibid., p. 61.

pursuing genuine national freedom.[48] A fundamental change seems to have occurred here, insofar as the author no longer expects, as Moltke and Yorck did originally, that the National Socialist system of domination will consume itself. Any lengthy continuation of the Nazi regime would subject broad segments of the population to "an intellectual and physical bolshevization" and replace the legal, economic, and institutional structures with a Darwinist struggle of all against all. Even a revolution "from below," which the author still sees as a possibility, would produce nothing but devastation and would destroy the basis for all meaningful political activity.[49]

The memorandum apparently reflects prior discussions among the members of the inner circle. It proposes the creation of a "unified, ideologically-oriented and unanimous group," that is, the Kreisau group, which, together with the army (in other words, by means of a military dictatorship) and possibly with the support of the workers, was to set up an alternative governmental system.[50] Its chief goal would be to combat the trend toward social atomization in mass society that had led, in the opinion of the Kreisau circle, to a total loss of social responsibility by individuals. Its task was to lay new foundations for "an inner attitude and constitution, in the German individual, that would be capable of responsibility for the whole."[51]

It would be a mistake to dismiss the cultural criticism of the memorandum as merely derivative from Weimar neoconservatism and from the ideas of Otmar Spann. It would likewise be an error to criticize its strongly speculative character. For the list of charges—the systematic "destruction of German humanity," the loss of the sense of personality, the loss of the spontaneous capacity and willingness to be responsible, the decline to a level of "amoral vitality," the destruction of the love for one's homeland, the danger of a "German bolshevization"—all these corresponded exactly to the social and moral realities of the Third Reich.[52] Further, the general decay had been accelerated by the war and by the Allied air campaign. The movement toward a "barracks society," the devastation of family structures, the extensive erosion of bourgeois associational life, the nazification of occupational associations at all levels, and the interruption of normal communications as a consequence of Gestapo terror all led to the same result: society lost all inner coherence, and individuals, thrown back upon their own devices, became disoriented.

[48] Ibid., p. 62.

[49] Ibid., p. 63.

[50] Ibid., p. 64. New here is the perspective of wanting to attain "a position of responsibility through the army in connection with a rather large, economically significant civilian group, preferably the workers." The Kreisau circle expected to play a leading, albeit indirect, political role.

[51] Ibid., pp. 66–67.

[52] Ibid., pp. 63–64.

In his well-known letter to Lionel Curtis, Helmuth James von Moltke remarks that the first priority is to restore "the image of humanity in the hearts of our fellow citizens."[53] This goal reflects the total destruction of the inherited social norms by the National Socialist system. Contrary to the theory of totalitarian dictatorship, the everyday reality of the Third Reich was characterized far less by ceaseless indoctrination than a first impression would suggest. Propaganda messages were taken less and less seriously. Sometimes this had tragic results, as in the case of the trivialization of the threats directed at the Jews. What predominated was, rather, a cynical mentality of sheer survival, of passivity, and of conformism. One grew accustomed to moral indifference and gradually lost the ability to articulate one's own opinions.[54] The constant mobilization of the population, along with the consequences of the war, led to a widespread destruction of the private sphere, the prerequisite for the preservation of personal identity. This was one of the most significant social-psychological consequences of the fascist dictatorship.

Thus the ideas of the national conservative resistance, which in another context might seem apolitical, and which assigned to the problem of moral renewal clear priority over the short-term questions about preparing to overthrow the regime, were an appropriate response to the political and moral vacuum that National Socialist politics had brought about. Naturally, they also wanted to legitimize the overthrow by proposing a new social order and developing a clear alternative to the fascist system. The conditions under which resistance could be undertaken at all fundamentally challenged exclusively pragmatic, political-tactical orientations. Pragmatic politicians were almost totally absent from the ranks of the national conservative resistance. The constitutional lawyers who took part in the Kreisau discussions certainly showed no particular concern for the workings of political systems.[55] It took a perspective that went beyond the moment, a millenarian vision, in fact, to continue to pursue a coup that seemed ever more impossible. The insight that one could not wait for the end of the war (something which, by the way, Hitler's program never envisioned) in order to stop and prosecute the crimes of the regime came only slowly to Claus Schenk von Stauffenberg, who had

---

[53] Moltke et al. (n. 15 above), p. 185, letter of April 18, 1942; and Moltke (n. 17 above), pp. 460–61, letter of March 18, 1943.

[54] See Wolfgang Franz Werner, *"Bleib übrig": Deutsche Arbeiter in der national-sozialistischen Kriegswirtschaft* (Düsseldorf, 1983), pp. 362 ff.; and Ulrich Borsdorf and Mathilde Jamin, eds., *Über Leben im Krieg: Kriegserfahrungen einer Industrieregion, 1939–1945* (Hamburg, 1989), pp. 169 ff., 180 ff.

[55] See, e.g., "Gedanken zur europäischen Ordnung," in Bleistein, ed., pp. 127 ff.; and Ger van Roon, "Staatsvorstellungen des Kreisauer Kreises," in Steinbach and Schmädeke, eds. (n. 4 above), pp. 560 ff.

initially planned to wait out the war.[56] His change of mind arose not only from the ever more ominous military situation but also from an accurate assessment of the destructive force of a regime at home that, in the end, was based solely upon the parasitic undermining of traditional structures of power.

The recognition that an overthrow of the government was meaningless if it did not also succeed in restoring a sense of politics (Politikfahigkeit) in German society and in implementing long-overdue reforms gave a certain unity to the various tendencies in the national conservative resistance. On the other hand, there were considerable differences of opinion over the question of whether the inner preconditions for an overthrow of the regime were yet at hand. Moltke, for example, was still sarcastic about the activity of the "excellencies" even in 1943. At first he did not join the preparations for the assassination attempt. He held to his skeptical belief that matters still had to get qualitatively worse in order to bring about a general change in favor of introspection and soberness. Only then would conditions be right for a fundamentally new beginning.[57] For him the primary consideration was the need for a restoration of the ethical foundations of Western society. Only that could give an alternative regime durability and credibility.

In light of the experiences of the Third Reich, Moltke demanded a fundamentally new politics, one that did not consist exclusively in propagandistic manipulation and the sheer accumulation of power. Rather than bending to changing mass sentiments, this politics was meant to win the confidence of the individual, while forgoing useless indoctrination. Only the restoration of an original *auctoritas* would raise politics above the level of dirty work and make it possible to appeal to a community sentiment and to social responsibility. Only in this way could one combat the "me generation" (Ohne mich) mentality that was spreading even in the NS regime. In this sense one could describe the primary goal of the national conservative conspirators as follows: to restore the moral basis for political activity and to show to their fellow citizens a dimension of politics beyond corruption, cynicism, and the accumulation of power, a dimension that once again would make personal commitment possible.

The reform plans of the German resistance to Hitler went beyond the overthrow of the National Socialists and envisioned the restoration in

---

[56] See Christian Müller, *Oberst i.G. Stauffenberg: Eine Biographie* (Düsseldorf, n.d.), pp. 216, 245–46.

[57] See the letters to Freya von Moltke of January 22 and January 24, 1943 (Moltke, pp. 455–56), as well as the one dated August 4, 1943 (p. 519). Moltke feared that, after Wilhelm Leuschner's clear decision in favor of Goerdeler, things would "slide toward a Kerenki-solution." Then one could "bid farewell, in our lifetime at least, to the hope for a healthy, organic solution. . . . Really, a lot more will have to be reduced to dust and ashes, before the time is ripe."

religious, social, and political life of an existence commensurate with human dignity. The utopian element in these plans can be understood social-psychologically as a response to the extreme vulnerability felt by groups that had not fallen victim to fascist self-deception. In the end, what was at stake in the attempted assassination was no longer external success but, rather, as Henning von Tresckow testified, the need to give a sign that there was an alternative to the rule of cynical force and unlimited subjugation. By participating in the attempt to overthrow the National Socialist regime, under political conditions that rendered their practical prospects hopeless, the conspirators in the July 20 movement were engaged in a symbolic restoration of politics in the sense of a freely agreed upon common life without force or oppression. The same is true of the many other, less spectacular resistance activities that were undertaken in this unconditional manner, those of the Communists as well. Their enduring heritage lies not in their specific political plans and programs, many of which are historically outdated but, rather, in their insistence on a belief in human dignity and social justice.

The Role of the Resistance in Austria, with Special Reference to the Labor Movement

Herbert Steiner
Vienna

One of the stated purposes of this conference is to examine how every generation confronts its inherited moral values anew, with some greater or lesser awareness of the relationship of these values to perceptions of historical time. In Austria—particularly since 1988, given the fiftieth anniversary of the Anschluß, the controversy surrounding Kurt Waldheim's presidency, Simon Wiesenthal's eightieth birthday, and similar events—there appears to be a growing interest and an increasingly serious commitment among young people toward the study of National Socialism, indigenous fascism, anti-Semitism, racism, and contemporary right-wing political activities.[1]

However, the reaction of those who experienced or participated in the events of 1933–38 or 1938–45 has been, on the whole, somewhat different. For the small minority of the population that actively participated in the resistance against Austrofascism and National Socialism, this period seems to rank easily as one of the most significant of their lives. Most of them now wish to convey the monumental importance of their experiences to the current younger generation. Universities, schools, the Austrian Ministry of Education, and various social organizations have helped these witnesses (*Zeitzeugen*) communicate their living message of the past by providing venues for them to speak and other forms of assistance. More than a few survivors of Nazi persecution—most are more than seventy years old—are very disappointed with the current Austrian political climate and do not participate as active citizens. The vast majority of elderly Austrians, however, participated in the Nazi war machine as soldiers, armament industry workers, etc. These individuals have preferred to keep quiet as Austrian circumstances of the 1930s and early 1940s have become the focus of somewhat more critical historical inquiry; most of them feel they had no

---

[1] The interest in these issues has been expressed in the form of numerous conferences and seminars, as well as Austrian television and radio productions. Notable among the latter have been the television documentary series "Österreich I" and "Österreich II." These programs, the fruit of a team of scholars and technicians assembled by Hugo Portisch, have garnered considerable public interest.

This essay originally appeared in the *Journal of Modern History* 64, suppl. (December 1992).

alternative but to act in the capacities in which they did, given the circumstances of 1938–45.[2] They refuse to bear witness to the past and would prefer that public discussion of these difficult years cease altogether. For many years the Second Republic's government, its political parties, and various social organizations encouraged this silent majority not to engage in reflection on past problems.

There can be no doubt that when the German army entered Austria on March 12, 1938, it was greeted enthusiastically—in some cases with hysterical fervor—by the greater part of the Austrian population.[3] At the time, about five hundred thousand Austrians were hopelessly unemployed in a population of approximately 6.5 million; many fostered the hope that absorption into the Third Reich would bring work and prosperity. Indeed, by autumn 1938 unemployment almost ceased to exist in Austria, as work in the German armaments industry and on large-scale construction projects (airfields, *Autobahnen,* etc.) offered employment to both skilled and unskilled labor.

If Hitler had organized his plebiscite for the Anschluβ in March 1938 instead of on April 10, he quite likely would have received 99 percent support. Despite the overwhelming support unification received even in April, one must not gloss over the repressive measures that followed the Germans' entrance into Austria on March 12. Within twenty-four hours after the Germans crossed the Austrian border, more than seventy thousand Austrians were arrested by the Gestapo, the police, and assorted Nazi paramilitary organizations.[4] Their work was expedited when the collected files of the Austrian police, particularly the *Staatspolizei* (political police) of the Austro-fascist "Fatherland's Front" regime, were confiscated. Included in this huge initial sweep of actual and potential opponents were members of most of the known anti-Nazi groups: Socialists, Communists, functionaries of the Fatherland's Front, representatives of the Catholic youth and labor movements, and

[2] This explains, in part, the support that Waldheim's presidential candidacy received. Younger people seem to think differently—witness the speech that the present chancellor, Dr. Franz Vranitzky (a man too young to have participated in the war), delivered before the Austrian parliament in September 1991, in which he stressed that Austrians by and large supported the Nazi regime, even though many Austrians were persecuted for their religious and political beliefs.

[3] The consequences of the German annexation of Austria in March 1938 has been the subject of a number of historical works. Significant among them are Dieter Wagner and Gerhard Tomkowik, *Ein Volk, ein Reich, ein Führer: Der Anschluβ Österreichs 1938* (Munich, 1968) and Franz Daniman, *Finis Austriae: Österreich, März 1938* (Vienna, 1988).

[4] Collections of the final letters written by members of anti-Nazi groups prior to their execution between 1938–45 can be found in Herbert Steiner, *Zum Tode verurteilt* (Vienna, 1964) and *Gestorben für Österreich* (Vienna, 1968).

of course a great number of Austrian Jews.[5] Only a very few of those facing arrest managed to leave the country. Most of the democratic countries refused to offer asylum to Austrian refugees, and the great powers—bound by international agreements to guarantee Austrian sovereignty and independence—did nothing to oppose Hitler's incorporation of Austria into the Reich. Apart from the Soviet Union and Mexico, all countries with embassies in Vienna withdrew their staffs. The governments of France and Great Britain calculated that appeasement would turn German expansion eastward and preserve peace in the west.

Considerable debate continues today over whether Austria was the first victim or the first ally of Hitler. From the historical, political, and diplomatic points of view, there seems little doubt that Austria was the first country to be annexed outright by Germany—in complete violation of the treaties of Versailles and St. Germain. It was no accident that Hitler chose March 12 for his military and political gambit. The Austrian government of Dr. Kurt Schuschnigg had intended to hold its own plebiscite to determine Austria's fate on March 13.[6] Schuschnigg felt reasonably certain that a budding mass movement in favor of Austrian independence would preserve Austria's integrity, particularly because the erstwhile underground Revolutionary Socialist and Communist labor movements, the majority of Catholic clergymen, and many Austrian intellectuals indicated their intention to vote yes to Austrian independence. The Austrian Labor Movement, in the underground since 1934, would have been instrumental in achieving a strong, united front for the independence faction. In return for the restoration of freedom of the press, freedom of assembly, and the freedom to organize without hindrance, labor representatives vowed to appeal to the workers to support Schuschnigg's regime and to fight for a free Austria in the face of any and all Nazi threats. Had the vote proceeded on March 13, the likelihood that Schuschnigg would have secured a majority would have been greater.[7]

Hitler's propaganda machine and the enthusiastic welcome the German army received in Austria helped him to camouflage his true purpose. His principal aim was the absolute revision of the Versailles Peace Treaty and the

---

[5] In 1938 Austria's Jewish population totaled approximately one hundred eighty thousand people. About one hundred ten thousand were able to flee abroad and perhaps sixty-five thousand became victims of Nazi genocide. Unquestionably, the Jews were the largest group of Austrian victims of Nazi terror.

[6] See Kurt Schuschnigg, *Ein Requiem in Rot-Weiβ-Rot* (Vienna, 1978).

[7] The German ambassador in Vienna and his military attaché observed these developments with concern. Reports were relayed daily to Berlin that the movement for Austrian independence was steadily gaining strength. Reports from the German embassy in Vienna are found in Akten zur Deutschen Auswärtigen Politik, 1918–45, Sektion D, Band 1.

establishment of a National Socialist–dominated greater Europe. To achieve this, large-scale rearmament and the modernization of the German military, as well as the close cooperation of industrialists and bankers with the National Socialist leadership, were required. Austria's plentiful natural resources— timber, oil, iron ore, and magnesium—were of great importance for weaponry and other war-related products.[8] Moreover, the Austrian industries and banks controlled important industrial assets in eastern and southeastern Europe (dating back as early as the late nineteenth century), and the Österreichische Nationalbank possessed almost sixteen times the gold and foreign currency of the Deutsche Reichsbank in early 1938. This compelling economic data suggests the actual reason why Hitler valued the annexation of Austria and why the German industrialists and the military so strongly supported this action.

Approximately one hundred thousand Austrian Jews were displaced as a result of the Anschluß, and some sixty-five thousand were executed in the "Final Solution." This success in eliminating Austrian Jewry, although it was carried out by the National Socialist regime, cannot be considered apart from centuries of deeply rooted Austrian anti-Semitism. Those sentiments were crudely manipulated by the church hierarchy, Christian Social municipal authorities, and even aristocratic ruling circles to divert attention from other political and economic difficulties. Because of problems of professional competition, anti-Semitism was stronger among intellectuals than in the general population, and it proved particularly disruptive in the universities. Nonetheless, many Austrian Jews played an important role in the cultural and economic fields as well as within Liberal and Social Democratic circles between 1918 and 1938. The Nazis, too, manipulated anti-Semitic sentiments to corrupt and demoralize sections of the population, although most Austrians played no direct, personal role in the oppression of Jews and their deportation.[9] The percentage of Jews among professions such as medicine and the law was quite high, and those who filled the void during the Third Reich knew what had become of their Jewish colleagues. Additionally, the deportation of Jews served as a means to resolve a pressing housing shortage in larger Austrian cities, particularly Vienna. To preserve their gains, individuals who had benefited hoped that the Jews would never return to Austria. These are some of the most prominent reasons why representatives of this older

---

[8] The economic consequences of the Anschluß are examined in detail in several significant works, including Felix Romanik, *Österreichs wirtschaftliche Ausbeutung* (Vienna, 1966) and Norbert Schausberger, *Der Griff nach Österreich* (Vienna, 1978).

[9] A great number of monographs on the subject of Austrian Jewry and anti-Semitism have been published recently. Perhaps the strongest among these contributions is Herbert Rosenkranz, *Verfolgung und Selbstbehauptung: Die Juden in Österreich, 1938–45* (Vienna, 1978).

generation have not relished discussion of the Nazi period during the Second Republic.[10]

The Austrian resistance movements, especially that of organized labor (both Revolutionary Socialists and Communists), had experienced four years of underground struggle against the Dollfuß-Schuschnigg regime prior to the Anschluß. Communist organizations were represented in many factories and municipal services (e.g., fire brigades and public transportation) and within the Austrian Federal Railway (*Österreichische Bundesbahn*). Many Socialist activists joined KPÖ-led groups and followed their Communist colleagues into concentration camps. Although the Revolutionary Socialists and the Communists expressed rather different goals for Austria's post-Nazi future, they did agree on one fundamental issue: both wanted Austria to be reconstituted as an independent, free, and democratic country, and it was during this period that the first genuine expressions of Austrian identity developed. Suffering crossed political camp and class barriers, and the death of almost one hundred thousand Austrians (two-thirds of them Jews) through execution or incarceration, the dislocation of many others, and the privation of the last years of the Third Reich strengthened Austrian sentiments during the difficult years of reconstruction following April 1945.[11]

In recent years many books and articles have been published in Austria about resistance and persecution. At the universities and secondary schools, resistance against National Socialism has become a matter of considerable interest among younger people.[12] The Dokumentationsarchiv des österreichischen Widerstandes (DöW–Altes Rathaus, Wipplingerstraße 8, A-1010 Wien), with its permanent exhibits, large library, and ever-expanding archival

---

[10] Gerhard Botz of the University of Salzburg has investigated the housing problem and other social issues in his *Wien vom Anschluß zum Krieg: Nationalsozialistische Machtübernahme und politisch-soziale Umgestaltung am Beispiel der Stadt Wien 1938–39* (Vienna, 1978). The most extensive publication addressing these questions, based on newly accessible sources, is Emmerich Tálos, Ernst Hanisch, and Wolfgang Neugebauer, eds., *NS-Herrschaft in Österreich, 1938–45* (Vienna, 1988).

[11] In addition to a large number of German-language publications on the Austrian resistance, several excellent English-language studies have been produced, such as C. Gwyn Nuttall, *An Exercise in Futility: The Austrian Resistance to the Nazis, 1938–1940* (Atlanta, 1972); Walter B. Maas, *A Country without a Name* (New York, 1979); and Radomir V. Luža, *The Resistance in Austria, 1938–1945* (Minneapolis, 1984).

[12] Various new publications examining the concentration camp Mauthausen in Upper Austria and its subcamps (*Nebenlager*) have contributed to this surge in interest, as well as the series *Widerstand und Verfolgung,* a multivolume project covering resistance in the different provinces published by the Dokumentationsarchiv des österreichischen Widerstandes. The DöW also has issued a series of documentary volumes on Austrian exiles and Austrians in the concentration camps of Auschwitz, Buchenwald, and Dachau.

holdings, has become the focal point for most Austrian antifascist research work. It not only deals with historical problems but also attempts to understand the sources and consequences of contemporary neofascist, anti-Semitic, and revisionist tendencies within Austria. Unlike many similar institutions in other European countries, the DöW is still growing and attracting the interest of a wide public.

Acts of Resistance: The White Rose in the Light of New Archival Evidence*

Christiane Moll
Freie Universität Berlin

On June 18, 1943, approximately three weeks before his execution, Alexander Schmorell wrote a farewell letter to his Russian girlfriend Nelly from his prison in Stadelheim. He wrote, "It was my fate to leave the earthly existence earlier than we all thought. We worked with Wanja [Hans Scholl] against the German government, we were discovered and condemned to death."[1]

In this terse and sober diction Alexander Schmorell summarized the course of action of the White Rose resistance group and its deadly consequences. At the same time, he articulated his understanding of the White Rose resistance actions, which mainly consisted of the composition and dissemination of six leaflets between June 1942 and February 1943 and ended with the spectacular action of the Scholls at Munich University on February 18, 1943. In two trials, the People's Court (*Volksgerichtshof*) in Munich sentenced the six main actors, Hans Scholl (twenty-four), Sophie Scholl (twenty-one), Alexander Schmorell (twenty-five), Christoph Probst (twenty-three), Willi Graf (twenty-five), and Professor Kurt Huber (forty-nine) to death for preparation for treason, support of the enemy, and subversion of military preparedness. Their confidants and supporters were sentenced, as accessories, to prison terms between six months and ten years.[2] At the end of May 1943—the Scholls and Christoph Probst had already been executed on February 22—Chief Prosecutor Lautz at the People's Court opposed a pardon for Alexander Schmorell, Kurt Huber, and Willi Graf. He opined that "the proceedings at hand constitute one of the most serious cases of treasonous handbill propaganda which occurred on German territory during the war."[3]

---

* Translated from the German by Betsy Mayer and Michael Geyer.

[1] Alexander Schmorell, letter to his Russian girlfriend, Nelly, June 18, 1943, from the personal papers of Dr. Erich Schmorell.

[2] These two White Rose trials took place on February 22 and April 19, 1943, in Munich at the People's Court (*Volksgerichtshof*). The trial documents are deposited with the Bundesarchiv Potsdam/Abt. Zwischenarchiv Dahlwitz-Hoppegarten (hereafter BAP), under the call numbers ZC 13267, vols. 1–15 (Prozess gegen die Geschwister Scholl und Christoph Probst), and NJ 1704, vols. 1–33 (Prozess gegen Alexander Schmorell, Willi Graf, Professor Kurt Huber, u.a.). A further trial on account of nonreporting treason against Manfred Eickemeyer, Wilhelm Geyer, Harald Dohrn, and Josef Söhngen took place on July 13, 1943, at the Special Court of the district court Munich I. The investigative reports can be found in the Staatsarchiv München (hereafter StAM), St.Anw. 12530; indictment and sentence are in BAP, NJ 534.

[3] Chief Prosecutor at the People's Court, letter to the Reich Ministry of Justice, May 31, 1943, in BAP, NJ 1704, vol. 33, p. 95.

In the historiography of resistance during the Third Reich,[4] as well as in the vast commemorative literature,[5] the White Rose is often interpreted as the symbol of "pure and moral resistance, neither power nor interest-oriented"[6] and, hence, diametrically opposed to groups such as that which planned the July 20 military uprising. It was thus inevitable that the White Rose's legacy was—and still is—instrumental for various political and religious movements.[7]

Surprisingly, a detailed and encompassing scholarly treatment of this resistance group is missing to this day.[8] Since the mid-sixties different authors

---

[4] See, among others, Wolfgang Benz, "Deutsche gegen Hitler: Widerstand, Verweigerung, Kampf gegen die NS-Herrschaft," in his *Herrschaft und Gesellschaft im nationalsozialistischen Staat: Studien zur Struktur und Mentalitätsgeschichte* (Frankfurt, 1990), pp. 180–96, esp. p. 187.

[5] See Ernst Fleischhack, *Die Widerstandsbewegung "Weiße Rose": Literaturbericht und Bibliographie, Sonderdruck aus Jahresbibliographie der Bibliothek für Zeitgeschichte* (Frankfurt, 1971), pp. 494–97; and Michael Kißener, "Literatur zur Weißen Rose, 1971–1992," in *Hochverrat? Die "Weiße Rose" und ihr Umfeld,* ed. Rudolf Lill (Konstanz, 1993), pp. 175–77.

[6] Peter Steinbach, "Erinnerung—aktives Gedenken: Annäherungen an den Widerstand," in *Die Weiße Rose und das Erbe des deutschen Widerstandes: Münchner Gedächtnisvorlesungen, 1983–1992* (Munich, 1993), p. 132.

[7] Kißener, p. 164.

[8] After the Second World War the literature on the White Rose was shaped by the reports of survivors, family members, and friends of the group. The Institut für Zeitgeschichte in Munich (IfZ) collected these reports in the sixties under the call number Fa 215, vols. 1–5. In the early fifties a first monograph appeared by Inge Scholl about her siblings, which told the story of the events from memory. This book, which has been translated into many languages, remains a classic. The latest German edition is Inge Scholl, *Die Weisse Rose: Erweiterte Neuausgabe,* 3d ed. (Frankfurt, 1993). Histories tended to concentrate on the Scholls. The genre of historical recollections of the events and personalities prevailed into the recent past; see, e.g., Richard Hanser, *A Noble Treason* (New York, 1979); Annette E. Dumbach and Jud Newborn, *Shattering the German Night: The Story of the White Rose* (Boston, 1986); Harald Steffahn, *Die Weiße Rose mit Selbstzeugnissen und Bilddokumenten,* 2d ed. (Hamburg, 1993). In the eighties the letters and diaries of Hans and Sophie Scholl as well as of Willi Graf were published: Inge Jens, ed., *Hans Scholl, Sophie Scholl: Briefe und Aufzeichnungen* (Frankfurt, 1984); Anneliese Knoop-Graf and Inge Jens, eds., *Willi Graf: Briefe und Aufzeichnungen* (Frankfurt, 1988). Individual portraits can be found in Hermann Vinke, *Das kurze Leben der Sophie Scholl: Mit einem Interview mit Ilse Aichinger,* 2d ed. (Ravensburg, 1987), Clara Huber, ed., *Kurt Huber zum Gedächtnis: "... der Tod ... war nicht vergebens"* (Munich, 1986); and, among others, Anneliese Knoop-Graf, *"Jeder Einzelne trägt die ganze Verantwortung"—Willi Graf und die Weiße Rose,* Gedenkstätte Deutscher Widerstand—Beiträge zum Widerstand, 1933–1945 (Berlin, 1991); Anneliese Knoop-Graf, "Hochverräter? Willi Graf und die Ausweitung des Widerstands," in Lill, ed., pp. 43–88. Aspects of a history of reception and of a critical historical reconstruction have been studied as well. See Günther Kirchberger, *Die "Weiße Rose": Studentischer Widerstand gegen Hitler in*

in East and West Germany have struggled to reach a more systematic understanding of the history of the White Rose and the motives and objectives for its leaflets and graffiti actions. West German authors, concentrating more on the first four leaflets and less on the fifth, have tended to emphasize the unpolitical Christian-ethical character of the White Rose actions.[9] East German authors who conceded the White Rose's Christian humanist character accentuated the importance of the fifth leaflet and the political development of the group, yet interpreted their objectives to fit East German ideology.[10] They marginalized the Scholls' daring action of February 18, while in West Germany it was sometimes interpreted as an act of personal self-sacrifice, an "unpolitical manifestation" meant to arouse the students of Munich to resistance.[11] This kind of assessment was made without any detailed knowledge of the event, which now, however, is available for the first time.

Newly Discovered Documents about the "White Rose"

Two years ago, after the White Rose Foundation had just finished the English version of the White Rose exhibition, the foundation received a call from a pastor in Lübeck informing us that he had found interesting material about the trials of the White Rose in an East Berlin archive. We were incredulous. Up to that point, of the two main trials against the White Rose, we had access only to the indictments and findings of the judgments, the clemency petitions and writs of execution of the accused from the second trial, and the records of the interrogations of Willi Graf, Kurt Huber, Falk Harnack, and Traute Lafrenz. Parts of the latter two were not public domain. For fifty years the documents concerning the first trial had been believed lost. Why should this pastor, of all people, have discovered this material?

Thus it was several months before I flew to East Berlin to find out what all this was about. In February 1992, the new source material was spread out in front of me in the former National Socialist archives, once a part of the

---

München (Munich, 1980); and Wilfried Breyvogel, "Die Gruppe 'Weiße Rose': Anmerkungen zur Rezeptionsgeschichte und kritischen Rekonstruktion," in *Piraten, Swings und Junge Garde: Jugendwiderstand im Nationalsozialismus,* ed. Wilfried Breyvogel (Bonn, 1991), pp. 159–207.

[9] Christian Petry, *Studenten aufs Schafott: Die Weiße Rose und ihr Scheitern* (Munich, 1968); and Heike Bretschneider, *Der Widerstand gegen den Nationalsozialismus in München 1933 bis 1945,* Miscellanea Bavarica Monacensia (Munich, 1968), pp. 179–99.

[10] Klaus Drobisch, ed., *Wir schweigen nicht! Eine Dokumentation über den antifaschistischen Kampf Münchner Studenten, 1942/43,* 4th ed. (Berlin, 1983); Karl-Heinz Jahnke, *Die Weiße Rose contra Hakenkreuz: Der Widerstand der Geschwister Scholl und ihrer Freunde* (Frankfurt, 1969).

[11] Petry, p. 151.

ministry for Staatssicherheit in East Germany. The young man assisting me had no idea why I was getting so excited: In front of me were the complete files of the first White Rose trial—the interrogations of Hans and Sophie Scholl and of Christoph Probst, their clemency petitions and writs of execution, Gestapo reports for the National Security Headquarters in Berlin on preliminary inquiries and investigative measures, and material that would illuminate the events of February 18. I had only a few hours to get acquainted with the material—the archives were being relocated—but I soon realized that we could now obtain a better understanding of the White Rose activities. By means of cautious and critical evaluation we could start verifying the written records to distinguish between what had become a legend over the years and what had really taken place.

I continued my quest and found additional interrogation records of members of the White Rose group who were sentenced in the second trial. Only recently the investigation records of Alexander Schmorell were discovered in the so-called Special Archive in Moscow. Together with the investigation records of the third White Rose trial, which was conducted by the Special Court (*Sondergericht*) in Munich on July 13, 1943, we can now analyze and evaluate nineteen (of twenty-one) interrogation transcripts consisting of approximately one thousand pages of testimony by the defendants in the three White Rose trials.[12] On the basis of these newly available

---

[12] The minutes of the interrogations of Manfred Eickemeyer, Wilhelm Geyer, Harald Dohrn, and Josef Söhngen have been available for some time in StAM. Together with the minutes of the interrogations of Kurt Huber, Wilhelm Graf, and Falk Harnack, in BAP, NJ 1704 (n. 2 above), vols. 7–9, and of Heiner Guter, in BAP, NJ 6136, available since the eighties, the records of Hans and Sophie Scholl and Christoph Probst, in BAP, ZC 13267 (n. 2 above), vols. 2–4, and those of Traute Lafrenz, Eugen Grimminger, Gisela Schertling, as well as Katharina Schüddekopf, in BAP, ZC 13267, vols. 6–7 and 15, are also available. In addition, the records of Alexander Schmorell's investigation are in the Special Archive Moscow, 1361-1-8808; those of Hans Hirzel's investigation are in BAP, ZC 14 116, vol. 1; and those of Helmut Bauer's investigation are in BAP, ZB II A 27. This documentation has been partly examined in the study of Michael C. Schneider and Winfried Süß, *Keine Volksgenossen: Studentischer Widerstand der Weißen Rose: The White Rose* (Munich, 1993). It should be noted that the use of Gestapo investigation and interrogation records as a source for history is controversial. Already in 1951 Günther Weisenborn rejected the use of these documents categorically. He stated that "today, everybody should know the circumstances in which Gestapo interrogations took place, that statements were forced through blackmail and torture, that the apprehended persons were completely helpless. Whoever considers this material as authentic and uses it, opts for the Gestapo, if he does not bring to bear the point of view of the victims. It is self-evident that the truth was not always said in these minutes, that prearranged statements were put down; self-evidently, factual findings were distorted; self-evidently, the commissars wanted to

records a more precise discussion of the White Rose activities is possible. The purpose of this essay is to elaborate and assess anew the sequence of events, motives, and intentions of the White Rose beyond the juxtaposition of a "merely moral" and a "political" resistance.

With this goal in mind the activities of the White Rose group can be subdivided into three clearly distinguishable phases. The first phase included June and July 1942, during which the first four leaflets appeared. The second phase was between November 1942 and January 1943, during which the fifth leaflet was prepared and distributed. The third phase in February 1943 consisted of graffiti activities and the composition of the sixth leaflet, which was distributed by mail and, ultimately, on February 18, scattered in the main hall of Munich University.

THE FIRST PHASE: "THE LEAFLETS OF THE WHITE ROSE"

We now know for certain that the first four "Leaflets of the White Rose" were distributed by Hans Scholl and Alexander Schmorell between June 27 and

---

hear incriminating evidence and misrepresented in turn; and self-evidently, the concluding statement of the Gestapo presents a garbled tableau of events" (letter to the editor, *Stern* [April 10, 1951]). Until recently, there were historians of the White Rose who warned against the use of interrogation reports, including the newly found ones of Hans and Sophie Scholl. It is rather strange in this context that the arraignments and the findings of the judges in the White Rose trials are used in the literature without further reflection as authentic material. They entered the historical record without further elaboration, as is the case, e.g., in the dating of the first four leaflets and the origins of the name White Rose. An alternative assessment of interrogation records is available in Bernd-A. Rusinek, *Gesellschaft in der Katastrophe, Terror, Illegalität, Widerstand Köln 1944/45*, Düsseldorfer Schriften zur Neueren Landesgeschichte und zur Geschichte Nordrhein-Westfalen, Bd. 24 (Essen, 1989), pp. 50–74. Rusinek comes to the conclusion that interrogation records can be more useful for historical research than arraignments and findings. In using the interrogation records of the White Rose, it is important to remember that they are "texts of repression"; that is, they are the products of extreme psychological pressure and fear, though actual physical mistreatment during the interrogations has not been reported. It is certain, though, that the interrogations were accompanied by threats of beatings as well as the threat of sending family members into a concentration camp. Nonetheless, as records of the interrogators they are the palimpsests of the interrogated, and it is possible as Rusinek states "to reconstruct an image of the interrogated through the web of interrogation" (p. 61). That is, while one is less likely to get linguistic authenticity from these records, a substantive authenticity that verifies key facts is feasible. Thus, it seems possible to clarify the course of events and some motives and goals of the group and to differentiate among the activities of its various members beyond and in correction of what is known today. This leads to a reassessment of the records of the arraignments and findings that have entered the literature without serious debate.

July 12, 1942, in other words, within a period of only sixteen days.[13] Schmorell and Scholl secretly produced the leaflets in Schmorell's room at Benediktenwandstraße 12, where he was living with his parents. It is impossible to reconstruct who bought the duplicating machine. But it was Schmorell who, on short notice, would repeatedly borrow the typewriter, a Remington portable used for all six leaflets, from a childhood friend. This friend still lives and the typewriter still exists.[14]

As was already known, Scholl and Schmorell wrote these leaflets together. But during his interrogation Scholl declared that he formulated the first and the fourth leaflet alone and that it was Schmorell who devised the latter half of the second and the third leaflet.[15] According to this evidence, Schmorell phrased in a more direct and nonideological style those sections in the second leaflet that dealt with Germany's deadly elimination politics against Jews and Poles and the Germans' joint guilt, and those of the third leaflet that prescribe concrete ways to enact passive resistance. Scholl's passages, by contrast, are more concerned with justifying the legitimacy of resistance as a consequence of the illegitimacy of the violent Nazi state, while demanding a spiritual and moral reversal reminiscent of the metaphysical argumentation and apocalyptic vision of his mentor Theodor Haecker (1879–1945).[16]

We can now more precisely determine the social group these leaflets tried to address as members of the "Christian and Occidental civilization" and "German intelligentsia."[17] Scholl wanted to mobilize the academic intelligentsia. He thought it was time to remind this part of the bourgeoisie of its political responsibilities, because they were the elite of a people and were called to leadership.[18] According to Scholl, it was not the masses who had failed politically since 1918 but this part of the intelligentsia. Schmorell shared this elitist view when he said, "The man in the street can't comprehend everything or decide everything; he isn't that presumptuous, he trusts his leaders, the educated classes, who understand things better than he does." In this context, he insisted on the implicit agreement between leaders and followers. "Under all circumstances, these classes must be deeply rooted in

---

[13] This date can already be found in the finding of the third White Rose trial, July 13, 1943, in BAP, NJ 534 (n. 2 above), p. 4. It is now verified by a Gestapo list of recipients of the White Rose leaflets, in BAP, ZC 13267, vol. 1, pp. 22–23.

[14] Interrogation of Alexander Schmorell, February 25, 1943, in Special Archive Moscow, 1361-1-8808, pp. 7 ff.; and interrogation of Karl Pötzel, March 10, 1943, in ibid., p. 28; interrogations of Hans Scholl, February 20 and 21, 1943, in BAP, ZC 13267, vol. 2, pp. 21, 26, and vol. 1, pp. 66–76.

[15] Interrogation of Hans Scholl, February 21, 1943, in BAP, ZC 13267, vol. 2, p. 26.

[16] See Inge Jens, "Die 'Weiße Rose': Biographische und kulturelle Traditionen," in Breyvogel, ed., pp. 202–21, esp. p. 204.

[17] First and second leaflet of the White Rose, in BAP, NJ 1704, vol. 32, pp. 1–2.

[18] Interrogation of Hans Scholl, February 20, 1943, in BAP, ZC 13267, vol. 2, p. 21.

the people, must think and feel like the people, because otherwise these classes will never understand the people and they conduct their own politics without reference to the common man, without pursuing his interests; that is, the interests of all those who form the majority in any case."[19]

Kurt Huber's influence is palpable. Hans and Sophie Scholl attended his lecture series "Leibniz and His Times" during the summer of 1942,[20] in which Huber illustrated the national responsibility of the academic intelligentsia, pointing to Wilhelm Leibniz (1646–1716) as an example.[21] Hans Scholl also reflected the ideas of Carl Muth (1867–1944), who had interpreted the rise of National Socialism as a result of the crisis of liberalism—a crisis that Muth saw in the apostasy from faith and the turn to "an empty economic liberalism, devoid of meaning."[22] In order to appeal credibly to the educated classes, the two leaflet writers used quite deliberately their language, quoting authorities like Schiller and Goethe but also Lao-tzu, the Bible, Novalis, and Aristotle.

The Gestapo had a list of some recipients of the leaflets; it mainly included writers, professors, school principals, owners of bookstores, and doctors from Munich and the outlying areas.[23] Scholl and Schmorell wanted these people to duplicate the leaflets and distribute them to a broader public. Even "acquaintances from lower classes," as is suggested in the third leaflet, were to be enlightened.[24] Scholl and Schmorell seemed to have been intent on publicity. Café, restaurant, and grocery owners received the leaflets too. Scholl wanted the leaflets to become popular, saying, "I hoped that owners will pass them on to their customers."[25] In addition Hans Scholl apparently attempted to win over publisher Heinrich Ellermann to his ideas in June and July 1942.[26] Friends, fellow students, and relatives also received the leaflets. Even though Scholl asserted the opposite during his interrogations, he and Schmorell seem

[19] Political confession of Alexander Schmorell, March 8, 1943, in Special Archive Moscow, 1361-1-8808, p. 30.

[20] Matriculation list for the lecture of Kurt Huber, Summer 1942, in Stadtarchiv Munich (StadtAM), Nachlaß Prof. Kurt Huber.

[21] Inge Köck and Clara Huber, eds., *Kurt Huber: Leibniz: Der Philosoph der universalen Harmonie*, 2d ed. (Munich and Zürich, 1989), esp. p. 307.

[22] Nicole Andrea Speer, *Der Widerstand der Gruppe "Weiße Rose": Zu Genese, Umfeld und Wirkung Studentischen Widerstands gegen den Nationalsozialismus*, Magisterarbeit (Freiburg, 1990), p. 84; and Karl Muth, "Die Stunde des Bürgertums," *Hochland* 28, no. 1 (October 1930–March 1931): 1–14.

[23] Gestapo list of recipients of the White Rose leaflets, in BAP, ZC 13267 (n. 2 above), vol. 1, pp. 22–23.

[24] Third leaflet of the White Rose, in BAP, NJ 1704 (n. 2 above), vol. 32, p. 3.

[25] Statements of Hans Scholl, February 20, 1943, in BAP, ZC 13267, vol. 2, p. 21; and Gestapo list of recipients of the White Rose leaflets, in ibid., vol. 1, pp. 22–23.

[26] Interrogation of Traute Lafrenz, March 25, 1943, in BAP, ZC 13267, vol. 6; and statements of Katharina Schüddekopf, March 24, 1943, in ibid., vol. 15, p. 9.

to have known the recipients well enough to assume that they "would sympathize with our cause," as Schmorell put it.[27]

The target group was relatively small. No more than one hundred leaflets were probably mailed each time.[28] It seems to have been the students' original intent to send all four leaflets to the same addressees, a list of "subscribers" to a kind of intellectual periodical.[29] Being realistic in their assessment of the totalitarian state, Schmorell explained their systematic procedure as follows: "In order to make sure the leaflets were being distributed by mail, we sent them to ourselves and therefore knew that our method worked."[30]

During this stage, the circle of initiates apparently included only Sophie Scholl, Traute Lafrenz (a friend of Hans Scholl), and Christoph Probst.[31] According to George Wittenstein, a friend of the group, he himself edited the third and fourth leaflets. To what extent Sophie Scholl participated in the actions of this phase remains unclear. According to Fritz Hartnagel, her fiancé, in May 1942 he was asked by Sophie to get a copy machine for her. Although during her interrogation she admitted to having actively participated in the campaigns during the winter of 1942–43 and, to protect friends, said she took part in actions she could not have been involved in, she vehemently denied having played a part in producing the first four leaflets.[32]

In order to test the effect of the leaflets, Scholl and Schmorell discussed the leaflets with friends and acquaintances without acknowledging their authorship openly.[33] They learned, as Schmorell recounted, "that some were for and some were against our leaflet."[34] Scholl and Schmorell not only succeeded in

[27] Interrogation of Hans Scholl, February 20, 1943, in BAP, ZC 13267, vol. 2, p. 21; statement of Alexander Schmorell, February 25, 1943, in Special Archive Moscow, 1361-1-8808 (n. 12 above), p. 7.

[28] Interrogation of Alexander Schmorell, February 25, 1943, in Special Archive Moscow, 1361-1-8808, p. 7; and interrogation of Hans Scholl, February 20, 1943, in BAP, ZC 13267, vol. 2, p. 21.

[29] Statements of Hans Scholl, February 20, 1943, in BAP, ZC 13267, vol. 2, p. 21.

[30] Statements of Alexander Schmorell, February 25, 1943, in Special Archive Moscow, 1361-1-8808, p. 7.

[31] Traute Lafrenz, in Scholl (n. 8 above), p. 132; and Gestapo list of recipients of the White Rose leaflets, in BAP, ZC 13267, vol. 1, pp. 22–23. Some of the addressees lived in and around Ruhpolding, where Christoph Probst and his family resided.

[32] Vinke (n. 8 above), p. 107. Statements of Sophie Scholl, February 18 and 20, 1943, in BAP, ZC 13267, vol. 3, pp. 9, 16; and statements of Traute Lafrenz, March 15 and 25, 1943, in ibid., vol. 6.

[33] Statements of Traute Lafrenz, March 15, 16, and 25, 1943, in BAP, ZC 13267 (n. 2 above), vol. 6; and interrogations of Katharina Schüddekopf, March 23, 24 and 26, 1943, in ibid., vol. 15, pp. 5, 8, 11; and excerpts from the interrogation of Alexander Schmorell, February 25, 1943, in StAM, St.Anw. 12530 (n. 2 above), p. 16.

[34] Statement of Alexander Schmorell, February 25, 1943, in Special Archive Moscow, 1361-1-8808, p. 7.

aiming their first four leaflets at a specific audience within the short time of two weeks but also had planned how to keep the campaign under control. Hence we are not surprised that Scholl, who during his interrogations turned out to be a rather calculating political pragmatist, explained the name of the White Rose differently from the version we have had up to now: "The name 'White Rose' was chosen at random. I was convinced that a compelling propaganda must include certain terms that in themselves mean nothing but sound good and stand for a program. It's possible that the choice of this name was instinctive because I was reading the Spanish romances, *The Rosa Blanca* [of Clemens von Brentano?], and was impressed by them."[35] Scholl was less concerned with the origin of the name "White Rose" than with its potential effectiveness in successful propaganda.

The results were far from unequivocal. Of the approximately one hundred recipients of the leaflets, thirty-five passed them on to the Gestapo. We now know that Scholl and Schmorell were aware of this fact, though not of its extent.[36] Therefore it remains open whether they would have continued distributing their leaflets had they not been sent to Russia at the end of July 1942. During his interrogation on February 20, 1943, Scholl voiced doubts about whether this method was the "correct way."[37] Away in Russia he undoubtedly also reflected on distributing the leaflets when he wrote to his family: "Surely the last weeks in Munich were wonderful and precious. But due to swiftness of time, some ideas did not mature."[38]

THE SECOND PHASE: THE FIFTH LEAFLET, "LEAFLETS OF THE RESISTANCE MOVEMENT IN GERMANY"

As early as summer 1942, according to Sophie Scholl's statement, the group wanted to "have an impact on a large part of the population."[39] But the fifth leaflet was not issued until the end of January 1943, six months later.

---

[35] Interrogation of Hans Scholl, February 20, 1943, in BAP, ZC 13267, vol. 2, p. 22. The version prevalent until now relied on a misleading abbreviation of the statement of Hans Scholl, which entered the arraignment of February 21, 1943, in ibid., vol. 1, p. 37: "The name 'White Rose' is accidental and dates back to reading a Spanish novel with this title." In the literature, reference was made to B. Traven, *Die Weisse Rose* (Berlin, 1931).

[36] Gestapo list of recipients of the White Rose leaflets, in BAP, ZC 13267, vol. 1, pp. 22–23; statements of Hans Hirzel, February 22, 1943, in BAP, ZC 14 116 (n. 12 above), vol. 1, p. 8; and statements of Hans Scholl, February 20, 1943, in BAP, ZC 13267, vol. 2, p. 20.

[37] Interrogation of Hans Scholl, February 20, 1943, in BAP, ZC 13267, vol. 2, p. 22.

[38] Hans Scholl, letter to his mother and sisters Inge and Sophie, from Russia, September 2, 1942, in Jens, ed., *Hans Scholl, Sophie Scholl* (n. 8 above), p. 87.

[39] Statement of Sophie Scholl, February 18, 1943, in BAP, ZC 13267, vol. 3, p. 8.

After their three-month stay in Russia, the active core of the resistance group in Munich had been enlarged by Sophie Scholl, Willi Graf, Christoph Probst, and Kurt Huber. The core group attempted to recruit acquaintances in other cities for a new campaign, the production and distribution of the fifth leaflet. This time the campaign was well prepared by several discussions about its purpose and distribution methods. The following account illustrates the long-term planning that had gone into the campaign: As early as November 1942, Scholl and Schmorell informed Hans Hirzel, an eighteen-year-old high school student from Ulm and friend of the Scholls, of a leaflet campaign in Munich and other cities. They did not want to launch one in Ulm, because the Scholl parents were too conspicuous there.[40] Apparently the date envisaged for distribution was January 30. After Hirzel agreed to distribute the leaflets in Stuttgart, he received some envelopes from Scholl as early as the Christmas holidays.[41]

The fifth leaflet had a new heading: "Leaflets of the Resistance Movement in Germany" and was addressed to "all Germans." The leaflet probably originated in mid-January 1943, as Willi Graf's entry into his diary on January 13, 1943, indicates: "Visit with Hans; I am still there in the evening; we start with our work; things are beginning to move."[42] This time Scholl and Schmorell showed drafts of the leaflets to Professor Kurt Huber, who rejected Schmorell's draft as "sounding too Communist." But he did approve of Scholl's draft, edit it, and help formulate the second half, which is the more political part.[43]

In Germany this leaflet was distributed in Augsburg, Stuttgart, and Frankfurt, and in Austria in Salzburg, Linz, and Vienna. The addresses were obtained from address books in the "German Museum" in Munich.[44] It was probably no coincidence that these cities were chosen. There had been

[40] Robert Scholl, the father of the siblings, was sentenced to four months in prison and subsequent expulsion from his profession by the Special Court in Ulm on account of "treachery" (*Heimtücke*).

[41] Interrogation of Hans Hirzel, February 22, 1943, in BAP, ZC 14 116, vol. 1, pp. 8, 12, and p. 2; statements of Alexander Schmorell, March 13, 1943, in Special Archive Moscow, 1361-1-8808 (n. 12 above), p. 23.

[42] Diary entry of Willi Graf, January 13, 1943, in Knoop-Graf and Jens, eds. (n. 8 above), pp. 99, 308 ff.; now also interrogation of Sophie Scholl, February 18, 1943, in BAP, ZC 13267, vol. 3, p. 9.

[43] Interrogation of Kurt Huber, March 2, 1943, in BAP, NJ 1704 (n. 2 above), vol. 7, p. 15; and the concluding statement of Kurt Huber at the People's Court, April 19, 1943, in Petry (n. 9 above), p. 187; and interrogation of Alexander Schmorell, March 1, 1943, in Special Archive Moscow, 1361-1-8808, p. 18.

[44] Interrogation of Sophie Scholl, February 20, 1943, in BAP, ZC 13267 (n. 2 above), vol. 3, p. 15; and statements of Alexander Schmorell, February 25, 1943, in Special Archive Moscow, 1361-1-8808, p. 8.

discussions in which Huber and Scholl emphasized that the south had a more liberal tradition and a stronger sense of justice than northern Germany. Huber thought that National Socialism in the north was "more radical," which to him meant "more Bolshevist." He believed that if Germany was invaded, its defense would have to be conducted from the south. They even considered separating northern from southern Germany. But Huber dismissed this idea because of its economic and national implications.[45]

This much is certain: The political ideas of the fifth leaflet bespoke traditionally southern concerns. It promoted a sound federal constitution for Germany and Europe and rejected Prussian militarism. Its sources included not only Kurt Huber's conception of politics but also Haecker's massive opposition against Prussia as the hegemonic Protestant power.[46] In a nutshell, the flyer called for an expedient separation from National Socialism in view of impending defeat. "Otherwise the Germans would suffer the same fate as the Jews," the leaflet argued, picking up on popular apprehensions.[47]

This time a total of six to nine thousand leaflets were produced.[48] In her interrogation Sophie Scholl gave a detailed account of how she transported the leaflets on the express train on January 25: "I had about 250 letters addressed to people living in Augsburg. . . . About 100 of these letters didn't have stamps, so I bought 100 8-pfennig stamps at the post office near the Augsburg train station, put stamps on them and put them in the mailbox there. I put about

---

[45] Concluding statement of Kurt Huber at the People's Court April 19, 1943, in Petry, p. 184; interrogation of Kurt Huber, February 27, 1943, in BAP, NJ 1704, vol. 7, p. 8; interrogation of Katharina Schüddekopf, March 23, 1943, in BAP, ZC 13267, vol. 15, p. 5; interrogation of Manfred Eickemeyer, April 7, 1943, in StAM, St.Anw. 12530 (n. 2 above), p. 23; interrogation of Harald Dohrn, April 2, 1943, in ibid., p. 44.

[46] See Speer (n. 22 above), pp. 84 ff.; and Jens, ed., *Hans Scholl, Sophie Scholl*, pp. 265-66.

[47] Ian Kershaw, "Resistance without the People? Bavarian Attitudes to the Nazi Regime at the Time of the Weiße Rose," in *Die Weiße Rose: Student Resistance to National Socialism 1942/43*, Forschungsergebnisse und Erfahrungsberichte: A Nottingham Symposium, ed. Hinrich Siefken (Nottingham, 1991), p. 58.

[48] The exact number of copies of the fifth leaflet remains unclear. The numbers differ in arraignments and in the findings. They are likely based on statements of Sophie Scholl and on the summary report of Kriminalsekretär Mahler on February 19, 1943, in BAP, ZC 13267, vol. 1, p. 15, which, in turn, relies on the statements of Hans Scholl. In her interrogation on February 18 and 20, 1943, in BAP, ZC 13267, vol. 3, pp. 9, 13, Sophie Scholl stated that altogether six thousand leaflets were produced, of which two thousand were distributed on the night of February 28, 1943. In his interrogations on February 18 and 20, 1943, in BAP, ZC 13267, vol. 2, pp. 13, 16, Hans Scholl confessed that altogether four thousand five hundred leaflets were distributed by mail and five thousand were dispersed. The statement of Hans Scholl entered the arraignment of February 21, 1943. According to Alexander Schmorell's statement on February 25, 1943, in Special Archive Moscow, 1361-1-8808, pp. 8, 11, two to three thousand leaflets were mailed and one thousand five hundred were distributed.

half of the letters into the mailbox inside the post office, and the other half into the mailbox in front of the building."[49] Afterward she took the train to Ulm and handed Hans Hirzel about two thousand leaflets, a part of which he and his friend Franz Müller sealed and stamped. Together with his sister Susanne, Hirzel distributed them in Stuttgart on January 27.[50] The second courier was Schmorell, who drove first to Salzburg on January 26 with several hundred letters, then to Linz, where he brought about one to two hundred letters to the post offices at the train stations. Later that evening he drove to Vienna, checked into a hotel under his real name and put the rest of the letters into several mailboxes, also posting leaflets to Frankfurt am Main the next day.[51] According to Sophie Scholl, there was a plan for the leaflets to appear in these various cities simultaneously to have a greater impact and give the impression of an extensive organization. When they took trains to distribute the leaflets in other cities, it was also to save money—they needed only 8-pfennig instead of 12-pfennig stamps.[52]

This strategy was not designed to distract the Gestapo's attention from Munich, which is what the Gestapo later assumed, as the White Rose group intended to mail letters in Munich, too.[53] But when they ran out of envelopes, they chose an even riskier alternative, which up to now had not been known.[54] On the night of January 28 they scattered leaflets in a circumscribed area in Munich, the center of which was, according to the Gestapo's report, the main train station.[55] Scholl approached it from the north and Graf from the south,

---

[49] Statement of Sophie Scholl, February 18, 1943, in BAP, ZC 13267, vol. 3, p. 9.

[50] Interrogations of Hans Hirzel, February 22 and 27, 1943, and March 11 and 23, 1943, in BAP, ZC 14 116 (n. 12 above), vol. 1, pp. 10–11, 18, 39–40, 47. See also Hans Hirzel, "Flugblätter der Weißen Rose in Ulm und Stuttgart," in Lill, ed. (n. 5 above), pp. 89–119.

[51] Statements of Sophie Scholl, February 18, 1943, in BAP, ZC 13267, vol. 3, p. 9; and statement of Alexander Schmorell, February 25, 1943, in Special Archive Moscow, 1361-1-8808 (n. 12 above), pp. 8–9.

[52] Statements of Sophie Scholl, February 18 and 20, 1943, in BAP, ZC 13267, vol. 3, pp. 9, 13; statements of Alexander Schmorell, February 25, 1943, in Special Archive Moscow, 1361-1-8808, p. 8; statements of Willi Graf, March 2, 1943, in BAP, NJ 1704, vol. 8, p. 20; statements of Hans Scholl, February 20, 1943, in BAP, ZC 13267, vol. 2, p. 20.

[53] Interrogation of Sophie Scholl, February 20, 1943, in BAP, ZC 13267, vol. 3, p. 13.

[54] Statements of Alexander Schmorell, February 25, 1943, in Special Archive Moscow, 1361-1-8808, pp. 8, 11.

[55] See esp. the report of Staatspolizeileitstelle Munich to Reichssicherheitshauptamt Berlin, February 5, 1943, in BAP, ZC 13267 (n. 2 above), vol. 1, pp. 1–3; and Chief Prosecutor Munich I, letter to the Reich Ministry of Justice in Berlin, February 5, 1943, in BAP, NJ 1704 (n. 2 above), vol. 33, p. 3. Statements of Hans Scholl, February 18, 1943, in BAP, ZC 13267, vol. 2, p. 13; statements of Sophie Scholl, February 18, 1943,

while Schmorell probably worked the area to the northeast. According to the reports of the Gestapo, the area where they scattered the leaflets extended about three miles from north to south, covering a stretch of approximately ten square miles. They dispersed somewhere between two and five thousand leaflets, of which the Gestapo claimed to have collected thirteen hundred.[56] They carried their operation out between 11:00 P.M. and 1:00 A.M. and afterward regrouped in the Scholls' apartment, from which they had set out. Early in February, Sophie Scholl went even a step further: she distributed a small number of leaflets during the day, in telephone booths and on parked cars.[57] This time the students were not able to gauge the effect the leaflets had, because, as Schmorell put it, "We didn't have the opportunity to talk to anybody and hear what they thought."[58] Soon they realized that they had not provoked the response they had hoped for.[59]

Thus the fifth leaflet was designed for people living in southern German and Austrian cities. It was a large-scale production, had a much larger distribution list, and had been planned and organized systematically long before.[60]

THE THIRD PHASE: THE SIXTH LEAFLET, "FELLOW STUDENTS!" AND THE GRAFFITI ACTIVITIES

As is well known, it was the official news of Germany's disastrous defeat in Stalingrad on February 3 that triggered the sixth leaflet. Gauleiter Giesler's offensive speech during a celebration for Munich University at the German Museum on January 13, 1943, caused an uproar among the students present and prompted the White Rose to mobilize yet another group with their next leaflet. This time, the group targeted their fellow students because, as Sophie Scholl put it during her interrogation, "we were of the opinion that most of the students were revolutionary and enthusiastic, but above all that they would have the courage to act."[61] According to Otl Aicher, Sophie believed that "revolutions arise, they are not preprogrammed. . . . History gains nothing from those who speculate about revolutions but only from those who set them

---

in ibid., vol. 3, p. 9; statements of Alexander Schmorell, February 26, 1943, in Special Archive Moscow, 1361-1-8808, p. 11; and the statements of Willi Graf, February 26, 1943, in BAP, NJ 1704, vol. 8, pp. 10–11.

[56] See n. 55.

[57] Sophie Scholl confessed this action to the Gestapo in her interrogation on February 18, 1943, in BAP, ZC 13267, vol. 3, p. 10.

[58] Statement of Alexander Schmorell, February 25, 1943, in Special Archive Moscow, 1361-1-8808, p. 9.

[59] Statement of Hans Scholl, February 20, 1943, in BAP, ZC 13267, vol. 2, p. 18.

[60] Petry (n. 9 above), p. 114. Petry is wrong in his assessment that the actions were never systematically planned but, rather, left to chance.

[61] Statement of Sophie Scholl, February 20, 1943, in BAP, ZC 13267, vol. 3, p. 14.

into motion. They need not begin as spectacular events. Revolutionary movements gather force, once there are people who start out with minor actions."[62]

This time the students did not write the leaflets themselves but chose Kurt Huber, their academic mentor, to compose it "like a young student would."[63] In February 1943 he was the only professor at Munich University who in his lectures still managed to fascinate an audience consisting of all disciplines.[64] According to Huber's statements, a controversy arose on February 9 when he handed Hans Scholl and Alexander Schmorell his draft, as they insisted on crossing out the following passage: "Students—you willingly joined the German *Wehrmacht* in front-line actions and at the bases; you faced the enemy and helped the wounded, worked at your desks and in laboratories. There can be no other goal for us all than to destroy Russian Bolshevism in every respect. Join forces with our wonderful *Wehrmacht*."[65] Huber said that when he left Scholl and Schmorell he was annoyed. According to Schmorell's testimony an argument did not arise, but Huber agreed to leave out a number of other passages they had criticized. It was only after Huber had left them that they crossed out, according to Schmorell, "a passage where Professor Huber stated our wonderful *Wehrmacht* must be saved."[66]

On Friday, February 12, 1943, the leaflets—a total of two to three thousand—were produced by Scholl, Schmorell, and Graf in the Scholls' apartment.[67] Sophie was taking care of her ailing mother in Ulm from

---

[62] Otl Aicher, *Innenseiten des Kriegs* (Frankfurt, 1985), p. 144.

[63] Statement of Kurt Huber, February 27, 1943, in BAP, NJ 1704, vol. 7, p. 11.

[64] On the development of the Philosophical Institute at the University of Munich and the increasingly difficult position of Kurt Huber on the faculty, 1933–43, see Claudia Schorcht, *Philosophie an den bayerischen Universitäten, 1933–1945* (Erlangen, 1990), pp. 162–68 and 232–55.

[65] Statement of Kurt Huber, March 1, 1943, in BAP, NJ 1704 (n. 2 above), vol. 7, p. 13.

[66] Statements of Alexander Schmorell, March 1, 1943, in Special Archive Moscow, 1361-1-8808 (n. 12 above), p. 19.

[67] Diary entry of Willi Graf, February 12, 1943, in Knoop-Graf and Jens, eds. (n. 8 above), pp. 106, 324; see also statements of Alexander Schmorell, February 25, 1943, in Special Archive Moscow, 1361-1-8808, p. 9. According to the statements of Hans Scholl, February 18, 1943, in BAP, ZC 13267 (n. 2 above), vol. 2, p. 13, eight hundred leaflets were mailed and one thousand two hundred were dispersed at the university. According to Sophie Scholl's statements on February 18, 1943, in BAP, ZC 13267, vol. 3, p. 10, one thousand two hundred were mailed and one thousand five hundred to one thousand eight hundred were distributed at the university. Alexander Schmorell's statements on February 25, 1943, in Special Archive Moscow, 1361-1-8808, pp. 9–10, corroborate those of Sophie Scholl. Sophie Scholl's information was entered in the findings for the first and the arraignment for the second trial.

February 5 to February 14.[68] The leaflet's original heading probably was "German Students!"[69] After a number of copies had been made, the stencil tore and Scholl and Schmorell changed its title to "Fellow Students!" When they prepared the leaflets for mailing on Monday, February 15, they again ran out of envelopes. So they folded the leaflets and wrote the addresses on the outside.[70] They copied the addresses from a list of students who had attended Munich University during the winter semester of 1941–42, which Huber had given them.[71]

The events surrounding Stalingrad were seen by the German population as the turning point of the war and the "beginning of the end." For the first time people's belief in Hitler's myth and invincibility was shaken.[72] The obvious change of mood that took hold of the public caused the White Rose friends to risk the more daring activities of graffiti, in order "to approach the masses," as Schmorell explained.[73]

According to Gestapo reports, during the night of February 3, Schmorell and Scholl used black tar paint to draw the slogan "Down with Hitler" and a crossed-out swastika on walls of public buildings in twenty-nine different locations. They used a huge stencil that Schmorell had designed and made. According to Scholl's statements, they had not planned where they were going to paint their slogans: "we simply tested the plaster on the walls [to see] whether it was suitable." On their way home, they painted the word

---

[68] Jens, ed., *Hans Scholl, Sophie Scholl* (n. 8 above), pp. 234 ff.

[69] Among others, statement of Kurt Huber on March 1, 1943, in BAP, NJ 1704, vol. 7, p. 13; and the graphological report of the police laboratory concerning the sixth leaflet, which refers to the same title, in BAP, ZC 13267, vol. 5. However, Hans Scholl contradicts this statement in his interrogation of February 18, 1943, in BAP, ZC 13267, vol. 2, p. 13; as does Alexander Schmorell in his interrogation of February 25, 1943, in Special Archive Moscow, 1361-1-8808, p. 9. Both insist that the sixth leaflet originally had the title "Studentinnen! Studenten!"

[70] Statements of Gisela Schertling, March 31, 1943, in BAP, ZC 13267, vol. 15, pp. 20–21; statements of Willi Graf, February 26, 1943, in BAP, NJ 1704, vol. 8, p. 11; statements of Sophie Scholl, February 20, 1943, in BAP, ZC 13267, vol. 3, p. 13; and statements of Alexander Schmorell, February 25, 1943, in Special Archive Moscow, 1361-1-8808, pp. 9–10.

[71] Statements of Kurt Huber, March 4, 1943, in BAP, NJ 1704, vol. 7, p. 16; and statements of Sophie Scholl, February 20, 1943, in BAP, ZC 13267, vol. 3, p. 15; and interrogation of Alexander Schmorell, February 25, 1943, in Special Archive Moscow, 1361-1-8808, pp. 9–10.

[72] Secret report of the SS, February 4, 1943, in *Meldungen aus dem Reich: Die geheimen Lageberichte des Sicherheitsdienstes der SS, 1938–1945,* ed. Heinz Bobe-rach (Herrsching, 1984), 12:4751; Kershaw (n. 47 above), p. 53.

[73] Statement of Alexander Schmorell, February 25, 1943, in Special Archive Moscow, 1361-1-8808, p. 11.

"Freedom" in letters about one foot high on both sides of the university entrance without using a stencil.[74] Five days later, during the night of February 8, Hans Scholl and Willi Graf used green paint they had stolen from Eickemeyer's studio to write the slogans "Down with Hitler" and "Freedom" on both sides of the university entrance.[75]

Seven days later, during the night of February 15, Scholl, Schmorell, and Graf launched their most dangerous operation, which entailed two different activities.[76] At 11:00 P.M. they carried approximately eight to twelve hundred leaflets in briefcases to various post offices in downtown Munich. At the same time they carried with them the stencil, a bucket of paint, and a brush to write "Down with Hitler" on the walls of the Bavarian Ministry and three other buildings. They wrote "Down with Hitler" and "Hitler mass murderer" on the walls of the Hugendubel bookstore. They used black tar paint, and the letters they painted without the stencil were more than three feet high. Scholl probably was carrying an army pistol with him, even though he denied having done so.[77]

Before we proceed to discuss the events of February 18, it is worth pursuing briefly the Gestapo's investigation of the leaflet and graffiti actions, and whether the Gestapo had already succeeded in tracing the events back to the White Rose group before February 18. This is of some importance, not least because the Gestapo's assessment figured quite prominently in the unfolding events.

The Gestapo began its examinations of the leaflet actions in the summer of 1942. However, the investigations of "these antistate endeavors and conduct,

---

[74] This information goes back to the report of the special commission of the Gestapo, February 19, 1943, and the report of Staatspolizeileitstelle Munich, February 20, 1943, in BAP, ZC 13267, vol. 1, pp. 13–15; and Chief Prosecutor Munich I, letter to the Reich Ministry of Justice in Berlin, February 5, 1943, in BAP, NJ 1704, vol. 33, p. 3. In addition, the statements of Alexander Schmorell on February 25, 1943, in Special Archive Moscow, 1361-1-8808, pp. 10–11; as well as the statements of Hans Scholl, February 20, 1943, in BAP, ZC 13267, vol. 2, pp. 18 ff.

[75] See n. 74 and statements of Willi Graf, March 2, 1943, in BAP, NJ 1704 (n. 2 above), vol. 8, p. 22; interrogation of Gisela Schertling, March 31, 1943, in BAP, ZC 13267, vol. 15, p. 21; statements of Manfred Eickemeyer, April 9, 1943, in StAM, St. Anw. 12530 (n. 2 above), p. 25.

[76] See n. 74 and statements of Willi Graf, February 26, 1943, in BAP, NJ 1704, vol. 8, pp. 11–12.

[77] Interrogation of Hans Scholl, February 20, 1943, in BAP, ZC 13267 (n. 2 above), vol. 2, p. 20; see, however, the statement of Alexander Schmorell on February 26, 1943, in Special Archive Moscow, 1361-1-8808 (n. 12 above), p. 16: "As much as I know, only Hans Scholl carried a pistol during the graffiti actions. He would have used it, if caught red-handed." See also the report by the Gestapo, February 18, 1943, on the house search of the Scholls' apartment, in BAP ZC 13267, vol. 2, p. 1: the Gestapo found a pistol and approximately two hundred cartridges.

unbecoming to morale" (*sinnabträgliches Verhalten*) came to nothing and were abandoned soon after.[78] It was only after the dispersal of fliers during the night of January 28, 1943, in Munich that a more serious investigation was launched and decisive measures were initiated. These actions can be summarized as follows: The Gestapo realized that the train station was the center for the distribution of the leaflets and concluded that their suspects were "traveling perpetrators" who had taken the train from Vienna, where leaflets had been found on January 27.[79] This is why Dr. Max Stefl, a former member of the Munich University Library, who was in Vienna during these "critical days," was the Gestapo's first suspect. He had been fired in 1934 because of his "hostility towards the state." He was now under surveillance for a few days, without any results. Stefl had been a close friend of Theodor Haecker's since 1919.[80]

On February 1, a search of all trains was launched in a number of cities in the south of Germany, as was a manhunt in Munich on the basis of a student's description. These efforts remained without results. After the Munich Headquarters for Criminal Investigations ascertained that all five leaflets had been written on the same typewriter, the Gestapo concluded that the perpetrators were from Munich and the outlying areas. On February 5, 1943, an ad was placed in a number of Bavarian newspapers that called for the public's assistance in the search for a "criminal."[81] The reward was 1.000 marks (today's equivalent would be about $6,000).

The group's graffiti activities were closely watched by the Gestapo. As of February 9, the university was under constant surveillance. Somewhere between February 5 and 11, a special investigative commission was formed under Robert Mohr. On February 17 and 18, a specialist in Greek philology, Professor Harder, was commissioned to do a philological analysis of the six leaflets to examine their historical and political background to get a grasp on the authors' identities. Thus the Gestapo of Munich had not yet found a clear trace of the White Rose group before February 18.

---

[78] Note of July 9, 1943, in the secret monthly report of Oberbayerischen Verwaltung, in Drobisch, ed. (n. 10 above), p. 25; and report of Robert Mohr, Kriminalobersekretär of the Gestapo Munich, in Scholl (n. 8 above), p. 171.

[79] The following summary results from the reports of the Gestapo of Munich, February 5 and 11, for Reichssicherheitshauptamt Berlin; the memorandum of the police laboratory, February 18, 1943; and the memorandum of Professor Harder of February 17 and 18, 1943, in BAP, ZC 13267, vol. 1, pp. 1–5, 9, and 16–18.

[80] Hinrich Siefken, ed., *Theodor Haecker, 1879–1945.* Mit einer Haecker-Bibliographie von Eva Dambacher, *Marbacher Magazin*, vol. 49 (1989), pp. 16 ff., and esp. p. 48.

[81] "Gewaltverbrecher gesucht: 1000 RM Belohnung," *Münchener Neueste Nachrichten* (February 5, 1943), p. 5.

However, in Stuttgart, police headquarters had been able to pick up a trace. On January 10, 1943, Hirzel had confided in two fellow members of the Hitler Youth that the White Rose was planning to distribute leaflets in Stuttgart on January 30. One of them reported him to the police authorities on January 29, and Hans Hirzel was interrogated by the Gestapo on the afternoon of February 17; he was confronted with the name of Sophie Scholl. Hirzel then warned the Scholl family in Ulm.[82]

On Thursday, February 18, 1943, the Scholls approached the main entrance of the university at approximately 10:45 A.M. They were carrying a brown suitcase and a briefcase containing copies of the sixth leaflet and a small number of the fifth. They ran into their friends Traute Lafrenz and Willi Graf in the university.[83] The Scholls placed stacks of leaflets in front of the closed auditoriums and in the corridors. At the rear entrance they turned around and went up to the second floor, where they deposited several more stacks, and then up to the third floor, where Sophie tossed the remainder of the leaflets over the railing. Sophie's explanation reads as follows: "It was either high spirits or stupidity that made me throw 80 to 100 leaflets from the third floor of the university into the inner courtyard, which is the reason why my brother and I were discovered."[84] The university janitor, Jakob Schmid, saw the leaflets tumbling down from the left balustrade and ran up to the Scholls, grabbed them, and told them to come with him. Hans tried to defend himself by saying, "But that's ridiculous. It's an impertinence to be arrested inside the university!"[85]

In the end, we will never find out why Sophie Scholl decided to throw the leaflets into the inner courtyard. This much we can tell from the new evidence: Hans Scholl and Schmorell had planned to deposit the leaflets in front of the auditoriums and in the corridors of the university. Willi Graf was also aware of the plan.[86] But, as Schmorell's statement in front of the Gestapo reads, "We

[82] Notice against Hans Hirzel by Wolf Tröster and Gerhard Munz at the Staatspolizeileitstelle Stuttgart on January 29, 1943, and interrogation of Hans Hirzel, February 17, 1943, in BAP, ZC 14 116 (n. 12 above), vol. 1, pp. 2–4; also Hirzel (n. 50 above), pp. 109–11.

[83] See esp. interrogation of Hans Scholl, February 18, 1943, in BAP, ZC 13267, vol. 2, pp. 13–14; and statements of Sophie Scholl, February 18, 1943, in ibid., vol. 3, p. 10. See also report of Traute Lafrenz, in Scholl, p. 134.

[84] Interrogation of Sophie Scholl, February 18, 1943, in BAP, ZC 13267, vol. 3, p. 10.

[85] Statements of Jakob Schmid, February 18, 1943, in BAP, ZC 13267, vol. 1, p. 6.

[86] Statements of Hans Scholl, February 18, 1943, in BAP, ZC 13267, vol. 2, p. 13; interrogation of Willi Graf, February 26, 1943, in BAP, NJ 1704 (n. 2 above), vol. 8, p. 12; statements of Alexander Schmorell, February 25 and 26, 1943, in Special Archive Moscow, 1361-1-8808, pp. 10, 13; statements of Gisela Schertling, March 31, 1943, in BAP, ZC 13267, vol. 15, p. 20.

hadn't decided on the specifics. We hadn't decided when we were going to do it or who was going to do it."[87] Thus Schmorell was taken by surprise on February 18, around noon, when in a streetcar on his way to the university, he was informed by an acquaintance that two students had been arrested in the university for spreading leaflets.[88]

There is another explanation for what happened. As before, the friends had sent the sixth leaflet to themselves as well to make sure their method still worked. But neither Schmorell nor Scholl received theirs. The Gestapo claimed to have confiscated eight hundred of the twelve hundred leaflets sent by mail.[89] Was it possible that on the morning of February 18 Scholl realized that the leaflets had been intercepted by the Gestapo? Were his suspicions confirmed that he had been under surveillance?[90] In any case, he seems to have felt time was running out and that he and his sister had to act without informing their friends.

The interpretation has been offered that tossing the leaflets was a deliberate act of self-sacrifice to encourage other students to resist the regime.[91] But this does not make sense since a vast amount of material incriminating their friends was not destroyed beforehand.[92] Furthermore, the statements of Sophie Scholl and Schmorell indicate that they intended to continue their method of spreading leaflets.[93] Thus Hans and Sophie's throwing the leaflets into the inner courtyard seems to have been a spontaneous act caused by their extreme mental and physical exhaustion or a euphoric, daring mood, or both.

Thus the preparation and production of the sixth leaflet apparently did not entail a long and intricate planning stage. The student address list they used

[87] Statement of Alexander Schmorell, February 26, 1943, in Special Archive Moscow, 1361-1-8808 (n. 12 above), p. 13.

[88] Ibid.

[89] Statement of Hans Scholl, February 18, 1943, in BAP, ZC 13267 (n. 2 above), vol. 2, p. 13; and statement of Alexander Schmorell, February 26, 1943, in Special Archive Moscow, 1361-1-8808, ibid.; report of the special commission of the Gestapo Munich, February 19, 1943, in BAP, ZC 13267, vol. 1, p. 15.

[90] Statement of Wilhelm Geyer, April 5, 1943, in StAM, St.Anw. 12530 (n. 2 above), p. 34: "They repeatedly talked about being observed." Josef Söhngen, in Scholl (n. 8 above), p. 128, also reports that Hans Scholl felt he was observed by the Gestapo. He said Hans Scholl was warned by an informer of the Gestapo.

[91] Kirchberger (n. 8 above), p. 40, shows how this image prevailed immediately after the war. See also the report of Falk Harnack, in Scholl, p. 149; Petry (n. 9 above), p. 119.

[92] See the list of incriminating evidence of the Gestapo and the results of the house search of February 20, 1943, in BAP, ZC 13267, vol. 1, p. 11, and on February 18, 1943, in ibid., vol. 2, p. 1.

[93] Statement of Sophie Scholl, February 18, 1943, in BAP, ZC 13267, vol. 3, p. 10; and statement of Alexander Schmorell, February 25, 1943, in Special Archive Moscow, 1361-1-8808, p. 10.

was old, and there were differences of opinion within the central group. The graffiti activities in February seem spontaneous and very risky, even somewhat reckless, culminating in the events of February 18.

MOTIVES FOR RESISTANCE

It goes without saying that the goals and motives of the White Rose group were complex and widely varied. Hitherto, the literature has described consistent motives that influenced with different emphasis the various members, shaping their attitudes during the years of 1942 and 1943. The strongest motivation seems to have been a Christian ethical outrage over the violent crimes against the Jews and the Poles in the East and Germany's politics in the occupied countries. Willi Graf's turn to resistance, in particular, was influenced by the war of annihilation in Russia whose beginnings in 1941–42 he alone of the group observed firsthand.[94] The German crimes were felt to be a mortgage on the future. Thus Hans Scholl supposedly said, "Our state isn't a state, it is a state consisting of criminals."[95]

But what triggered the actions of the White Rose in June 1942? As of spring 1942, Scholl had heard about the violent crimes in the *Generalgouvernement* from the architect Eickemeyer.[96] But he seems to have felt scruples against taking the step from theoretical opposition to practical resistance, because his concept of *ordo* (order) as being bound to a divine world order did not legitimize intervening in the process of history.[97] For the time being he discussed the situation with friends and vented his rage among them. But finally he decided that discussions were fruitless.[98]

Hans Scholl came to the conclusion "that I had to act out of my inner conviction and I believed that this inner obligation was more binding than the oath of loyalty which I had given as a soldier."[99] Schmorell had similar ideas.

---

[94] Unpublished diary, which reveals that Willi Graf was stationed, since October 1941, in the central sector of the eastern front in the area of Wjasma-Ghatsk, approximately one hundred miles west of Moscow. On the location of the Einsatz- and Sonderkommandos in this area in October 1941, see Helmut Krausnick, *Hitlers Einsatzgruppen: Die Truppe des Weltanschauungskrieges 1938–1942,* 2d ed. (Frankfurt, 1989), pp. 159–60.

[95] Hirzel (n. 50 above), pp. 96–97; statements of Katharina Schüddekopf, March 23, 1943, in BAP, ZC 13267, vol. 15, p. 5.

[96] Petry, pp. 40 ff; and Hirzel. Hirzel states that Hans Scholl was informed about these criminal actions already in winter 1941–42.

[97] Hirzel.

[98] Statements of Traute Lafrenz, March 19, 1943, in BAP, ZC 13267, vol. 6; and statements of Sophie Scholl, February 18, 1943, in ibid., vol. 3, p. 8.

[99] Interrogation of Hans Scholl, February 18, 1943, in BAP, ZC 13267 (n. 2 above), vol. 2, p. 15.

During his interrogation, Scholl explained why the White Rose wanted to mobilize the small circle of the educated bourgeoisie with their leaflets at the end of June 1942: "I was of the opinion that it was high time to point out the political obligations most seriously to this part of the bourgeoisie."[100] This notion of "high time" or a "last hour" is ambiguous. It may articulate Carl Muth's and Theodor Haecker's vision that a spiritual collapse was imminent.[101] Very commonly this apocalyptic message was taken as the decisive reason for the resistance activities of summer 1942. And since the leaflets, indeed, portray National Socialism as an ahistorical and apolitical force and use eschatological images, it is usually assumed that the authors of the leaflets were apolitically following their consciences.[102] However, the phrase might just as well connote a more practical sense of the political situation. Their sense of urgency was a result of the military-political situation in Germany at the end of June 1942. Indeed, it seems that day-to-day political considerations, which reflected the changing military situation, were far more important for the actions of the White Rose than previously assumed.

As we have seen, the White Rose's leaflets appeared between June 27 and July 12, 1942, during a period of time in which the expansion of the Axis forces had reached its limit and the turning point of the war for Germany became visible. On the one hand, the British air strikes were becoming intense and threatening—the first leaflet mentions the Royal Air Force's bombing raid on Cologne at the end of May—and, on the other hand, Rommel's victorious campaign had come to a halt near El Alamein on July 3, 1942. Furthermore, food was becoming scarce in Germany. Thus, when the first leaflet appeared, the public's mood was insecure. According to Security Service (*SD*) reports, the interpretation of the late start of the summer offensive against the Soviet Union on June 28, 1942, was that the Germans would be unable to achieve a decisive victory against the Russians before the onset of winter.[103] The fourth leaflet, dispatched on July 12, 1942, gives a realistic assessment of this military situation: "During the past few weeks Hitler celebrated military victories in Africa and in Russia. . . . Meanwhile Germany's attack against Egypt has come to a halt . . . but still the Germans continue to advance in the

[100] Statement of Hans Scholl, February 20, 1943, in BAP, ZC 13267, vol. 2, p. 21.

[101] See, among others, diary entries of Theodor Haecker, May 12, 1940, and January 1, 1943, in Hinrich Siefken, ed., *Theodor Haecker Tag- und Nachtbücher, 1939–1945,* first complete and commented ed., Brenner Studien, vol. 9 (Innsbruck, 1989), pp. 58, 211; Konrad Ackermann, *Der Widerstand der Monatszeitschrift Hochland gegen den Nazionalsozialismus* (Munich, 1965), pp. 72 ff.

[102] See Kirchberger (n. 8 above), pp. 22–23; and Petry (n. 9 above), pp. 54 ff., esp. p. 58.

[103] See Secret reports of the SS, esp. June 25 and 29, 1942, and July 9 and 13, 1942, in Boberach (n. 72 above), 10:3872–73, 3880 ff., 3922 ff., 3934 ff.

East. The sacrifices that led to this ostensible victory were truly horrible so that they cannot be described as advantageous. We therefore warn anyone against being optimistic."[104]

The leaflets' formulations, such as "before it's too late" or "in this last hour," thus not only reflect eschatological dimensions but also give us an idea of how Schmorell and Scholl assessed the military situation.[105] Obviously they saw a space for action and wanted to show the intellectual elite what was at stake when they wrote, "The individual must recognize his responsibility as a member of Christian and Western civilization and put up as strong a fight as he can in this last hour, act against the scourge of humanity, against Fascism and any similar system that symbolizes an absolute state."[106] Their orientation was opposed to any totalitarian state.[107]

The turning point of the war is also reflected in the leaflets' appeal to the Christian intelligentsia. In the name of a Christian sense of responsibility, the group called for a spiritual and moral reversal and at the same time for sabotage on all levels to shorten the war. Scholl and Schmorell referred to their idealistic and philosophical cultural heritage to write politically radical passages such as this from the third leaflet: "The meaning and the objective of passive resistance is to bring National Socialism to a Fall, and in this battle no one should refrain from any means or any action—in all areas, wherever they may be. . . . This non-state must be given its final blow—a victory of Fascist Germany in this war would have immeasurable, horrible consequences. Germans should not be concerned foremost with military victory over Bolshevism; our first concern is a defeat of National Socialism."[108]

This heated call for action probably originated in the complex personal background of Alexander Schmorell, which further elucidates the complexity of motives that entered the leaflets. Being half Russian, with a pro-Russian but anti-Communist and anti-Nazi position, in June 1942 Schmorell was, as he said, "in a complicated situation, because I was interested in destroying Bolshevism and avoiding Russia's having to lose land. . . . Ultimately, a part of me is of German blood, and that part is being destroyed in this war. There were two factors that moved me to do something. On the one hand, I wanted to protect the German people from the dangers of a major conquest of land and the arising conflicts. On the other hand, I wanted to save Russia from losing

[104] Fourth leaflet of the White Rose, in BAP, NJ 1704 (n. 2 above), vol. 32, p. 4.

[105] First leaflet of the White Rose, in BAP, NJ 1704, vol. 32, p. 1.

[106] Ibid.

[107] Michael Probst, "Zuversicht und Klarheit: Der Widerstand der 'Weißen Rose,'" Sonderdruck aus Dokumentationsband zum 88. Deutschen Katholikentag, München 4.–8. Juli 1984 (Paderborn, 1984), pp. 353–54.

[108] Third leaflet of the White Rose, in BAP, NJ 1704, vol. 32, p.3.

too much land."[109] This is probably why Schmorell wanted to promote passive resistance not only at the home front but also in the field on the eastern front. Such were his declared goals even before the president of the People's Court.[110]

Since Scholl and Schmorell were aware that only a military power could topple the government, which is what the fourth leaflet states, what were their goals in the leaflets? Certainly they intended to shake up the intellectual elite, to encourage individuals to transcend timidity and passivity, and "to bring about . . . an increasingly public consciousness of the true character of National Socialism and of the actual [German] situation."[111] But with the war at a turning point, they also wanted to show what was at stake for Germans: the decline of Occidental-Christian civilization. The two sides remain inseparable and cannot be played out against one another. Thus, the estimation of the military situation was sober. Scholl and Schmorell aimed for publicity calculated to attract attention and to generate resistance against the regime inside Germany. It also seems that they attempted to attract attention in the United States and Great Britain by giving testimony to the presence of "a different Germany." At the same time, the two students picked up Haecker's political theology, which interpreted the impending catastrophe of the Third Reich as an indication of the demise of the Antichrist.[112]

During their three months at the eastern front in the summer and fall of 1942, and through the mediation of Schmorell, Scholl and Graf became well acquainted with the Russian people and the beauty of the Russian landscape.[113] Scholl evidently revised his concept of the Communist system. To the surprise of Huber, Scholl came to the conclusion that the peasants were not Bolshevist, that their economic situation was better than under the tsar, and that they had maintained their religious customs. The peasants considered Bolshevism to be the lesser of two evils.[114] Schmorell was even more extreme. He thought the Communist system had been transcended.[115] After his three-month stay in Russia—which fulfilled in him a deep yearning for his

[109] Statement of Alexander Schmorell, February 26, 1943, in Special Archive Moscow, 1361-1-8808 (n. 12 above), p. 13.

[110] Findings of the second White Rose trial of April 19, 1943, in BAP, NJ 1704, vol. 2, p. 120; and report of Falk Harnack, in Scholl (n. 8 above), p. 156.

[111] Scholl, p. 97.

[112] See once again the interpretation of Kirchberger (n. 8 above), p. 46.

[113] The image of Russia was strongly influenced by the Youth Movement; see Jens, "Die 'Weiße Rose' " (n. 16 above), pp. 211 ff.

[114] Statements of Kurt Huber, February 27, 1943, in BAP, NJ 1704 (n. 2 above), vol. 7, p. 8.

[115] Alexander Schmorell, letter to his parents, August 5, 1942, from the personal papers of Dr. Erich Schmorell.

Russian mother, who had died when he was young—he was determined to return there as soon as possible. On December 9, 1942, he wrote to his Russian girlfriend from Munich: "If I did not have obligations here, I could not stand it any longer. Only these obligations give me the moral right to stay."[116]

After this new assessment of Russia and its political system, the motives and the objectives that prompted the White Rose to write the fifth leaflet sound surprising. I will quote Scholl in full because crucial parts of the beginning of this quotation were left out in the rendering of this passage in East Germany:

> Realizing a German victory was impossible after our defeat on the Eastern Front and the incredible increase of the military strength of England and America, I decided after much painful deliberation that there was only one way to maintain the European idea, and that was to shorten the war. On the other hand, I was horrified by the way the occupied territories and the people were being treated by us. I couldn't imagine that after the way we governed there it would yet be possible to start a peaceful restructuring of Europe. These deliberations increased my skepticism against this state, and because as a citizen of this state I wasn't going to be indifferent toward its fate, I decided to manifest my fundamental beliefs in actions, not only in thoughts.[117]

In Scholl's estimate the war was lost—as a consequence of the defeat at the eastern front and the superior military strength of America and England, whose invasion they "expected in the West," as stated in the fifth leaflet.[118] Scholl's statement shows that his motivation was now strongly determined by his vision of the future. The criminal occupation policies in Eastern and Western Europe would prevent the Germans from playing a role in a peaceful reconstruction of Europe after the war. The objective was now the defense of "the European idea," that is, the historical, religious, and philosophical ideas

---

[116] Alexander Schmorell, letter to his Russian girlfriend, Nelly, December 9, 1942, from the personal papers of Dr. Erich Schmorell.

[117] Statement of Hans Scholl, February 18, 1943, in BAP, ZC 13267 (n. 2 above), vol. 2, p. 12. In the East German literature this statement was abbreviated to read as follows: "After much painful deliberation I decided that there was only one way, that was to shorten the war. On the other hand I was horrified of the way the occupied territories and the people were being treated by us. I could not imagine that after the way we governed there it would be possible to start a peaceful restructuring of Europe. These deliberations increased my skepticism against this state, and because as a citizen of this state I was not going to be indifferent toward its fate, I decided to manifest my fundamental beliefs in actions, not only in thoughts." See, e.g., Jahnke (n. 10 above), p. 49, who quotes Hans Scholl, following Paul Verner, "Die Geschwister Scholl," in *Deutschlands Junge Garde* (Berlin, 1954), p. 289; first traces of this tradition can be found by Paul Verner, "Geschwister Scholl: Der Opfergang einer Jugend," in *Neues Deutschland,* Berlin (February [?] 1948). Paul Verner (1911–86) was head of the youth secretariat of the Central Committee of the SED in 1948.

[118] Fifth leaflet of the White Rose, in BAP, NJ 1704, vol. 32, p. 6.

that had been evoked in the first four leaflets and that made up the group's interpretation of Occidental civilization.

As we know, in the fifth leaflet Scholl and Huber showed an alternative political framework for Europe after the war, in which this European idea was to be realized: a confederation of European states, the destruction of Prussian militarism, a reasonable socialism, and the guarantee of human rights and material goods for all.

Christoph Probst's draft that was found among his investigation reports indicates how the White Rose group envisioned a realization of these ideas.[119] At the end of November or in early December 1942, after the Western Allies had landed in French North Africa and the Sixth Army had been encircled in Stalingrad, Scholl asked Probst to write a manuscript, "the contents of which would be suitable to open the German people's eyes to the fact that only if we approach the Anglo-American States and England will we be saved." Probst gave Scholl his draft on January 31, 1943, after the fifth leaflet had already surfaced.[120] After listening to BBC broadcasts, Probst quoted in his draft Roosevelt's demand for an unconditional surrender on January 24, 1943, emphasizing that this demand was not directed against the people but against the political systems of the Axis powers. The positive example he referred to was the clearance of the German-Italian troops on January 23, 1943, in Tripoli by the British, which was carried out without senseless sacrifices. Probst wrote, "What did the English do? They let the lives of the citizens continue in their usual tracks. They even keep the police and the civil servants." The other extreme, Probst wrote, was the senseless sacrifice of two hundred thousand German soldiers in Stalingrad "for the prestige of a military con-man." National Socialist propaganda had concealed the humane nature of the Russian demands of surrender. Probst then appealed to the Germans: "Today Germany is as encircled as Stalingrad was. Will all Germans be sacrificed to the harbinger of hate and destruction (*Vernichtungswillen*)? To him, who tortured the Jews, who eradicated half of the Poles, who desired the annihilation of Russia—to him who took away liberty, peace, happiness (*Familienglück*), hope and joy, and gave us inflationary money instead? This ought not, this must not be. Hitler and his regime must fall so that Germany can live. Make your decision, Stalingrad and downfall, or Tripoli and a hopeful future. And once you have decided, act."[121] A desire for a "hopeful

---

[119] Draft of the leaflet, which Christoph Probst was forced to reconstruct during his interrogation, in BAP, ZC 13267, vol. 4, p. 7.

[120] Interrogation of Christoph Probst, February 20, 1943, in BAP, ZC 13267, vol. 4, p. 4; and also diary entry of Willi Graf, January 31, 1943, in Knoop-Graf and Jens, eds. (n. 8 above), pp. 104, 319.

[121] Christoph Probst's draft, in BAP, ZC 13267, vol. 4, p. 7.

future" must have been especially strong for Probst, who had a family and whose third child had just been born on January 21, 1943.[122]

Statements of Helmut Bauer and Wilhelm Geyer, two acquaintances of the group, refer to conversations with Hans Scholl and Willi Graf around New Year's 1942–43 that reflect the strong hope they had for England as a political force that would guarantee certain rights after the defeat of Germany and the resulting chaos. One can even find deliberations considering a separate peace settlement with the West.[123]

Probst's draft was never published. Nor did his ideas enter into the sixth leaflet. Did the White Rose friends understand that Roosevelt and Churchill, with their demand for an unconditional surrender, wanted to strengthen their alliance with Russia, avoid cooperation with German resistance groups, and seek a separate peace settlement with Germany? Or did the official announcement of the catastrophe of Stalingrad on February 3, 1943, kill any hope for a quick end to war and for cooperation with the Western Allies?

In any case, the defeat of Germany at Stalingrad, to which the Nazi regime reacted with a total mobilization of all forces and increased terror, produced different reactions among the main instigators of the White Rose. Schmorell reported, "While Scholl was very depressed about the events in Stalingrad, I, who was for Russia, was happy about the war situation that had evolved for the Russians."[124] On February 5, 1943, Probst wrote to his stepmother from Austria: "It's an apocalyptic time and we all have yet to be shaken to the core so that peace can finally take hold in this half-destroyed world."[125] On April 18, 1943, Huber gave a retrospective account of his resistance in a letter to his friend Karl Alexander von Müller. Huber, too, seems to have lost hope for a quick end to war by the Western Allies: "The blow at Stalingrad, which I overestimated, has become my fate, too. I admit—I was nervous, overworked and broken—but at some point I would have come into open conflict with the Nazi state's development, which, even with a passive attitude, I cannot tolerate any longer." This development, Huber explained earlier, consisted in the Nazis' drift to the Left.[126] The explanation of his motives shows that the military catastrophe of Stalingrad triggered the writing of his

---

[122] On January 21, 1943, Katharina Probst, called Katja, was born.

[123] Statements of Helmut Bauer, March 5, 1943, in BAP, ZB II A 27 (n. 12 above), p. 11; and statements of Wilhelm Geyer, April 5, 1943, in StAM, St.Anw. 12530 (n. 2 above) p. 35; and interrogation of Harald Dohrn, April 2, 1943, in ibid., p. 44.

[124] Statements of Alexander Schmorell, February 25, 1943, in Special Archive Moscow, 1361-1-8808 (n. 12 above), p. 9.

[125] Christoph Probst, letter to his stepmother, Elisabeth Probst (geb. Rosenthal), February 5, 1943, from the personal papers of Dr. Michael Probst.

[126] Kurt Huber, letter to Karl Alexander and Irma von Müller, April 18, 1943, in Huber, ed. (n. 8 above), p. 71.

leaflet. But it also reveals that Huber had already been in conflict with the Nazi state because of what he took to be its drift to the Left or, as he stressed repeatedly, "the continual Bolshevization of the German people,"[127] which to him meant "the destruction of material and spiritual freedom and all moral substance."[128]

What objectives did Huber strive for in the sixth leaflet? A battle against the politics of the Nazi party, an appeal to Germany's youth and university students to seek revenge against Nazi tyranny, a fight for the right of self-determination and to establish a new spiritual Europe. This last objective reminds one of the fifth leaflet. Huber's contributions, already in evidence in the fifth leaflet, open up yet another horizon for resistance. Germans were caught in the "here and now"; they were forced to topple the Nazi regime without outside help. Huber recalled in this situation the experience of the wars of liberation against Napoleon in 1813 and thus appealed to German students and youth in a spirit of revolutionary nationalism.[129]

CONCLUSION

The war in its various stages was extremely important for the campaigns the White Rose launched, and not just for the sixth leaflet. The activities of the White Rose reflected military and political events and the politics of the Allies. To this extent, the motivations and objectives of their actions were not only moral and idealistic but also political.

During the first phase, the White Rose directed their leaflets toward the members of an intellectual and Christian elite, hoping to reach people in Germany and abroad. In doing so, they were motivated by Germany's total loss of legitimacy resulting from the Nazi regime's criminal acts and the terror it spread in Germany and abroad, which was at odds with their own values. These leaflets were disseminated during a time at which the turning point of the war for Germany was becoming apparent. If one analyzes their diction and the composition of their addressees, it seems that the authors of the leaflets recognized the military and political situation.

The second phase was also characterized by an evaluation of the military situation as leading inevitably to Germany's defeat. But the White Rose group hoped for a quick end to war and an alliance with the Western forces to retain Christian values, which, for Hans Scholl, were manifested in the European idea. The attempt was made to broaden the campaign and enlarge the circle of

---

[127] Political confession of Kurt Huber, March 8, 1943, in BAP, NJ 1704 (n. 2 above), vol. 7, p. 21.

[128] Sixth leaflet of the White Rose, in BAP, NJ 1704, vol. 32, p. 5.

[129] Ibid.

leaflet recipients to prepare the population in southern German and Austrian cities for "the day after." This campaign ostensibly also wanted to send a signal to the Western Allies.

Following the final defeat at Stalingrad and the increasing terror of the system, the White Rose entered a third phase in which it was thrown back on itself and on its fellow students. The campaigns during this phase show that they aspired to bring about the toppling of the Nazi system. Since their actions did not show a recognizable success, a desperate sense of radicalness and impatience set in, as well as the awareness of surveillance. Their will to topple the system and their ingenuity drove them to ever more reckless campaigns. Thus we can say that on February 18, 1943, they reacted to total war without and total terror within. It was the same day on which Goebbels proclaimed total war—*"den totalen Krieg"*—in Berlin.

Dietrich Bonhoeffer and the Decision to Resist

Raymond Mengus
Université de Strasbourg

Resistance does not happen unless persons actually resist. The story of Dietrich Bonhoeffer (1906–45), the German Protestant theologian who was hanged in the concentration camp at Flossenbürg in the last days of the National Socialist regime, may still provoke some reflections on human destiny and moral choices. Even today this man represents a very poignant case of the gradual involvement in resistance.

Although Bonhoeffer's way was unique, his motives and inspiration remain exemplary. His highly personal decisions were grounded ethically and religiously and are still perceived as stimulating in analogical contexts today.[1] As a mediator between a dramatic past and our own time, Bonhoeffer enlightens our understanding of the moral complexities of his situation as well as provides a significant insight into our own moral challenges.

In the first section of this essay, I wish to discuss resistance with respect to Hitler's dictatorship. Second, I shall examine Bonhoeffer's motivations for taking part in the resistance against National Socialism. And finally I will attempt to trace the stages of his increasingly radical engagement and to evaluate some consequences of his decision to resist.

EMERGENCE AND MEANING OF ANTITOTALITARIAN RESISTANCE

Although we will be discussing the development of one person, we must be careful not to lose a sense of proportion for the wider history of our time. There is, of course, more to our century than the relatively brief reign of Hitler and the even briefer period of the Second World War. Nor does the Third Reich exhaust German identity. We have to guard ourselves against too-quick assessments and generalizations which fail to distinguish among the victims, the victimizers, and the silent majority. Nevertheless these twelve years deserve a special, renewed attention. They not only contain political and military events but also offer keys to a better understanding of people's hearts and minds, especially through the study of opposition by Germans and non-Germans alike.

---

[1] To cite only two examples: *Genf '76: Ein Bonhoeffer-Symposion*, ed. C. Kaiser (Munich, 1976); R. Mengus, *Entretiens sur Bonhoeffer*, ed. Beauchesne (Paris, 1978).

This essay originally appeared in the *Journal of Modern History* 64, suppl. (December 1992).

Debate continues on many aspects of the Nazi period, even in the reading of such basic matters as the French attitude toward German occupation or the scale of French resistance (see also Tony Judt's reflections on this subject in this volume). Even in 1990, public controversy in France persists on the exact role of Jean Moulin, the great "incarnation" of French resistance.[2] And many years after the demythologizing picture *Le chagrin et la pitié,* by André Harris and Alain de Sédouy, a nation of would-be resisters still has to come to terms with its actual nonresistance—another sign of our French difficulty. For everybody who experienced the German occupation, "winners" and "losers" alike, the past presents itself once again as an unchallenged chapter of our lives.

In other parts of our world today we can also observe governments analogous to Hitler's totalitarian state. Thus, resistance to such regimes is clearly not a thing of the past. As long as we face intolerable situations—that is, as long as human history exists—we have to find the courage to say no, for radical opposition. To prepare such an eventual resistance, an example like Bonhoeffer's is of great value, particularly at a time when we notice a certain emptiness, a vacuum of deeply rooted convictions in our Western society. How do we face up to modern or postmodern threats of a subtly totalitarian nature in our developed countries? Our situation demands primarily not a political but rather an anthropological and ethical choice. This is why the life and thought of a consciously reflecting person such as the radical resister Bonhoeffer remains so precious for us. His story interests us beyond all historical particularities as one paradigm of a general human disposition to say no to any form of repression. Bonhoeffer is to be placed in the wider development of human rights; in a sense, the French Declaration of 1789 may be read as a recognition of and an appeal for resistance against every oppression.

Bonhoeffer may also be located in the history of Christianity insofar as this history can be seen (among other perspectives) as a series of resistances, though more episodic than institutional. This history began and culminated with Jesus of Nazareth who, as a free man, resisted many sides of the then-existing political and religious order but was soon himself accused of subverting this order. Probably never since the great persecutions of early Christianity have faith and resistance been joined so closely as during the Nazi time in Germany. Motivated by either political or religious convictions, many individuals and communities came together in a common fight for life and death. As in the famous poem of Eluard, both "celui qui croyait au ciel et celui qui n'y croyait pas" went beyond their ideological differences to link their resources on unexpected battlefields.

---

[2] Daniel Cordier, secretary and now biographer of Jean Moulin, and Henri Frenay represent two opposite interpretations of the French inner resistance.

Theology suddenly acquired a unique temporal, even political efficiency. To recall once more the French case: some of the leading Catholic thinkers of their generation now stood up to develop a risky "theology of resistance." As early as 1940 great names like Henri de Lubac and Gaston Fessard questioned the near general acceptance of their nation's "collaboration" with the occupant force.[3] Their Jesuit colleague Yves de Montcheuil, who joined his Paris students in the maquis and lost his life in the Vercors in 1944, is still the very symbol of the Christian "intellectuel engagé."[4] Jacques Maritain, the lay refounder of modern Thomism, was held in America in 1939 by the declaration of war but did not hesitate to make the decision to resist: from New York, he fought to the end with philosophical and spiritual weapons.[5] During these dramatic years the best of the French Catholic tradition yielded fruits of resistance.

A similar strengthening of the old faith under the pressure of an unprecedented dictatorship was to occur in the other great Western church, on the other side of the Rhine. The German Protestant Dietrich Bonhoeffer was younger than the French Catholics already mentioned; the cardinal de Lubac, for example, was nine years his senior. Yet, beyond any boundary, in the 1930s and 1940s a strong communion between men of the same fundamental orientation developed in the underground.

From Pacifism to Radical Resistance

Bonhoeffer's development toward theological, political, and even armed resistance was perhaps best expressed one year after his execution by one of his former fellow prisoners at Berlin-Tegel who had survived the Third Reich. After the war, the Italian engineer and reserve officer Gaetano Latmiral had located Bonhoeffer's brother-in-law Gerhard Leibholz, then professor at Oxford University. In a letter dated March 6, 1946, and first published in December 1989, Latmiral offered the fresh, living, condensed recollection of

---

[3] See H. de Lubac, *Résistance chrétienne à l'antisémitisme: Souvenirs, 1940–1944* (Paris, 1988), and *Théologie de l'histoire*, vol. 2, *Questions disputées et résistance au nazisme* (Paris, 1990); G. Fessard, "Du sens de l'histoire: Conférence à Vichy" (1940), in *De l'actualité historique* (Paris, 1960), 1:77–93. As early as 1936 this Catholic philosopher expressed a method to interpret present history: *Pax Nostra: Examen de conscience international* (Paris, 1936).

[4] On this "French Bonhoeffer" one can now read *Spiritualité, théologie et résistance: Yves de Montcheuil, théologien au maquis du Vercors* (Grenoble, 1987).

[5] In addition to J. Maritain's war writings *Les droits de l'homme*, new ed. (Paris, 1989), *Christianisme et démocratie*, new ed. (Paris, 1989), see his remarkable correspondence with Général de Gaulle, in *Cahiers Jacques Maritain* (Kolbsheim, 1988).

his experience with a singular fellow inmate. In this testimony the main lines of Bonhoeffer's biography and theology appear:

> He spoke to me about the tragic fate of the German people, whose defects and values he knew; he said to me that it had cost him a great effort to desire his [country's] defeat but that it was necessary. . . . . He said that as a pastor he considered his duty not only to console or to take care of the victims of exalted men who drove madly a motor-car in a crowded street, but also to try to stop them. He said that he was sure not to see the end of these events, because he feared that, in the event he were transferred to a concentration camp, he would be killed with the other political prisoners before the end. He said that in this case he hoped to face death without fear, being convinced it was for the sake of the right and the Christian faith.[6]

In this statement Bonhoeffer's own tragic fate is clearly and strongly contained. But even more forceful is the last written sentence of Bonhoeffer's final hours (April 9, 1945) in the Bavarian concentration camp Flossenbürg to which he had been transferred: "I am dying as a silent testimony of Christ among the brothers." This expresses at once the end and the culmination of Christian existence, of a silent yet—through life and death—forceful theology.

When we consider his earlier life, this man seems not at all destined to proceed in this direction. Therefore we must abstain from supposing that his destiny followed a predetermined course. At Bonhoeffer's cradle, in his family, in his confessional and national traditions there was no preformed inclination toward resistance. Moreover, there was no trend toward theology either. His many decisions were highly personal, beyond all probability and theory, as we hear from his own later confessions. Thus in his youth he opted consciously for an evangelical faith and church. He turned early to a consideration of "the last things": God, his Word, and his grace. The Gospel of Christ became the organizational principle of Bonhoeffer's existence, even his raison d'être. Whereas his older brothers chose academic careers and established themselves in business, young Bonhoeffer was not satisfied until he embraced the final step, what he later called the ultimate, the last things, beyond the mediation of worldly goods. Thus his decision to attend divinity school and then enter the ministry was in no way politically motivated in either the twenties or early thirties.

Moreover, at first, he displayed no signs of any oppositional attitude. Although within a few years he would adopt extreme and risky positions, he began by approaching the public domain with reserve and distance. If he drew attention to himself at this point, it was more through submission than

---

[6] *Die Begegnung: Festgabe für Gaetano Latmiral zum 80. Geburtstag* (Düsseldorf, 1989), Bonhoeffer-Rundbrief 31.

resistance. The Lutheran theory of the two kingdoms—the spiritual and the temporal—was often interpreted as separating them, or even as involving the submission of the first to the latter, even to the point of justifying the unjustifiable. Karl Barth and the reformed doctrine of the church-state relationship were soon to encourage Bonhoeffer to choose a different way and to practice theological opposition at a time when legal opposition was no longer possible.

Bonhoeffer's tendency toward pacifism also supports the thesis that he might not necessarily have adopted a position of resistance. As a young boy he had experienced the Great War in which he lost his older, promising brother; this incident purged him of inflated collective hopes resulting from national exaltation or the cult of power. His systematic theological reflection, especially in the area of ecclesiology,[7] his initial pastoral responsibilities in Berlin and abroad, and his early and numerous ecumenical contacts all strengthened his inclination toward the ideal—or even obligation—of world peace.[8] In the aftermath of the Treaty of Versailles (1919), this young German felt pushed by reason and faith alike into the pacifist movement. This was yet a further obstacle in Bonhoeffer's way to embrace an ethics of armed opposition.

What happened? How did Dietrich Bonhoeffer change his course from such a foundation to the great decisions of his thirties? Here one must consider both external and inner factors. The key to his evolution may be found in a pregnant formulation which appeared in his last writings, particularly in the fragments of his *Ethics:* The ultimate pushed him into the penultimate.[9] For God's sake world and mankind had to be saved.

Bonhoeffer's inner development may be explained to some extent by his general disposition and theological conception. His way had to do with the personal convictions of a free and courageous person. On the one hand, his position is characterized by an unusual search for concreteness and a pronounced attention to reality. As a scholar at Tübingen and Berlin, Bonhoeffer became well acquainted with the temptations of dogmatism. His first publications—including both his doctoral thesis and his professional dissertation (*habilitation*)—are not immune to the tendency to explain

---

[7] His dissertations both give indications in this sense: Dietrich Bonhoeffer, *Sanctorum communio* (1927–30), new ed. (Munich, 1960), and *Akt und Sein* (1931), new ed. (Munich, 1964).

[8] Bonhoeffer made his strongest declaration of pacifism as international secretary of an ecumenical youth association: "Zur theologischen Begründung der Weltbundarbeit" (1932), in *Gesammelte Schriften* (hereafter cited as *GS*) (Munich, 1958), 1:140–61.

[9] Dietrich Bonhoeffer, "Die letzten und die vorletzten Dinge," in *Ethik* (Munich, 1962), pp. 128–52.

everything from one intellectual point of view. However, early on he began to develop a "theology of reality" (André Dumas). He became open to the nonconceptual elements of life and Christian faith. He integrated history and society into his reflection on faith, and thus he made himself vulnerable to the suspicious looks of his theological colleagues.

Was he not scientific enough? Or can one miss the reality even by being thoroughly academic? In any case one may well come to the conclusion that German university professors in this period were among the last to understand their own world, to discover the signs of their time. Has not the one who participates in the actual historic process more opportunity to disclose truth than the one who studies it only from an academic distance?[10]

In addition, his basic disposition included a more and more pronounced ethical component. This dimension was alive in his personal conduct as well as in his understanding and treatment of reflective ethics. On both levels an acute sense of tradition was mixed with spiritual independence, self-consciousness with relentless pursuit of God's concrete commandment (as I have emphasized elsewhere already in some detail).[11] As a faithful man and as a theologian, Bonhoeffer cultivated both his autonomy and his allegiance to an absolute, revealed divine will. His ethics, then, could not be simply deductive nor just obliged to higher authority. Unlike so many moral treatises and handbooks of his time—or of ours—Bonhoeffer's work had a place for themes such as a responsible approach to reality, the free relation to the actual world, and resistance.

Moreover, an intense relation to Christian community and church was characteristic of Bonhoeffer's manner of making theology. In 1932 Barth had published the first volume of his *Church Dogmatics* with a very unusual epithet for such a context: "kirchlich." The theology of his German disciple and friend was also church-oriented, from his dissertation of 1927 through his final fragments. Bonhoeffer's main themes, both academic and spiritual, stood permanently in close connection with the ecclesial realm. The spectrum they covered reached concretely from the area of his Berlin parish over the German evangelical church to the then emerging ecumenical movement. On every level of his thought, discipleship, "cheap and expensive grace," justification and sanctification, culpability and representative suffering, participation in the

---

[10] From his prison Bonhoeffer would formulate for himself the difference between both of these approaches in a series of adjectives which he put side by side, speaking of "unsere beweglichere, lebendige, *weil letztlich wirklichkeitsgemässere* theologische Haltung" (letter to Eberhard Bethge, February 21, 1944, in *Widerstand und Ergebung: Briefe und Aufzeichnungen aus der Haft,* ed. E. Bethge, Neuausgabe [Munich, 1970] [WENA], p. 244; emphasis mine).

[11] R. Mengus, *Théorie et pratique chez Dietrich Bonhoeffer* (Paris, 1978), pp. 51–109.

fate of Jesus Christ—all these themes had inseparable worldly and religious implications. For Bonhoeffer, what was at stake in Christianity was nothing other than the general human condition. On the other side, authentic humanity, especially in dark times, found its most natural ally in the church.

As Barth, once again the master, definitely showed in his famous essay of 1938, "Justification and Justice" have to do with each other.[12] The reciprocity here is decisive. Bonhoeffer took it most seriously. Even more resolute than Barth, he went beyond doctrinal boundaries like the traditional theory of the two kingdoms in order to institute the exclusive and universal lordship of Christ. These beliefs made available fundamental personal and intellectual dispositions. Bonhoeffer's next task was to find the accurate conjunction between his moral stance and the elements of his times—between event, information, and decision.

In Hitler's Germany there was no lack of dreams, illusions, speculations, or compromises. There were a few attempts, or "half political actions," at resistance to the regime.[13] Only a very few committed themselves completely. Count von Stauffenberg remains their military exponent, pastor Bonhoeffer their theological symbol. In Bonhoeffer's case, outside events quickly influenced his inner disposition and brought him step by step to extreme political commitment. The first stages of his resistance appeared soon after the establishment of the National Socialist regime.

Bonhoeffer's first impetus to resistance was provoked by the first Berlin measures against the Jews. At that time his closest friend was pastor Franz Hildebrandt, a half Jew, through whom Bonhoeffer was informed and affected by the discriminatory legislation. In a radio broadcast of February 1938, Bonhoeffer labeled the führer a "Verführer" (a seducer)—and the emission was interrupted on the spot.[14]

Günter Grass has recently forged the sentence "Never did Germans do such a thing."[15] The writer's assessment applies to the suicidal behavior of the German electorate in the fateful year 1933 as well as to the courageous initiatives of a handful of citizens whose perceptiveness partially—or at least symbolically—compensated for the passivity of the masses before the dictator. Not many alternatives were left to those Germans who did not participate in the general acclaim. Apart from simple abstention from public activity or exile, people could choose to focus themselves on their private

[12] K. Barth, *Rechtfertigung und Recht* (Zurich, 1938).

[13] E. Bethge, *Dietrich Bonhoeffer: Theologe, Christ, Zeitgenosse* (Munich, 1967), pp. 476 ff.

[14] Bonhoeffer gave a conference on the same topic at the Berlin Hochschule für Politik (March 1933): "Der Führer und der einzelne in der jungen Generation," in *GS* (1959), 2:22–38.

[15] "Nie haben Deutsche so etwas getan."

cause or duty. They could also try to manifest in one way or another their solidarity with threatened or distressed people. For Bonhoeffer, all began with his deep empathy for a specific group of compatriots, church ministers with a Jewish origin. Their exclusion was for him simply intolerable. Once kindled in this context, his active compassion then extended itself to wider circles.

In 1933 and 1934 it seemed for a while that a resolute attitude of opposition would be adopted by most of the evangelical church leaders and members. The *Kirchenkampf* ignited soon after the Nazis came to power. The alternatively subtle and brutal fight against religion pushed Germany's two main confessions to dramatic choices: either to surrender or to proclaim the "status confessionis"—submission to a pagan, totalitarian state, or resistance on genuinely Christian grounds. While the Roman Catholic community as a whole stood united behind its bishops, Protestant churches splintered. Significant numbers of individuals and parishes, both Lutheran and Reformed, responded to the Third Reich challenge and to the collaborating "German Christians" by creating a defensive and offensive front: the Confessing Church.

At the national synods of Barmen and Dahlem, where this strategy was defined and the church opposition structured, Bonhoeffer was pastor of the German parish at London. From 1934 to the end, nevertheless, he would be one of the most radical and consequential representatives of the Confessing Church. He was to be adamantly loyal to it even in the prewar years when he found it shaky, wavering, in quest of legalization, and ready to make many kinds of compromises, including acceptance of the personal oath to the führer.

Bonhoeffer's main criticism of his confessing brothers was an essential one. Having made a first—religious—step, they refused to draw its consequences; they hesitated to make a second step into social, public resistance. For him, to stop before moving from the ecclesiastic to the political level meant merely to betray the Barmen Declaration. The only course available to the authentic defenders of the 1934 decisions was to thwart the Hitlerian power through total, if desperate, opposition, whether in 1937 (before Austria's and the Sudetenland's annexation), in 1939 at the beginning of the Second World War, or in 1941/42 at the climax of the Nazi military triumphs.

Did Bonhoeffer maintain such a significant posture? His development was complex. He did not immediately turn himself against the oppressor. Like so many others, he was not immune to the illusion of apolitical, purely ideological dissent. As long as he could he took care of the wounded without directly or systematically attacking the culprit, the wounder. As time passed and information exposed the aims of this singular Reich, he like others sought for alternatives to the established (dis)order. But there seemed no organized counterforce visible or possible. Motivated individuals and small groups had to find their way and take their own risks. Very few went as far as Dietrich

Bonhoeffer in combining "conviction ethics" and "responsibility ethics" so closely; perhaps the Weberian binomial was never so intimately united.

In this dramatic situation "the consciences stood up"[16] to deny the leaders of the German fatherland and instead to testify for another Deutschland, for another humanity—despite the remote chances of overthrowing the National Socialist tyranny.

For such an extreme enterprise the moralist Bonhoeffer became the theoretician of extreme responsibility. He, who had taken the irreversible step, could bring first ethical and eventually theological help to both friends and unknown resisters. At stake was much more than just the chance of success: at stake was a moral investment before history, and God.

In Bonhoeffer's biography, one notes clearly a turning point in 1939 during a stay in the United States. After a first sojourn in 1930–31 at Union Theological Seminary in New York City, he had been invited back by a few friends and divinity schools. Through a precious notebook from June 1939 we gain insight into his state of mind during those perilous weeks. He debated of course whether he ought to return to Germany or not. His hesitation finally ended on June 20.[17] His place was at home for decisive if unimaginable fights. A farewell letter to Reinhold Niebuhr, the German-American friend who had obtained him the invitation, clearly and sharply stresses the point:

I have made a mistake in coming to America. I must live through this difficult period of our national history with the Christian people of Germany. I will have no right to participate in the reconstruction of Christian life in Germany after the war if I do not share the trials of this time with my people. . . .

Christians in Germany will face the terrible alternative of either willing the defeat of their nation in order that Christian civilization may survive, or willing the victory of their nation and thereby destroying our civilization. I know which of these alternatives I must choose; but I cannot make that choice in security.[18]

[16] "Das Gewissen steht auf"—with this eloquent title appeared later in Germany two big, well-illustrated, moving volumes containing portraits of and testimonies on main representatives of the German resistance.

[17] Bonhoeffer analyzed his state of mind on the spot. "It probably means more for me than I can see at the moment. God alone knows what. . . . The reasons one gives for an action to others and to one's self are certainly inadequate. One can give a reason for everything. In the last resort one acts from a level which remains hidden from us. So one can only ask God to judge us and to forgive us" (*The Way to Freedom: Letters, Lectures and Notes, 1935–1939, from the Collected Works of Dietrich Bonhoeffer*, vol. 2, ed. and introduced by Edwin H. Robertson, trans. Edwin H. Robertson and John Bowden [London, 1966], p. 233). The day after, this habitually so self-conscious man added: "Ich kenne mich nicht mehr aus. Aber Er kennt sich aus" (*GS*, 1:303–5).

[18] Bonhoeffer, *GS*, 1:320.

Toward an Ethics and Aesthetics of Resistance

From the time of his return to Germany until his arrest and imprisonment in April 1943, Dietrich Bonhoeffer became more and more involved in anti-Nazi activity. He went as far as to participate in searching for a "radical solution," that is, to eliminate Adolf Hitler. He stood in resolute and encouraging relation with persons and groups who prepared the conjuration leading to July 20, 1944. Under these overwhelming conditions he developed ideas and wrote down notes for an ethics of resistance, which implied a certain aesthetics of resistance. His new life and role were largely restricted to the underground, with permanent camouflage in order to keep useful, even official key positions. The opportunities he enjoyed to travel, to have money, and to visit foreign missions allowed him to maintain legally a net of illegal relations; it also brought him into ambiguity and the appearances of a double life. His activities were tied up with evident dangers. They could not bring him the least immediate satisfaction, credit, or honor.

Between the summer of 1939 and June of 1940, Bonhoeffer undertook the decisive step at the most contrary time. He joined the resistance movement at its lowest stand, without idea or possibility of return. His complicity began with a constant and perilous quest for information. In detailing Bonhoeffer's activities in these months, Eberhard Bethge, his friend and later biographer, remarks that information "was for him the first act—so he could maintain independence of judgment."[19]

Beyond that he had a specifically ethical responsibility. Amid his co-conspirators, the pastor and professor of divinity had to think about the moral justification of their common purpose. It was vitally important to find a spiritual basis for approbation so that he could offer reasons for liberating the consciences of his friends—as well as his own. He did not hesitate long before accepting the need to work with the armed forces and in some cases to wear the uniform. He knew from his family and informers that only a conspiracy that included the military would be able to unite a great variety of resisting groups and places.

To reach this goal, it was necessary to act with all kinds of people and under a great variety of circumstances. The former pacifist was now engaged in counterespionage within the official framework of the Abwehr. There the moralist-turned-activist found access to R-Marks, trips, contacts—plus other less official enterprises. His goal was no less than overthrowing a dictatorship and building a new future. Exceptional civil courage was needed. Bonhoeffer best analyzed the mental and strategic situation in a synthetic, confidential assessment composed at a turning point in his life: "Nach zehn Jahren.

---

[19] Bethge, pp. 701–2.

Rechenschaft an der Wende zum Jahr 1943." In these pathetic and at times prophetic reflections on the dramatic decade 1933–42, he stressed the ethical and political necessity for strengthened human values, for unselfish, far-sighted, even hopeless action, and for passion; and he firmly asserts God's presence and involvement in man's history.

A few months later, Bonhoeffer's activity in the underground resistance was discovered. On April 9, 1943, he was arrested. During his detention while awaiting trial, first in the Wehrmacht prison of Tegel and later in the stricter prison of the Gestapo, Bonhoeffer's energy was concentrated on protecting himself and his net, on attempting to downplay the significance of all documents that testified to his implication in the coup attempt. In the aftermath of the assassination attempt, Bonhoeffer's close link with the conspiracy was discovered and he had to fight for his survival. The dramatic self-evaluation he had sketched shortly before his detention then became bitter reality. "Who stands fast? Only the man whose final standard is not his reason, his principles, his conscience, his freedom, or his virtue, but who is ready to sacrifice all this when he is called to obedient and responsible action in faith and in exclusive allegiance to God—the responsible man, who tries to make his whole life an answer to the question and call of God. Where are these responsible people?"[20] Even more pathetic sounds his question: "Are we still of any use? . . . Will our inward power of resistance be strong enough, and our honesty with ourselves remorseless enough, for us to find our way back to simplicity and straightforwardness?"[21]

As for himself, in the same document Bonhoeffer best provided the key to his own ethics and spirituality of resistance. The formula is: "We are not Christ, but if we want to be Christians, we must have some *share in Christ's large-heartedness by acting with responsibility* and in freedom when the hour of danger comes, and by showing a real sympathy that springs, not from fear, but from the liberating and redeeming love of Christ for all who suffer. . . . The Christian is called to sympathy and action, not in the first place by his own sufferings, but by the sufferings of his brethren, for whose sake Christ suffered."[22]

But the decision to resist does produce immediate benefits. First one has to note the actual emergence of "new solidarities beyond long-standing boundaries of class and denomination."[23] This was evident in the case of Dietrich

---

[20] Dietrich Bonhoeffer, *Letters and Papers from Prison,* ed. Eberhard Bethge (London, 1971), p. 5.

[21] Ibid., pp. 16–17.

[22] Ibid., p. 14; emphasis mine.

[23] Michael Geyer, personal communication.

Bonhoeffer. A new, deeper relation developed within his own family, particularly with his brothers-in-law Hans von Dohnanyi and with Rüdiger Schleicher, who shared his fate until prison and summary execution. A similar preoccupation with human dignity and rights brought the bourgeois Bonhoeffer nearer to other social classes; through his resistance network he was in contact and cooperated with a few trade unionists and socialists. A new solidarity developed as well on the ecumenical field; former relations revived; the interdenominational interest extended to Catholicism (parts of Bonhoeffer's *Ethics* were written in the Benedictine abbey of Ettal in Bavaria);[24] the imposing and concrete plans for a new Christianity after the war applied to all existing churches.[25] National boundaries, finally, had to be crossed for the sake of the German nation. Bonhoeffer's trips to Switzerland were among the most risky and important of his activities as an Abwehr conspirator. Through all this, his long-held idea of "Sanctorum communio" came to realization: "Christus als Gemeinde existierend."

In the eyes and hearts of German anti-Nazis like Bonhoeffer, resistance—with or without any prospect of immediate success—promised and brought another series of benefits. It was the most responsible though dangerous means to ensure for later the recovery of the best German values and traditions. As a citizen and as a Christian, the theologian was convinced that he best served his fatherland by radically opposing the "bad drivers" of his land. The clearest, longest, and strongest testimony for this vision and energizing hope is to be found in the marvelous letter that Bonhoeffer sent from prison in May 1944 for the christening of Dietrich Bethge, the son of his friend Eberhard and his niece Renate Schleicher.[26] These moving pages contain a little treatise on the need to maintain old values and a fertile tradition. To oppose the extreme right of National Socialism, it was not necessary to respond from the left or extreme left. Not in Germany, France, or Italy was resistance the specialty of an exclusive (communist) party. An open, moderate, critical conservatism offered ground enough to resist.

---

[24] If Bonhoeffer stood in relation to Catholic institutions, it does not seem that he knew Catholic personalities who could have been very near to his own spirit and thinking. With the exception of the politician Joseph Müller, I did not find signs of any contact with representatives of Catholic resistance like Alfred Delp, Msgr. Lichtenberg, Reinhold Schneider, or Romano Guardini.

[25] Bonhoeffer, *Widerstand und Ergebung,* pp. 413–16.

[26] Ibid., pp. 321–22. Why not confess here as a matter of fact that I came to the reading and study of Bonhoeffer's work through this door? Nearly thirty years ago, the Danish theologian Regin Prenter, who was at the time guest professor at Strasbourg University, spoke to me of this christening letter. Who may have been the man, I asked then and still do now, smart and free enough to compose such a document?

"Revolutionary traditionalism" characterizes Bonhoeffer's vision of a possible and desirable future for both his country and his faith. As for many others, total involvement followed by loss of liberty opened the door to a pure, inner freedom.[27] Bonhoeffer, the theoretician and practitioner of responsibility for others before God, could not do less than to imagine alternative futures. In tragic conditions he calmly expressed his (rather traditional) vision of a postwar Germany, and his (rather revolutionary) interpretation of faith and church in a world that had come of age.

This man had not only a vision; he had intellectual means, moral courage, and the theological ability to express his vision. Thanks to him, those who did not experience such extremity can see what he saw. The historian is not simply a bird of prey. Remembrance ends in gratitude.

[27] Compare Bernadette Morand, *Les écrits de prisonniers politiques* (Paris, 1976), which sketches an interesting typology for the mental evolution of most prisoners in very diverse situations. After various psychological stages often comes a passionate projection into the future.

"We Have Discovered History": Defeat, Resistance, and the Intellectuals in France

Tony Judt
New York University

> I lived through the thirties in the despair of French decline. . . . In essence, France no longer existed. It existed only in the hatred of the French for one another. [RAYMOND ARON]

The Third Republic, it is said, died unloved. Few sought seriously to defend it in July 1940, and it passed away unmourned. Recent scholarship suggests this judgment may need to be nuanced as regards the general population, but so far as the intelligentsia were concerned, it remains a fair comment upon their disengagement from the Republic and its values.[1] Those who had sympathized with the communists were disillusioned by the compromises of the Popular Front, the refusal to intervene in Spain and, finally, by the party's about-face in August 1939, following the Molotov-Ribbentrop Pact. Looking to the socialists, so hopeful in 1936, they would have found similar loss of faith, accentuated by a division within the socialist community over pacifism and the correct response to German expansion. To the right there was the fear and loathing crystallized by the memory of June 1936, bringing conservatives and reactionaries ever closer in a coalition cemented by anticommunism, increasing antirepublicanism and an ever-more-confident and aggressive anti-Semitism. As to intellectuals of the "center," they were rare. Those few men who would speak, after Munich, in defense of the Republic and against fascism, did so in the name of values that they continued to hold in spite of the Third Republic and its shortcomings, but which they had mostly ceased to associate with that political regime and its institutional forms.

The notion that the Republic and the world that it represented were rotten and unsavable was widespread. Writing in 1932, in the first editorial of his new journal *Esprit,* Emmanuel Mounier observed, "The modern world is so utterly moldy that for new shoots to emerge, the whole rotten edifice will have

---

[1] See J.-L. Crémieux- Brilhac, *Les français de l'an 40,* 2 vols. (Paris, 1990); J.-P. Azéma, *1940, l'année terrible* (Paris, 1990); Pierre Laborie, *L'opinion française sous Vichy* (Paris, 1990); René Rémond and Janine Bourdin, eds., *La France et les français* (Paris, 1978).

This essay originally appeared in the *Journal of Modern History* 64, suppl. (December 1992).

to crumble."[2] For Mounier the metaphor spoke above all to questions of sensibility, an aesthetic distaste for the cynical worldliness of late Third Republic France; it did not commit him to any particular political position, and after an initial flirtation with Italian fascism (also on aesthetic grounds), he came out firmly against Nazism and was to be a critic of Munich. On the other hand, his vision of an organic, communal alternative to Republican anomie (Mounier and his generation reflected some of Durkheim's suspicion of modernity, albeit on rather different grounds) kept him and his colleagues in *Esprit* constantly critical of modern democracy. What was needed was a new elite to lead and renew a tired nation.[3]

Mounier's outlook was shared by many others, each in his own terms. Noting the seductive appeal of totalitarian systems, Denis de Rougemont confided to his journal in 1938 the following reflection: "The first task for intellectuals who have understood the totalitarian peril (from right and left) is not to 'join up' with some sort of antifascism but to attack the sort of thinking from which both Fascism and Stalinism necessarily grow. And that is liberal thought."[4] This was a characteristic response—fascism might be the immediate threat, but liberalism was the true enemy. Mounier and Rougement were intellectuals of the Left (insofar as this distinction applied during the thirties), but what they were thinking was echoed on the intellectual Right. J.-P. Maxence echoed their distaste for the mundane world of democratic France: "While most countries of Europe are being led toward greatness and adventure, all our leaders are inviting us to transform France into an insurance company."[5] All in all, the sensibility of the contemporary intellectual when faced with the condition of France was thus very much that of Drieu de la Rochelle (an author admired on Left and

[2] "La moissure du monde moderne est si avancée, si essentielle qu'un écroulement de tout sa masse vermoulue est nécessaire à la venue des nouvelles pousses" (Emmanuel Mounier, "Refaire la Renaissance," *Esprit*, vol. 1 [1932]).

[3] John Hellman, *Emmanuel Mounier and the New Catholic Left* (Toronto, 1981), p. 82.

[4] "La première tache des intellectuels qui ont compris le péril totalitaire (de droite ou de gauche) ce n'est pas d'adhérer à quelque anti-Fascisme, mais de s'attaquer à la forme de pensée d'où vont necessairement sortir le Fascisme de le stalinisme. Et c'est la pensée libérale" (Denis de Rougemont, *Journal d'une époque, 1926–1946* [Paris, 1968], p. 374).

[5] "Tandis que la plupart des pays d'Europe sont dirigés par leurs chefs vers la randeur et vers l'aventure, nous sommes invités par les nôtres à transformer la France en une société d'assurances" (J.-P. Maxence in *Combat* [October 1936], quoted in G. Leroy, "La revue combat [1936–1939]," in "Des années trente: Groupes et ruptures" [Actes du colloque organisé par l'antenne de l'URL, no. 5, Université de Provence 1, May 5–7, 1983], p. 129).

Right alike): "The only way to love France today is to hate it in its present form."[6]

Separated as we are from the world of the thirties by the barrier of war and collaboration, it is easy to underestimate the importance and appeal of the intellectual Right at the time. Political weeklies like *Candide* (circulation 339,000) had a wide audience. The daily *Action Française* published 100,000 copies and had a much wider audience than this *tirage* would suggest. Indeed, the influence of Charles Maurras, the founder and guiding spirit of *Action Française,* was immense, comparable in its impact on contemporary young intellectuals to that of Sartre a decade later. Maurras's particular contribution to contemporary alienation from the Republic lay in "his violent and contemptuous attitude toward his opponents,"[7] which formed a generation of writers in whom an aggressive distaste for the compromises of democratic politics became a commonplace. Like the Communist party of the postwar years, Maurras and his movement constituted a sort of *plaque tournante,* a stage through which passed a surprising number of writers later associated with quite different political positions. Jean-Marie Domenach, a contributor to *Esprit* and later its editor, would admit, some twenty years later, to having been seduced (albeit, as he put it, in "une manière enfantine et intense") by the fascist mood of the thirties, and he was far from alone.[8]

The gleeful schadenfreude with which right-wing intellectuals would greet France's downfall in 1940 was echoed, in muted form, in the feelings of people who were themselves by no means on the Right. For many Catholics, who took no responsibility for the deeds and misfortunes of a political system that had devoted time and effort to expelling them from its midst, 1940 was at best a well-merited tragedy, if not a punishment for the sins of the past three generations. But even for their erstwhile opponents, the event was also not without its redeeming dimensions, an apocalypse half-welcomed, deliverance through catastrophe from a political and moral system they could no longer defend. Left and Right alike shared a common distaste for the lukewarm and

---

[6] "Il n'y a qu'une façon aujourd'hui d'aimer la France, c'est de la détester telle qu'elle est." See Drieu de la Rochelle in *Combat* (April 1937). See also Emmanuel Mounier, reviewing *Gilles* in *Esprit* (April 1940): "La France d'avant-guerre avait besoin de muscles et d'un peu de sauvagerie," quoted in Michel Winock, *Nationalisme, anti-sémitisme et fascisme en France* (Paris, 1990), p. 371.

[7] "Son violent et méprisant à l'égard de l'adversaire" (Julien Benda, *Belphégor: Essai sur l'esthétique de la société française dans la première moitié du vingtième siècle* [Paris, 1947], p. 209).

[8] Thus, Jean-Marie Domenach: "J'ai vécu, de 1934 à 1939, d'une manière enfantine et intense, la vague fasciste qui secouait alors l'Europe," quoted from an interview with *l'Express* in 1959. See Eric Werner, *De la violence au totalitarianisme: Essai sur la pensée de Camus et de Sartre* (Paris, 1972), p. 41, n. 1.

were fascinated by the idea of a violent relief from mediocrity.[9] Robert Brasillach, later to be executed at the Liberation as the symbol of intellectual collaboration and who in the thirties wrote pointed, often scabrous columns for extreme right-wing papers, frequently expressed his reluctant admiration for the "hard" Left. Himself drawn to fascism, he could appreciate the appeal of Moscow to his opponents; as he would note, reflecting on the experience of the interwar years from the perspective of 1940: "It was a time when everyone looked to foreign countries, seeking there . . . warnings and examples."[10] The disaffected, antibourgeois tone of the reactionary intellectual echoed and sometimes even inspired that of his progressive contemporaries: the "nausea" of Drieu's *Gilles* at the prospect of France's old ruling class has more than a little in common with that of Roquentin.

* * *

This crossing of the lines, the intersection at the extremes of radical sentiments from Left and Right, did not, of course, begin with the thirties. Proudhon and Péguy were icons for the syndical Left and the integrist Right alike because they had addressed, in their very different ways, the limitations and frustrations of parliamentary republicanism that had occupied the thoughts of earlier generations as well.[11] It was in the 1920s that Georges Valois had unsuccessfully attempted a combination of nationalism and socialism in a movement to be devoted to attacking "individualism, liberalism" and the parliamentary regime, and among those who had been initially attracted was Paul Nizan. Even before the First World War Edouard Berth (in *Les méfaits des intellectuels*) had proposed something similar, a union of Left and Right against democracy "for the salvation of the modern world and the grandeur of our Latin humanity."[12] The difference after 1932 was that a new generation of intellectuals adopted these vague ideas and tried to give them tangible form and programmatic content.

This generation has now been consecrated in the historical literature as that of the "nonconformists" of the thirties, representing a special mood and outlook.[13] Just how new or original it really was is perhaps open to question—Nizan, by then a committed Marxist, described it as a middle-class

---

[9] Claude Roy, *Moi, Je* (Paris, 1969), p. 215.

[10] "C'est le temps où chacun se tourne vers les pays étrangers, où il y cherche . . . quelques avertissements et quelques instructions" (Robert Brasillach, *Notre avant-guerre* [Paris, 1941], p. 204).

[11] Ibid., p. 163.

[12] "Pour le salut du monde moderne et la grandeur de notre humanité latine" (quoted in Winock, p. 252).

[13] See J.-L. Loubet del Bayle, *Les non-conformistes des années 30* (Paris, 1969).

elite, distilling half-understood "thick foreign philosophical currents."[14] But however superficial its contribution to political or philosophical speculation, it most assuredly shared a common sense of the need for renewal and expressed a widely held longing for something new and confident. Between 1930 and 1934 there appeared a steady flow of books, pamphlets, clubs, plans, journals, and circles, all peopled by men and women in their twenties and thirties; some came from the political Right, others from the Left (like the Révolution Constructive and Plan groups within the Socialist party and the Confédération Générale du Travail), though most made a point of asserting their indifference to existing political divisions and organizations. Few of the movements and periodicals survived the early thirties (*Esprit* is the most important exception), and much of what they published neither deserved nor acquired a wide audience. There were also important distinctions among them (not always clearly seen at the time): Mounier and his circle sought to construct a new morality, antibourgeois and spiritually refreshed, while others saw capitalism as the problem, and worked to devise alternative social and economic programs for national renewal. What they shared, however, was what François Mauriac (in a different context) called "an idea at once just and tainted";[15] the nation was in a parlous condition and only wholesale change could save it. This condition of France was taken to include (and in part to derive from) its republican and democratic forms, its emphasis on the rights of the individual at the expense of the duties and interests of the community. Hence the ease of communication across traditional nineteenth-century barriers, and hence, too, a certain ambivalence in the face of antidemocratic challenges, at home and abroad.

These challenges only surfaced openly in the wake of the events of February 6, 1934, for many young intellectuals on Left and Right the moment at which their aesthetic and philosophical leanings were shaped into political commitment. With the Popular Front there came a further exercise in sentimental education, the moment at which those of the Right parted company definitively from the "socialist and Jewish" Republic. On the Left there was a momentary truce, as many of the "nonconformists" of the early thirties placed their hopes in the promise of radical social transformation from above. With the failures of Leon Blum's government and its heirs there came a renewed alienation from republican politics, this time definitive. By 1938, the common sentiment of French intellectuals is described (and echoed) in

[14] Paul Nizan, quoted in Hellman (n. 3 above), p. 73.

[15] "Une idée à la fois juste et corrompu." According to Mauriac, Drieu, like others, "sentaient vivement que le concept de nation, au sens étroit que les Jacobins français lui donnaient, était atteint" (François Mauriac, *Journal,* vol. 4 [Paris, 1950], entry for September 25, 1945).

Arthur Koestler's characteristically disabused commentary: "What an enormous longing for a new human order there was in the era between the two wars, and what a miserable failure to live up to it."[16]

The end of the thirties was marked, furthermore, by the growing significance of pacifism.[17] From the early twenties, the desire for a secure peace had marked the whole of the French community, exhausted and drained by its "victory" in the war and collectively sensitive to Paul Valery's famous rumination on the fragility of civilizations. The intellectual community of the twenties expressed its war weariness most forcibly in a collective retreat from political affiliation, but even those on Right or Left who remained politically involved shared a universal longing for an end to military involvement. The Right sought to achieve this through the (illusory) strength of the French armed forces; the Left, through the hunt for collective security. Indeed, writing in the late twenties, Thibaudet remarked that "Today one could say that 'socialism equals the search for peace.' One is a socialist by virtue of the priority given to this problem over all others."[18] But by the thirties, lines that had once been clear were again blurred. The Communists, until 1935 adamantly opposed to any form of national defense, were from then until August 1939 the most ardent and consistent proponents of antifascism (before joining the integral pacifists once again in their opposition to any "capitalist" war). The Right, while remaining in principle as germanophobic as ever, was confused in its allegiance by a sympathy for Hitler's Italian ally and by a virulent hatred of the post-1936 Republic, led by "outsiders" with interests of their own that risked embroiling France in a war she did not need. As for most intellectuals, they, like the political parties of the center Left, were cruelly divided. Some, the followers of Alain or heirs to the older socialist emphasis on antimilitarism at all costs, moved from antifascist committees into unconditional opposition to war at any cost. Others, a small minority, shared Raymond Aron's understanding of the nature of Nazism and the way in which Hitler's accession to power had altogether changed the terms of political choice.[19] And a considerable number found themselves somewhere in

---

[16] Arthur Koestler, *The Yogi and the Commissar* (New York, 1945), p. 102.

[17] See, notably, Antoine Prost, *Les anciens combattants et la société française, 1914–1939,* 3 vols. (Paris, 1977). See also André Delmas, *À gauche de la barricade* (Paris, 1950).

[18] "Aujourd'hui on dirait 'le socialisme, c'est la recherche de la paix.' On est socialiste aujourd'hui dans la mesure où l'on met ce problème avant les autres" (Albert Thibaudet, *Les idées politiques en France* [Paris, 1927], p. 203).

[19] According to Etiemble, he was tempted to follow Drieu, sharing his scorn for Left and Right alike, but was fortunate enough to be disenchanted by Hitler and Munich. See Etiemble, *Littérature dégagée, 1942–1953* (Paris, 1955), p. 193. See also J.-F. Sirinelli, *Génération Intellectuelle* (Paris, 1988), p. 640.

between: witness the paradoxical condition of a Bertrand de Jouvenel—half-Jewish, a friend of Blum and against the Munich compromise, but a member in 1936 of the neofascist Parti Populaire Français and constantly tempted by the appeal of order and stability associated with Nazi Germany.[20]

These intertwined and contradictory positions, adopted by various people or by the same people at different times, often in the midst of confusion and moral uncertainty (Blum's famous "lâche soulagement" at the news of Munich was probably typical of many), are inadequately captured in the notion of "commitment" or the opposition between democratic and undemocratic affiliation. Certainly, commitment, or "engagement," was the term of choice for many contemporaries. But it fails to distinguish between Left and Right—or, when making the distinction, exaggerates it; more to the point, it insists upon a discontinuity between the active engaged intellectual of the early and mid-thirties and the apparently disillusioned, disengaged, cynical stance of all but a few in 1940. What is lost here is the idea of engagement as an end in itself—the notion, common to intellectuals of the thirties and forties alike, that there was some sort of existential imperative to be involved. The specific direction of that involvement was less important; in politics as in battle, "on s'engage et puis on voit." Moreover, the emphasis on engagement/disengagement fails to catch the continuing commitment of intellectuals in 1940 and after, as we shall see. But whatever the nature of that engagement, it was not and had for some time not been committed to the democratic Republic.

The uncertainties and variations in intellectual life during the thirties also help explain the relative unimportance of the communist intellectual. In marked contrast with what was to come, communism did not yet exercise an irresistible charm for the thinking classes. Like fascism, Soviet communism's strongest suit was its condemnation of bourgeois society, in its rhetoric and in its actions (indeed, then as for decades to come, communist rhetoric was suffused with just that language of corruption, decay, and renewal that colored the writings of the thirties nonconformist intellectuals). But its practical, positive appeal was still limited: "The intellectual leans toward communism because he smells the scent of death hanging over the bourgeoisie and because capitalist tyranny exasperates him. But communism then requires of him that he subscribe to a program and methods that seem to him, respectively, stupid and ineffective."[21] With the withering away of the Popular Front, the

---

[20] See Bertrand de Jouvenel, *Un voyageur dans le siècle* (Paris, 1979).

[21] "L'intellectuel tend vers le Communisme parce qu'il sent sur la bourgeoisie l'odeur de la mort et que la tyrannie capitaliste l'exaspère. Mais le Communisme exige alors de lui qu'il souscrive à un programme et à des methodes dont l'un lui semble

Communist party and its syndicalist allies lost much of their recently acquired mass support, to the point of being little better off at the outbreak of war than they had been in 1934. Out of tune with the pacifist sentiments of the nation in 1938 and 1939, accused by former supporters like Gide of having hidden the truth about the Soviet Union,[22] embarrassed by the Moscow show trials and alienated from a radical intellectual constituency by their very moderation during the Popular Front years, the French communists by 1940 exercised little appeal to most intellectuals. Although some came to the party's defense during its persecution by Daladier in the *drôle de guerre,* the volte-face that precipitated that official harassment of the Parti Communiste Français (PCF) not only lost the party most of its remaining support but alienated from it some of its most influential intellectual adherents. Had men like Gabriel Péri and Paul Nizan not been killed in the war and occupation, they might well have returned to haunt the PCF in its postwar bid for cultural hegemony.

The German victory and the Pétainist coup of July 1940 thus found a French intellectual community in a political disarray symptomatic and reflective of the social and physical disarray of the nation itself. Even those who remained faithful to the Republic would be so shaken by the events of that year that they were driven to reflect on the disaster, finding in it evidence of a corruption and decay they had not previously understood.[23] It is worth noting that among those who did remain loyal, who were ostensibly immune to the mood of the thirties, were a disproportionate number of intellectuals from an older generation. Those on the Left who had come of age at the time of the Dreyfus Affair retained a loyalty to republicanism in its classic shape, whatever their growing criticisms of the practice of politics in Republican France. The younger generation, for whom not the defense of the rights of man but war had been the formative moment in the collective experience, was much more likely to prove sensitive to the appeal of pacifism and/or fascism.[24] This is a point of some significance, not so much for the thirties themselves as for what would follow. For not only was Vichy initially appealing to many in this generation, but it was this same cohort that emerged after 1944 as the dominant group within the intellectual community. Born between the turn of the century and 1913, they lacked any collective experience of successful democratic politics. They also had never had the occasion to unite, in good

---

stupide et les autres inéfficaces" (Emmanuel Berl, *Mort de la pensée bourgeoise* [1929; Paris, 1970], pp. 97–98).

[22] A. Gide, *Retour de l'URSS* (Paris, 1936).

[23] See Leon Blum, *À l'échelle humaine* (Paris, 1945); and Marc Bloch, *Étrange défaite* (Paris, 1946).

[24] See Sirinelli, pp. 463 ff.

faith and with clear conscience, in defense of democracy and rights. All their political experience consisted of opposition and disaffection.

The year 1940, then, marks not so much a break between a democratic and an authoritarian regime as the consummation of a process of decline and alienation, shared by many and articulated by a new generation of intellectuals in the last decade of the Republic. For many, Hitler's lightning victory constituted the verdict of history, a judgment upon the inadequacy and mediocrity of contemporary France (much as Stalingrad later would be seen as history's positive verdict upon communism). Many past and future democrats shared the view that, though hardly a "divine surprise," the accession of Pétain and his "National Revolution" provided an opportunity to begin the reconstruction of the nation, along lines drafted in the course of the debates of the thirties. Henri Massis, an intellectual of impeccable conservative credentials, could have been speaking for many from all points on the spectrum when he wrote, in December 1940, that the task now was to deliver the French from "the appalling abuse of trust to which they have fallen victim; it will be necessary to relearn how to use words truthfully, to restore to them their meaning and their value."[25]

If it is true, as Camus was to note in October 1944, that a "world ended" in June 1940, it should not be supposed, therefore, that this was a source of regret to many.[26] This is not, however, something one can easily discover from the memoir literature that deals with this period. Those who would go on to collaborate or abstain from public life are naturally inclined to minimize the pleasure they felt at the overthrow of the Republic, even though for many of them the war with Germany had been but an interlude in the much longer and more important conflict among the French. But the memoirs of those who had the good fortune to emerge on the victorious side in 1944 are not much better. There is something fundamentally disingenuous about Claude Roy's suggestion, for example, that he lived the years 1935 to 1939, ideologically speaking, as an "insomniac" trying to find a comfortable spot in bed.[27] He may have sensed that his true home did not lie with the men of *Action Française* and *Je Suis Partout* with whom he was then sharing column space; later he would have the same experience with his new communist friends. But uncomfortable or not, at the time he presumably shared the enthusiasm of his fellow right-wing intellectuals at the ignominious collapse of the Republic, so it is odd that his three-volume memoirs offer no echo of that enthusiasm. Others

[25] "L'effroyable abus de confiance dont ils ont été les victimes, il faudra reapprendre à être honnête avec les mots, en leur restituant leur sens et leur valeur" (Henri Massis, *Au long d'une vie* [Paris, 1967], p. 149). The passage quoted was written at Uriage in December 1940.

[26] Albert Camus in *Combat* (October 7, 1944).

[27] Roy (n. 9 above), p. 21.

among his contemporaries slide across the space between the collapse of France and the establishment of the Resistance some years later with similarly selective recollections.

This is an understandable human response to complicated and contradictory experience. But for the historian it leaves the moment of 1940 in shadow. This is in part the result of treating the events of the spring and summer of 1940 as the beginning of Vichy, the Occupation, and (by extension) the Resistance. On the contrary, they are best seen as the closing sequence in the intellectual adventure of the interwar decades, an experience composed of various shades of hope—positive, negative, forlorn, and ultimately lost. Intellectuals who had made a career out of describing and condemning the inadequacies of the Republic came face-to-face in 1940 with the fulfillment of their earlier demands for its overthrow. It is not really surprising that most of them, once they got over the shock of the defeat itself, saw in the National Revolution some hope for the future. This was especially and predictably the case for those who, during the early thirties, had espoused ideas about central planning, social "organicism," new moral orders, and an end to divisive emphases on the individual. To take a stand against Pétain at this early stage would have required not only considerable foresight (not to speak of courage); it also would have meant a willingness to defend, albeit in some modified form, the very values with which the deceased Republic had been associated.

This was not an attitude widely found in France, at this time, among any group of the population, and there is no reason why it should have prevailed to any greater extent among intellectuals. Indeed, for the reasons suggested above, the opposite is the case. If "a certain number of Frenchmen were already weary by 1940," there is no reason to exempt the intelligentsia.[28] To understand the impact of the years 1940–44 upon French intellectuals, it is thus important to have in mind the point of departure for that experience, which shaped the terms in which Vichy, the Resistance, and the postwar "revolution" would be understood. With respect to liberalism, democracy, the rights of man, and the heritage of republicanism, it was very, very difficult in 1940 to imagine, much less proclaim, a case for the defense. What was missing was a commonly accepted language in which to express and advocate such matters. The very men and women who might now have undertaken the task of rebuilding an ethos of democratic politics were, of course, in no position to do so for purely practical reasons. But this would pass. What endured, and colored so much that followed, was the sense of being politically inarticulate, of having been deprived—of having deprived oneself—of the ideological and linguistic means with which to construct a morally defensible

[28] Camus, *Combat* (October 7, 1944).

polity. It has been charged against the writers and thinkers of the thirties that their arguments, directed against the prevailing regimes, offered no guidance to others on how to react to political or moral dilemmas—the rise of Hitler, the crisis of appeasement, the advent of Vichy. This is true, but perhaps a little beside the point. The real problem was that these intellectuals provided no such guidance to themselves.

* * *

> In sum, we have discovered History and we claim that it must not be forgotten. [Maurice Merleau-Ponty]

It is not always easy to distinguish, in the biographies of prominent postwar figures, the precise circumstances or motives that impelled them to take a particular political or philosophical stance following the *débâcle* of 1940. Writing from the vantage point of 1945 and beyond, they often collapsed the years 1940–44 into a single experience. Placed in the path of History by the impact of combat, prison, German occupation, and intellectual or physical resistance, they recognized at the Liberation that their prewar concerns, notably those that had kept them aside from political engagement or public action, could no longer be recaptured. For some (Sartre, Merleau-Ponty) this was a philosophical observation before it became a political choice; for others like Mounier and his fellow Catholics it was—or seemed to be—a natural extension of their earlier spiritual critique of interwar society. What was not often conceded was that for most people this lesson had not been learned in 1940, but only in the course of the years that followed (years during which, it might be added, Sartre and a few others acquired a cultural prominence with remarkably little interference from the occupying authorities or their French collaborators). Not only did the intellectual resistance and the accompanying historical self-consciousness so much in evidence in 1945 not begin in 1940 but the fall of the Third Republic was in fact followed by a brief but important period of illusion and even optimism.

Those who sought to recover something positive from the defeat of France had first to give the new order a meaning beyond that imposed on it by German fiat. The events of 1940 had to be recast as an occasion to transcend old divisions, to remake France, and not simply an opportunity for revenge on the defeated Republic. With a greater or lesser degree of good faith, this is how pro-Vichy intellectuals of the nonfascist variety presented to themselves the opportunity of 1940, and it helps explain why men who would later join the intellectual resistance to Pétain and the Germans were at first swept along in the fantasy.

The best, because best-intentioned, example of the ambivalence that characterized initial responses to defeat can be found in the brief experiment at Uriage, in southeastern France. The outlines of this first French attempt to establish a training ground for a new moral and political elite are well known.[29] The group that came together in the autumn of 1940 with the ambition of building a new and exemplary community, something halfway between a scout camp and a *grande école,* carried distinctive echoes of early thirties ideas and attitudes. It was dominated by a younger generation of Catholics—soldiers, scholars, and teachers—and gave priority in its lectures and daily activities to ideas of responsibility, hierarchy, and national renewal. The emphasis on a specifically Christian renewal was accompanied, as it had been a decade earlier, by a markedly critical attitude toward the bourgeoisie (and the late unlamented "bourgeois Republic"). Mounier and other writers from *Esprit* were prominent among the early speakers, but also present were a new group from whom would emerge important public leaders of the Fourth and Fifth Republics (including Hubert Beuve-Méry, the founder and first editor of *Le Monde,* who would later bring to his new publication some of the ideals and quite a lot of the sanctimonious confidence of the Uriage community).

The ambivalent aspect of the Uriage experiment, which lasted little more than a year, lay in its acceptability to Vichy. Indeed, the new regime and the Uriage activists shared a symbiotic relationship. With the exception of the communists, these left-wing Catholics (the description is slightly anachronistic but not inaccurate) constituted the only group with a clear social and cultural identity to survive 1940 in a recognizable form (indeed, there is a certain significance to the fact that both Mounier and the communists sought official permission to continue printing their journal under the new regime; Mounier was accorded the right to do so). Although the growing insistence at Uriage on themes of freedom and morality eventually brought it into conflict with the authorities, the early concern with a remaking of the national "soul" echoed the language of the National Revolution. Mounier's rather delphic concept of *personnalisme* favored values like "service," leadership, efficiency, and community that some prominent officials around Pétain sought genuinely to apply to French public life.

Moreover, this sort of language also addressed a parallel sensibility within the secular community, and even within the political Left. Leon Blum, after all, had similar criticisms to offer of the spiritual shortcomings of the Third Republic (and his own and his party's role within it): one of the themes of *À l'échelle humaine* was the need for a liberated France to give itself a stronger

---

[29] Pierre Bitoun, *Les Hommes d'Uriage* (Paris, 1988).

executive power, to rid itself of the traditional distaste for control and direction that had undermined republican government. The representative institutions of the bourgeois republic had failed the nation, he would write, and his views were shared by a goodly number of younger socialist intellectuals who emerged in the Resistance.[30] Thus the Uriage group spoke to a widespread sentiment, and might be said to have combined for a brief period the concerns of the Left within the National Revolution and the moderates of the nascent intellectual resistance. This point is captured symbolically in the reading matter favored by the leadership at Uriage, which ranged from Proudhon to Maurras but took in Marx, Nietzsche, and Péguy, among others, along the way. Any and all critiques of bourgeois materialism were welcomed.[31]

Where the intellectuals at Uriage eventually parted company from the Vichy regime was in the latter's increasingly collaborative stance and the growing evidence that the National Revolution was at best an illusion, more likely and increasingly a cynical facade for persecution, dictatorship, and revenge. But it is important to note that the illusion of finding a "third way" between fascism and liberal democracy was not abandoned. As late as February 1941, by which time articles in *Esprit* were already being heavily censored and some of the original Uriage activists had gone underground, Emmanuel Mounier was attacking the newly forming Christian Democrats (that Catholic element within the Resistance that eventually would coalesce into the Mouvement Républicain Populaire [MRP]) for their overemphasis on democracy. Placing the "defense of democracy" at the masthead of opposition and renewal was, he wrote in a letter, "uncreative" and inflexible.[32] From then until his death in 1950 Mounier would remain suspicious and critical of the MRP and its ideals, preferring to retain the high ground of moral renewal rather than descend to the level of democratic political struggle, with all that this implied about a return to the ways of the Republic and the failure of the hopes vested in an alternative vision.

For Mounier's non-Catholic contemporaries the early Vichy experience offered less hope of change or national rebirth, but they did share with the men of Uriage the sense that 1940 had changed the rules of the game. Before 1940, even the most engaged intellectual could see himself as an isolated actor, making private choices and expressing preferences and objectives that were his alone and that he was free to adopt or abandon at will. The very

[30] See Blum (n. 23 above).

[31] See Janine Bourdin, "Des intellectuels à la recherche d'un style de vie: L'école nationale des cadres d'Uriage," in *Revue française de science politique* (December 4, 1959), p. 1041.

[32] See Emmanuel Mounier, "Lettre à Etienne Borne" (February 22, 1941), in his *Oeuvres* (Paris, 1961–63), 4:694–95.

relationship between writing and action had hitherto been fortuitous—only in rare instances like Malraux or St. Exupéry was the writer living, or appearing to live, the demands of his literary creations. With the defeat of France all this changed. Writers and artists were no longer free to say, publish, or perform whatever they wished. They risked, always in theory and often in practice, persecution and punishment for their ideas. Many of them were brought face-to-face, for the first time, with the need to think through the relationship between their private thoughts and their public lives; in the midst of a humiliating national tragedy, even the most solitary of writers could not help but feel affected by the fate of the community.[33]

It does not, of course, follow from this that the shape of intellectual life in wartime France was constantly colored by real dangers and the sort of clarity such dangers can bring to even the most clouded mind. Only a few of the men and women I am discussing here were ever exposed to real risks during this period; indeed, those who went to the most trouble to theorize this situation tended to be the ones whose positions were least exposed and whose careers were least affected. But this does not diminish the significance of their interpretation of the times. What Sartre in 1945 would call being "en situation dans son epoque" was something all could feel. Whatever was now going to happen would in a sense be their responsibility, especially if they chose to abstain from choice by pretending to an irresponsibility that no longer existed.[34] It is not clear just how much intellectuals actually felt "brusquement situés" from the very start, but even if it is an ex post facto account of their condition it is not for that reason false.[35]

Being a part of History—having no choice but to respond to your circumstances and take charge of them—meant breaking with the aesthetic impulse of some thirties intellectuals to be "ailleurs qu'est la foule," and it meant taking seriously the idea of evil, the possibility that human existence might hang in the moral balance and must be defended and reclaimed.[36] Once again, it should not be supposed that no one had thought of this before 1940; but as we have seen, the intellectual ethos of the late thirties precluded the sort of ethically grounded political defense of freedom (at least in the republican form in which the French had hitherto conceived of it) that such a stance might

---

[33] See, e.g., Raymond Aron, in *France libre* (London; June 15, 1941).

[34] "Jamais nous n'avons été plus libre que sous l'occupation allemande" (Jean-Paul Sartre, *Les lettres françaises* [September 9, 1944]); see also Simone de Beauvoir, "Oeil pour oeil," in *Les temps modernes* (February 5, 1946), pp. 814 ff.

[35] In "Q'est-ce que la littérature?" Sartre writes of having had his eyes opened by the crisis of 1938—"du coup nous nous sentimes brusquement situés." This seems a little doubtful. See *Situations* 2 (1948): 242–43.

[36] See Drieu de la Rochelle, "Récit secret," quoted in Louis Bodin, *Les intellectuels* (Paris, 1964), p. 70.

entail.[37] After the fall of France, however, and especially after 1942, when excuses for collaboration or compromise became harder to find, intellectuals would find themselves discovering, in the very act of political disobedience, the freedom they would later defend. The dilemma between "being" and "doing" that had seemed so significant before the war collapsed. To do was to be: no longer a universal consciousness vested in a singular self, the intellectual was bound within the organic community, presented with apparently simple choices, all of which entailed action of one sort or another.[38] Being part of the common purpose, accepting as one's own the meaning given to a collective action, being offered certainty in place of doubt, the intellectual resister took on a mantle of confidence and shed the cloak of insecurity that had shrouded the previous generation.[39]

Why did some intellectuals find this confidence and others not? For some people, the explanation lies in their disillusion with the initial expectations placed in Vichy; others never harbored illusions in the first place but could only be brought to defend what became the values of the Resistance once they had recovered from the shock of defeat and had been sufficiently moved to protest at the policies and practices of occupiers and collaborators alike. A third category (in which should be included men such as Merleau-Ponty or Sartre) seem to have been waiting for some such moment all their lives, so enthusiastically did they welcome the chance to be part of a romantic commitment whose scope and meaning would both transcend, transform, and give practical effect to their earlier writings. In practice only a minority of intellectual resisters saw real action of any sustained sort, whether in the Free French armies, the armed resistance, or in clandestine networks of all kinds. For most of the rest, it was the association with the community of resisters that counted, the sense of being part of something larger than oneself—a circle of dissenting writers, a resistance group, a clandestine political organization, or History itself.

This sense of being part of something larger than oneself also had a politically radicalizing effect. In part this was the inevitable outcome of the one-sidedness of domestic Resistance politics and the increasingly reactionary and repressive nature of government policy. With the passage of time, and at an accelerated pace after 1942, people forgot their dislike of the republic and concentrated instead on the crimes and sins of the regime that had replaced it. In effect, the French now had been engaged in a civil war that by 1944 had

---

[37] According to J.-M. Besnier (*La politique de l'impossible* [Paris, 1988], p. 234), Georges Bataille at least did not need Hitler and the impact of his war to awaken him to the existence of evil.

[38] Maurice Merleau-Ponty, "La guerre a eu lieu," *Les temps modernes* (October 1, 1945), p. 64.

[39] See Maurice Merleau-Ponty's letter to the journal *Action* 74 (February 1, 1946).

lasted eight years, and the participants on the winning side were led by the force of their own experience to rethink their commitments and to state them in ever starker forms. The absence of any possibility of compromise (and, later, of any need for it) encouraged the emergence of a political and moral vocabulary keyed to absolutes—the absolute defeat of one's adversaries, the nonnegotiable demands of one's own side. Once it had become clear that there was nothing to be retrieved from the Vichy experience, Resistance intellectuals of every kind devoted their attention instead to constructing the future, taking it as given that one began with a tabula rasa.

Curiously, this did not mean abandoning once and for all the republican past, since the national political imagination (and contemporary circumstances) offered few alternative sources for a rethinking of France. On the contrary, the lost illusions of 1940 helped cast the once-despised Third Republic in a better light. True, as Camus put it in August 1944, the Resistance had not made so many sacrifices only to resume the bad habits of a country "that had been preoccupied so long with the morose contemplation of its own past."[40] That past, La France de M. Herriot, of boutiques, *bureaux de tabac,* and "banquets législatifs, une France sans obligation ni sanction," which had made of the words *député* and *gouvernement* symbols of derision, was gone and should not be revived. But, as an anonymous editorialist noted in the clandestine journal *Après,* published in Toulouse, "A few years of the French state and the Vichy dictatorship will have sufficed to endear the Republic to those who had no love for it in the past."[41] Compared with what one had just seen, heard and experienced, the Republic did not look so bad.[42]

Intellectuals who had identified with the Resistance, then, emerged from the war years with an oddly paradoxical sense of themselves and their purpose. In the first place, their experience was of interest and value to them precisely to the extent that it denied the previous isolation of the intellectual condition and merged it with the actions and movement of a whole society. Yet at the same time their engagement on the side of a historical movement as intellectuals bequeathed to them a special sense of duty, the obligation to articulate and

---

[40] "Qu'on a voulu maintenir si longtemps dans la rumination morose de son passé" (Camus, *Combat* [August 24, 1944]).

[41] "Quelques années d'État français et de dictature de Vichy auront en effet suffi à faire aimer la République par ceux-là mêmes que ne l'aimaient pas autrefois." See ibid. (June 27, 1945); and the editorial in *Après* (July 2, 1943), quoted in H. Michel and B. Mirkine-Guetzévitch, *Les idées politiques et sociales de la Résistance* (Paris, 1954), p. 87.

[42] Mauriac, on March 15, 1945, commented with reference to "nos anciens adversaires" and their incurable phobias: "La haine de la démocratie, une peur animale, une peur viscérale du communisme, l'attachement aux privilèges de l'argent et aux régimes qui mettent la force brutale au service de ces privilèges, l'injustice à l'égard de la classe ouvrière" (n. 15 above).

pursue what they understood to be the lessons of the war years, both in politics and in their own professional activities as responsible intellectuals. Second, they had undergone a political radicalization very unlike that of the thirties, since it was shorn of ambiguity and arrière-pensée, and yet the local form of political life to which that radicalization now committed them resembled the same Third Republic that most of them had shunned just a few years earlier (the continuity with the Third Republic accentuated, of course, by de Gaulle's insistence on treating the Vichy regime as nothing more than an illegitimate interlude). The years of resistance and clandestinity (for some) had obscured these paradoxes, but they would emerge with embarrassing clarity as soon as the war was over.

Superficially, Resistance-era intellectuals were divided in many ways. On the one hand there were the Catholics, themselves split along political lines and also by generation (the intellectual and cultural gulf separating François Mauriac from the *Esprit* circle, e.g., was quite unbridgeable); then there were the unattached intellectuals soon to be associated with Sartre and *Les temps modernes.* Beyond these there were the "politicals"—socialists, communists, and Gaullists, and beyond them an important if disparate group of intellectuals whose distinctive identity was formed in the Resistance itself, men like Claude Bourdet or Albert Camus. In practice, most of these people had experienced the Resistance years in one of two ways. If they had been part of the organized communist or Gaullist movements, they inclined toward a collective view of the recent past, seeing the organizations and activities of the years 1940–44 as a paradigm for a better France. On the other hand, as individual resisters or as members of movements more loosely shaped (and often resolutely nonparty political), the rest tended rather to recall the war years as a sequence of individual choices, exemplary and binding upon themselves, but above all a private experience, lived in public. The implications of this distinction would be felt in later years, in the uses to which wartime memory was put and the causes it could be made to serve.

There were, however, two aspects of the war years that were common to all. One of these was well expressed in a speech in 1945 by Albert Camus: "The hatred of the killers forged in response a hatred on the part of the victims. The killers once gone, the French were left with a hatred partially shorn of its object. They still look at one another with a residue of anger."[43] This seems to me a remarkably acute observation. The civil war did not come to an end

---

[43] "A la haine des bourreaux a répondu la haine des victimes. Et les bourreaux partis, les Français sont restés avec leur haine en patie inemployée. Ils se regardent encore avec un reste de colére" (Camus, speech at La Mutualité [March 15, 1945], reprinted in Albert Camus, *Actuelles* [1950; Paris, 1977], 1:116).

in 1944—it simply lost its external targets and shape. In the writings of all French intellectuals of these years there lurks a hidden and half-admitted fury. It would be too easy to treat this as the redirection of self-hatred, and insufficient to ascribe it to straightforward motives of resentment and revenge. Many of the angriest men and women may have been overcoming feelings of inadequacy (there was an occasional inverse correlation between the publicly stated desire for vengeance and the absence of any marked record of heroism or physical engagement); but they do seem to have been speaking, in their way, for the emotions of the nation. Pursuing a line of thought already characteristic of the later Third Republic, and now shaped into a moral language by the struggle against Vichy, they divided all experience, all choices, all of humanity indeed into binary categories: good or evil, positive or negative, comrades or enemies. A natural and normal practice in time of war, this angry Manichaeism continued to mark France long after the resolution of the conflict with Germany.[44]

The second universally shared sentiment was one of urgency—urgency to join the winning side in 1944 ("so many were afraid, at that point, to miss the bus of history"),[45] but also the desire to make up for lost time. This was true at the personal level, of course, with many intellectuals frenetically writing and publishing their way into a literary or journalistic career, and it is in large measure accounted for by the fact that most of the prominent figures of the intellectual community were still not much over thirty years of age. But it also marked the political and social thought of the day, and the policies and positions derived from it. Having rediscovered their faith in certain truths (if not transcendent, then at least self-evident), the French intelligentsia were in a collective hurry to see these applied. Once again extrapolating from the Resistance years, the only experience of collective action most of them had ever known, they looked upon inaction as the worst of all options. Indeed, like the generation of the thirties, they saw "revolution," in this case the continuation and completion of the experience and objectives of the Resistance, as the only solution, the only way to prevent France from slipping backwards. But unlike their predecessors (or, in some cases, themselves at an earlier stage) they were now in a position, if not to make a revolution, at least to impose upon their own society the language and symbolism of urgent and wholesale upheaval.

* * *

[44] See Paul Wilkinson, *The Intellectual Resistance in Europe* (Cambridge, Mass., 1981), p. 265.

[45] "Combien ont eu peur, à ce moment, de manquer la patache de l'histoire" (Pierre Emmanuel, "Les oreilles du roi Midas," *Esprit* [December 1956], p. 781).

Curiously, the political ideas and programs of the Resistance itself were not notably revolutionary. Or, rather, they were implicitly radical in content (and in the context of French social and political history) but were expressed for the most part in remarkably mild language.[46] Some of them consisted of the continuation of the social program of the Popular Front; others proposed significant legal and political innovations; some even sought to pursue and perfect certain administrative and institutional reforms inaugurated by Vichy itself. One can ascribe this to the need for compromise between different political parties and movements, or to the search for a consensus around which to reunite a divided nation. But whatever the causes, the consequence was a series of proposals and ideas remarkably moderate in their overall tone. Most of the spokesmen for the Resistance certainly saw the Liberation as an opportunity for dramatic economic changes, for more and better planning, and socially controlled distribution of goods and services. But beyond this, and vague calls for political "renewal," there was no consistent and clearly articulated Resistance "vision."

One reason for this was the desire to avoid overly programmatic designs, easily drawn up and as easily abandoned. François Mauriac probably spoke for many when he noted, in August 1944, that "We know all too well the uselessness of these panaceas, these hastily typed fantasy programs,"[47] even if his own rather exalted perspective took insufficient account of the practical problems facing the new governments. Perhaps even more representative is the opinion of Claude Bourdet, reflecting a few years later on the remarkably nonideological nature of the Resistance in which he played an active part: "Clandestinity, and then prison, sharpened in most of us the sense of the certain collapse of a whole society . . . but they did not lead us to think in plans or schemas; the Resistance had learned to rely on a combination of voluntarism and empiricism: un-French approaches, but ones that had succeeded elsewhere."[48]

A further source of this moderation was the total concentration, at least in the internal Resistance, on fighting the enemy. A large part of the initial program of the Conseil National de la Résistance (CNR) was concerned with

[46] For the programs of the Resistance, see H. Michel and B. Mirkine-Guetzéevitch (n. 41 above).

[47] "Nous sommes payés pour connaître l'inutilité de ces panacées, de ces programmes mirifiques, tapés à la machine" (François Mauriac, *Mémoires politiques* [Paris, 1967], p. 150).

[48] "La clandestinité, puis la prison avaient accentué chez la plupart de nous ce sentiment de l'effondrement certain de toute une société . . . mais cela ne conduisait pas à penser en plans et en schémas; les résistants . . . avaient appris à compter sur la volonté active jointe à l'empiricisme; procédés peu français, mais qui ont fait leurs preuves ailleurs" (Claude Bourdet, *L'observateur* [August 21, 1952]).

practical problems to be faced in the daily struggle, with longer-term solutions to France's chronic weaknesses to be addressed once the battle was won.[49] Members of the Resistance, intellectuals and politicians alike, had no shared background experience, no common view of the future and its possibilities. The Resistance program was primarily a moral condition and a bond of experience and determination. Something better had to come from the sacrifices of the struggle, but the shape of that vision was left to individuals and political groups to articulate. If there was a general sentiment, it was probably something along the lines of Camus's desire for "the simultaneous instauration of a collective economy and a liberal polity."[50]

In these circumstances, it might be thought, the wider hopes vested in the Resistance were doomed from the start. This may be so; certainly in France, as in Italy, the dream of a single all-embracing Party of the Resistance, breaking old political allegiances and committed to nonpartisan national reconstruction, never really got off the ground. But even before the disillusion of 1945, political reality had intervened. It was in 1943 that Jean Moulin allowed (some would say encouraged) the re-formation of political parties within the CNR, largely to appease those who resented the presence of communist political networks in their midst. Thus the main organization of the Resistance fostered the reconstitution of the major parties of the defunct Republic, with the notable addition of the MRP. This return to party politics occasioned some comment and disapproval, but it was not until later, seeing the ease with which postwar France seemed to have slipped into the comfortable old clothes of its predecessor, that intellectuals directed criticism at the parliamentarians for betraying the ideals of a united national renaissance.[51]

Of all the newly reemergent political parties, it was the communists whose appearance mattered the most for the intellectual community. This is not because the PCF could count on a significant membership among the haute intelligentsia—quite the contrary: the impermeable, deathless commitment of an Aragon ("My Party has restored to me the meaning of the times / My Party has restored to me the colors of France") was only ever a minority taste.[52] But for many younger intellectuals, the party had not only redeemed itself in action since 1941 but it represented in France, both symbolically and in the

---

[49] See Jacques Debû-Bridel, "La Quatrième République est-elle légitime?" in *Liberté de l'esprit* (October 1952), p. 220.

[50] "La mise en train simultanée d'une économie collective et d'une politique libérale" (Camus, quoted in Jeanyves Guérin, *Camus et la politique* [Paris, 1986], p. 231).

[51] See H. Michel and B. Mirkine-Guetzéevitch (n. 41 above).

[52] "Mon Parti m'a rendu le sens de l'épopée / Mon Parti m'a rendu les couleurs de la France."

flesh, the transcendent power and glory of Stalin's Soviet Union, victorious in its titanic struggle with Nazi Germany, the unchallenged land power on the European continent and heir apparent to a prostrate Europe. A sense of having experienced the prelude to an apocalypse was widespread among those for whom the Occupation had been their formative political experience. Older left-wing intellectuals might vote communist and even place their hopes in a Marxist future, but they could not wholly forget the Molotov-Ribbentrop Pact, nor even the problematic Soviet domestic record of the thirties. Younger ones, however, ignorant of the past or anxious to put it behind them, saw in the party a political movement responding to their own desire for progress, change, and upheaval.[53] Thus Pierre Emmanuel wrote in 1956: "I dreamed of an ideal communism through fear of real communism, fascinated as I was, like so many others, by the imminent apocalypse rising out of the chasm into which Europe had just been swallowed up."[54] It helped that communism asked of its sympathizers not that they think for themselves but merely that they understand the case for adopting the authority of others. For intellectuals who sought so passionately to melt into the community, communism's relative uninterest in their own ideas was part of its appeal.

Moreover, communism was about revolution; this was the most important part of its attraction. It was the source of some confusion: intellectuals dreamed of revolution in the immediate and in the abstract, while Lenin's heirs dutifully maneuvered on the terrain of tactical practice, where revolution in the future could always justify passivity in the present. But these crossed purposes, even when conceded, had no impact upon the commitment of intellectuals to the idea of revolution itself, even if they led to occasional ingenuous criticisms of the PCF for its lack of insurrectionary fervor in the years 1945–47. For most postwar French intellectuals, the term "revolution" contained three distinct meanings, none of which depended upon the communists or their doctrine. In the first place, "revolution," it seemed, was the natural and necessary outcome, the logical terminus ad quem of the hopes and allegiances of the wartime years. If France in 1945 was to go in any direction at all, it would only be propelled there by a revolution: "If we call ourselves revolutionaries, it is not just a matter of hot words or theatrical gestures. It is because an honest analysis of the French situation shows us it is revolutionary."[55]

---

[53] J. Verdès-Leroux, *Au Service du Parti* (Paris, 1983), pp. 100 ff.

[54] "Je rêvais d'un Communisme idéal par peur du Communisme réel, fasciné que j'étais, comme tant d'autres, par l'imminente apocalypse qui se levait de l'abîme où venait de s'engloutir l'Europe" (Emmanuel [n. 45 above], p. 781).

[55] "Si nous disons révolutionnaires, ce n'est pas par échauffement verbal ni par goût du théâtre. C'est parce qu'une analyse honnête de la situation française nous la montre

We should not take too seriously Emmanuel Mounier's claim to have undertaken an "honest analysis" of the contemporary French situation, nor suppose him as free of "échauffement verbal" as he imagined. He had, after all, been proclaiming the need for "revolution" ever since 1932. But the difference in 1945 was that the cumulative experience of the defeat, Vichy, the horrors of occupation and deportation, the sacrifices of the Resistance and the revelation of France's decline made it seem realistic to believe in a coming moment of catastrophic and total change, in a way that had not been the case before 1940. Not only could reasonable people now believe in the likelihood of utter collapse and destruction, but it seemed irrational to imagine that major change could be achieved in any other way. If French history from 1939 to 1945 meant anything, it seemed to warn against believing in the possibility of progressive improvement and human benevolence.

Second, "revolution" meant order (in this respect intellectuals and communists were in agreement). It had been a commonplace of the cultural critiques of the early thirties in France that capitalism and bourgeois society were a version of the Hobbesian vision of nature, a war of all against all in which the strong emerged victorious and all nonmaterial values were doomed. A new order was thus called for in the moral and the social realms alike. But disorder, after 1945, described not only the unregulated mediocrity of the Third Republic but also the unjust and arbitrary authority of foreign and domestic fascist power. Order, in contrast, would be the condition of society after a revolution of a very particular sort, one deriving its political coordinates from the lessons of history and its moral imperatives from the recent experience of political struggle and engagement.

Third, and this was Sartre's special contribution, though it expressed the views of many others at the time, revolution was a categorical imperative. It was not a matter of social analysis or political preference, nor was the moment of revolution something one could select on the basis of experience or information. It was an a priori existential requirement. Revolution not only would alter the world but it constituted the act of permanent re-creation of our collective situation as the subjects of our own lives. In short, action (of a revolutionary nature) is what sustains the authenticity of the individual. In the early postwar years Sartre, still at this time committed to his writing, would seek to deculpabilize himself and his social class for their intrinsic social marginality by claiming that writing *was* action. By revealing, writing transformed, and in transforming it revolutionized its objects, a view that is seen at its most developed in *Qu'est-ce que la littérature?*[56] Later, of course,

---

révolutionnaire" (Mounier in 1945, quoted in Anna Boschetti, *Sartre et "Les temps modernes"* [Paris, 1985], p. 239).

[56] See *Situations* 2 (1948).

he would abandon this indirect approach and commit himself to direct action (or as direct as his personal limitations allowed).

The abstract and protean quality of "revolution" thus described meant not only that almost any circumstance could be judged propitious to it and any action favorable to its ends; it also meant that anything that qualified under the heading "revolutionary" was necessarily to be supported and defended. The Manichaean heritage of the Resistance did the rest—to be on the side of the good was to seek "the revolution," to oppose it was to stand in the way of everything for which men had fought and died. Within France this reductionism could do relatively little damage, since the threat of real revolution after 1945 seemed to be ever diminishing. Thus it cost little to be "for" the revolution, and was hardly worth the effort to be against it, in this abstract form. But elsewhere in Europe the impact of war and (real) revolution was still being felt, and there one's stance on the meaning of revolutionary language and acts really mattered.

Because the dream of revolution was so pervasive in the discourse of postwar intellectuals, it is worth looking ahead to note the moral price that was exacted. The case of Mounier is exemplary, precisely because he and his circle were not attached to any political movement, had few if any foreign entanglements, and represented, in their own eyes, a moral position purer than that of their contemporaries, beholden to no one and driven only by a wish for spiritual renewal and a love of truth and justice. Writing in 1944, Mounier urged on the French community a thoroughgoing spiritual and political revolution, whatever the cost. All revolutions, he wrote, are "full of ugliness"; the only question is, "Should the crisis come to a head, and if so as soon as possible?" We are engaged in radical upheaval, he insisted; we cannot go back now. As for a precipitous historical transformation, "the only way to neutralize its risks is to bring it about." The French have the chance, he went on to suggest, to abolish human suffering and lay the basis for happiness and something more besides. This challenge cannot be met by a "parliamentary democracy of the chatty, liberal sort, but . . . it should be organically bound to a real democracy, with firm structures."[57]

All this sounds harmless enough, a typical article of its time, combining an invocation of revolutionary possibilities with general political prescriptions drawing on the language of the thirties' nonconformists. But buried just below the surface one can already detect the omelette thesis, the belief that a

---

[57] "Farcies de laideur." "Faut-il que la crise aboutisse, et aboutisse aussi vite que possible?" "Le seul moyen d'en neutraliser les dangers, c'est de la faire aboutir." "Démocratie parlementaire de type libéral et bavard, mais . . . elle devra sourdre organiquement d'une démocratie réele, aux structures fermes" (Emmanuel Mounier, "Suite française aux maladies infantiles des révolutions," *Esprit* [December 1944]).

sufficiently important historical advance is worth the price we may have to pay to bring it about. This is stated a little more openly in an article published two years later, but is rendered explicit in the editorial commentary published by *Esprit* on the occasion of the Prague coup in February 1948.[58] Because this, the last communist takeover in central Europe, made little pretense of representing the desires of the majority or of responding to some real or imagined national crisis, Mounier's response to it is illustrative of the moral price he was driven to pay in order to sustain his faith in the intrinsic value of revolutionary action. It is worth quoting at length: "In Czechoslovakia the coup masks a retreat of capitalism, the increase of workers' control, the beginnings of a division of landed property. There is nothing astonishing in the fact that it was not undertaken with all the ceremonial of a diplomatic move, nor that it is the work of a minority. None of this is unique to communism: there is no regime in the world today or in history that did not begin with force, no progress that was not initiated by an audacious minority in the face of the instinctive laziness of the vast majority."[59] As to the victims of the coup, the Czech socialists and their social-democratic allies, Mounier had no regrets. The social-democrats in particular he described as "saboteurs des Libérations européenes." Their cause is lost, their fate richly deserved—"they belong to a dead Europe."[60]

Mounier and his colleagues on *Esprit* are significant precisely because they did not claim to share the communists' worldview. But a revolution was a revolution, its goals *ex hypothesi* laudable, its enemies and victims in principle the servants of the past and the enemies of promise. One source of this favorable prejudice, and it is a point that has received wide attention in recent years, was the problematic status of the term "revolution" in the history of French political thought and language. One hundred fifty years after Saint Just, the rhetorical hegemony exercised by the Jacobin tradition not only had not diminished but had taken from the experience of the Resistance a renewed vigor. The idea that revolution—the Revolution, any revolution—constitutes not only a dramatic break, the moment of discontinuity between past and future, but the only possible route from the former to the latter, so pervaded

---

[58] Emmanuel Mounier, "Débat à haute voix," *Esprit* (February 1946), pp. 76–77.

[59] "En Tchécoslovaquie le coup d'état masque un recul de capitalisme, l'accroissement du contrôle ouvrier, le début du partage des terres. Qu'il ne la fasse point avec le cérémonial d'une démarche diplomatique, qu'il ne s'exprime sans doute qu'une minorité, il n'y a pas là de quoi s'étonner ni mettre en cause specialement le Communisme: il n'est pas un régime au monde et dans l'histoire qui n'ait débuté par un coup de force, pas un progrès qui n'ait été déclenché par une minorité audacieuse contre la paresse instinctive du grand nombre" (Emmanuel Mounier, "Prague," editorial in *Esprit* [March 1948]).

[60] "Ils appartiennent à l'Europe morte" (ibid.).

and disfigured French political thought that it is hard to disentangle the idea from the language that it has invested with its vocabulary and its symbols.

Thus Mounier and his generation are hardly to be blamed for their adoption of such a vision and the venerable language that accompanied it. The disdain felt by Simone de Beauvoir, for example, at all mention of "reformism," her desire to see social change brought about in a single convulsive moment, or else not at all, was a sentiment she shared not only with her contemporaries but with fin-de-siècle socialists, Commune-era feminists, and the Blanquist fringe of French socialist thought throughout the previous century.[61] As the last and most enduring of the myths of the Enlightenment, the idea that an intrinsically evil order only could be replaced by one founded on nature and reason, revolution was always likely to become a dominant passion of the intellectuals, in France as in Russia. The special quality of the postwar era was the immediate possibility it seemed to offer for the enactment of this last great historical drama.

It is this that made all the more poignant the rapid disillusion of these years. Indeed, almost before the revolutionary moment seemed to have come, there were those who could already sense its passing. As early as December 1944 an *Esprit* editorialist was lamenting that there was nowhere in France to be found the smack of firm and new political authority. In the same journal, Jean Maigne drew readers' attention to the dead and deported Resistance leaders and the mediocrity of the political chiefs now emerging: "We see all of a sudden that the Resistance is but a shadow of itself."[62] Of course, in some circles a certain dolorous pleasure was taken in proclaiming the hopelessness of the situation, even as the same writers called for change and upheaval. But in this case the sentiment really was widespread. By 1947 it was universally held to be the case that the Liberation had "failed." The best-known symptom of this was the failure to follow through on the *épuration* of collaborators and the purge of tainted political and economic leaders.[63] The demand for justice, or vengeance, had been integral to the revolutionary vision of communists,

---

[61] See de Beauvoir's comments throughout her writings from this period, notably in her memoirs, *La force des choses* (Paris, 1963).

[62] "Nous nous apercevons tout à coup que la Résistance n'est plus que le déchet d'elle même" (Jean Maigne in *Esprit* [December 1944], quoted in Jean Galtier-Boissière, *Mon journal depuis la libération* [Paris, 1945], p. 81). See also the editorial in *Esprit* (December 1944): "Ce que l'on cherche partout en vain c'est une doctrine politique neuve et ferme."

[63] For detailed figures on the French *épuration*, see, e.g., Hilary Footitt and John Simmonds, *France, 1943–1945* (New York, 1988). Whereas in Norway, Belgium, and the Netherlands, the numbers of persons sentenced to prison for collaboration varied from 400 to 640 per 100,000 inhabitants, in France in the figure was just 94 per 100,000. See also Peter Novick, *The Resistance versus Vichy* (London, 1968), esp. app. C, pp. 202–9.

intellectuals, and even some within the political center; a final settling of scores with France's past was the necessary condition of a better future. Even those like Jean Paulhan who thought that the *épuration* had been a hypocritical exercise in private revenge conceded that, as a movement for revolutionary change, the Liberation had lacked the courage of its convictions and represented a lost opportunity.[64] In January 1947 Mauriac, perhaps recalling his own hopes of 1944 and his biting condemnations of the Third Republic, noted sourly, "Everything is beginning again. Everything remains hopelessly unchanged. . . . The Third Republic lives on; it is the Fourth that is dead." "Who," as Camus lamented a few weeks later, "today cares about the resistance and its honor?"[65]

The skeptical disaffection of 1940, the revolutionary hopes invested in the liberation of France, and the rapid disillusion that followed so soon after, are an important part of a number of stories about contemporary France. They cast a revealing light upon the emphasis that was placed in the first postwar years upon "the honor of the resistance," the need for a vengeful justice, and the half-acknowledged desire to prolong by all possible means the certainties and harmonies of the Resistance experience itself. This entailed on the one hand reconstructing that experience as something both more significant, more morally self-aware than it had been, and on the other extracting from it political and moral positions which could then be applied in other situations and to other conflicts and choices. Had the actual experience of resistance and liberation been more decisive, had the Fourth Republic been the child of something more recognizably decisive and radical by way of birth pangs, things might have been different. As it was, the intellectual community in postwar France remained unhealthily fixated upon its wartime experience and the categories derived from that experience, with significant and enduring consequences.

[64] Jean Paulhan, *Lettre aux directeurs de la Résistance* (Paris, 1952).

[65] "Tout commence. Tout demeur désespérément pareil. . . . La troisième République continue; c'est la quatrième qui est morte" (François Mauriac, *Journal*, vol. 5 [Paris, 1953], entry for January 28, 1947). "Qui se soucie aujourd'hui de la Résistance et de son honneur?" (Camus, *Combat* [March 22, 1947]).

NACHHOLENDER WIDERSTAND—

RESISTANCE AFTER 1945

"A Beacon in the German Darkness": The Anti-Nazi Resistance Legacy in West German Politics*

David Clay Large
Montana State University

In 1946 Alexander Abusch, the leftist writer and recently returned émigré, identified the small minority of Germans who had actively opposed Hitler as a "beacon in the German darkness" whose light must be kept burning to show the way to a democratic future for postwar Germany.[1] But it soon became apparent that this beacon did not provide a clear and steady point of orientation for most Germans in the post-Nazi era. Indeed, attempts to steer by it yielded almost as much confusion and discord as comfort or inspiration. The following article explores some of the efforts to use the resistance legacy as a moral guide and as a source of historical legitimacy for the new political experiments in Germany. Though it focuses primarily on the Federal Republic of Germany (FRG), it draws also on developments in the German Democratic Republic (GDR) for purposes of comparison.

Alexander Abusch notwithstanding, when it came to establishing a West German state in 1949, the German framers of that new political order did not find—indeed they did not look for—a major source of inspiration in the wartime resistance movement. It is true that three of the state constitutions—those of Hesse, Bremen, and West Berlin—contained provisions for "resistance" against unconstitutionally exercised governmental authority, but until 1968 the federal constitution, the *Grundgesetz,* did not. A proposition for such a resistance clause was advanced in the constitutional debates but was rejected on the grounds that it would introduce a plebiscitary element into the governmental system—something that the Weimar experience prompted the framers to avoid at all costs. Moreover, opponents of a resistance clause pointed out that it made no sense to enshrine such a "right" in the constitution, since by definition it could apply only in situations where the constitution had broken down. *Widerstand* in the true sense, it was argued, stood outside legal norms. How could one "normify the unnormifiable?"[2]

---

*An earlier version of this article appeared in *Contending with Hitler: Varieties of German Resistance in the Third Reich*, ed. David Clay Large (Cambridge: Cambridge University Press, 1991). Portions © 1991 Cambridge University Press reprinted with permission.

[1] Alexander Abusch, *Der Irrweg einer Nation* (Berlin, 1946), p. 260.

[2] For a discussion of the debate on codifying a right to resistance in the *Grundgesetz,* see Christoph Böckenförde, "Die Kodifizierung des Widerstandsrechts im Grundgesetz," *Juristenzeitung* 25 (1970): 168–72.

This essay originally appeared in the *Journal of Modern History* 64, suppl. (December 1992).

As for the populace as a whole, public opinion polls taken in the first years of the Federal Republic registered an attitude ambivalent at best toward the phenomenon of German resistance. A survey taken in 1952 showed that only 20 percent of the respondents believed that Hitler's opponents should have resisted during wartime; 34 percent insisted that the resisters should have "waited until after the war"; and 15 percent said there should have been no resistance at all. To the question, "How should the men of the Twentieth of July be judged?" 40 percent answered positively, and 30 percent answered negatively; the rest had no opinion. Over 50 percent were opposed to naming a school after Count von Stauffenberg.[3] In these same years liberal newspaper columnists often complained that the resistance cause "had not found a secure place in the German heart" and that the Twentieth of July seemed already "forgotten."[4]

Some Germans, however, appeared to have remembered this dimension of their recent past only to condemn it in the old Nazi fashion. There was in the early 1950s considerable open talk of the July 20 assassination attempt as a "treasonous" act. Right-wing former-officers' associations like the Bruderschaft and the Freikorps Deutschland took this line; so did respected ex-generals like Heinz Guderian and Franz Halder. A Deutsche Partei Bundestag delegate named Wolfgang Hedler won an enthusiastic following in Schleswig-Holstein with his claims that the German war effort had been crippled by anti-Nazi defeatists. By 1951 West German newspapers were warning of a "new stab-in-the-back legend";[5] and in October of that year the federal cabinet in Bonn felt obliged to issue an official statement defending the July 20 resisters against "libelous slander." "The men and women of the Twentieth of July," said the statement, "proved to the world that not all Germans had been taken in by National Socialism. Their act helped establish the basis upon which a Germany could be rebuilt in cooperation with the free world."[6]

Such formal statements from Bonn, however, did nothing to discourage further attacks on the resistance legacy from the extreme right. The Sozialistische Reichspartei (SRP) politician Otto-Ernst Remer, who in July 1944 had helped foil the anti-Nazi putsch in Berlin, declared at an SRP rally in 1952 that

---

[3] Erich-Peter Neumann and Elisabeth Noelle, *Jahrbuch der öffentlichen Meinung, 1947–1955* (Allensbach, 1956), p. 138.

[4] Heinz Holldack, "Gedanken am 20. Juli," *Süddeutsche Zeitung* (July 20, 1951); "Der vergessene 20. Juli," *Schweizer National-Zeitung* (July 21, 1951).

[5] R. Eggert, "Neue Dolchstosslegende im Kommen?" *Welt am Sontag* (Hamburg) (February 22, 1951); "Neue deutsche Dolchstosslüge," *Das freie Wort* (Düsseldorf) (August 31, 1951).

[6] "Bonn bekennt such zum Widerstand," *Stuttgarter Zeitung* (October 3, 1951).

the Twentieth of July resisters were traitors who had been "paid from abroad." He added that he hoped that the plotters who had survived Hitler's just revenge would one day have to face a German court and pay for their crimes.[7]

In fact it was Remer who had to go to court; in 1952 he was convicted of defaming the honor of the July 20 resisters and their families. The prosecutor in the case was determined to use this event to free the resistance legacy once and for all from the "stigma of treason." Though the much publicized trial, which featured *Gutachten* on the meaning of the resistance from noted theologians, jurists, and historians, may have helped to create a somewhat more positive public image of the anti-Hitler opposition, it also had the less salutary effect of narrowing the definition of "resister" to someone who had opposed the regime in its fundamentals and actively tried to overthrow it.[8]

The implications of this development quickly became apparent when the Bundestag voted in 1953 to include resistance survivors or their families in the Federal Indemnification Law, which materially compensated victims of nazism. According to the law, compensation might be awarded only to those men and women who, motivated by repugnance for the Nazis' abuses of human rights, had actively campaigned against the regime as such, and whose oppositionist efforts, at least in the resisters' eyes, had a significant chance of fundamentally undermining the Nazi system. Obviously this left out all those practitioners of occasional, intermittent, conditioned, or partial resistance—in other words, the vast majority of those who had bothered to oppose the regime. Explicitly excluded, too, were any citizens whose political ideology rejected the "free democratic order." This meant that as of 1956, when the Kommunistische Partei Deutschlands (KPD) was declared illegal, veterans of the communist resistance were ineligible for compensation.[9] The relatively few citizens who were qualified to receive compensation eventually got payments that were considerably smaller than the sums given the so-called *Kriegsgeschädigten,* the people who had been victimized by the war, primarily by Allied bombing.

Another source of malaise among the resistance survivors was the conviction that they were not accorded the degree of political influence in the new state commensurate with their services and sacrifices to the nation. They

[7] Horst W. Schmollinger, "Sozialistische Reichspartei," in *Parteienhandbuch: Die Parteien der Bundesrepublik Deutschland, 1945–1980,* ed. Richard Stöss, 2 vols. (Oplanden, 1984), 2:2274–76.

[8] Peter Steinbach, "Widerstandsforschung im politischen Spannungsfeld," *Aus Politik und Zeitgeschichte* 28 (July 8, 1988): 5.

[9] Ibid., pp. 6–7.

charged that although some of them had found important positions in the government and parties—Jakob Kaiser, Robert Lehr, Otto Lenz, and Eugen Gerstenmaier were cases in point—all too many of them were being used primarily as "window-dressing" (*Aushängeschilder* or *Persilscheinausstel-ler).* One resistance veteran, Rudolf Pechel, even insisted that former resistance figures were deliberately excluded from real power because they made their colleagues "uncomfortable"—they were a "living reproach" to those who had not stood up against the Nazis.[10]

When resistance figures complained, as they often did, that genuine power in the Federal Republic was exercised by people who had "wintered over" during the Third Reich, they were undoubtedly thinking primarily of West Germany's first chancellor, Konrad Adenauer. Adenauer, of course, had been no Hitler supporter. He had been thrown out of his job as mayor of Cologne by the Nazis, for whose policies he had nothing but contempt. During his enforced exile from political life he had contact with some figures in the Catholic resistance. But when one of them, Jakob Kaiser, told Adenauer of his conspiratorial plans involving a group of generals and invited Adenauer to join the conspiracy, the latter declined. "Have you ever seen a smart general?" he asked.[11] Clearly Adenauer had little faith in the efficacy of a military resistance, and even less in the machinations of another leading figure in the opposition, Carl Goerdeler, whom he considered a careless fool. Adenauer, on the other hand, was anything but careless. He knew he was being watched by the Gestapo, and he believed—perhaps correctly—that he could not be of much use to the plotters. But whatever the justification for his cautious stance, people who had actually risked their lives in the resistance naturally resented it when Adenauer's party, the Christlich Demokratische Union (CDU), eventually associated him directly with the resistance legacy.

It was Adenauer, however, who took the lead in the Federal Republic's belated discovery of the resistance legacy as a source of moral and political inspiration, as well as a kind of ticket for readmission to the community of civilized nations. He and several of his governmental colleagues took the tenth anniversary of the July 20, 1944 assassination attempt as an opportunity not just to honor the anti-Nazi resisters but also to extract some political mileage from their example. Speaking at Bonn's newly constituted Foreign Office, Adenauer declared that the martyred resisters who had belonged to the German Foreign Office in the Third Reich had "given their lives . . . so that the unjustifiable condemnation [of the Foreign Office] at home and abroad

[10] Claus Donate, "Deutscher Widerstand gegen den Nationalsozialismus aus der Sicht der Bundeswehr" (Ph.D. diss., Freiburg University, 1976), p. 394.

[11] Hans-Peter Schwarz, *Adenauer: Der Aufstieg, 1876–1952* (Stuttgart, 1986), p. 406.

might be reversed."[12] He also took pains to recall that Foreign Office personnel like Ernst von Weizsäcker had urged the Western powers to stand up to Hitler, in which case he might have been overthrown from within; the West, however, had chosen to "save" Hitler at Munich. Adenauer's colleague, Eugen Gerstenmaier, said on the same occasion that it was high time that the Foreign Office be recognized as a bastion of the "other Germany."[13] But it was President Theodor Heuss, speaking at the new Free University of Berlin, who made the most sweeping claim of all: "The blood of the martyred resisters," he insisted, "has cleansed our German name of the shame which Hitler cast upon it." The resistance was therefore "a gift to the German future."[14]

These claims were not without validity, and many people, both in West Germany and abroad, were pleased that Bonn seemed finally to have found something in the recent German past to be proud of, some "tradition" that might help give the young republic an added measure of legitimacy. Bonn's evocation of the Twentieth of July legacy, however, could not simply be applauded as a welcome recognition of the anti-Nazi resisters' tragic service to the nation. The government's expropriation of this inheritance was open to charges of hypocrisy, since some of the chancellor's closest associates, most notably Hans Globke and Theodor Oberländer, were themselves implicated in Nazi crimes. Moreover, in inscribing the resistance movement in the Federal Republic's pantheon, Bonn's leaders were obliged to interpret this phenomenon rather selectively, to downplay its antipluralistic, anticapitalist, and less democratic sides. They also had to overlook the painful fact that some of those who had tried to assassinate Hitler had also helped bring him to power in the first place. In this context, we might recall that President Theodor Heuss himself, who certainly became a committed opponent of the Nazis, was one of those parliamentarians who voted in March 1933 for the Enabling Law that helped Hitler break through to dictatorial power.

Moreover, however selectively Bonn's leading politicians interpreted the Twentieth of July conspiracy, their almost exclusive focus on this particular dimension of the anti-Hitler opposition betrayed an eagerness to overlook the more prolonged and systematic resistance that came from the radical Left, particularly from the communists. And one can sense also in the claims of Adenauer and company an anxiousness both to shift some of the blame for Hitler from the Germans to the Western powers and to exaggerate the extent

---

[12] *Bulletin des Presse- und Informationsamtes der Bundesregierung* (July 22, 1954), p. 1211.

[13] Ibid., p. 1209.

[14] Theodor Heuss, *Dank und Bekenntnis: Gedenkrede zum 20. Juli 1944* (Tübingen, 1954), pp. 30, 25.

to which conservative institutions like the Foreign Office represented cohesive bastions of the "other Germany."

But whatever objections we might have to the selective way in which Bonn interpreted the resistance, the various official speeches marking the tenth anniversary of the Twentieth of July seemed to suggest that West Germany's ruling establishment had now taken this legacy firmly into its heart. Another occurrence at that same time, however, showed that memories of the resistance were still capable of arousing passionate controversy. On July 20, 1954, Otto John, a former resister and now president of Bonn's Verfassungsschutz (Office for Constitutional Protection), slipped over the border into East Germany. Immediately thereafter he went on the radio to say that Stauffenberg had not "died for the Federal Republic," which he accused of fomenting a neo-Nazi revival.[15] In the investigation that followed, it turned out that John had worked on behalf of Admiral Canaris's resistance group in Madrid and had had contact with the British Secret Service. The British, in fact, had recommended him for his post as head of the Verfassungsschutz. He may also have had ties to the underground communist resistance, the *Rote Kapelle*.

These revelations inspired a new wave of recrimination in West Germany against the resistance veterans in general, and in particular against those resisters who had operated in foreign countries or later served the occupation powers. John's bitter rival, Reinhard Gehlen, who headed the Bundesnach-richten Dienst (Federal Intelligence Agency), made the acid comment: "Once a traitor, always a traitor."[16] In the parliamentary debate on the John Affair, Hans Joachim von Markatz of the conservative Deutsche Partei declared that a man like John, who had "served the enemy," should have been automatically disqualified from any official position. He insisted that an investigation be opened to determine if anyone else with a background like John's was employed in a sensitive position.[17]

These attacks opened the way for a broader witch-hunt directed against Germans who had fled the Reich to work in resistance organizations abroad, and then returned after the war to join in the effort to rebuild their country. Among this group were prominent figures in the Sozialdemokratische Partei Deutschlands (SPD)—Erich Ollenhauer, Fritz Heine, Herbert Wehner, Willy Brandt—and they were now tarred by the nationalist Right with the brush of treason. So vicious was the attack that even some CDU leaders, including Adenauer and the future chancellor Kurt Georg Kiesinger, felt obliged to

[15] "Ich habe mich ergeben," *Der Spiegel* (December 21, 1955), p. 11.
[16] Ibid.
[17] Deutscher Bundestag, 42. Sitzung, September 16, 1954, p. 1985.

denounce this slur on the socialist emigrants. But Kiesinger, interestingly enough, drew the line at those who had given evidence against Germans in postwar trials: their presence in government, he said, was cause for "grave concern."[18]

It is instructive to examine the trials conducted in the Federal Republic in the 1950s involving former Nazi officials connected with the prosecution—or persecution—of the July 20 resisters following their abortive coup.[19] A certain Walter Huppenkothen, one of the Nazi prosecutors who had called for the death penalty for Hans Oster, Hans von Dohnanyi, and Wilhelm Canaris, faced charges of murder when he was released from American captivity in 1951. The Munich court in which he was tried acquitted him on the grounds that the men he had condemned had been guilty of treason under then-existing German law. An associate of Huppenkothen's, the SS judge Dr. Otto Thorbeck who had presided over the concentration camp courts that condemned some of the resisters to death, was also tried and acquitted by the same Munich court. The Bundesgerichtshof (Federal Court), however, refused to validate these verdicts, citing improper legal procedures, and turned the cases over to a court in Augsburg for new trials. The Augsburg court concluded in 1955 that the special tribunals in the Third Reich that condemned the resisters had been established only to provide pseudo-legal cover for political murder; it sentenced Huppenkothen to seven years in prison and Thorbeck to four. The two men appealed these judgments back to Federal Court, arguing that the Augsburg judge, who had himself been persecuted by the Nazis, harbored a "deep and abiding hatred for National Socialism" and was therefore biased. This time the defendants found a sympathetic ear at the Federal Court, for the new president of that body, one Hermann Weinkauff, had been a member of the Reich court between 1937 and 1945. In 1956 the court acquitted Thorbeck, declaring that a judge could not be expected to recognize as legitimate an accused person's plea that he was adhering to a "higher law" than that prevailing in the land at the time he was tried. Huppenkothen, on the other hand, was sentenced to six years in prison, but not because of his complicity in the executions of the resisters; his offense was a purely technical one, that of neglecting to secure confirmation for the death sentences from Ernst Kaltenbrunner, chief of the Reichssicherheitshauptamt. The lack of such confirmation, said the court, made the executions illegal. These verdicts, we should recall, were rendered two years after President Heuss had identified the resistance as a "gift to the German future."

[18] Ibid., p. 1961.

[19] On the trials, see Jörg Friedrich, *Die kalte Amnestie: NS-Täter in der Bundesrepublik* (Frankfurt, 1985), pp. 281–90.

While West German courts were dealing lightly with ex-Nazis who had helped to liquidate some of the leading resisters, West German parties were busy turning the resistance legacy into a bone of political contention. Adenauer's CDU was quick to stake its claim to this heritage, or at least to that part of it that the party wished to recognize. The CDU claimed that its "historical roots" could be found in the national-conservative resistance movement's ecumenical organization and its commitment to high ethical standards and traditional Christian values.[20] The CDU's main coalition partner, the Frei Demokratische Partei (FDP), also claimed to perpetuate certain dimensions of the resistance legacy, particularly its emphasis on individual dignity and personal freedom.[21] But this party was by no means unified on the advisability of honoring the men who tried to kill Hitler. The FDP's military specialist and chief liaison to the postwar veterans' movement, former General Hasso von Manteuffel, declared that he was proud not to have belonged to the Twentieth of July circle and to have done his duty to the bitter end. In 1948 he had advised Adenauer to have nothing to do with the men who had broken their oath to the führer.[22] In order to avoid an open split within the party over the resistance issue, the FDP leadership put together a compromise formula that officially documented its respect both for those who had resisted the Nazi state and for those who had loyally served it to the end.[23] The statement explicitly avoided according a higher moral or political value to the former posture than to the latter.

Meanwhile the chief opposition party, the SPD, was not about to leave the resistance legacy to the ruling conservative-liberal coalition. Kurt Schumacher, the party's leader until his death in 1952, had personally suffered gravely at the hands of the Nazis, and he strongly resented the occupation powers' and Bonn's tendency to ignore or dismiss the socialist resistance. "We Socialists would have been resisters, " he said, "even if the Americans and the British had become fascists."[24] Schumacher based the socialists' claim to a leading role in postwar Germany on his and his colleagues' opposition to the Nazis and on their continuing struggle against rightist-restorative forces. The SPD's failure to parlay what its leaders believed was socialism's moral superiority

---

[20] Torsten-Dietrich Schramm, *Der deutsche Widerstand gegen den Nationalsozialismus: Seine Bedeutung für die Bundesrepublik in der Wirkung auf Institutionen und Schulbücher* (Berlin, 1980), pp. 65–68.

[21] Ibid., p. 73.

[22] Hasso von Manteuffel, "Bekenntnis eines freimütigen Deutschen," Bundesarchiv-Militärarchiv, Freiburg, BW9/2118.

[23] See Erich Mende, *Die neue Freiheit, 1945–1961* (Munich, 1984), p. 321.

[24] Schumacher quoted in Ulrich Buczylowski, *Kurt Schumacher und die deutsche Frage: Sicherheitspolitik und strategische Offensivkonseption von August 1950 bis September 1951* (Stuttgart, 1971), p. 26.

into effective political power in the early years of the Federal Republic only exacerbated the socialists' bitterness, their sense that the true resistance legacy, which they recalled had included commitments to socialization of the economy and national unity, was being betrayed by Bonn's new rulers.

The unity issue introduces the problem of Cold War politics, which had a significant influence on the interpretation and exploitation of the resistance legacy in the Federal Republic (and the GDR) during the fifties. Of course the Cold War perpetuated the tendency in Bonn to exclude the communist and socialist anti-Nazi opposition from acceptance into the resistance canon. The emerging theory of totalitarianism, which stressed the similarities between communism and National Socialism, allowed the ongoing opposition to Russian-imposed communism in East Germany to be equated with the earlier resistance against Hitler. Thus the uprising in East Berlin on June 17, 1953, was widely interpreted in the Federal Republic as a latter-day July 20, 1944.[25] Commemorative speeches honoring the Twentieth of July legacy from July 1953 through the early sixties placed these two dates on a common footing: they were described as two noble, albeit abortive, efforts to overthrow a tyranny.[26] At a ceremony on July 20, 1953, marking the unveiling of a monument to the Twentieth of July resisters in the former Oberkommando der Wehrmacht (OKW) headquarters in the Bendlerstrasse, West Berlin mayor Ernst Reuter declared: "We must continually attempt to grasp German history anew. . . . We must try to make connections between what is happening now and our past actions or inactions, [we must] see present events in light of the historic struggle against tyranny that we are honoring today."[27] But while West German commemoration speakers generally encouraged the Federal Republic's citizenry to see the July 20, 1944 assassination attempt as a historical event, which hardly needed emulation in the West German Rechtsstaat, they hoped that their fellow Germans in the GDR would regard this heritage as an invitation to perpetual resistance. As Ernst Lemmer, Minister for Greater German Questions, put it in 1962, a year after the building of the Berlin Wall: "Sixteen million of our countrymen are still living under an oppressive fate that the men and women of the Twentieth of July tried to cast off for ever."[28]

From the mid-sixties through the seventies, as CDU domination in Bonn gave way to the Grand Coalition in 1966 and then to the SPD-FDP partnership

---

[25] See, in particular, Hans Rothfels, "Das politische Vermächtnis des deutschen Widerstands," *Vierteljahrshefte für Zeitgeschichte* 2 (1954): 329–43.

[26] Ulrike Emrich and Jürgen Nötzgold, "Der 20. Juli in der öffentlichen Gedenkreden der Bundesrepublik und in der Darstellung der DDR," *Aus Politik und Zeitgeschichte* 26 (June 30, 1984): 3–12.

[27] Reuter quoted in Steinbach (n. 8 above), p. 4.

[28] Quoted in Emrich and Nötzgold, pp. 5–6.

in 1969, official speeches commemorating the resistance movement shifted emphasis from this legacy's Cold War applications to its possible uses in building new bridges to the East. When the Brandt government was concluding the first phase of its *Ostpolitik* through the normalization of relations with the Soviet Union, West German politicians suddenly recalled that Count von Stauffenberg had also made overtures to the Russians and had advocated ties to the communist resistance. Thus on the eve of the signing of the Treaty of Moscow (August 1970), the West German minister of justice, Gunther Jahn, delivered a Twentieth of July commemoration speech in which he placed a recent meeting in Erfurt between Brandt and the East German politician Willi Stoph in the tradition of Stauffenberg's attempt at an opening to the East.[29] Clearly, this was meant to give Brandt's *Ostpolitik,* which was under fire from conservatives in the West, added legitimacy. In the same vein President Gustav Heinemann, long a partisan of closer ties between the two Germanies, used the main Twentieth of July commemoration in 1969 to emphasize the contributions of workers and communist politicians to the resistance against Hitler.[30]

Ironically enough, the growing tendency in the FRG to recognize officially the contributions of leftist resisters was perceived in the East less as a sign of Bonn's belated enlightenment and fraternal intentions than as a cultural-political challenge, since the GDR had long come to regard the left-wing anti-Nazi resistance as its exclusive historical patrimony. We should recall in this connection that East Germany, which most of the world (even Moscow) did not consider the "real" Germany, was even more in need of validating historical traditions than the FRG. In order to bolster its self-image as a "socialist German nation," East Berlin laid claim to traditions, institutions, and personages from the German past that might suggest continuity with the present communist state. Among these was the communist and socialist working-class opposition to Hitler, which B. H. Scheel, vice-president of the Academy of Sciences, insisted was "an essential part of our pre-history."[31] On the other hand, the GDR's cultural arbiters tended to condemn most of the Twentieth of July conspirators as Johnny-come-lately reactionaries whose goals included striking a nefarious deal with the West that would allow a continuation of the Nazis' war against the Soviet Union.[32] In the late 1960s and 1970s, however, East German historians and political commentators

[29] *Bulletin des Presse- und Informationsamtes der Bundesregierung* (July 22, 1970), p. 969.

[30] Gustav Heinemann, "Eine Flamme am Brennen halten," in *Gedanken zum 20. Juli 1944,* ed. Forschungsgemeinschaft 20. Juli (Mainz, 1984), pp. 67–69.

[31] Scheel quoted in Emrich and Nötzgold, p. 9.

[32] Ibid., p. 10.

began to separate Stauffenberg from the rest of the conservative resistance, taking care to emphasize his rejection of a "one-sided West orientation."[33] Thus just as Bonn began to recognize the importance of the communist resistance, East Berlin not only tightened its hold on this legacy but also laid claims to Stauffenberg and other "progressive" bourgeois resisters, while happily leaving strongly anti-Soviet figures like Goerdeler and Beck to the West. A prominent East German historian wrote in 1979 that "Goedeler belongs to Bonn, Brussels, and Washington, but Stauffenberg belongs to Berlin. By Berlin we do not mean the Kurfürstendamm, but the capital of the German Democratic Republic."[34]

The resistance legacy had a prominent place not only in the two German states' often competitive campaigns for historical legitimacy but also in their varying constitutional arrangements. The GDR constitution contained from the outset a *Widerstand* provision giving every citizen "the right and the duty to resist measures that contravene directives of the peoples' legislature." But clearly this law was intended—and understood by everyone to intend—to protect the state from the people, rather than vice versa.[35] It provoked little controversy because East German citizens realized that they could not invoke it against the regime without risking persecution for "antistate" activities. The history of a constitutional codification of resistance in the FRG, on the other hand, is rather more complicated and therefore needs further explication.

As noted above, the charter *Grundgesetz* did not contain a formal resistance clause, though there had been attempts to include one. Many politicians, particularly in the SPD, continued to believe that an absence of a constitutional *Widerstandsrecht* left the young democratic order insufficiently protected against potential abuses of power by state authorities. Anxieties on this score grew after the Adenauer government proposed in 1958 to take over the emergency powers originally vested in the Western Allies. Critics of such a *Notstandsverfassung* were prepared to countenance it only if it included some form of resistance provision.[36] In 1968, following the outbreak of extensive student rioting in West German cities, the Bundestag managed to pass a series of emergency laws granting the government broader powers to deal with political violence. As a counterweight to this expansion of government power,

---

[33] Ibid.

[34] K. E. von Schnitzler, "Der Mythos des 20. Juli," *Horizont* 29 (1979): 18 (quoted in Emrich and Nötzgold, p. 10).

[35] Peter Schneider, "Widerstandsrecht und Rechtsstaat," in *Widerstandsrecht,* ed. Arthur Kaufmann and Leonard E. Backmann (Darmstadt, 1972), p. 366.

[36] On these developments, see Böckenförde (n. 2 above), pp. 169–71.

the parliament duly included a new clause in the Basic Law that said: "All Germans shall have the right to resist any person or persons seeking to abolish the constitutional order, should no other remedy be possible."[37]

Here, then, was the "right to resist" finally enshrined in the federal constitution, but exactly what it meant and how far it went were the subjects of much acrimonious debate. Some conservative jurists reconciled themselves to the statute because they saw that "resistance" might be defined not only as resistance *against* the state but also (in GDR fashion) as resistance *by* the state against transgressions among the citizenry.[38] Following this logic, the police themselves invoked the "right to resist" when after the Schleyer kidnapping in 1977 they raided hundreds of apartments and houses without search warrants.[39] The objects of police attention, the "Red Army Faction" (RAF) terrorists and their sympathizers, also claimed to be operating within a framework of "resistance" against an allegedly oppressive political and social order. Soon all sorts of leftist or "alternative" groups—house-squatters, gay rights crusaders, ecological activists, outraged feminists, peace demonstrators, anti-nuke campaigners—claimed sanctification for their protests by invoking the ideal of *Widerstand.*

These developments prompted a number of protests against a perceived "inflation" or "perversion" of the resistance ideal. In one such instance, Count Peter von Kielmansegg, whose father had had connections to the Twentieth of July conspiracy, denounced the self-professed resisters of the contemporary era for claiming a moral inheritance to which they had no title. "We Germans," he said, "who have had the opportunity to learn what resistance against a tyranny really means, ought to be the last people to allow themselves this confusion."[40]

But if one could justly worry about the increasing reduction of the resistance ideal to a kind of conceptual hodge-podge without rigor or historical validity, the opposite danger was also present. In 1977 the Kuratorium 20. Juli invited—and then disinvited—the socialist (and former

---

[37] The clause is Section 4, Article 20 (see *The Basic Law of the Federal Republic of Germany* [Bonn, 1981], p. 23). For a technical discussion of the *Notstandsverfassung,* see Otto Lenz, *Notstandsverfassung des Grundgesetzes* (Frankfurt, 1971).

[38] Böckenförde, p. 171.

[39] Jane Kramer, "Hamburg: Terrorism in Germany," in her *Europeans* (New York, 1988), p. 131.

[40] Peter Graf von Kielmansegg, "Frieden geht nicht vor Demokratie," *Die Zeit* (October 7, 1983). For other protests against "misuse" of the resistance legacy, see Eberhard Bethge, "Widerstand—damals und heute," *Süddeutsche Zeitung* (July 25/26, 1981); Karl Dietrich Bracher, "Verwirrung um Widerstand," *Rheinischer Merkur* (January 8, 1982); Ernst Nolte, *Widerstand im Nationalsozialismus und Widerstand heute—legitimer Vergleich oder Anmassung?* Schriften der Hermann-Ehlers-Akademie, no. 18 (Kiel, 1985).

communist) politician Herbert Wehner to speak at that year's commemoration of the military resistance in the Bendlerstrasse. Stauffenberg's son argued that Wehner, whose resistance to Hitler had been exercised from his Moscow exile, would not be an appropriate speaker.[41] (On the other hand, the younger Stauffenberg had no objection to inviting Hans Karl Filbinger, a prominent CDU politician who while serving as a Navy judge in the last days of World War II had sentenced several young sailors to death for desertion.) The symbolism of the Twentieth of July, Stauffenberg seemed to be saying, did not belong to the entire people but only to a particular political group.

The controversy over this incident showed that historically conscious Germans still were not in agreement over what their resistance against Hitler really meant and to whom it belonged. And the fight continued into the 1980s, when it featured in the *Historikerstreit* and the debate over how to portray the Third Reich and the resistance legacy in Bonn's projected museum of German history.[42] Thus it was thoroughly appropriate that President Weizsäcker, in his famous speech to the German people on May 8, 1985, insisted that it was important to honor the memory of *all* those Germans who had sacrificed their lives resisting Hitler.

Whether Weizsäcker's appeal had much resonance among the populace at large is doubtful. In a public opinion poll taken the year before, only 30 percent of the respondents designated "Der deutsche Widerstand" as an achievement in which the German people ought to take pride; this figure placed the resistance behind "the bravery of German soldiers" and the "reconstruction after World War II," not to mention "West German automobiles."[43]

Yet whatever its meaning for the man in the street, the resistance legacy continued to figure prominently in the rhetoric of German politics, especially as the two German states began their rush toward national unity in 1989–90. In its first (and last) official commemoration of the Twentieth of July putsch, the East German parliament issued a statement in July 1990 recognizing the resisters' legacy as an "admonition to resist dictatorships in every form and to maintain peace in Germany and Europe forever."[44] At the most recent annual

---

[41] Erich Kosthorst, "Didaktische Probleme der Widerstands-Forschung," *Geschichte im Wissenschaft und Unterricht* 9 (1979): 554.

[42] On the debate over the new museum, see Charles S. Maier, "A Usable Past? Museums, Memory, and Identity," in his *The Unmasterable Past* (Cambridge, Mass., 1988), pp. 121–59.

[43] Allensbach poll (September/October 1984), reprinted in Harro Honolka, *Schwarzrotgrün: Die Bundesrepublik auf der Suche nach ihrer Identität* (Munich, 1987), p. 209.

[44] "Verpflichtung für den Frieden," *Frankfurter Allgemeine Zeitung* (July 21, 1990).

commemoration ceremony at the former OKW headquarters in West Berlin, mayor Walter Momper insisted that the resistance legacy was more relevant than ever, since enthusiasm for unity might breed a dangerous new chauvinism. "Beware of the beginnings!" he warned.[45] One could only hope that this time someone was listening.

[45] "Gedanken an den 20. Juli 1944," *Frankfurter Allgemeine Zeitung* (July 21, 1990).

German Communism, the Discourse of "Antifascist Resistance," and the Jewish Catastrophe

Jeffrey Herf

German Marshall Fund of the United States, Washington, D.C.

From Weimar to the DDR, the meaning of resistance for German Communists was inseparable from the master narrative of antifascism. Marxism-Leninism defined that narrative before Nazism came to power, and after it was defeated.[1] After 1945, the narrative was one of historical vindication, success, and victory. The fate of Europe's Jews did not fit into the dialectical optimism of the Soviet victory over fascism. Their story was pushed to the margins of discourse. It never emerged from the shadows of the main Marxist drama of class struggle.[2]

The following essay looks at two Marxist interpretations of Nazi Germany from the Weimar Republic to the first decades of the German Democratic Republic, with particular focus on the wartime resistance and its postwar consequences. It examines the dominant tradition articulated by the Moscow-based Communists led by Walter Ulbricht (1893–1973) and Wilhelm Pieck (1876–1960), as well as a minority tradition articulated by Paul Merker (1894–1969), the member of the politburo of the German Communist party who was the leading figure of the German Communist wartime emigration in

---

[1] Jeffrey Herf, "Multiple Restorations: German Political Leaders Interpret Nazism, 1945–1946," *Central European History* 26, no. 1 (1993): 21–57.

[2] On the German Communist party's analysis of "fascism" and the development of the "social fascism" attack on the Social Democrats in the last years of the Weimar Republic, see the comprehensive and important work by Heinrich August Winkler, *Der Weg in die Katastrophe: Arbeiter und Arbeiterbewegung in der Weimarer Republik 1930 bis 1933* (Berlin and Bonn, 1987). Also see Siegfried Bahne, *Die KPD und das Ende von Weimar: Das Scheitern einer Politik, 1932–1935* (Frankfurt am Main, 1976), and "Sozialfaschismus in Deutschland: Zur Geschichte eines politischen Begriffs," *International Review of Social History* 10 (1965): 211–45; Franz Borkenau, *World Communism* (Ann Arbor, Mich., 1962); Karl Dietrich Bracher, *Die Auflösung der Weimarer Republik,* 5th ed. (Konigstein, 1978); Ossip K. Flechtheim, *Die Kommunistische Partei Deutschlands in der Weimarer Republik* (Offenbach, 1948), and 3d ed. (Frankfurt am Main, 1973); Albert S. Lindemann, *A History of European Socialism* (New Haven, Conn., 1983), chap. 8; and Barbara Timmerman, *Der Faschismus-Diskussion in der Kommunitischen Internationale (1920–1935)* (Ph.D. diss., University of Cologne, 1977). For the official East German narrative, see Walter Ulbricht, *Zur Geschichte der Deutschen Arbeiterbewegung,* Bd. 1 (East Berlin, 1953); Institut für Marxismus-Leninismus beim Zentralkomitee der SED, Autorenkollektiv, *Walter Ulbricht* (u.a.), *Geschichte der Deutschen Arbeiterbewegung,* Bd. 4, *Von 1924 bis Januar 1933* (East Berlin, 1966).

Mexico City.[3] It then explores the consolidation of the dominant tradition as well as the suppression of the minority tradition during Merker's denunciation, expulsion, imprisonment, and partial rehabilitation in East Germany from 1950 to 1956. It draws on the published official history of German Communism during the Nazi era, which Ulbricht and Pieck did so much to establish, as well as materials only recently available from the archives of the East German Communist party and the Stasi, which reveal the details and the significance of the Merker case.

RESISTANCE, THE PERSECUTION OF THE JEWS, AND THE DEFEAT OF ANTIFASCISM

In the Communist resistance to the rise of Nazism and in the historical literature on the subject, the issue of the persecution of the Jews has been a minor theme, compared to the great debates about capitalism and fascism, the split between Communists and Social Democrats, Moscow's determination of the German Communist party's policies toward Nazism, and the shifts in the Comintern line from left to right through the Third Period (1928–35), Popular Front (1935–39), the Hitler-Stalin nonaggression pact (1939–41), and the years of the anti-Hitler coalition (1941–45).[4] The issue of anti-Semitism was considered primarily as an instrument in the context of the main drama: the class struggle of the ruling capitalist class against the working class.[5] The East German regime after 1945 defined itself as the heir of the "antifascist resistance" extending from Weimar through the Third Reich.[6]

---

[3] On the German Communists in the Soviet Union and in Moscow, see Wolfgang Leonhard, *Die Revolution entlässt ihre Kinder* (Cologne and West Berlin, 1955). An impressive group of leading German Communists, including a future minister of culture in the DDR, Alexander Abusch, the writer Anna Seghers, along with Merker, found refuge in Mexico City, where a government grateful for the contributions of the Communist participation in the Spanish Civil War opened its doors to German Communist émigrés. On the group's journal, *Freies Deutschland,* and the *Bewegung Freies Deutschland* in Mexico City, see Wolfgang Kießling, *Alemania Libre in Mexiko,* Bd. 1, *Ein Beitrag zur Geschichte des antifaschistischen Exils (1941–1946)* (East Berlin, 1974); and F. Pohle, "'Freies Deutschland' und Zionismus: Exilkommunistische Bündnisbemühungen um die jüdischen Emigranten (Mexiko)," *Babylon: Beiträge zur jüdischen Gegenwart,* no. 3 (1988), pp. 88–96.

[4] See n. 2 above.

[5] See definitions for "Faschismus" and "Anti-faschismus," in *Kleines Politisches Wörterbuch* (East Berlin, 1967), pp. 37–38, 196–98.

[6] In the era of fascism, the Communists viewed themselves, and the Soviet Union, as the primary target of and source of deliverance from European fascism. After 1945, they defined the German Democratic Republic as an "anti-fascist democratic order." See "Antifaschistisch-demokratische Ordnung," and "Widerstands-bewegung (antifaschistische)," in *Kleines Politisches Wörterbuch,* pp. 36–37, 730–31.

In the early years of the East German government, the publication of collected essays and speeches by Wilhelm Pieck and Walter Ulbricht established the framework of the official history of Communist resistance to National Socialism. Ulbricht was the most powerful member of the German Communist party (KPD) and then Socialist Unity party (SED) after World War II, as well as the leader of the East German government from 1949 to 1971.[7] His *Zur Geschichte der Deutschen Arbeiterbewegung* (1953; On the history of the German labor movement) and *Zur Geschichte der neuesten Zeit* (1955; History of the recent period) dealt with his essays, speeches, and important party documents covering the period from Weimar to the mid-1950s.[8] Pieck's career began with the founding of the KPD in 1918–19, continued through his tenure as chairman of the Communist party in exile, and closed with his presidency of East Germany from 1949 to 1960. Collections of his essays covering the period from 1908 to 1950 appeared in 1951.[9] Ulbricht's and Pieck's collections established the canonical texts and outlined the postwar narrative of the era of fascism and resistance.

Three features of the KPD's antifascism are of particular note. First, in the Third Period, from 1928 to 1935, German Communist resistance to fascism meant attacks against the Nazi party as well as against "social fascism," that is, the German Social Democratic party.[10] Second, from 1930 to 1933, the

[7] See Carola Stern, *Walter Ulbricht: Eine Politische Biographie* (Cologne and Berlin, 1963); and "Walter Ulbricht," in *Wer war Wer: Ein Biographisches Lexikon* (Berlin, 1992), p. 461; and "Walter Ulbricht," in *Wer ist Wer in der SBZ: Ein Biographisches Handbuch* (Berlin-Zehlendorf, 1958), p. 266.

[8] See Walter Ulbricht, *Zur Geschichte der Deutschen Arbeiterbewegung, Aus Reden und Aufsätze, Band II: 1933–1946,* 2d ed. (East Berlin, 1953), *Zur Geschichte der Neuesten Zeit: Die Niederlage Hitlerdeutschlands und die Schaffung der antifaschistische-demokratischen Ordnung,* 2d ed. (East Berlin, 1953); and Institut für Marxismus-Leninismus beim Zentralkomitee der SED. For purposes of historical reconstruction of the formative years of East German political culture, Ulbricht's two volumes of 1953 (1st ed., 1951) and 1955 are of far greater significance than the multivolume history not published until the 1960s.

[9] Wilhelm Pieck, *Reden und Aufsätze: Auswahl aus den Jahren 1908–1950,* 2 vols. (East Berlin, 1951). See "Wilhelm Pieck," in *Wer war Wer,* pp. 349–50; and "Wilhelm Pieck," *Wer ist Wer in der SBZ,* p. 195.

[10] On "social fascism," and the KPD's attacks on the SPD in the last years of the Weimar Republic see Winkler. At times they went so far as to call the Social Democrats "their major enemy (*Hauptfeind*) in the proletariat" (cited by Winkler, pp. 444–45). In October 1932, e.g., Ernst Thälmann, the chairman of the KPD, said of Social Democracy and Nazism that one ought not equate "both wings of fascism," but any "tendency to weaken our principled struggle against the SPD leaders or to adopt a liberal juxtaposition of fascism and social fascism was utterly inadmissable" (Ernst Thälmann, *Im Kampf gegen die faschistische Diktatur: Rede und Schlußwort des Genossen Ernst Thälmann auf der Parteikonferenz Oktober 1932* [Berlin, 1932], pp. 4, 12, 16). Also see Siegfried Bahne, *Die KPD und das Ende von Weimar,* and

Communists extended the labels *fascist* and *fascism* to include the last governments of the Weimar Republic.[11] The third and less frequently noted element of the KPD's antifascism was an indefatigable political optimism that found elements of "growing resistance" even as the Nazis rose, seized, and then consolidated power.[12] Indeed, even in 1934, Pieck, who had become chairman of the KPD after Thälmann's arrest, insisted that the ten months of fascist dictatorship had "confirmed the prediction of the Communist International," that fascism would not usher in a period of reaction and that "the establishment of the Hitler dictatorship may indeed temporarily hinder but cannot put a stop to the development of revolutionary forces."[13] The shattering of this Marxist optimism during the Third Reich was one of the most important developments in the history of German Communist resistance to National Socialism.

It was not until after the initial strategy of Communist antifascist resistance had been defeated—that is, after the Nazis had destroyed the aboveground

---

"Sozialfaschismus in Deutschland"; Borkenau; Bracher; Flechtheim; Lindemann. For the official East German narrative see Ulbricht, *Zur Geschichte der Deutschen Arbeiterbewegung;* and Institut für Marxismus-Leninismus beim Zentralkomitee der SED. Also still important are Leon Trotsky's unsuccessful criticism of the Third Period's denunciations of "social fascism." See Isaac Deutscher, *The Prophet Outcast: Trotsky: 1929–1940* (New York, 1963).

[11] In the Reichstag on February 11, 1930, Ernst Thälmann (1886–1944), the leader of the KPD, and its candidate for the presidency in 1925 and 1932, said that "fascism rules in Germany." See Ernst Thälmann, *Verhandlungen des Reichstags* (February 11, 1930), vol. 426, p. 3940; reprinted in Ernst Thälmann, *Im Kampf gegen den Deutschen und den Amerikanischen Imperialismus: Drei Reichstagsreden* (East Berlin, 1954), pp. 75–98. Also see Ernst Thälmann, *Im Kampf gegen die Faschistische Diktatur: Rede und Schluβwort des Genossen Ernst Thälmann auf der Parteikonferenz der KPD. im Oktober 1932* (Berlin, 1932); and *Ausgewählte Reden und Schriften in zwei Bänden* (Frankfurt am Main, 1976).

[12] "Resolution der Parteikonferenz der KPD über das 12. Plenum des EKKI und die Aufgaben der KPD" (October 15–17, 1932), reprinted in Flechtheim (n. 2 above), pp. 285–94.

[13] See Wilhelm Pieck, *We Are Fighting for a Soviet Germany* (Executive Committee Communist International) (New York, 1934). Pieck also continued to denounce the Social Democrats. He said that on German Social Democracy "alone rests the tremendous guilt, by splitting the working class and by its criminal policy, for having assisted fascism to power and having made possible the fascist dictatorship. When in 1918 it struck down the proletarian revolution, it swindled the masses with talk of the democratic peaceful development to socialism, without the dictatorship of the proletariat. It led the masses to fascism. It bears the blame for the fact that Hitler and his gangs have tortured hundreds of revolutionary fighters to death and that hundreds of thousands have been cast into concentration camps" (pp. 62–63). *We Are Fighting for a Soviet Germany* was not republished in Pieck's collected works in the DDR. Pieck was a cofounder of the KPD in 1918–19, and of the SED in 1946 in Berlin. He was the president of the DDR from 1949 until he died in 1960. See "Wilhelm Pieck," *Wer war Wer,* pp. 349–50; and also in *Wer ist Wer in der SBZ,* p. 195.

KPD and sent up to one hundred thousand German Communists to prisons and concentration camps—that the "ultraleftism" of the Third Period came to an end at the Comintern's Seventh Congress in Moscow in August 1935. It was replaced with a call for a popular front against fascism that would bring together Communists with Social Democrats and with liberals opposed to Nazism.[14] Pieck abandoned the rhetoric of revolutionary optimism for a sobering assessment of Communist misjudgments, both in the attacks on the Social Democrats and in the underestimation of the potentials of Hitler and the Nazi movement.[15]

In October 1935, the German Communists, meeting in Moscow, issued what became known as the resolution of the Brussels conference.[16] Now antifascist resistance meant "unity of action" (*Aktionseinheit*) between Communists and Social Democrats. Outside Paris in January and February 1939, at what was called the Bern Conference, the KPD gave a nationalistic tone to the meaning of resistance to fascism.[17] Pieck urged the twelve of fifteen members of the KPD politburo in attendance to stress the "conflict between the policy of Hitler fascism and the interest of the German nation."

[14] For an excellent discussion of the analysis of fascism in the Comintern, see Timmermann (n. 2 above); and Theo Pirker, *Komintern und Faschismus: Dokumente zur Geschichte und Theorie des Faschismus* (Stuttgart, 1965). For the official East German history see Institut für Marxismus-Leninismus beim Zentralkomitee der SED (n. 2 above), 10:108–9.

[15] Pieck included among the "errors" of Communist policy in the Third Period "the absolutely false idea that all of the bourgeois parties were fascist, that there were 'not two methods of bourgeois rule,' and that it was not proper for Communists to defend the remnants of bourgeois democracy." See Wilhelm Pieck, "Der Vormarsch des Sozialismus: Bericht, Schlußwort und Resolution zum 1. Punkt der Tagesordnung des Kongresses: Rechenschaftsbericht über die Tätigkeit des Exekutivkomitees der Kommunistischen Internationale," in *VII Weltkongreß der Kommunistischen Internationale, Moskau/Leningrad 1935* (Milan, 1967), p. 40; cited by Timmermann, pp. 409–10; also see *VII Weltkongreß der Kommunistischen Internationale: Referat, Aus der Diskussion, Schlußwort, Resolution* (Frankfurt am Main, 1971). Neither *We Are Fighting for a Soviet Germany* nor Pieck's critique of the Third Period in Moscow in August 1935 were printed in his collected works published in East Germany. Walter Ulbricht, emerging as the leading figure in the KPD, while placing primary responsibility on the SPD for splitting the working class and thus making possible the Nazi rise to power, conceded that the KPD had "directed its main blows against Social Democracy at a point at which it should have directed them against fascism" (see Walter Ulbricht, "Der VII. Weltkongreß der Komintern und die Kommunistische Partei Deutschlands," *Bolschewik* [Moscow], no. 18 [September 1935]; reprinted in *Zur Geschichte der Deutschen Arbeiterbewegung*, 2:71).

[16] "Das Program der Kommunistischen Partei Deutschlands zum Sturz des Hitlerregimes: Die Brüsseler Parteikonferenz der KPD," in Institut für Marxismus-Leninismus beim Zentralkomitee der SED, 10:112–28.

[17] "Die Berner Konferenz der Kommunistischen Partei Deutschlands und das Programm des neuen demokratischen Republik," in *Geschichte der Deutschen Arbeiterbewegung*, 10:216–24.

The Communists should not avoid words like *Nation* and *Volk.* "Saving the nation from catastrophe means saving it from traitors and destroyers, Hitler fascism and big capital. This is the highest national deed of our era."[18] However, from the days of Weimar elections through the Bern Conference, the KPD's efforts to establish its German nationalist credentials appeared to conflict with emphatic identification with the great Other, the Jews. With the signing of the Hitler-Stalin pact on August 23, 1939, the Popular Front era came to an end. German Communist antifascist resistance ended until the Nazi invasion of the Soviet Union in June 1941.[19]

Throughout the years spanning the Third Period, Popular Front, and the Hitler-Stalin pact, the persecution of the Jews did not play any role in these major intra-Communist debates and played only a minor role in Communist thinking about resistance in general.[20] But the Jewish question was important for the Communists because they saw in anti-Semitism one of the most dangerous bourgeois efforts to confuse, divide, and weaken the working

[18] Wilhelm Pieck, "Die Gegenwärtigen Lage und die Aufgabe der Partei," in *Geschichte der Deutschen Arbeiterbewegung,* 10:217–18. In fact, before 1933, resistance to fascism, and hence anti-imperialism, had often included nationalist attacks, e.g., on the Versailles Treaty, and Dawes and Young plans. On this see "Programm/Erklärung" zur nationalen und sozialen Befreiung des deutschen Volkes, (August 24, 1930)," in *Geschichte der Deutschen Arbeiterbewegung.*

[19] On the KPD and the nonaggression pact, see Horst Duhnke, *Die KPD von 1933 bis 1945* (Cologne, 1972); and Wayne Thompson, *The Political Odyssey of Herbert Wehner* (Boulder, Colo., 1993), pp. 72–75. For the KPD's Central Committee response to the pact, see "Aus der Erklärung des Zentralkomitees der Kommunistischen Partei Deutschlands zum Abschluss des Nichtangriffspaktes zwischen der Sowjetunion und Deutschland," in Walter Ulbricht, *Zur Geschichte der Neuesten Zeit* (n. 8 above), pp. 330–33. The Hitler-Stalin pact was a blow to the German Communist emigration in Moscow because it meant that three thousand of the four thousand German Communists in the USSR, including Jews, were forced to return to imprisonment or death in Germany. On German Communists in the Soviet Union and Nazi Germany, see Margarete Buber, *Under Two Dictators* (London, 1949).

[20] In the words of a leading historian of the subject, KPD in Weimar had a very "small number of Jewish members, a tiny number of Jewish voters and a minimal interest for the Jewish question" (Edmund Silberner, *Kommunisten zur Judenfrage: Zur Geschichte von Theorie und Praxis des Kommunismus* [Opladen, 1983], p. 264). Until 1929, up to 10 percent of the leadership was of Jewish origin, though a 1927 survey indicated that the Jewish percentage of an organization composed of the working class and the unemployed was 0.7 percent, or one thousand out of 143,000. Six of the sixty-two Communist members of the Reichstag in 1924 were Jewish. By 1933, there were no Jews among the one hundred Communist representatives, p. 265. Also see, Hans-Helmuth Knütter, *Die Juden und die deutsche Linke in der Weimarer Republik, 1918–1933* (Dusseldorf, 1971). On the Jews, Communism, and anti-Semitism after 1945 in Europe see Francois Fejto, *Les Juifs et l'Antisemitisme dans les Pays Communistes* (Paris, 1960), German trans., *Judentum und Kommunismus in Osteuropa* (Vienna, Frankfurt am Main, and Zurich, 1967).

class.[21] The association of the Jews with capitalism, and of German Jews with the bourgeoisie, remained a strong current in the KPD.[22] The German Communists, guided by Stalin's 1913 essay on the national question, which had denied Jews the prerequisites of nationhood, did not consider the Jews as Jews to be an oppressed or persecuted nationality.[23] Neither the Brussels Resolution of 1935 or the Bern Resolution of 1939, both of which sought to appeal to the broadest possible base of potential antifascists, focused on the persecution of the Jews.

The great exception to the Communist lack of focus on the persecution of the Jews was found in a special issue of *Die Rote Fahne,* the party's clandestine newspaper, in response to the Nazis' anti-Jewish pogrom of November 9, 1938.[24] The Central Committee passionately denounced the pogrom, "which has covered Germany's honor with the deepest disgrace in the eyes of the whole of humanity." All "honorable Germans" rejected the attacks on defenseless Jews. The German people had "nothing in common with those who set fire to synagogues, with the plunderers of Jewish

---

[21] "Kommunismus und Judenfrage," in *Der Jud ist Schuld . . . ?* Diskussionsbuch über die Judenfrage (Basel, Berlin, Leipzig, and Vienna, 1932), pp. 272–86. The essay, the only extensive discussion of the Jewish question before 1933, was written by an anonymous member of the party leadership and never widely circulated. See discussion in Silberner, pp. 279–86. The essay also attacked Zionism, as a movement that threatened the interests of the majority of Jews and served only the interests of a reactionary, imperialist group of Jews in league with the English bourgeoisie, and British, American, French, and German imperialism in struggles against the colonial liberation movements of the Arabs. After a wartime and early postwar hiatus, this early Communist anti-Zionism returned to dominance after 1949 in East Germany.

[22] See Julius Carlebach, *Karl Marx and the Radical Critique of Judaism* (London, 1978); and recently Liah Greenfeld, *Nationalism: Five Paths to Modernity* (Cambridge, Mass., 1992).

[23] The Jews, he had argued, lacked the commonalities of language, territory, economic life, and cultural characteristics that were the prerequisites of nationhood, and were thus not a nation (Josef Stalin, "Marxismus und nationale Frage," in *Werke,* 12 vols. [East Berlin, 1950], 2:226–333.

[24] "Gegen die Schmach der Judenpogrom! Erklärung des Zentralkomitees der KPD," *Die Rote Fahne: Sonderausgabe gegen Hitlers Judenpogrome* (November 1938), p. 1. A version of Wilhelm Pieck's essay was reprinted in East Germany in the 1950s. See Wilhelm Pieck, "Nicht nur Entrüstung, sondern Taten! Gegen die Judenpogrome," in Pieck, *Reden und Aufsätze* (n. 9 above), 1:326–29. Walter Ulbricht did not include the document in his collection of essays and documents published in the early 1950s. It was discussed briefly in the 1969 fifteen-volume official history. See "Der Kampf zur Sturze der Faschistischen Diktatur und fur die Verhinderung des Krieges durch die Schaffung der Aktionseinheit der Arbeiterklasse und aller Antifaschistischen, 1933–1939," in Ulbricht, *Geschichte der Deutschen Arbeiterbewegung,* 2:7–416; and Institut für Marxismus-Leninismus beim Zentralkomitee der SED (n. 2 above), 10:213–16.

businesses and apartments, with harassment, torture and murder of Jewish fellow citizens." The Nazi leadership had prepared and organized the pogrom and used the slogan "The Jew is guilty" in order to "divert the growing anger of the people against the National Socialist dictatorship."[25]

In ringing tones, the Central Committee expressed its solidarity with the persecuted Jews of Germany and linked the fate of the Jews to that of the Germans fighting Nazism.

Therefore, the struggle against the Jewish pogrom is an inseparable part of the German struggle for freedom and peace against the National Socialist dictatorship. Hence, this struggle must be conducted with the most complete solidarity with our Jewish fellow citizens by all who have been subjected to the tyranny of the Hitler dictatorship. . . .

The Communist Party appeals to all Communists, Socialists, Democrats, Catholics, and Protestants, to all decent and honorable Germans: *Help our tortured Jewish fellow citizens with all means!* With a wall of iron contempt, isolate from our people the good-for-nothings who carry out the pogrom. . . .

The *German working class* stands at the front of the battle against the persecution of the Jews. . . .

The liberation of Germany from the shame of the Jewish pogrom will coincide with the hour of the liberation of the German people from the brown tyranny. . . .

Solidarity in sympathy and in assistance for Jewish compatriots, solidarity with persecuted Communists and Socialists, solidarity with threatened Catholics, solidarity of all of those who work to undermine and overthrow the hated Nazi regime by the creation of the broadest German popular front movement—this is what the hour demands for all peace and freedom loving Germans![26]

The statement was unique in the history of German Communism. Never, before or afterward, did the Central Committee of the KPD, or later the SED, give the Jewish question such a central role in the resistance to the Nazis, or so forcefully proclaim its solidarity with the Jews.

Pieck, still the revolutionary optimist, argued that the pogrom was due to Hitler's fear of popular antagonism in response to his war provocations of September 1938, and to the Nazi regime's efforts "to intimidate the German people as a whole and thus to break its growing resistance."[27] It was, he

[25] "Gegen die Schmach der Judenpogrome!" p. 1. A statement at the top of p. 1 read, "Comrade! Give *Rote Fahne* only to a reliable friend—no uncontrolled distribution. Convey the contents orally to others."

[26] Ibid.; emphasis in original.

[27] Wilhelm Pieck, "Unser Volk gegen die barbarischen Judenpogrome," *Die Rote Fahne: Sonderausgabe gegen Hitlers Judenpogrome,* no. 7 (November 1938), p. 2. A slightly longer version of the article was published in the German Communist exile newspaper in Basel, *Rundschau* (November 24, 1938). It is reprinted in Pieck, "Nicht nur Entrüstung, sondern Taten!"

continued, not only the Jews who were the Nazis' victims. "It is the *working masses as a whole against whom these excesses are directed.*"[28] The working class and the Communists not only rejected the attack on the Jews "*but feel bound in solidarity with the persecuted Jewish population, and see in their defense, the preservation of their own interests.*"[29] Pieck's expression of moral solidarity with the Jews was impressive, yet it also contained hints of a far less generous conception of resistance. The Nazis had not attacked the Jews as part of an assault on the working class. They had not been part of the Communists' natural constituency, and many in the German working class and in the KPD identified German Jewry with Social Democracy or, worse, with German capitalism.

In the same issue, Ulbricht described the pogrom as a "weapon of fascist war policy," and a tool of Nazi domination.[30]

The Jewish pogrom, which was carried out under the slogan "against Jews, Catholics, and Communists" is directed at *all civilized people. The witch hunt against the Jews is intended to split the mass opposition, and prevent the unification of workers and peasants, intellectuals and the middle class, and of all freedom loving people in Germany.*

The cause of the persecuted and murdered Jews is the cause of all moral men and women. The cause of the Jews is the cause of peace, freedom and humanity. One cannot successfully fight for peace and freedom without decisively fighting against fascist racist insanity (*Rassenwahnsinn*).[31]

It was "under the mask of anti-Semitism" that Hitler was conducting a fight against "all free and progressive forces in France and England." The terms "mask," "tool," "weapon," and "means" were ubiquitous in the Communist response to Nazi anti-Semitism. Moral solidarity was intertwined with an inability or refusal to understand or believe that the attack on the Jews was an end in itself, that is, not primarily a means to some other, presumably more fundamental end, defined by the narratives of class struggle or anti-Sovietism.

Especially in light of the militantly anti-Israeli policies Ulbricht pursued from 1949 to 1971 as the leader of Communist East Germany, his November 1938 statement is particularly striking because of the meaning he gives to anti-imperialism. He saw a "*connection between anti-Semitic agitation and*

[28] Pieck, "Unser Volk."

[29] Ibid.

[30] Walter Ulbricht, "Die Pogrome—eine Waffe der faschistischen Kriegspolitik," *Die Rote Fahne* (November 1938), p. 2. The article was not reproduced in Ulbricht's *Zur Geschichte der Deutschen Arbeiterbewegung.*

[31] Ibid.; emphasis in original.

[German] *colonial demands.* Every day, German radio agitates against the Jews in Palestine and in the colonies. Though stirring up race hatred, it seeks to strengthen fascist influence among the Arabs and to prepare the capture of colonies by German fascism."[32]

Ulbricht did not include this article in his essays collected in the second volume of *Zur Geschichte der Deutschen Arbeiterbewegung.* Instead, he reprinted a brochure entitled *Kriegsschauplatz Innerdeutschland* (Theater of war inside Germany) distributed in 1938 by the Communist underground in Germany.[33] Three pages of that essay dealt with "lies and racial persecution" (*Rassenhetze*) as an instrument of war preparation.[34] The German people, he said, noting that the Nazis linked all of their opponents to the Jews, "will be able to offer successful resistance against Hitler's war policy only when and if they become aware of the dangers of this barbaric racial persecution."[35]

The emphatic solidarity with the plight of the Jews evident in the November 1938 issue of *Die Rote Fahne* did not reappear in the wartime appeals of the Moscow-based German Communists, even though wartime Moscow had a large number of Jewish Communists who were willing—and briefly able—to speak out as Jews about the Jewish catastrophe.[36] During the war and Holocaust, antifascist resistance meant first and foremost the battle of the Red Army against the *Wehrmacht.* It was among the German Communist émigrés in wartime Mexico City, not Moscow, that the Jewish question was most fully discussed, indeed more fully discussed than at any other time in the history of German Communism. In the remainder of this essay I document the migration of this discussion to Mexico City, seek to explain its absence in Moscow, and examine why the promises of solidarity made by the Communists to the Jews

---

[32] Ibid.

[33] Ibid., pp. 188–89. "Kriegsschauplatz Innerdeutschland" was published under the code title "Deutsche Scholle" (German Earth). For the reprinted version see Walter Ulbricht, "Faschistische Kriegsvorbereitung," in Ulbricht, *Zur Geschichte der Deutschen Arbeiterbewegung* (n. 2 above), 2:186–89. Ulbricht often used the term *Rassenhetze* or *Judenhetze* instead of *Rassenhass* (racial hatred), *Judenhass* (hatred of the Jews), or *Anti-Semitismus* (anti-Semitism). *Hetze* is a more general term that encompasses "hatred" but also evokes persecution, agitation, witch hunt, that is, the active implementation of a program. I have translated *Rassenhetze* as "racial persecution" in keeping with Ulbricht's view of the active, instrumental use of such sentiments. "Race hatred" sounds too much like an end in itself rather than a means to other ends, something that would conflict with his view of the instrumental purposes of Nazi anti-Jewish policies.

[34] Ulbricht, "Faschistische Kriegsvorbereitung," pp. 186–89.

[35] Ibid., pp. 188–89.

[36] See "An die Juden der ganzen Welt," *Freies Deutschland* (Mexico City) (June 15, 1942), pp. 1–2, the statement of the "Second Congress of Representatives of the Jewish People" held in Moscow on May 24, 1942.

in 1938 were not kept in postwar East Berlin. We now turn to the discourse of wartime resistance in Moscow and Mexico City.

RESISTANCE IN THE FACE OF NONRESISTANCE: THE COMMUNISTS IN MOSCOW

Ulbricht's *Zur Geschichte der Neuesten Zeit: Die Niederlage Hitlerdeutschlands und die Schaffung der antifaschistische-demokratische Ordnung* (The history of the recent period: The defeat of Hitler's Germany and the creation of an antifascist-democratic order), published in 1955, was the East German master narrative of wartime resistance to and victory over Nazism.[37] Ulbricht dedicated it to the "fighters of the Soviet army, to whom the German people are indebted for their liberation from fascism, and also to the nameless heroes of the illegal antifascist struggle."[38] Yet the work contains very little about the German resistance to Nazism. Only six of the 616 pages of volume 2 of *Zur Geschichte der Deutschen Arbeiterbewegung,* his previously published essays and speeches covering the period of 1933 to 1946, dealt with "antifascist opposition in Germany."[39] In fact, antifascist resistance between 1933 and 1945 within Germany was a minor episode in Ulbricht's official history.[40] Just as the German invasion of the Soviet Union of June 22, 1941, was "the greatest crime of German history," so the Red Army was the primary source of resistance to fascism.[41] It was only after the "blows of the Soviet army" destroyed the legend of the invincibility of the German army that "broad circles of the German people were willing to listen to arguments for reason and to face reality."[42] The word "resistance" first appears in Ulbricht's history in relation to the first setbacks for the German army in the Soviet Union in 1941: "Brest-Litovsk resisted heroically for nine days. The battle for Smolensk lasted a month. Odessa resisted for seventy days."[43] In Ulbricht's

[37] Ulbricht, *Zur Geschichte der Neuesten Zeit* (n. 8 above).
[38] Ibid., p. 5.
[39] Walter Ulbricht, "Die antifaschistische Opposition in Deutschland," in Ulbricht, *Zur Geschichte der Deutschen Arbeiterbewegung,* 2:213–19; originally published in Moscow in *Bolschewik* (January 1939).
[40] Walter Ulbricht, "Der Eroberungskrieg des Faschistischen Deutschen Imperialismus und die Zerschlagung der Hitlerarmeen durch die Sowjetarmee," in Ulbricht, *Zur Geschichte der Neuesten Zeit,* p. 8. The Communist party of Germany was, he wrote, "the only (*die einzige*) political force in Germany" that had revealed Hitler's aggression to be an "imperialist policy of domination, organized resistance," and explained to the German working class and German people why this policy "must lead to catastrophe."
[41] Ibid., p. 9.
[42] Ibid., p. 10.
[43] Ibid., p. 12.

view, fissures and cracks opened up within German society and resistance emerged as a response to the setbacks and then defeats of the German army in the Soviet Union from 1943 on.

In *Zur Geschichte der Neuesten Zeit,* Ulbricht reprinted "What is the nature of the turn in the war after the defeat of the German army in Stalingrad?" a report he had written in February 1943.[44] The German defeat at Stalingrad, he argued, demonstrated the military, political-moral, and economic superiority of the Soviet Union over Hitler Germany. It would generate "further contradictions within the German bourgeoisie" and encourage officials and officers who had doubts about Hitler to further distance themselves from him. To the extent to which the military defeat at Stalingrad became known in Germany, "opposition in the ranks of working people against Hitler fascism will grow. The conditions for organizational cooperation of anti-fascist forces in Germany have become more favorable." Finally, the United States and Great Britain would be more interested in forming a second front in Europe so that the Soviet army alone would not defeat Nazi Germany.[45] Just as the German Communist party was "the only" real antifascist force within Germany, so the Soviet Union, in his view, was the leader of antifascist resistance among the warring states of World War II. If resistance within Germany increased it was in response to the change in the balance of power in the war driven by Soviet victories on the eastern front.[46]

Ulbricht did briefly refer to a number of resistance groups with Communist affiliations inside Germany.[47] Their heroism and sacrifices, he wrote, preserved "the honor of the German people . . . in spite of the eruption of barbaric Nazi ideology into the broad circles of the German people."[48] However, he dismissed the efforts of the conspirators of July 20, 1944, as "the projects and

---

[44] Ulbricht, *Zur Geschichte der Neuesten Zeit,* pp. 16–17; also Walter Ulbricht, "Worin besteht die Wendung in der Kriegslage nach der Niederlage der deutschen Armeen bei Stalingrad?" Moscow (February 1943); reprinted in Ulbricht, *Zur Geschichte der Deutschen Arbeiterbewegung* (n. 2 above), 2:302–3.

[45] Ulbricht, *Zur Geschichte der Neuesten Zeit,* pp. 16–17.

[46] Raymond Aron offered telling insights into the mixture of Clausewitzian realism and Marxism-Leninism. See his still important *Peace and War: A Theory of International Relations,* trans. Richard Howard and Annette Baker Fox (Malabar, Fla., 1981).

[47] Ibid., pp. 28–29. Ulbricht referred to a group of Jewish Communists led by Herbert Baum in Berlin. "Comrade Baum taught the members to see that the essence of fascism was not only in terror against the Jews, but rather was in the oppression of the whole German people, and that therefore they must fight actively for the overthrow of fascism." On the Jewish and Jewish Communist resistance see Helmut Eschwege, "Resistance of German Jews against the Nazi Regime," *Leo Baeck Yearbook 25* (1970): 143–80.

[48] Aron, p. 29.

efforts of German monopolists to preserve their power beyond the lost war and to find a way out at the cost and to the detriment of the German and other peoples."[49] As first articulated by Ulbricht, the dominant East German narrative of antifascist resistance was a realist's assessment of the power of states, not a romantic legend of resistance. For Ulbricht, resistance to Nazism meant first and foremost Stalin, the Red Army, and Soviet power, not antifascist resistance among the Germans. This judgment grew out of a deep and bitter disappointment with the failure of the Germans themselves to successfully resist Nazism.

The German Communists in Moscow sought to undermine the Nazi war effort and encourage the German soldiers and citizens to overthrow Hitler. Their work took the form of radio broadcasts and leaflets directed at German soldiers fighting in the *Wehrmacht,* and lectures and meetings with German prisoners-of-war in the Soviet Union. Wilhelm Pieck's addresses on the German-language edition of Moscow radio, which were published in his collected essays after the war, document the collapse of his hopes for an internal German resistance against the Nazis.[50] Disillusionment and disappointment with the German people was at times the dominant theme as it became evident that Nazism was not going to be overthrown by an indigenous German revolt.

In April 1942, Pieck called on the Germans to restore Germany's name, which had "been disgraced in the whole world by Hitler's and his barbarians' war crimes."[51] In July 1942, he repeated his appeal, stressing that "the Hitler clique" was "the deadly enemy of the German people."[52] The war was being waged in the interest of "a small band of robbers, of plutocrats and Nazi big shots."[53] The "greatest national crime against the German people" was the

---

[49] Ibid., p. 39.

[50] For some of Wilhelm Pieck's wartime addresses, see his *Reden und Aufsätze* (n. 9 above), 1:356–79.

[51] Wilhelm Pieck, "Appel zur Einigung und Aktivität für den Sturz Hitler" (Rede in der deutschsprachigen Sendung des Moskauer Rundfunks, April 8, 1942), in *Wilhelm Pieck: Gesammelte Reden und Schriften,* Bd. 6, *1939 bis Mai 1945* (East Berlin, 1979), pp. 90 and 92. Pieck's major wartime radio addresses are found in this volume. Also see Wilhelm Pieck, NL 36/417 Stiftung Archiv der Parteien und Massenorganisationen der DDR im Bundesarchiv, Berlin, Zentrales Partei Archiv (hereafter SAPMO-BA, ZPA); and Wilhelm Pieck, "Schafft die Kampfeinheit gegen Hitlers Kriegsverbrechen!" (Rede in der deutschsprachigen Sendung des Moskauers Rundfunks, April 30, 1942), in *Wilhelm Pieck: Gesammelte Reden und Schriften,* 6:93–94.

[52] Wilhelm Pieck, "Anklage gegen die Hitlerclique" (Rede in der deutschsprachigen Sendung des Moskauer Rundfunks, July 26, 1942), *Wilhelm Pieck: Gesammelte Reden und Schriften,* 6:103–5.

[53] Ibid., p. 102. The word "plutocrat" appeared in Nazi discourse and found its way into some German Communist language as well.

"imperialist war of plunder against the Soviet Union," which broke the nonaggression pact of 1939 and led to the deaths of 3,500,000 German soldiers. The German people could save themselves, and save Germany from ruin, by overthrowing this "clique."[54] If, he warned in September 1942, the Germans waited for Nazism to be defeated from without, then they would be "burdened with a heavy guilt for having stuck with this band of criminals until the end."[55] He urged the Germans to wage a broad-based armed revolt to "annihilate the Hitler band before it is too late!"[56]

Pieck's most extensive wartime statement on Nazi criminality from his radio addresses to the Germans was "Against the Hitler Barbarism," delivered on September 15, 1942.[57] He reported the murder of the inhabitants of Lidice and Lezaky in Czechoslovakia. In Poland, he said that "more than 900,000" Poles had been murdered or died from hunger since 1939. Several hundred thousand had been taken to concentration camps. Almost two million had been shipped to forced labor in Germany. "However, the SS bandits in Poland were especially intent on annihilating the Jewish population. 700,000 Jews have already been murdered. Hundreds of thousands of Jewish families have been crammed together into concentration camps and are dying of hunger and disease." In Yugoslavia, over 350,000 people had been executed, and thousands of hostages shot in France, Belgium, Holland, and Norway.[58] Typically, although he mentioned the attack on the Jews, he did not see it as a defining or central feature of Nazi policy but as one among a number of crimes. His descriptions, moreover, were most vivid, specific, and detailed when he described the "unheard of crimes the Nazi band committed against the Russian civilian population." There was, he said, "no bestiality imaginable which the SS

---

[54] Ibid., pp. 104–5.

[55] Wilhelm Pieck, "Wie muß dem Krieg ein Ende gemacht werden?" (Rede in der deutschsprachigen Sendung des Moskauer Rundfunks, September 1, 1942), in *Wilhelm Pieck: Gesammelte Reden und Schriften,* 6:106.

[56] Ibid., p. 107.

[57] Wilhelm Pieck, "Gegen die Hitlerbarbarei" (Rede in der deutschsprachigen Sendung des Moskauer Rundfunk, September 15, 1942), in *Wilhelm Pieck: Gesammelte Reden und Schriften,* 6:108–12. The issue of American and British failure to stop the Holocaust has engaged historians for many years. Pieck's radio addresses call attention to the issue of what the Soviet government and the extensive Communist underground and intelligence network in Europe knew about the Holocaust and Nazi death camps, when they knew it, and how much of what they knew they shared with the United States and England. Given the proximity and enormous size of the Soviet air force, the issue of what the Soviet Union could have done to destroy the death camps from the air deserves further examination.

[58] Ibid., pp. 108–9.

bloodhounds will not commit against the Russian people."[59] Again, there was "only one way" that the Germans could regain the respect of other peoples: overthrow the Nazis, "take revenge on the Hitler clique, liberate the world from the disease of Hitler barbarity, and thus bring honor again to the German name."[60]

In July 1943, in Moscow, the National Committee for a Free Germany (*Nationale Komitee Freies Deutschland* or NKFD) was founded.[61] The NKFD was composed of German Communist émigrés and captured German army officers and soldiers. Its purpose was to encourage revolt and undermine morale within the *Wehrmacht*.[62] In Pieck's address to the assembled captured *Wehrmacht* officers, Red Army officers, and fellow German Communist émigrés, he raised the issue of what would happen if the Germans themselves did not revolt against the Nazis.[63] If, he said, the Germans followed Hitler to the end, then Germany would be devastated not only by a land war but would lose its unity and national independence to foreign control. Only a revolt from within could prevent this "catastrophe."[64]

---

[59] Ibid., pp. 109–11. Pieck was especially appalled to read letters from German women to their husbands at the front urging them "to engage in robbery and plunder and to participate in destroying the Russian people. Can one image a more terrible human degeneration as that which emerges from these letters? . . . Germans will be hated and despised as long as they remain silent about these barbarities and tolerate them, and so long as they do not take up open struggle."

[60] Ibid., p. 111. Also in 1942, Pieck collected his thoughts in a pamphlet on "Hitler Fascism and the German People." It repeated the themes of his radio addresses. It contains nothing about the attack on the Jews but calls on workers, farmers, intellectuals, and soldiers to rise up against the Nazis. See Wilhelm Pieck, "Der Hitlerfaschismus und das deutsche Volk, 1942," in *Wilhelm Pieck: Gesammelte Reden und Schriften*, 6:120–83.

[61] See the material on the Nationalkomitee Freies Deutschland, Schulung Deutscher Kriegsgefangener, in Wilhelm Pieck Papers, NL 36/582 SAPMO-BA, ZPA (n. 51 above). For lectures and course outlines from the Communist party school in wartime Moscow, see Walter Ulbricht Papers, NL 182/827 SAPMO-BA, ZPA.

[62] For files on the Nationale Komitee Freies Deutschland, and wartime courses for German prisoners of war in the Soviet Union, see the files in the SED archives for Wilhelm Pieck, 36/582 SAPMO-BA, ZPA.

[63] Wilhelm Pieck, "Es darf kein neues 1918 geben! Wie kann der heraufziehenden Katastrophe Einhalt geboten werden?" (Rede auf der Gründungskonferenz des Nationalkomitees Freies Deutschland, July 13, 1943), in *Wilhelm Pieck: Gesammelte Reden und Schriften* (n. 51 above), 6:195–205. On the *Nationale Komitee Freies Deutschland*, see Herman Weber, *Geschichte der DDR*, 3d ed. (Munich, 1987); Bodo Scheurig, *Freies Deutschland: Das Nationalkomitee und der Bund Deutscher Offiziere in der Sowjetunion, 1943–1945* (Cologne, 1984).

[64] Pieck, "Es darf kein neues 1918 geben!"

At the same meeting, the NKFD issued a "Manifesto to the Wehrmacht and the German People," appealing to the Germans to save "the fatherland" by anti-Nazi resistance.[65]

> If the German people continues to permit itself to be led to ruin without will and without resistance, then with every passing day it becomes not only weaker, and powerless but also guiltier. Then Hitler will only be overthrown by the weapons of the [Allied] coalition. Such an outcome would mean the end of our national freedom and of our state. It would bring about the dismemberment of our fatherland. And we could not bring an indictment against anyone but ourselves.
>
> If however, the German people quickly pulls itself together and proves through its deeds that it wants to be a free people, and is determined to liberate Germany from Hitler, it wins the right itself to determine its own future destiny, and the right to belong to the world.
>
> THAT IS THE ONLY WAY TO SAVE THE SURVIVAL, THE FREEDOM, AND THE HONOR OF THE GERMAN NATION.[66]

The appeal for resistance now contained an indictment of the Germans and a warning of postwar consequences for failure to revolt.

At the same congress, Erich Weinert, a writer, German Communist, and Spanish Civil War veteran, was chosen to be president of the NKFD.[67] Weinert also spoke of the possibility of national salvation by revolt.[68] Under the impact of Hitler's early successes in the war, he said, many Germans paid no attention to whether or not the war was just. Despite the warnings of the anti-Nazi opposition, the vision of "Lebensraum" in the East was more powerful than the demands of morality. "This is a bitter criticism of our people but it must be said."[69] It was, he continued, the setbacks in Moscow in the winter of 1941–42, then the growth of the power of the Red Army, and

[65] "Manifest an die Wehrmacht und an das deutsche Volk," in Ulbricht, *Zur Geschichte der Neuesten Zeit* (n. 8 above), 1:355–61. The manifesto was also printed in 1944 by the Mexico City National Committee for a Free Germany. See *Deutsche Wohin? Protokoll der Gruendungsversammlung des National-Komitees Freies Deutschland und des Deutschen Offiziersbundes,* with a foreword by Paul Merker (Mexico City, 1944).

[66] Ibid., pp. 356–57; emphasis and capitalization in original. The manifesto precluded any peace with Hitler. It called for formation of a democratic German government that would immediately end the war, withdraw German troops, give up all conquered territories, enter peace negotiations, and create a new "free Germany." Such a new government would eliminate all racist legislation; restore political rights and freedom of speech, press, organization, and religion; secure the right to work and to "legally gained property"; and return stolen property to its rightful owners.

[67] See "Erich Weinert," in *Wer war Wer* (n. 7 above), pp. 476–77.

[68] Erich Weinert, "Protokoll der Gruendungsversammlung," *Deutsche Wohin?* pp. 15–24.

[69] Ibid., p. 17.

finally the "catastrophe in Stalingrad" that "shook the certainty of victory among the German people and shattered Hitler's credibility and faith in his ability as a military leader."[70] It was then, and only then, that the German people and German soldiers began to turn away from the Nazis. Like Ulbricht, Weinert saw resistance to Nazism more as the product of the shifting fortunes of war than as a result of outraged conscience.[71]

The theme of German national salvation by revolt and resistance, or national disaster and shame through continued subservience, was evident in Weinert's subsequent NKFD statements.[72] It was, he said, not only Himmler's terror and the SS that kept Hitler in power. It was also, he continued, "your [the Germans'] obedience, your fateful bond [to Hitler] . . . your cowardly silence and hesitation which still always gives Hitler the possibility to preserve his power." The Germans, he insisted, had means—strikes, work slowdowns—to "break his power. . . . You must only have the will to use them."[73] During the war, the absence of a successful or consequential German resistance to Nazism strained the credibility of the Communist analysis of fascism as rule by a small clique of capitalists, militarists, and Nazi functionaries without significant popular support.

In the NKFD German Communists worked with German officers. Yet in the public and published documents, Ulbricht and Pieck display no evidence of having made public statements of resistance to Nazism in common with Soviet Jewish Communists who were speaking as Jews. In May 1942, ten months before Soviet hopes were raised by the victory at Stalingrad, Soviet Jewish Communists declared that "with pride, we Jews of the Soviet Union speak to Jews of the whole world."[74] The statement spoke very specifically

---

[70] Ibid., p. 17.

[71] For an interesting recent set of essays that also focuses on Stalingrad as the starting point of disillusionment, see Martin Broszat, Klaus-Dietmar Henke, and Hans Woller, *Von Stalingrad zur Währungsreform: Zur Sozialgeschichte des Umbruchs in Deutschland* (Munich, 1990).

[72] Erich Weinert, "Nationalkomitee Freies Deutschland, Anweisungen Nr. 2," in Wilhelm Pieck, NL 36/577 SAPMO-BA, ZPA (n. 51 above). The pamphlets, leaflets, and radio broadcasts of the *NKFD* directed at the Wehrmacht and at the German home front were written under the direction of Pieck and Ulbricht; Anton Ackermann, another German Communist émigré and future member of the SED Central Committee, and Erich Weinert. For the Moscow Communists' anti-Nazi wartime propaganda from 1941 to 1945, see Wilhelm Pieck, NL 36/569 (Frontagitation, 1941–42), NL 36/570 (Frontagitation, 1942–43), and NL 36/577 (Nationalkomitee Freies Deutschland—Aufrufe und Flugblätter, 1941–42, July 1943–March 1945), SAPMO-BA, ZPA.

[73] Weinert, "Nationalkomitee Freies Deutschland, Anweisungen Nr. 2."

[74] "An die Juden der ganzen Welt" (n. 36 above). The statement was used for fund-raising efforts abroad. Some of the signers of the statement, such as Solomon Michoels and Schachno Epstein, were subsequently executed in the anti-Semitic

about the Jews of Europe and the Soviet Union who "are beaten, tortured, and murdered by the beastial Hitlerites," called the Red Army the "hope of all humanity," and warned that in the summer of 1942, "the fate of all humanity . . . and also the fate of the Jewish people" would be decided.[75] Yet, in contrast to the German Communists in Mexico City, there was no public or published German Communist dialogue with the Jewish question in Moscow.

In lectures on anti-Semitism for German prisoners-of-war or for purposes of internal education, they and their Soviet colleagues examined anti-Semitism as a ruling-class tool to divert popular dissatisfaction onto the Jews and to weaken popular German resistance to Nazism.[76] Johannes R. Becher (1891–1958), a future member of the SED Central Committee and minister of culture in the DDR, in his 1944 essay denounced "The Race Theory of German Fascism" as a scientifically worthless tool in the service of German aggression. He examined anti-Semitism as a part of a larger racist complex of colonialism and imperialism and offered little analysis of the history of anti-Semitism or its particular significance in the Nazi regime.[77] The German Communists in Moscow did little to distinguish between a generalized German racism directed against the peoples of Eastern Europe and the Soviet Union, and anti-Semitism. While they worked with anti-Nazi, captured German officers, they seemed to distance themselves from explicit identification with the Jewish tragedy. Perhaps, conscious of the spread of anti-Semitism among the Germans, they thought that successful appeals to the "honor of the German nation" required reticence about Nazi attacks on the Jews.

In a radio address from Moscow on May 4, 1945, Wilhelm Pieck expressed the ambivalence of the moment.[78] Every "honorable and true German," he

---

attacks on Soviet Jews between 1948 and 1952. See Lionel Kochan, *The Jews in the Soviet Union since 1917* (New York and London, 1978). On the Jews during World War II in the Soviet Union, see Vassily Grossman's very important novel, *Life and Fate,* trans. Robert Chandler (New York, 1985).

[75] "An die Juden der ganzen Welt."

[76] See "Einführungskurs, 1942," in Wilhelm Pieck, NL 36/582 SAPMO-BA, ZPA. For lectures and course outlines for German prisoners of war, see Wilhelm Pieck, NL 36/582 SAPMO-BA, ZPA. For lectures and course outlines of the Communist party instruction for party cadres in Moscow during the war see Walter Ulbricht, 182/827 SAPMO-BA, ZPA. See "Nation und Rasse" and "Nation," in "Program für den Kriegsgefangene, 1942," in Wilhelm Pieck, NL 36/582 SAPMO-BA, ZPA.

[77] Johannes R. Becher, "Zur Rassentheorie des Deutschen Faschismus," reprinted in his *Publizistik II, 1939–1945* (Berlin and Weimar, 1978), pp. 384–90. The essay was first published in 1978 in Becher's collected works. Becher's analysis of fascism's racial theory was literally engraved in stone in 1958 in his inscriptions in the Buchenwald memorial to victims of fascism.

[78] Wilhelm Pieck, "Berlin von Hitler befreit!" in his *Reden und Aufsätze* (n. 9 above), 1:423–26.

said, was filled with joy at the Red Army's victory "over the forces of darkness, racist insanity and genocide embodied in Hitlerism. . . . Yet the joyful news is mixed with the bitter, tortured consciousness that the German people themselves did not free themselves from this band of murderers, but instead followed them to the end, and supported them in their war crimes."[79] The Germans had refused to listen to the warnings of the antifascists, were blinded by Hitler's apparent successes, and adopted the "Nazi poison of imperialist ideology of plunder. . . . You [the Germans] became the tools of Hitler's wars and thus have taken a great shared guilt and responsibility. Now you will bear this guilt towards other people and must again clear the German name from the filth heaped on it by the Hitler band."[80] The other people Pieck had in mind were the people of the Soviet Union. Later that month, Georgi Dimitroff, Pieck's longtime colleague in the Comintern, told Pieck that the majority of Germans "would have been happy if Hitler had won the war."[81] The German Communists also knew that what little resistance the Germans offered, noble or heroic as it may have been, was not decisive in the defeat of Nazi Germany. By 1945, the Communists were not romanticists of a German antifascist resistance but realists who thought first of all of the Soviet Union and the Red Army when they thought of resistance to fascism. They returned to Berlin disillusioned.

These lessons of the war were apparent in the Communists' "appeal" to the German people of June 11, 1945, which echoes the bitterness of the returning exiles.[82] It recalled the unheeded warnings of the German Communists concerning the dangers of Nazism and spoke of the Germans' shared guilt (*Mitschuld*) and shared responsibility (*Mitverantwortung*) for the war and its consequences. "The greatest and most fateful of Hitler's war crimes was the malicious and treacherous attack on the Soviet Union." It stressed the role of the Red Army in destroying Nazism. The statement referred to Nazi death camps but did not mention the Jews who perished in

---

[79] Ibid., p. 423.

[80] Ibid., p. 424.

[81] "Besprechung mit Dimitroff (May 25, 1945)," in Wilhelm Pieck, NL 36/500 SAPMO-BA, ZPA.

[82] Zentralkomitee der Kommunistischen Partei Deutschlands, "Aufruf der Kommunistischen Partei," *Deutsches Volkszeitung* 1, no. 1 (June 13, 1945): 1–2; reprinted in Ulbricht, *Zur Geschichte der Neuesten Zeit* (n. 8 above), 1:370–79. The appeal was written by Anton Ackermann, a member of the KPD's Central Committee who had played a major role in radio propaganda of the National Committee for a Free Germany directed against the Wehrmacht during the war and would be a major figure in East German Communism. Also see Weber (n. 63 above), pp. 47–54; Leonhard (n. 3 above).

them. It called for *Wiedergutmachung* for damage the Nazis had done to "other peoples."[83]

As the NKFD Manifesto of 1943 suggested, a postwar dictatorship oriented to Moscow could be presented as the price that had to be paid for the Germans' failure to overthrow Nazism themselves, as a necessary act of prudence needed to keep a wary eye on the Germans, or, for the Communists themselves, as a welcome deliverance into the arms of Soviet liberators. Celebration of the antifascist resistance after the war was also a permanent rebuke to the majority who, for whatever reason, did not resist.

PAUL MERKER AND ANTI-NAZI RESISTANCE IN MEXICO CITY, 1942–45

It was in wartime Mexico City, thousands of miles from the Soviet and KPD leaders in Moscow, that the Jewish question entered into the public discourse of German Communist resistance to fascism or, at least, into the public discourse of one leading figure of the German resistance to Nazism. Unlike any other leading German Communist, Paul Merker (1894–1969) placed anti-Semitism and the Jewish catastrophe at the center of his conception of resistance to Nazism. His denunciation, expulsion, and imprisonment in East Germany (1950–56) amounted to the suppression of a possible alternative Communist understanding of resistance to Nazism and the Jewish question.[84]

Merker was a member of the left-wing KPD in the 1920s, and a member of the Prussian legislature.[85] He was one of the leaders of the German Communist underground in France before he escaped to Mexico City in 1942.

[83] "Aufruf der Kommunistischen Partei." "Hitler-Germans' (Hitlerdeutschen) hands are stained with the blood of millions of murdered children, women and elderly people. Day after day, in the death camps, the extermination of human beings was carried out in gas chambers and ovens. Burning living bodies, burying living bodies, cutting living bodies up into pieces—this was how the Nazi bandits ravaged. Millions of prisoners of war and foreign workers seized and taken to Germany were worked to death, and died of hunger, cold and disease."

[84] On the Merker case see Karl Wilhelm Fricke, *Warten auf Gerechtigkeit: Kommunistische Säuberungen und Rehabilitierungen, Bericht und Dokumentation* (Cologne, 1971), and *Politik und Justiz in der DDR: Zur Geschichte der politischen Verfolgung, 1945–1968, Bericht und Dokumentation* (Cologne, 1979); Rudi Beckert and Karl Wilhelm Fricke, "Auf Weisung des Politbüros: Aus den Geheimprozeßakten des Obersten DDR-Gerichts, Teil III: Der Fall Paul Merker" (Deutschlandfunk, Zur Diskussion/Geschichte Aktuell, Hamburg, January 10, 1992); George Hermann Hodos, *Schauprozesse: Stalinistische Säuberungen in Osteuropa 1948–1954* (Frankfurt am Main, 1988); and Sigrid Meuschel, *Legitimation und Parteiherrschaft* (Frankfurt am Main, 1992), pp. 101–16.

[85] "Paul Merker," in *Wer war Wer* (n. 7 above), p. 308. For Merker's "ultra-left" contributions to the attack on Social Democracy as "social fascism," see Paul Merker, "Der Kampf gegen den Faschismus," *Die Internationale* 13, no. 3 (February 1930):

There, from 1942 to 1945 in the Mexico City version of *Freies Deutschland,* he wrote numerous articles on Nazism, anti-Semitism, *Wiedergutmachung* for the Jewish victims of Nazism, the course of World War II, and the shape of a future democratic Germany.[86] Merker also wrote a remarkable two volume analysis of Nazi Germany, *Deutschland: Sein oder Nicht Sein.*[87] It was the first and only work by a leading German Communist to place Nazi anti-Semitism at the center of an analysis of National Socialism, and of the prospect for democracy in postwar Germany. Merker, a loyal Communist, could envisage a blend of communism and democracy. He could not envisage a Germany that was anti-Semitic and democratic, and he believed that German Communists after the war should do all they could to restore the Jewish community in Germany, which the Nazis had destroyed. He was an unusual German Communist.

Paul Merker was not Jewish.[88] He did have a strong appreciation for the role German Jews had played in German history in general as well as within the socialist and communist tradition, and he associated the struggle against anti-Semitism in German history with the struggle for democracy. He spent the years 1931 to 1933 in the United States, meeting and working in trade

---

65–69, and "Der Kampf gegen den Faschismus," *Die Internationale* 13, nos. 8/9 (1930): 259–66.

[86] Some of the most important are the following: Paul Merker, "Hitlers Anti-Semitismus und wir," *Freies Deutschland* 1, no. 12 (October 1942): 9–11, "Die Verantwortung der Deutschen," *Freies Deutschland* 2, no. 1 (November–December 1942): 8–9, "Nationalisierung der deutschen Grossindustrie und Wiedergutmachung," *Freies Deutschland* 2, no. 6 (May 1943): 6–8, "Brief an einen Freund: Die Bewegung Freies Deutschland und die Zukunft der Juden," *Freies Deutschland* 3. no. 5 (April 1944): 5–7, "Die Juden und das neue Deutschland," *Freies Deutschland* 4, no. 11 (October 1945): 7–8, "Lord Vansittart, Friedrich Stampfer und die deutsche Untergrundbewegung," *Freies Deutschland* 3, no. 7 (June 1944): pp. 7–9; "Demokratische Kraefte in Deutschland? Die Kernfrage nach der militaerischen Niederlage Hitlers," *Freies Deutschland* 4, no. 6 (May 1945): 6–8. On Merker's Mexican writings, see L. Maas, "Unerschüttert bleibt mein Vertrauen in den guten Kern unseres Volkes: Der Kommunist Paul Merker und die Exil-Diskussion um Deutschlands Schuld, Verantwortung, und Zukunft," in *Deutschland nach Hitler: Zukunftspläne im Exil und aus der Besatzungszeit, 1939–1949,* ed. Thomas Koebner, Gert Sautermeister, and Sigrid Schneider-Grube (Opladen, 1987).

[87] Paul Merker, *Deutschland—Sein oder Nichtsein?* Bd. 1, *Von Weimar zu Hitler* (Frankfurt am Main, 1973; reprint, Mexico City, 1944), Bd. 2, *Das Dritte Reich und sein Ende* (Frankfurt am Main, 1972; reprint, Mexico City, 1945).

[88] The following draws on Merker's "Position on the Jewish Question" written for the Central Party Control Commission of the SED in 1956 as he—unsuccessfully—sought full political rehabilitation after having been imprisoned since 1952 on espionage charges that were subsequently dropped. Paul Merker, "An die Zentrale Kontrollkommission des ZK. der SED, Berlin: Stellungnahme zur Judenfrage," in Paul Merker, NL 102/27, SAPMO-BA, ZPA.

unions with many Jewish Communists in New York and Chicago. Their support for equality for American blacks and their opposition to white racism within the American working class left a lasting impression. While in the Communist underground in Berlin, in March–April 1934, he found that Jews, both party members and nonparty members, readily made their homes and apartments available to "illegal comrades" and gave them assistance.[89] As a result of these experiences, he opposed Nazi anti-Semitism not only out of "political and national but also from human motives." As the Nazi persecution of the Jews deepened, he concluded that "the struggle of the German working class against anti-Semitism had been inadequate. It seemed to me to be the special duty of non-Jewish people to decisively stand up against anti-Semitism."[90]

After the anti-Jewish pogrom of November 1938, he began to write about anti-Semitism while he and Franz Dahlem (1892–1981), another member of the KPD politburo, directed the foreign secretariat of the KPD in France from 1939 to 1942. Merker was troubled that German Socialists and Communists, unlike the French socialists and liberals during the Dreyfus case or the Russians under Lenin and Plekanov, had not made the fight against anti-Semitism central to the fight for democracy.[91] With a visa attained with the assistance of an "antifascist" committee in New York that was helping Jews and leftists to escape from southern France, Merker arrived in Veracruz, Mexico, in June 1942 on a boat from Casablanca.[92]

Soon after arriving in Mexico City, Merker published "Hitler's Anti-Semitism and Us," which appeared in the Mexico City edition of *Freies Deutschland* in October 1942. It was followed by a steady stream of essays on related issues.[93] Merker was the only leading figure of German Communism to produce such a body of work during the war and Holocaust. In "Anti-Semitism and Us," he wrote,

If all of the German rivers flowed with ink, and all the German forests were made of quill pens they would not suffice to describe the immeasurable crimes which Hitler

[89] Ibid.

[90] Ibid., p. 4.

[91] Ibid., p. 6.

[92] The circumstances of Paul Merker's activity in the Communist underground and his exit from France were very complex and became the subject of an intensive inner-party investigation after 1945. For Merker's own account see Paul Merker, "Fragebogen," and "Mein politischer Lebenslauf," in ZPKK IV/2/II/V, SAPMO-BA, ZPA, pp. 1–54.

[93] Merker, "Hitlers Anti-Semitismus und wir." Two previous essays on anti-Semitism in *Freies Deutschland* were Leo Katz, "Anti-Semitismus als Barometer," *Freies Deutschland* 3 (January 1942): 13–14; and Ernst Abusch, "Der gelbe Stern und das deutsche Volk," *Freies Deutschland* 3 (January 1942): 17–18.

fascism has committed against the Jewish people. Where is there today a Jewish family from Germany which has not been robbed and deeply humiliated, whose relatives have not been locked in concentration camps, murdered or driven to forced suicide? . . .

The campaign of extermination of Hitler fascism against the Jewish citizens of Germany was only the beginning. It has been extended to all of the countries and areas conquered by Hitler. An unprecedented flood of anti-Semitic propaganda has poured over these countries and more or less also over the Western world as well. The victims of this flood number in the hundreds of hundreds of thousands. As a result, Hitler Germany will be enshrined in history as the country of the most gigantic degree of state sponsored and cowardly murderousness. Because the German people permitted the crimes of its dominant class against the Jewish people, it has taken on itself a heavy responsibility.[94]

In the German Communist tradition of antifascist resistance, passages such as this one were exceptional. Merker was unique in addressing the Nazi attack on the Jews with such specificity and detail. Those responsible included not only monopolists, militarists, and Junkers but also intellectuals, writers, politicians, professors, scientists, and artists "who incited the masses of the people against the Jewish population through the development and spread of racist nonsense and false documents such as the 'Protocols of the Elders of Zion' "; the Weimar politicians who due to "their many years of capitulation to reaction, opened the way to the restoration of its rule, prevented the unity of the German working class, and made impossible a broad battle front of the people against fascism."[95] Only those "antifascists" who had risked their lives and freedom in the fight against Hitler's fascism, Merker continued, were not burdened with the responsibility. They had long recognized the "driving forces of anti-Semitism" and sought to erect a dam against it. They freely assumed responsibility "insofar as it is at all possible to bring about restitution for the crimes committed against their Jewish fellow citizens."[96]

Like Johannes R. Becher, Merker saw the so-called race theory of Hitler fascism, in part, as an instrument for Nazi global imperialist ambitions.[97] "Anti-Semitism" was "blackest reaction. It was directed not only against the Jews, but also against the interests of the German working classes as well as against all other peoples. The stance of a cultivated individual towards anti-Semitism is the measure of whether or not he is progressive or reactionary." Just as all "progressive forces" opposed anti-Semitism, "the place of Jewish fellow citizens is on their side, in their ranks. Their deadly

[94] Merker, "Hitlers Anti-Semitismus und wir," p. 9.

[95] Ibid.

[96] Ibid.

[97] Ibid. Merker also saw the Nazi attack on the Jews as an assault on Christianity "because all religious communities with international relations and political influence were a barrier to realization of his plans for world domination."

enemy is the same. Their struggle and their destiny correspond to one another."[98] For Merker, resistance to fascism brought Jews and "progressive forces" closer together to form the nucleus of a future German democracy.

Aware of arguments within the KPD that exempted wealthy German Jews from Communist empathy, he noted that some wealthy Jews had separated themselves from the "democratic and socialist oriented masses" and had become "more or less reactionary." Yet nineteenth-century bankers and Jewish capitalists in Weimar had also become victims of anti-Semitism. Hence, the fate of the Jews as a whole people was "inseparable from the freedom struggle of the workers and the middle classes" and was "dependent on victory over Hitler fascism and [on] the destruction of its basis: the economic monopoly of the few." In seeking to include even "capitalist Jews" among those who numbered among the victims of fascism, Merker made an argument that would come back to haunt him in postwar Berlin.[99]

Further, Merker departed from Stalin's views on the national question, noting that Hitler's anti-Semitism had strengthened "Jewish national feeling." He raised the issue of a Jewish state, of restoration of Jewish rights of citizenship in Germany, and of "restitution" (*Wiedergutmachung*) for the moral and economic damage suffered by the Jews. He stressed "that above all non-Jewish anti-fascists, among whom I include myself, must decisively be engaged in support of the Jewish people who are in such distress as a consequence of [the Nazis'] world wide pogrom," both in the interest of the Jews and "in the interests of their own fight for an international solution to problems created by the persecution of the Jews."[100]

The first decrees of "the coming German peoples government" should declare that anti-Semitism and all race hatred is a crime, and perpetrators of past anti-Semitic acts would be tried by special courts with the power to impose life sentences or the death penalty. All efforts would be made to reintegrate Jews into German society should they desire to return to it. Expenses for Jews to return to Germany would be covered by the state, as would the emigration costs of German Jews who freely chose to go to another country. Economic losses of Jewish citizens would be compensated whether they decided to return to Germany or remain abroad. He sought to assure "our Jewish friends and comrades in struggle" that a new democratic regime would find ways to "destroy anti-Semitism in Germany forever."[101]

---

[98] Ibid., p. 10.
[99] Ibid. Merker painted a glowing picture of the end of anti-Semitism, and of equality for Jews in the Soviet Union.
[100] Ibid.
[101] Ibid., p. 11.

"Hitler's Anti-Semitism and Us" evoked critical letters to *Freies Deutschland* and a response by Merker, which appeared in the March 1943 issue.[102] First, his critics said he wanted to "give back millions to Jewish bankers and big capitalists." He responded that he advocated the nationalization of the economy to eliminate fascism in Germany. Naturally "the Rothschilds" would not regain their monopolies, but the material compensation of the Jews would have to be enough to make possible their "full, equal reintegration into the economic and social life of Germany in as short a time as possible."[103] Second, his critics asserted that postwar compensation should take into account the class position of victims. Merker responded that the Nazis had "plundered all Jews regardless of their class position." In matters of compensation, he continued, neither the class position nor the moral character of the individual could play a role. "Only the extent of material and moral damage" was decisive. While an upper limit of compensation would be established, in many cases, Jewish artisans, small and medium-sized industrialists, doctors, and professionals would receive what had been taken from them.

Third, why, he was asked, should only the Jews receive restitution? Did not the politically persecuted, that is, the Communists, who were "fighters" against fascism, have an even greater claim? There was, he wrote, an important difference between the Jews and those persecuted because of their political activity. The Jews were persecuted because they were a "defenseless, national, religious or caste-like minority" that "Hitler fascism" used to divert attention from its own plans for world domination.

Without restitution (*Wiedergutmachung*) for this injustice and the complete elimination and destruction of anti-Semitism the victory of freedom and the securing of democracy is impossible. In my view, the Jewish people have the same right to restitution of the damage done to them as do all of the nations Hitler invaded and oppressed.

Those persecuted because of their political views are not a national, religious or caste-like minority. They stand in struggle against the Hitler dictatorship. They have taken up this struggle voluntarily and on the basis of their convictions. They are therefore regarded by the Nazis as deadly enemies, which in fact they are. Anti-fascist fighters cannot expect material compensation for the sacrifices that result. They fight for the destruction of Hitler fascism and for the freedom of peoples. This fight demands the highest commitment. The compensation for anti-fascist fighters is every successful battle and the final victory, the erection of a democratic power.[104]

---

[102] Paul Merker, "Das Echo: Diskussion ueber 'Hitlers Anti-Semitismus und Wir,' " *Freies Deutschland* (Mexico City) 2, no. 4 (March 1943): 33.
[103] Ibid.
[104] Ibid.

Fourth, Merker was asked why he focused only on the German Jews and not the Jews of countries Hitler had invaded. He answered that "everything" that he said against Hitler's anti-Semitism and for *Wiedergutmachung* for the German Jews applied in equal measure for the Jewish population of the countries the Nazis had invaded.

Merker's offense against orthodoxy in this passage was to assert that the Jews were no less deserving of restitution than "all of the nations Hitler invaded and oppressed." It was an argument for equality for the Jews, not for a monopoly of empathy or special treatment, among the various victims of fascism. It contradicted Stalin's arguments denying Jewish nationhood. Further, Merker placed *Wiedergutmachung* for the Jews and the elimination of anti-Semitism at the center of his definition of successful resistance and victory over fascism. This response was held against him in the party purges and secret political trials after the war. In postwar Berlin, Merker worked on restitution policy for victims of fascism, which included both Communists and Jews. But his wartime comments, suggesting that Communist resistance fighters, unlike Jewish victims, should consider victory over fascism its own reward, were held against him. In postwar Berlin, the KPD and then the SED placed Communist "anti-fascist resistance fighters" at the top of the hierarchy of "victims of fascism."[105]

When Merker was meeting with American Communists in 1931–33, the participation of black Communists in the black church impressed upon him how important religion could be to political activity.[106] In Mexico City and in postwar Berlin, Merker suggested that Jewish members of the Communist party join in the activities of the Jewish community. Merker saw German-Jewish contact and dialogue as a valuable legacy of the Mexican emigration when boundaries between Jews and Germans, Communists, and non-Communists became fluid under the pressures of wartime resistance.[107] The

---

[105] As Communist hostility to the West and to Israel intensified, the victimization of the Communist "fighters" came to predominate over that of the Jewish "victims" in postwar memorials. For an early postwar discussion of who was a victim of fascism for purposes of political prestige, pension, employment, housing, health, and welfare benefits, see Carl Raddatz, *Wer ist Opfer des Faschismus?* (Weimar, 1946), pp. 3–14. Raddatz was the secretary of the Executive Committee of "Victims of Fascism" and was later active in the leading Communist organization of former resistance members, the Vereinigung des Verfolgten des Naziregimes. On the application of the term "fascism" to the Adenauer government in West Germany, see Carl Raddatz, *Faschismus und Krieg—Das Programm der Adenauer-Regierung: Tatsachen und Dokumente über das Wiedererstehen des Faschismus in Westdeutschland* (Fascism and war—the program of the Adenauer government: Facts and documents on the reemergence of fascism in West Germany) (East Berlin, 1952).

[106] Paul Merker, "Stellungnahme zur Judenfrage" (n. 88 above), pp. 19–20.

[107] Ibid., p. 25.

Communist statements at the Brussels and Bern conferences, calling on the German people to resist the Nazis, contained a discourse of reconciliation framed politically, between Communists and Social Democrats, not culturally, between Germans and Jews.

Merker had spent six years in France and four in Mexico. In the anti-Nazi resistance he had met Communists from different countries, and he had met and talked with many non-Communist anti-Nazis. He had written with enthusiasm about the wartime alliance between the Soviet Union, the United States, and Great Britain. The resistance and the broad political spectrum of the anti-Hitler coalition, more than his own distinctive theories of radical democracy, left Merker with a more inclusive definition of antifascist resistance than his colleagues on the KPD politburo who spent the war years in Moscow. When the wartime alliance gave way to the Cold War, this expansive conception of resistance involving contact with non-Communists and with religious institutions became grounds for suspicion and accusations of espionage.

Perhaps because he devoted more effort than Ulbricht to examining the mechanisms of repression and terror within Nazi Germany, Merker was able to combine a clear moral judgment concerning German postwar responsibility to punish the guilty and aid their victims with the hope that the Germans did have the resources to build a postwar democracy. While asserting the "shared responsibility" of the German people for Nazi crimes, Merker argued that returning German Communists ought not give up hope for a democratic element among the Germans, despite the absence of an internal revolt against the Nazis. A public exchange of letters in May and September 1945 in *Freies Deutschland* between Merker and Wilhelm Koenen (also a member of the KPD in Weimar, and a future member of the SED Central Committee from 1946 until his death in 1964) dealt with the issue of whether there were democratic and progressive forces in Germany at the end of the war.[108] Koenen wrote bitterly about the "reactionary role of the German people" and the "betrayal of the German proletariat" who had "closed their eyes" to the crimes taking place and who had obeyed when asked to do so.[109] By contrast, Merker spoke of "we anti-Nazi emigrants" who shared with "the whole German people" the responsibility for the "Hitler gangster regime." Merker then took issue with Koenen's pessimism about the Germans. In his view, it would not lead to a new democracy but would make permanent the "spirit of

---

[108] Paul Merker, "Demokratische Kraefte in Deutschland? Die Kernfrage nach der militaerischen Niederlage Hitlers, An meinen Bruder in London," *Freies Deutschland* 4, no. 6 (May 1945): 6–8.

[109] Wilhelm Koenen, "An meinen Bruder in Mexiko," *Freies Deutschland* 4, no. 10 (September 1945): 37–39.

subservience" Koenen purported to criticize. The returning German anti-Nazis could not, Merker continued, help democracy to sink roots in postwar Germany if they considered themselves no more than "reliable administrators for the occupation authorities."[110]

In an essay published in October 1945 in *Freies Deutschland* before he returned to Berlin in summer 1946, Merker again returned to the issue of "the Jews and the New Germany."[111] The problem now faced by Jewish survivors was whether or not the military victory over fascism had also delivered a "decisive blow against anti-Semitism." Unfortunately, he wrote, the answer was negative, and this would be so as long as "capitalist monopolies and trusts" continued to exist.[112]

Merker returned to Berlin in 1946 and reassumed his position as a member of the politburo of the KPD; later he moved on to the Central Committee of the SED when it was founded in 1946. He worked on land reform, social welfare, and refugee resettlement issues. Most important, he was the leading figure in the SED Central Committee to raise the issue of fighting anti-Semitism and to make the case for restitution (*Wiedergutmachung*) to the Jewish victims of Nazism both as an inherent moral imperative and as essential to the construction of a postwar democracy.[113] Against fierce resistance within the East German Communist administration at times, he argued for a law of restitution that treated Jews on a equal plane with Communists, and that would compensate Jews as Jews, regardless of their class backgrounds.[114] He welcomed the creation of the state of Israel as the result of the Jewish people's just struggle against British imperialism, American oil interests, and Arab "fascists."[115]

[110] Ibid., p. 43.

[111] Paul Merker, "Die Juden und das neue Deutschland" (n. 86 above).

[112] Ibid., pp. 7–8.

[113] See Sekretariat Lehmann, IV/2027/29-33, SAPMO-BA, ZPA (Wiedergutmachung gegenüber den Verfolgten des Naziregimes, 1945–1950). For discussions of *Wiedergutmachung* and of the relationship of the East German state to the small (15,600 in 1945) Jewish community of East Germany, see Erica Burgauer, *Zwischen Erinnerung und Verdrängung—Juden in Deutschland nach 1945* (Hamburg, 1993), pp. 139–43; Robin Ostow, *Judisches Leben in der DDR* (Frankfurt am Main, 1988); Julius H. Schoeps, *Juden in der DDR: Geschichte—Probleme—Perspektiven* (Duisburg, 1988); and Jerry E. Thompson, *Jews, Zionism and Israel: The Story of the Jews in the German Democratic Republic since 1945* (unpublished diss., Washington State University, 1978); and Angelika Timm, "Der Streit um Restitution und Wiedergutmachung in der Sowjetischen Besatzungszone Deutschlands," *Babylon: Beiträge zur jüdischen Gegenwart,* nos. 10–11 (October 1992), pp. 125–38.

[114] See Sekretariat Lehmann, IV/2027/29-33, SAPMO-BA, ZPA (Wiedergutmachung gegenüber den Verfolgten des Naziregimes, 1945–1950).

[115] Paul Merker, "Der Krieg in Palastina" (probably August 1948), in Paul Merker, NL 102/45, SAPMO-BA, ZPA. On Merker in postwar Berlin, see memoirs of East

In 1950, the SED's Central Party Control Commission denounced Merker as an agent of American imperialism because of his wartime contact with Noel H. Field, who was then described as an American spy. The Field case took place in an atmosphere of fear and paranoia about "cosmopolitans" in the Communist parties of the Soviet bloc. Merker was expelled from the Central Committee and from the SED. Several Jewish Communists he had known in Mexico City were also expelled, and some were sent to prison. In the fall of 1952, Rudolf Slansky, Merker's old friend Andre Simone (Otto Katz), and other leading Jewish Communists in Prague were convicted of espionage for the United States, Israel, and Zionist organizations and executed. In December 1952, Merker was arrested and also accused of being a member of the same espionage conspiracy.[116] He was imprisoned and interrogated from 1952 to 1955. In a secret political trial in the East German supreme court in March 1955, he was sentenced to eight more years in prison, even though all of the charges had been dropped in the Noel Field affair in 1954.[117] To support their guilty verdict, the judges stressed Merker's contact with "émigré Jewish capitalist circles," that is, the Jewish émigrés in Mexico City, his support for *Wiedergutmachung* for the Jews, and his argument that victory over fascism would, in itself, be adequate compensation for German Communists.[118]

In 1956, following Khrushchev's secret speech to the Twentieth Party Congress and subsequent de-Stalinization, Merker was released from prison and wrote a statement, "Position on the Jewish Question," for the SED

German and Jewish historian Helmut Eschwege, *Fremd unter meinesgleichen: Erinnerungen eines Dresdner Juden* (Berlin, 1991), esp. pp. 51–131.

[116] For the Central Committee's denunciation of Merker and others as agents of Zionism and American imperialism, see Herman Matern, "Lehren aus dem Prozess gegen das Verschwörerzentrum Slansky," in *Uber die Durchführung des ZK der SED Lehren aus dem Prozess gegen das Verschwörerzentrum Slansky* (East Berlin, 1953), pp. 48–70. Also see the excellent discussion of antifascism, nationalism, and anti-Zionism in the Communist attack on "cosmopolitanism" in Meuschel (n. 84 above), pp. 101–16.

[117] The Stasi files on Merker's arrest in 1952, his imprisonment and interrogations from 1952 to 1955, and the verdict in the secret political trial have recently become available. See Ministerium für Staatssicherheit (hereafter M.f.S.) Untersuchungsvorgang 294/52, Paul Merker, Archiv 192/56, Bande 1–3. The files of the Ministerium fur Staatssicherheit or Stasi contain very important records of political justice in the DDR. I wish to express my gratitude to the staff of the Abteilung Bildung und Forschung of the Bundesbeauftragte für die Unterlagen des Staatssicherheitsdienstes der ehemaligen Deutschen Demokratischen Republik, known as the "Gauck Behörde," for facilitating access to the Merker file. This office is performing valuable work for historians working on East German history.

[118] "Oberstes Gericht der Deutschen Demokratischen Republik: In der Strafsache gegen den Kellner Paul Merker" (March 29 and 30, 1955), M.f.S. Untersuchungsvorgang 294/52, Paul Merker, Archiv 192/56, Bd. 3, pp. 522–35.

Central Party Control Commission in an effort to gain full "political rehabilitation." Merker wrote that his KGB and Stasi interrogators were convinced he must have been an agent for the United States or Israel because he was not Jewish and nevertheless took such a strong position on the Jewish question during World War II. Why, they wondered, unless he was an agent of American imperialism, or of Zionists and Jewish capitalists, would any German Communist pay so much attention to the Jewish question?[119] His answer summarizes a strategy of resistance and a resulting policy that was to remain exceptional.

I am neither Jewish, nor a Zionist, though it would be no crime to be either. I have never had the intent to flee to Palestine. I have not supported the efforts of Zionism. I have . . . occasionally said that among the Jews, after having been plundered by Hitler fascism, most deeply humiliated, driven from the homelands, and millions of them murdered, only because they were Jews, the feeling of a deepest bond and the desire for their own, Jewish country emerged among Jews of different countries. This feeling was the expression of those most deeply harmed and outraged. Moreover: Hitler fascism emerged among us. We [Germans] did not succeed through the actions of the working masses in preventing the erection of its rule and hence the commission of its crimes. Therefore, especially we Germans must not and ought not ignore or fight against what I call this strengthening of Jewish national feeling.[120]

In the same statement, he recalled Soviet support for a two-state solution in 1947, Soviet Foreign Minister Gromyko's criticism of the influence of American oil interests on American Middle East policy, and pointed to the role played by the Israeli Communists in Hagannah in the fighting with the Arab Legion.[121] "No one," Merker boldly told his former colleagues on the SED's Central Committee, "will want to claim that the Soviet government was an 'agent of American imperialism.'"[122] Merker argued that the logical result of Communist resistance to Nazism was support for the Jewish state, a view that by then was diametrically opposite to Soviet and East German policy toward

---

[119] Paul Merker, "An die Zentrale Kontrollkommission des ZK. der SED, Stellung-nahme zur Judenfrage (June 1, 1956)," (Zentrale Parteikontrollkommission), IV 2/4/111, SAPMO-BA, ZPA. Merker wrote that "the Soviet and the German interro-gators repeatedly said that it was completely incomprehensible to them that a non-Jew, such as myself, would become active on behalf of the Jews unless he was in their pay or being paid by Jewish organizations, all of which, in the opinion of these examiners were without exception agents of the imperialist powers. Therefore, a non-Jew, could only be active on behalf of the Jews as an agent of imperialism. For them, my engagement on behalf of Jewish people, who were going through the most horrible persecution by the Hitler fascists was by itself sufficient proof that I must be an agent of imperialism and an enemy of the working class. The prosecutor and the [supreme] court agreed" (p. 3).

[120] Ibid., p. 16.

[121] Ibid., p. 18.

[122] Ibid., p. 19.

Israel. Paul Merker's rehabilitation remained incomplete. He never attained a position of political influence after his release from prison in 1956 until his death in 1969. His conception of anti-Nazi resistance was one of the important lost causes of the history of the East German Communist regime. In the resistance to Nazism, some "antifascists," like Merker, became "cosmopolitans"; that is, they talked to and became friends with Jews, non-Communists, and non-Germans. This contact with Otherness of various kinds proved dangerous in the formative years of the DDR.

RESISTANCE WITHOUT TEARS

It was Ulbricht, Pieck, and the other German Communists in Moscow exile, not Merker and some of the Mexican émigrés, who determined the meaning of "antifascist resistance" in the Soviet zone of occupation from 1945 to 1949, and then in the founding decades of the German Democratic Republic. The Holocaust did not change their minds concerning the instrumental character of Nazi anti-Semitism. It was, they continued to insist, a tool for other purposes. Antifascist resistance, therefore, continued to mean primarily opposition to capitalism. It also formed, as it had before 1945, a key element of Communist self-definition and legitimation. Just as fascism in the 1920s had been a highly elastic concept, so after 1945 the discourse of antifascist resistance became part of the ongoing politics of the Cold War. Antifascism after the war meant eliminating capitalism and the Junkers in the East, and fighting the Cold War against the West. The East German Communists felt no additional obligation to make restitution to Jewish survivors living abroad or to refrain from Soviet bloc attacks on Israel. Merker's arguments were expelled from the canon of acceptable Communist discourse and defamed as the consequence of the impact of Zionists and "Jewish capitalist circles." While Merker had appealed for "equality of memory" for the Jews of Europe, official memories of resistance and victimization pushed their fate to the margins.[123] One ironic consequence of the dominant Communist understanding of antifascist resistance was an enduring East German hostility to Israel.

Immediately after the war, Walter Ulbricht published *Die Legende vom Deutschen Sozialismus* (The legend of German socialism), which became the most important East German text analyzing Nazism. Fifty thousand copies

[123] The dominant German Communist version of resistance to fascism had, as one of its practical results, a deep and enduring hostility to the state of Israel, and a no less enduring support for Israel's Arab adversaries. The mobilization of the German conception of antifascist resistance in the service of such a policy is an important irony of East German history that, however, goes beyond the scope of this essay. On East German–Israeli relations, see Inge Deutschkron, *Israel und die Deutschen: Das schwierige Verhältnis* (Cologne, 1991); and Peter Dittmar, "DDR und Israel," *Deutschland Archiv* 10, no. 7 (July 1977): 736–54; 10, no. 8 (August 1977): 848–61.

were printed by December 1945.[124] By January 1947, three hundred thousand more copies had been published by the official party publishers.[125] It was reissued in the 1950s under the title *Der Faschistische Deutsche Imperialismus (1933–1945)*.[126] Its third edition alone, published in 1956, went through an additional 340,000 copies.[127] It was Ulbricht's major public statement of "coming to terms with the Nazi past" and set the framework for subsequent East German discussions.

Ulbricht wrote that, after 1933, "Hitler fascism" began with the destruction of the Communist and Social Democratic parties and trade unions. Pogroms against the Jews spread racial hatred "as preparation for the planned annihilation of members of other peoples in war."[128] He referred to annihilation camps, gas chambers, ovens, and mass graves in Poland but not to Jews in particular.[129] He presented the Soviet Union as the primary victim of Nazism, as well as the primary source of deliverance from the Nazi yoke.[130] The significance of this choice is easily overlooked, since it seems so self-evident. Having lost the German people to Nazism, the East German

[124] Walter Ulbricht began his socialist engagement before World War I, participated in a Soldier's Council in 1918, was a cofounder of the Communist party in Leipzig, was a member of the German Communist Party Central Committee since 1923, and was a member of the Reichstag. He was forced into emigration in 1933 and worked in Paris and Prague before going to Moscow in 1938. From 1943 to 1945 he was the leading figure of the Nationale Komitee Freies Deutschland in Moscow. He was the director of the Central Committee of the KPD on its return to Berlin in 1945, and (under different titles, chairman, general secretary, first secretary) was the dominant figure of the SED from 1946 until he left power in 1971. See "Walter Ulbricht," in *Wer war Wer* (n. 7 above), p. 461; and in *Wer ist Wer in der SBZ* (n. 7 above), p. 266.

[125] "Verlag Neuer Weg, Plan der in Arbeit und in Vorbereitung befindliche Verlagserscheinungen, Stand am 12. Dezember 1945," "Aufstellung der vom 9. Mai 1945 bis 31.11 1947 im Verlag Neuer Weg bzw im Verlag JHW Dietz Nachf. GmBH erscheinen Titel," IV 2/9.13/5 Verlag Neuer Weg, SAPMO-BA, ZPA.

[126] Walter Ulbricht, *Der Faschistische Deutsche Imperialismus (1933–1945) (Die Legende vom "deutschen Sozialismus")*, 4th ed. (Berlin, 1956).

[127] But also see Ulbricht, *Zur Geschichte der Neuesten Zeit* (n. 8 above). This work included Ulbricht's analysis of the defeat of Nazi Germany by the Soviet Union, as well as statements made by the German Communists and the "Committee for a Free Germany" in Moscow during the war.

[128] Ibid., p. 107.

[129] Ibid., p. 24. "Himmler organized mass annihilation of the civilian population and the prisoners of war in Poland and in the occupied Soviet territories. He created the annihilation camps with their gas chambers, death wagons, gallows, piles of corpses, mass graves, ovens for burning human beings in which millions of innocent men, women and children fell victim." Elsewhere, Ulbricht wrote that Hitler and his associates waged wars of annihilation in which foreign countries and the "German homeland" were destroyed. "Annihilation of human beings in hells of torture and gas wagons, through murder and rape, and in gas ovens—this characterized decaying German imperialism" (p. 110).

[130] Ibid., p. 109.

Communists now placed their hopes with the Soviet state and the Red Army, the source of deliverance from fascism, and the bulwark against its "renaissance" in Bonn.[131] For a realist student of the balance of power such as Ulbricht, this was consistent with long-held convictions. The restoration of Communist thinking after 1945 coexisted with the eclipse of Communism as a movement as it had emerged in World War I and continued to the end of Weimar. As the Jews all but vanished from postwar Communist images of gas chambers and mass graves, so, for the victorious Communists, had the Germans as agents of their own destiny. Hence Ulbricht's main effort consisted in separating his Socialism from National Socialism. The Nazi "class struggle from above" had produced "exploitation and enslavement" of the working class, not a "genuine people's community" (*Wahre Volksgemeinschaft*). He regretted that some German workers, "blinded by the colorful fireworks of 'German socialism,'" supported Hitler and his system and thus supported the power of the German industrialists, bankers, and "armament plutocrats." Nazism was neither "national" or "socialist" but instead was the "deadly enemy" of the German people. In this, his major work on Nazism, Ulbricht sought to eliminate any connection between National "Socialism" and socialism in the DDR, and to stress the capitalist elites behind Hitler's throne rather than the masses who supported the regime. He saved the people from utter condemnation, only to make plain that they, individually and collectively, could never be trusted again. Ulbricht emerged from the failure of German resistance as an East German Robespierre to impose yet another dictatorship on a dangerous people.

In the German Democratic Republic, the second Sunday of each September was set aside for ceremonies honoring the memory of the heroes of the resistance. Especially in the early years, many tears must have been shed at the "days of recollection of the victims of fascism." However, the photo archive of the SED in Berlin contains only two pictures of unheroic, simple human grief and mourning, both taken on September 9, 1951. The first shows representatives of Berlin's Jewish community, their faces taut and somber, laying a wreath covered with the Star of David.[132] The second is of a

---

[131] For the East German Communists, resistance to fascism did not stop after 1945. It continued in the form of the Cold War and an enduring attack on "fascism" in the Federal Republic of Germany. See Raddatz, *Faschismus und Krieg* (n. 105 above), p. 8; Albert Norden, *Um die Nation: Beiträge zu Deutschlands Lebensfrage* (East Berlin, 1952), and *Die Nation und wir: Ausgewählte Aufsätze und Reden, 1933–1964,* 2 vols. (East Berlin, 1965); and Michael Lemke, "Kampagnen gegen Bonn: Die Systemkrise der DDR und die West-Propaganda der SED, 1960–1963," *Vierteljahreshefte für Zeitgeschichte* 41, no. 2 (April 1993): 153–74.

[132] "Tag der Opfer des Faschismus am 9. Sept. 1951 in Berlin: Kranzniederlegung durch Vertreter der Jüdischen Gemeinde von Berlin," Bildarchiv 1274/79N, SAPMO-BA, ZPA.

Fig. 1.—A delegation of former French resistance fighters who had been imprisoned in the Nazi concentration camp in Buchenwald participate in memorial ceremonies on September 9, 1951. (Source: ZPA Bildarchiv 399/71N, SAPMO-BA.)

delegation of "former resistance fighters" honoring the memory of members of the French resistance who died in Buchenwald. Not far from the usual flags of victory and militance, two women are wiping away tears while the men appear to be reflecting on their lost comrades more than on the bright socialist future (fig. 1).[133] These displays of individual grief and loss were the exception.

More typical are photos of determined men, women, and militant children and teenagers marching in the former concentration camps, carrying red flags in the "struggle for peace." The ceremonies began with mourning fallen martyrs but ended with redemption of the Germans through the victory of communism and the Red Army.[134] The "days for women" evoked the female

[133] "Eine Delegation ehemalige Widerstandskämpfer im ehemalige KZ Buchenwald: 9 Sept., 1951: Am Ehrenhain Französische Widerstandskämpfer," Bildarchiv 399/71, SAPMO-BA, ZPA.

[134] Much work remains to be done on the history of memory of World War II, including issues of manliness and heroism in postwar East Germany and the entire Soviet bloc. For some points of comparison see Jeffrey Herf, *Reactionary Modernism: Technology, Culture and Politics in Weimar and the Third Reich* (New York, 1984); and esp. George L. Mosse, *Fallen Soldiers: Reshaping the Memory of the World Wars* (New York, 1990).

heroes of the resistance, those who did not break under torture and were brave beyond the point of endurance.[135] In September 1950, the day of memory was marked by a huge peace rally in Berlin.[136] The incorporation of women and teenagers into the heroic mode of recollection was captured in two striking photos taken in September 1952 at the "women's peace demonstration" at the former Nazi concentration camp in Ravensbrück. In a remarkable and disturbing image, teenagers presumably in the uniform of the *Freie Deutsche Jugend,* the Communist youth organization, are walking and carrying flags past one of the ovens at the camp.[137] Another photo at the same event shows Irma Thälmann, Ernst Thälmann's daughter, with four other women, leading a march of women, many of whom are carrying flags as they march past the wall of the Ravensbrück camp.[138] The historian cannot presume to know what private grief and mourning consumed the women in this photo, but for the camera and for the public they put on the determined look of a progressive faith in History and in ultimate victory.

These ceremonies now displayed a relentlessly "progressive," forward-looking quality. Occasioned by losses in the past, they were devoted to victory in the present and future. Like the ubiquitous socialist realist statues of Ernst Thälmann, this discourse and these ceremonies combined public mourning with a more pervasive historical muscularity, strength, optimism, and confidence in the future.[139] They fostered an identity with victors and heroes of the antifascist resistance, not with those, like the Jews, whose deaths had no meaning in Hegelian narratives of German Communist history in which suffering was happily redeemed with success.

The dedication ceremonies of the former concentration camps at Buchenwald and Sachsenhausen, in 1958 and 1961, respectively, were the high point

---

[135] *Referentenmaterial, Deutsche Frauen im Widerstandskampf gegen das Naziregime: Gedenktag für die Opfer des Faschismus* (East Berlin, 1948).

[136] "Kundgebung für die Opfer des Faschismus in Berlin vor dem Alten Museum, Sept. 1950," Bildarchiv 713/71N, SAPMO-BA, ZPA.

[137] "Friedenskundgebung der Frauen in Ravensbrück am 13. September 1952," Bildarchiv 1269/80N, SAPMO-BA, ZPA.

[138] "Friedenskundgebung der Frauen in Ravensbrück am 13.9.1952," Bildarchiv 1267/79N, SAPMO-BA, ZPA.

[139] The postwar Ernst Thälmann cult, in its pedagogical-didactic as well as aesthetic and gender connotations, deserves much more extensive analysis in considerations of the meaning of resistance and heroism. See Parteivorstand der SED, *Programmhefte für Sozialistische Feierstunden Gedenk- und Erinnerungstage: Ernst Thälmann* (East Berlin, 1949); Wilhelm Pieck, "Ernst Thälmann: Das Vorbild der Jungen Friedenskämpfer," and Walter Ulbricht, "Ernst Thälmann," in *Ernst Thälmann: Vorbild der Deutschen Jugend* (East Berlin and Leipzig, 1951), pp. 5–12 and 13–25; Walter Ulbricht, *Wir Erfüllen Ernst Thälmann Vermächtnis* (East Berlin, 1953); and Marx-Engels-Lenin-Stalin Institut beim Zentral Komitee der SED, *Ernst Thälmann: Bilder und Dokumente Aus Seinem Leben* (East Berlin, 1955).

of the heroic mode of commemorating antifascist resistance. In Buchenwald in 1958, Grotewohl extolled the heroism of antifascist resistance fighters as an inspiration for the nation. The antifascist resistance fighters had emerged the victors. Their ideals were embodied in the East German state and its resistance to the policies of West German rearmament and American imperialism.[140] A widely reproduced photo of the occasion conveys the message of collectivist triumph. In the front of a large crowd, the hammer and sickle wave in the wind. In the middle of the crowd is one of the socialist realist frescoes of the Buchenwald memorial depicting muscular men and women, standing tall and carrying a flag.[141]

At the 1961 dedication of the DDR's memorial to victims of fascism at the former Nazi concentration camp at Sachsenhausen, Walter Ulbricht, speaking to a crowd of two hundred thousand people, again presented the DDR as the victorious fulfillment of the legacy of antifascist resistance. It is a legacy that continued in East Germany's "antifascist struggle for peace," against the danger of West German armament and American imperialism—and in the marginalization of the Jewish catastrophe. A striking photo shows Ulbricht, alongside other members of the SED Central Committee as well as Rosa Thälmann, Ernst Thälmann's widow, walking out of the Sachsenhausen memorial.[142] Ulbricht is waving a politician's wave of triumph.[143] The chimney of the Sachsenhausen camp is visible behind them. A large crowd is

---

[140] Otto Grotewohl, "Buchenwald Mahnt! Rede zur Weihe der Nationalen Mahn- und Gedenkstätte Buchenwald 14. September 1958," in his *Im Kampf um die Einige Deutsche Demokratische Republik: Reden und Aufsätze,* Bd. 6, *Auswahl aus den Jahren 1958–1960* (East Berlin, 1964), pp. 7–14.

[141] "Einweihung der Mahn- und Gedenkstätte Buchenwald am 14. September 1958," Bildarchiv 34/93N, SAPMO-BA, ZPA.

[142] "Einweihung der Nationalen Mahn- und Gedenkstätte Sachsenhausen am 23. April 1961," Bildarchiv 566/80N, SAPMO-BA, ZPA.

[143] The study from which this essay is taken includes a contrast with West German forms of official memory and forgetting. The most apt comparison in the early years is with the ceremonies dedicating the memorial at the former Nazi concentration camp in Bergen-Belsen at the end of November 1952. Bundespräsident Theodor Heuss and Nahum Goldmann, representing the World Jewish Congress, spoke. Heuss's address has none of the sense of triumph and militancy in East German antifascist recollection. See Theodor Heuss, "Diese Scham nimmt uns niemand ab: Der Bundespräsident sprach bei der Weihe des Mahnmals in Bergen-Belsen" (No one will lift this shame from us), *Bulletin des Presse- und Informationsamtes der Bundesregierung,* no. 189 (December 1, 1952), pp. 1655–56; reprinted in Theodor Heuss, *Der Grossen Reden: Der Staatsmann* (Tübingen, 1965). Goldmann's speech was a powerful narrative of Jewish suffering and resistance. See Nahum Goldmann (no title), Theodor Heuss, B122 2082/028, BA-Koblenz. A photo of Heuss and Goldmann conveys a somber, funereal mood. At the level of cultural history, the faces and discourse of Adenauer and Heuss were those of sobered yet intact bourgeois patriarchs who had seen too much to convey militant tales of a bright future, at least on such occasions as these.

Fɪɢ. 2.—Dedication of the National Memorial in Sachsenhausen, April 23, 1961. Front row: fourth from left, Irma Thalmann, Ernst Thalmann's widow; fifth from left, Walter Ulbricht. (Source: ZPA Bildarchiv 566/80N, SAPMO-BA.)

in the background while soldiers stare stiffly ahead on either side. It is a photo of German Communism rising like a phoenix from the ashes of catastrophe (fig. 2).[144]

The German Communists rightly drew attention to sufferings that the Nazis inflicted on the Soviet Union, and to the enormous contribution made by the Red Army to the defeat of Nazi Germany. Yet though they presented themselves as the representatives of the persecuted and oppressed, their memories of resistance reflected the realities of power in 1945. As Paul Merker had shown them, memory need not have been a competitive or zero-sum game in which attention devoted to the Jews would be subtracted

---

[144] Walter Ulbricht, "Walter Ulbricht bei der Einweihung der Gedenkstätte Sachsenhausen: Von der DDR wird stets der Frieden ausstrahlen," *Neues Deutschland* (April 24, 1961). Identification with past heroes rather than tragic victims was not limited to East German or Soviet official antifascism. Whatever the degree of active resistance among the European Jews, their history during the Holocaust was one of loss and tragedy rather than uplifting historical vindication, a story of winners rather than losers. On the Israeli mixture of identification and distance with the European diaspora see the comments on "Holocaust and heroism" in Tom Segev, *The Seventh Million: The Israelis and the Holocaust,* trans. Haim Watzman (New York, 1993), esp. pt. 3, pp. 113–86 and 421–45.

from that given to the other peoples of Europe and the Soviet Union. Flushed with victory, they were in no mood to reflect on their own mistakes, to share credit with others for the defeat of Nazism, or to accept Merker's more complex understanding of Nazism and the demands of resistance against it.

They forgot and repressed their attacks on social fascism of the Third Period, the embarrassing hiatus of the Hitler-Stalin pact, the failure of the internal German resistance, as well as their own briefly declared solidarity with the Jews of Germany and Europe. With Hegelian symmetry, the antifascist resistance had emerged from history's slaughterhouse to vindication by military victory in 1945. The Jews of Europe remained a tragic, unredeemed lost cause. The tragedy of the Holocaust did not fit the dialectic of militant optimism present at the postwar ceremonies of East German antifascist resistance. As in the entire history of German Communism, anti-Semitism and the Jewish catastrophe remained marginal to the master narrative of class struggle, resistance, and redemption.

From Resistance to Liberation Theology: German Theologians and the Non/Resistance to the National Socialist Regime

Werner G. Jeanrond
University of Dublin, Trinity College

In this article I wish to examine the connection between both Christian theology and Christian resistance to the National Socialist regime in Germany and the development of a new political theology in postwar Germany. By "theology" I mean the academic reflection upon the Christian faith; and by "resistance" I mean the opposition in word and action to Hitler's or any related form of ideological theory and praxis.

I wish to approach this complex subject matter from our current need to discuss the theological implications of the overall lack of organized *theological* resistance to the Nazi regime. Of course, the Barmen Declaration of 1934 and its spiritual father, Karl Barth, are well remembered for their brave attack on the Nazi regime; and the thoughts, actions, and long suffering of Dietrich Bonhoeffer, Martin Niemöller, and other individual Christians are not forgotten. But my thesis is that there was at first no constructive theology of resistance to the National Socialist revolution in the Third Reich. Moreover, at that time there was no solid theological foundation available upon which a theology of resistance could have been constructed. Dimensions of such a theology of resistance only emerged in response to the unfolding totalitarian nature of Hitler's regime—too late, however, to affect the regime itself in any significant way.

In the first section I shall reflect briefly on the political dimension of theology in Germany prior to 1933. In the second section I shall review theological motives in the emerging Christian resistance to the Nazi regime. In the third section I shall discuss contemporary approaches to theological resistance that have been developed in reaction to the failure of much of German theology during Hitler's reign.

THE POLITICAL DIMENSIONS OF GERMAN THEOLOGY BEFORE 1933

In Germany the political and cultural breakdown after the First World War did not give rise to a critical reflection upon the political dimension of Christian theology. The opposite was the case: Protestant and Roman Catholic theologians,

This essay originally appeared in the *Journal of Modern History* 64, suppl. (December 1992).

though for different reasons, responded to the collapse of imperial Germany either by concentrating on nonpolitical theological projects or by giving some support to an emergent *"völkische Theologie."* This latter group of theologians, which included Paul Althaus and Emanuel Hirsch, promoted the development of a "political theology" that sought to establish a synthesis between theology and aspects of the Nazi ideology and therefore remained largely uncritical toward the politics of the day.[1] Karl Barth quickly became the most influential figure among those Protestant theologians who opposed any synthesis between theology and politics. I begin my examination with a brief discussion of his theological method.

Karl Barth's Dialectical Theology

Karl Barth (1886–1968), born in Switzerland but trained mainly in Germany by teachers such as Adolf von Harnack and Wilhelm Herrmann, had spent the war years as a pastor in various Swiss cities before returning to Germany in 1921 as professor of theology. He had become famous overnight because of his book *The Epistle to the Romans* that was read as the manifesto of a renewed Protestant theology, now truly concerned with God's will, and therefore rejecting all the liberal Protestant syntheses between God's will and human action of the prewar decades. Barth's eagerness to bring God back to the forefront of theological reflection made him remove the world from his constructive theological program. Culture, religion, the world as a whole were now only considered as standing under God's judgment, and that meant for Barth that their ungodly nature had to be emphasized in order to see God's divine nature even more sharply. This change of primary focus from the liberal theologians' interest in this world to Barth's concentration on God did not provide a fertile horizon for any constructive theological consideration of the political realm of human life.[2]

Barth's personal involvement in political activity, such as his membership in the Swiss Socialist party (since 1915) and in its German equivalent (since 1931), must not divert our attention from this diagnosis: according to my reading, Barth's theological method makes the development of a political theology impossible.[3] This method aimed at exposing the radically human

---

[1] For a discussion of the development of this form of "political theology," see Klaus Scholder, *Die Kirchen und das Dritte Reich,* vol. 1, *Vorgeschichte und Zeit der Illusionen, 1918–1934* (Frankfurt am Main and Berlin, 1986), pp. 124–32.

[2] The term "dialectical" as a characterization of Barth's theology is misleading: in Barth's theology it really points to the radical difference between God and humankind, rather than to the nature of the relationship between faith (or theology) and Christian praxis.

[3] I differ here both from Friedrich Wilhelm Marquardt's and from E. Jüngel's readings of Barth. According to Marquardt's *Theologie und Sozialismus: Das Beispiel*

character of any form of thinking and at submitting such thinking to the judgment of God's Word. Any form of political organization or of an underlying political theory must be bracketed and supplied with the "divine minus sign outside the bracket." This divine minus sign outside the bracket "means that all human consciousness, all human principles and axioms and orthodoxies and -isms, all principality and power and dominion, are as such subjected to the destructive judgement of God."[4] While such a statement makes some sense when read against the previously untroubled symbiosis between state and faith as proposed by von Harnack, Herrmann, and other liberal theologians, it is incapable of promoting the development of a Christian understanding of the "positive" requirements of establishing any constructive, though, of course, critical, form of government. In this sense, one can say that the necessary critique of the previously uncritical relationship between theology and political existence was now stated in such an absolute way that any effort to develop a better political culture was radically called into question before it could even begin. Thus, Barth's rejection of a particular concept of political theology resulted in a total rejection of political theology as such. Apart from his negative verdict against all "isms," he could not furnish any fresh theological stimulus for a theological reflection on constructive political praxis. This led to a paradoxical situation: while fighting past syntheses between theological and political thinking, Barth's own theology was unable to promote any new synthesis and thus left the field wide open for the developers of *"völkische Theologie."*

Moreover, Barth's "revolutionary" understanding of theology as motivated and guided by faith alone helped to destroy the traditional German understanding of academic theology originally formulated by Friedrich Schleiermacher at the beginning of the nineteenth century. The critical but constructive nature of theology in the university was now transformed into a purely faith-oriented character without due consideration of the worldly meeting point between God's Word, on the one hand, and the conditions of human response, on the other. In the absence of any serious hermeneutical criteria to

---

Karl Barths, 3d ed. (Munich, 1985), Barth's theology could be interpreted as an example of Christian socialism, whereas Jüngel understands Barth's theology generally as a theory for Christian praxis, which is by nature political. Jüngel, *Barth-Studien* (Gütersloh and Zurich, 1982), p. 126: "Barths Theologie hatte immer eine starke politische Komponente, war aber seit dem ersten *Römerbrief* niemals mehr die Funktion eines übergeordneten politischen Grundsatzes. Kurz und knapp formuliert: Das Politische ist für Barth zwar Prädikat der Theologie, die Theologie aber niemals Prädikat des Politischen." I agree with Jüngel's critique of Marquardt's over-interpretation of Barth as a political theologian, but I fail to see how Barth's radical negation of any political program could still be called "political."

[4] Karl Barth, *The Epistle to the Romans,* trans. Edwyn C. Hoskyns (Oxford, 1968), p. 483.

guide the appropriation of God's Word and Will in the complex conditions of the Weimar Republic and later in the Third Reich, Barth's theology remained detached from the world that it wanted to see saved. Instead it concentrated on the Word of God whose active presence could not be understood in the terms of any institutional objectification, be this church or state. Again, the critical direction of this anti-ideological and anti-institutional theology must be appreciated. But at the same time this kind of approach could not inspire the formation of a theology of the world. Let me stress once more that what is true of his theology is not true of Barth himself. He resisted the National Socialist regime more than most university teachers of the time, but his theology did not at this time help promote a constructive resistance beyond the mere critique of all worldly movements.

Roman Catholic Theology during the Weimar Republic

Roman Catholic theology in Germany was, first of all, Roman, and as such obliged to follow the universally prescribed neo-scholastic canon of teaching and research. Scholastic theology included, of course, a particular approach to the world. Thomas Aquinas had developed a threefold natural order: reason, divine law, and politics.[5] As far as political systems were concerned, he favored a monarchical government and demanded "that subjects should obey their superiors: for there would otherwise be no stability in human affairs. So, therefore, the Christian faith does not dispense the faithful from the obligation of obeying temporal princes."[6] But at the same time he foresaw the possibility that civil disobedience or tyrannicide might be called for. If such rulers "command things to be done which are unjust, their subjects are not obliged to obey them."[7] In that sense we can speak of elements of a theology of resistance in scholastic thought.

The problem, however, with scholastic theology, and equally so with its late child, neo-scholasticism, was that it was conducted by theologians who worked in religious academies far removed from the people in the church, and also in a different language, namely, Latin. Therefore it did not become a real part of the wider German culture. Instead, its application to modern circumstances was administered by ecclesiastical authorities who had a predominantly legalistic self-understanding. The "success" of the publication of the new Canon Law in 1917 encouraged such legal thinking still further.

Authoritative figures such as the newly appointed nuncio to Bavaria, Eugenio Pacelli, himself a canon lawyer by training and coeditor of the new

---

[5] *Aquinas: Selected Political Writings,* ed. A. P. D'Entrèves, trans. J. G. Dawson (Oxford, 1959), p. 109.

[6] Ibid., p. 179.

[7] Ibid.

Canon Law, understood their task increasingly in terms of securing a legally defined and guaranteed place for the Roman Catholic church in a world struck by all kinds of revolutionary movements and events. Marxism celebrated its first major success simultaneously with the publication of the new Canon Law in 1917, and, until very recent days, was considered by Rome to be the greatest threat to Christianity. In the aftermath of 1917 the Vatican's and Pacelli's foremost political aim in Germany was a legal agreement (*Konkordat*) between the Holy See and the German states that would secure the foundations of the Roman Catholic Church in Germany. This political endeavor to reach an agreement between church and state did not help to promote a public theological debate between Christian theology, on the one hand, and the new ideological movements on either side of the political spectrum in Germany, on the other. The lay people in this church were considered to be fully dependent on theological guidance from above; not only was that guidance not forthcoming but, as a consequence of the *Reichskonkordat* of 1933, Rome was seen to be the very first legal partner of Hitler's regime. Therefore it must not surprise us that there was no development of a political theology in which the very foundations of Hitler's ideology could have been critically and publically discussed.[8] Instead, in Rome, one trusted in the political strength of the Catholic *Zentrumspartei,* a trust that in 1933, however, proved not to have been based on a realistic assessment of the revolutionary process in Germany.

Comparing Barth's and Rome's approach to the ideological conflict during the Weimar Republic, one recognizes in Barth a strong theological mistrust of human thinking that undermines all institutional realizations of faith in a political context; and, conversely, one finds in Rome a big trust in the institutional framework as legal guarantor of the possibility of a Christian faith within the limits of the church alone. Neither approach to the organization of Christian faith in Germany produced any form of coherent theology of resistance, and thus the activity of resisting the Nazi regime was left to a number of individuals.

THEOLOGICAL MOTIVES IN THE EMERGING CHRISTIAN RESISTANCE TO THE NAZI REGIME

The Political Conditions of Christian Theology during Hitler's Rule

As soon as Hitler's power became firmly established in 1933, there could be no doubt anymore that his ideological program left no real space for the free

---

[8] See Scholder, *Vorgeschichte und Zeit der Illusionen, 1918–1934,* pp. 184 ff.; and also Georg Denzler, *Widerstand oder Anpassung? Katholische Kirche und Drittes Reich* (Munich, 1984), pp. 35 ff.

development of Christian faith in its ecclesial setting, whether Catholic or Protestant. While the *Konkordat* with the Vatican allowed Hitler to restrict Roman Catholic expression by pointing to the clause in this agreement that emphasized very clearly the separation between church and politics, the fragmentation of the Protestant church in Germany meant that such a quick legal instrumentarium was not at hand. However, since Hitler wanted such a control mechanism, he propagated the development of a united (Protestant) German church. This move was correctly interpreted by many Protestant Christians as a sign of Hitler's real intentions, namely, to destroy an independent, and therefore potentially critical, Christian church in Germany.

Those pastors, theologians, and lay people who actively opposed both Hitler's ideology and its application against the church organized themselves eventually in 1934 as the Confessing Church in Germany. This step must be appreciated as an active moment of Christian resistance, but it came too late to convince a wider Protestant church whose members had been taught for centuries that a truly Protestant Christian must support the given worldly authorities. It was also more interested in the separation between church and state than motivated by an explicitly critical political theology or theology of resistance. Organized Christian resistance to civil authority had been ruled out by Martin Luther because it would only increase political turmoil and thus destabilize a God-given order. An active fight against Hitler, therefore, had to include first an element of inner-Christian critique and necessarily required a renewed attention to the world and the political realm as theological data. At this moment, the failure of dialectical theology to take the world seriously as God's world and as the place of God's presence proved fatal, even though the representatives of that theological movement, in particular Karl Barth, themselves underwent a dramatic change.[9] However, their personal theological conversion in this respect came too late to be effective during Hitler's rule.

---

[9] In order to appreciate the extent of Barth's "conversion" to a more explicit political theology, it may be fruitful to compare the final passages of his *Theologische Existenz heute!* (1933), ed. H. Stoevesandt (Munich, 1984), pp. 86–87, with his essay "The Christian Community and the Civil Community" (1946) in Karl Barth, *Against the Stream: Shorter Post-War Writings, 1946–52* (London, 1954), pp. 13–50. While in 1933 he had concentrated on emphasizing the limits imposed by the church on the state ("Sie [die Kirche] ist die naturgemäße Grenze jedes, auch des totalen Staates"), in 1946 he attempted to develop some features of a constructive program for a political theology. For instance: "The Church will not in all circumstances withdraw from and oppose what may be practically a dictatorship, that is, a partial and temporary limitation of these freedoms, but it will certainly withdraw from and oppose any out-and-out dictatorship such as the totalitarian State. The adult Christian can only wish to be an adult citizen, and he can only want his fellow citizens to live as adult human beings" (Barth, *Against the Stream,* p. 37).

Dietrich Bonhoeffer's Theology of the World

Dietrich Bonhoeffer's (1905–45) active resistance and theological reflection on the world were to have a wider impact on theology only after his death in one of Hitler's concentration camps. Only after 1945 could his prophetic witness both in theological thought and in political action against the Nazi regime serve as a major stimulus in Protestant and Roman Catholic theology. Since Bonhoeffer's theology of resistance has received special treatment elsewhere in this volume (see Raymond Mengus's essay), it will not be necessary to trace Bonhoeffer's personal and theological development once again in any detail. Instead I would like to point to some connections between his theological method and his understanding of the Christian's responsibility to resist Hitler.

It is often said that Bonhoeffer's theological method was quite traditional. What remains significant, however, is that he succeeded in retrieving the world as a fundamental aspect of his theology and thus was in a position to develop this aspect in view of his own experiences of resistance. This actual dialectic of theological theory and Christian praxis in Bonhoeffer's thought and writing allowed him to face the concrete problems of Christian witness in a very complex and confused cultural and political situation.

For Bonhoeffer, as for Barth, theology and Christian action had to be seen eschatologically. But while eschatology remained a mere critical principle for Barth, it entailed the urge for responsible action for Bonhoeffer, though not without the critical aspect. Bonhoeffer's own resistance to Hitler was motivated as a struggle in this "next-to-the-last time" (*im Vorletzten*).[10] This struggle, he insisted, must not be interpreted as a fight for the existence of the institutional church but as the struggle for the Word of God, which is to be proclaimed in such a way that the world will be transformed and renewed.[11] This is not a vote for the end of the church but an effort to retrieve its proper calling in and for this world, a world that Bonhoeffer understood to have come of age.[12]

Non/Resistance and Contemporary German Theology

Since the collapse of the Third Reich, Christian theologians have been faced with two crucial questions: first, why was there no theology of resistance that

---

[10] Dietrich Bonhoeffer, *Ethics,* ed. Eberhard Bethge, trans. Neville Horton Smith (London, 1971), pp. 103 ff.

[11] See Georg Kretschmar, "Dietrich Bonhoeffer," in *Klassiker der Theologie,* ed. H. Fries and G. Kretschmar (Munich, 1983), 2:376–403, esp. p. 399.

[12] Dietrich Bonhoeffer, *Letters and Papers from Prison: The Enlarged Edition,* ed. Eberhard Bethge (London, 1971), p. 342.

could have motivated more members of the Christian churches actively to oppose the ideological theory and totalitarian praxis of the Nazi regime? And second, how, if at all, can theology continue to speak of a loving God after Auschwitz? Jürgen Moltmann and Johann B. Metz, two influential German theologians, have tried to tackle both of these questions in developing a new approach to theology. In what follows, I would like to consider both approaches briefly and assess them as possible foundations for an adequate theological theory of resistance.

Jürgen Moltmann's Theology of Hope

In view of the eclipse of the world as a constitutive category in Karl Barth's earlier theological method and in contrast to Rudolf Bultmann's concentration on the individual believer's search for authenticity, Moltmann (born in 1926) has attempted to retrieve the world and human history as foundational concerns of a more adequate Christian theology.[13] He recognizes the conflictual nature of both the world and history, and in his theology sets out to discuss the political dimension of Christian faith that could then be the horizon within which to consider the various situations of human conflict. This political dimension of faith, then, requires a corresponding treatment in Christian theology.

A careful reading of Moltmann's work shows that there are two influences that led him to develop this politically conscious theology. One is the awareness of the continuing need for a properly defined theology of resistance in view of ongoing situations of oppression and slavery; the second is the stimulus offered by neo-Marxist philosophers such as Bloch and various representatives of the Frankfurt School.[14] The latter group of thinkers, most of them exiled from Germany by Hitler because of their humanist philosophy and their mostly Jewish background, were the first to consider possible dimensions of a new and critical political theory before, during, and after the Third Reich.[15] It is significant that the question of resistance does not appear solely from the perspective of what did or did not happen during the Nazi

---

[13] Jürgen Moltmann, *Theologie der Hoffnung: Untersuchungen zur Begründung und zu den Konsequenzen einer christlichen Eschatologie,* 10th ed. (Munich, 1977), pp. 43–66.

[14] See, e.g., Jürgen Moltmann, "Ernst Bloch und die Hoffnung ohne Glauben," in his *Das Experiment Hoffnung: Einführungen* (Munich, 1974), pp. 48–63, and *Der gekreuzigte Gott: Das Kreuz Christi als Grund und Kritik christlicher Theologie,* 4th ed. (Munich, 1981), pp. 209 ff., where Horkheimer's and Adorno's thoughts are discussed.

[15] See Rolf Wiggershaus, *Die Frankfurter Schule: Geschichte-Theoretische Entwicklung-Politische Bedeutung* (Munich, 1988). In this context the theologian Paul Tillich must also be mentioned. Before he went to his exile in the United States in 1935 he had taught at the University of Frankfurt and was closely associated with

period. Rather, according to Moltmann, the question of resistance imposes itself on the theologian because of contemporary experiences of political exploitation and racial repression such as the dominion over blacks by whites in South Africa or the economic exploitation of Latin Americans by northern Europeans and Americans.[16]

Moltmann's retrieval of the political dimension of theology and church. In the context of his discussion of the mixed reactions in West Germany to the decision by the Ecumenical Council of the Churches in 1970 to support among other groups also some of the liberation movements in southern Africa, Moltmann comes to the following diagnosis: "The negative reactions in West Germany have revealed both a disturbed relationship to power in the German traditions and also a Christian repression complex with regard to resistance to tyranny."[17] In Germany, he argues, there seemed to be a deep sense that it was better to affirm conservative forces than liberating forces, and that the power that guarantees order was preferred to active resistance even when that power was unjust and illegitimate. Moltmann recognizes that there was a discussion of the resistance against Hitler following the Second World War, but he claims that the insights from that discussion were quickly forgotten.[18] What is more necessary than ever is, therefore, a proper discussion of the criteria for the justified use of power. A Christian reflection on this question can look back to a long and detailed theological treatment within the Christian tradition. But what is most significant in Moltmann's discussion is that he advocates not only the right to resist, as the tradition also did (cf. Thomas Aquinas), but a duty to resist, a "revolutionary duty of all Christians."[19] For him, resistance against unjust regimes is a command that follows directly from the Christian command of love for one's neighbor. However, Moltmann hastens to add that any such resistance must be "legitimate" resistance, and that this qualification imposes an essential duty on those who resist, namely, to work for either (1) the reestablishment of legality, or (2) the reestablishment of the constitution, or (3) the establishment of a new constitution that guarantees human rights.[20]

From a theological point of view, any act of resistance to state authority involves the Christian in guilt, but in a guilt that follows from love for the neighbor and that for the greater good must be accepted. There is no innocent

---

Horkheimer and Adorno. For a recent appreciation of his political thought, see *Tillich Studies: 1975,* ed. John J. Carey (Chicago, 1975), pp. 27–74.

[16] Jürgen Moltmann, "Rassismus und das Recht auf Widerstand," in his *Das Experiment Hoffnung,* pp. 145–63.

[17] Ibid., p. 146 (my translation).

[18] Ibid.

[19] Ibid., p. 156.

[20] Ibid., p. 157.

resistance. "Guilt remains guilt, but in faith one can live with this guilt and does not have to commit suicide."[21] Moreover, Christian resistance has to be discussed in the wider context of Christian community, that is, the church. "The church is not only an institution whose purpose it is to proclaim the Word and administer the sacraments; it is also the concrete community of the faithful, and as such also the practical community of love."[22]

Moltmann emphasizes the "worldly responsibility of the Church" and stresses that any neglect of this responsibility ought to be termed "heretical."[23] Thus, according to Moltmann, the church must have a political character because Christian faith is essentially also political. And he urges the development of an ecumenical solidarity in trying to cope with this political and social responsibility of the Christian church.[24]

The theological foundation of Moltmann's theology of resistance.   So far we have concentrated only on Moltmann's explicit discussion of the political nature of faith, church, and theology, but we have not yet considered the wider theological program in which this theology of resistance is located. I see four major related aspects that may best characterize Moltmann's theology: the eschatological starting point, the revolution in the concept of God, the concept of creation, and the concept of human freedom.

Karl Barth had already attempted to retrieve the eschatological nature of Christian theology, but, as we have seen, failed to locate this eschatology in the actuality of time and space in this world and thus used it solely as a principle of negation in order to preserve God's divinity against any human hubris. Over against this rather transcendent eschatology, Moltmann retrieves history as the actual place for eschatological considerations. The category that for him characterizes best the eschatological situation of all human response to God's invitation to cooperate with God's will for this world is hope. Hope is thus a constructive attitude and always directed to the expectation of God's ultimate fulfillment of his overall creative project.[25] But human hope has to cope with conflict and the experience of radical failure. Moltmann asks most concretely: How can we have hope after Auschwitz? Does the experience of the death camp not prove the failure of any hope in God's promises? What sort of God is this who allowed the horrors of Auschwitz to take place?

---

[21] Ibid., p. 160 (my translation). Here Moltmann alludes to Martin Luther's *"Pecca fortiter, sed crede fortius."*

[22] Ibid., p. 163 (my translation).

[23] Ibid., p. 162.

[24] Ibid., p. 163.

[25] Compare Moltmann, *Theologie der Hoffnung* (n. 13 above), pp. 308–9: "'Präsentische Eschatologie' heißt nichts anderes als eben 'schöpferische Erwartung,' Hoffnung, die zur Kritik und Veränderung der Gegenwart ansetzt, weil sie sich der universalen Zukunft des Reiches öffnet."

At this point Moltmann rejects the traditional Christian concept of a God who is far removed from the course of this world. Over against this theistic concept of an apathetic God, Moltmann, developing Luther's theology of the cross, stresses the biblical understanding of a suffering God. The event that forces the Christian theologian to reconsider the traditional concept of God and thus to overcome classical theism is the cross of Jesus Christ.[26] Originally, Moltmann saw the cross as the event that opened the eschatological dimension of human existence. But more recently, he considers the suffering of God in the entire creation process, a suffering highlighted for Christians in the trinitarian interpretation of the cross of Jesus of Nazareth, but a suffering that is present wherever God's creation is attacked.[27] The trinitarian understanding of God points to the essential relatedness of God, to God's involvement in the continuing creation.

This understanding of God's presence in the world provides, of course, a radically different urgency for believers to resist any power that threatens to violate God's creative project. God has suffered in the cross of Jesus Christ and in the death of Jews and other victims in the death camps of Hitler's Germany. Human suffering is thus seen as being integrated into God's own suffering. This active presence of God in our human suffering opens the possibility for us to share in God's future, a future that found a first expression in the resurrection of Jesus Christ. God's unlimited love then ultimately overcomes the suffering that his creation inflicts on him. This love, however, does not undo human suffering; rather, it opens a different and wider horizon in which this suffering is taken into God's own history. This is the basis on which Moltmann can call for a "revolutionary theology," but, as should be clear by now, "without a revolution in the concept of God, [there can be] no revolutionary theology."[28]

The God who suffers and overcomes our suffering by his love and liberating action grants us a new spirit, namely, the spirit of creative freedom, and thus makes possible human freedom. This spirit of freedom opens new space and time for us and thus provides us with the renewed possibility of responsible action.[29]

Moltmann's approach to theology offers one way out of the dilemmas of Barthian theology. It shares with the latter the emphasis on the critique of all human ideology, but Moltmann, following Bonhoeffer, has also successfully retrieved the world and human history as the places in which God's creative

---

[26] See Moltmann, *Der gekreuzigte Gott* (n. 14 above), pp. 193 ff., esp. p. 214: "Gottes Sein ist im Leiden, und das Leiden ist in Gottes Sein selbst, weil Gott Liebe ist."

[27] See Jürgen Moltmann, *Trinität und Reich Gottes: Zur Gotteslehre* (Munich, 1980), pp. 67–68.

[28] Moltmann, *Das Experiment Hoffnung*, p. 110 (my translation).

[29] Compare Moltmann, *Trinität und Reich Gottes*, pp. 236 ff.

project needs to be promoted and not just proclaimed.[30] These dimensions of a radically political theology will be picked up by the developing liberation theologies, as we shall see in a moment. But before discussing these more recent approaches to a theology of resistance, I wish to examine Johann B. Metz's outline of a radically political theology and its response to the failure of German resistance.

Johann B. Metz's Theology of the World

Among Roman Catholic theologians in post–World War II Germany, Johann B. Metz (born in 1928), one of Karl Rahner's most brilliant students, was the first to retrieve the political dimension of Christian faith and theology. His overall program resembles that of Moltmann in many respects. Metz's theological project may be characterized by the same four aspects as Moltmann's: hope, a new understanding of God's presence in human history, creation, and freedom for the concrete praxis of Christian faith. Like Moltmann, Metz too considers resistance not so much in the context of theological historiography as in terms of the continuing struggle for human emancipation from various forms of oppression. And like Moltmann, Metz is influenced significantly by Bloch and the philosophers of the Frankfurt School on the philosophical level, and by Bonhoeffer on the theological level.[31]

Metz's retrieval of the world as the focus of Christian theology. In a number of publications, Metz has stressed the need to view the current process of radical secularization in Europe as an ambiguous move whose positive side reflects increasing attention to the historical development of the world as the horizon for any consideration of God's creative activity. It is his primary intention "to offer a theological interpretation of the secular world today, and this must determine the scope of my analysis of the Christ event."[32] Thus, incarnation is now seen to indicate that "God acts in such a way in relation to the world that he accepts it irrevocably in his son."[33] Hence, Metz too emphasizes the crucified Christ as the point of radical contact between God and the world. This action of God in the world discloses once and for all the eschatological character of the world and opens up the horizon of human freedom and Christian praxis in the world. "The relationship between the Christian faith and the world should be characterized from a theological viewpoint as a creative and militant eschatology."[34]

---

[30] Moltmann, *Der gekreuzigte Gott*, p. 60.

[31] See Johann B. Metz, *Theology of the World,* trans. William Glen-Doepel (London, 1969), pp. 128–29.

[32] Ibid., p. 21. See also Johann B. Metz, *Glaube in Geschichte und Gesellschaft: Studien zu einer praktischen Fundamentaltheologie,* 2d ed. (Mainz, 1978), pp. 23–25.

[33] Metz, *Theology of the World,* p. 22.

[34] Ibid., p. 91.

Again, like Moltmann, Metz stresses the role of the church as that community of believers that hopes for the future of the whole world. Here Metz quotes Moltmann: "The hope of the Gospel has a polemical and a liberating relation to man's present and practical life and to the [social] conditions in which man leads his life."[35]

Toward a theology of resistance. Having thus established the critical potential of his political theology, Metz uses it to develop a program of theological resistance against contemporary forms of human oppression. His attention focuses on oppressive moments within the Christian church as well as on those structures in human society that block the way toward human emancipation.

In this context Metz considers the significance of Auschwitz for contemporary Christian existence. He warns against any claim by Christians to have "understood" the horrors of Auschwitz and the suffering that German people have imposed on Jews. Instead Metz urges Christians to listen to the Jewish voices today and to learn from them—possibly for the first time. One of the insights Christians can gain from listening to Jewish voices today is the radically messianic nature of Jewish faith in God. And it is this messianic faith that can challenge the dangerous kind of triumphalist interpretation of history that has characterized Christian faith for far too long. Christians, Metz argues, have seen their religion too much in terms of a victorious movement with answers to every human question, and thus they lacked the passionate questioning present in Jewish thinking, acting, and praying. Metz asks: "Rather is it not that even Christians still have something to hope for and to fear—not only for themselves, but also for the world and the whole of history?"[36] Metz continues: "If I see the danger of Jewish messianism to consist in its continuing suspension of all reconciliation at the present time, then I see the danger of messianism in a Christian sense to consist in its tendency to limit the reconciliation in Christ too much to our presence and to accredit the respective generation of Christians with moral and political innocence."[37]

In such an attitude Metz recognizes the basis for the lack of Christian resistance to Hitler's regime. He asks: "Does not the history of our Christianity show a drastic deficit in political resistance and a surplus of political adaptation? Here lies for me the crucial point of the reflection by Christians and theology on themselves in view of Auschwitz."[38] The

---

[35] Ibid., p. 95. Compare Moltmann, *Theologie der Hoffnung* (n. 13 above), p. 304.
[36] Johann B. Metz, *Jenseits bürgerlicher Religion: Reden über die Zukunft des Christentums* (Munich and Mainz, 1980), p. 37 (my translation).
[37] Ibid., p. 38 (my translation).
[38] Ibid., p. 39 (my translation).

reduction of Christian discipleship to a mere bourgeois religion with a firm set of beliefs has destroyed the Christian sense of the mystical and the political nature of a Christian praxis. *"Here,* in this collapse of the messianic religion into a purely bourgeois religion I see one of the decisive roots in contemporary Christianity for the Christian failure with regard to the Jewish question, and ultimately also for the Christian inability really to mourn and really to repent, and for the churches' failure to resist our society's grand repression of guilt during the years after the last war." [39] Metz concludes this discussion by insisting that no Christian theology can ever move back behind Auschwitz, and that we as Christians will never be able to move beyond Auschwitz on our own, but only together with its victims. [40] Accepting this insight, it would seem to me to be essential for Christian theologians to consider very carefully recent reflections by Jewish thinkers on the Holocaust and human resistance to oppression. [41]

Even this brief examination of Metz's theology clearly shows how the insight into the failure of Christians to resist Hitler has moved Metz to reassess the political nature of theology as well as the historical and theological foundations for a theology of resistance today. Resistance can only emerge from the praxis of active and "costly discipleship." Metz uses this term that Bonhoeffer had introduced to theological discourse. [42] However, Metz's understanding of discipleship is characterized now by the continuous challenge to Christian theology that comes from the memory of the suffering at Auschwitz and the failure of Christianity to prevent it. Thus nonresistance now becomes the basis for the formulation of resistance both to the process of *Verbürgerlichung* in the church and to all oppression of human beings that results either directly from human action or indirectly from unjust structures operated by human beings.

Again, like Moltmann's, Metz's approach to theology has provided a major stimulus for theologians throughout the world to formulate theologies of liberation and emancipation for their particular contexts.

Theologies of Liberation and the Problem of Resistance

It would be impossible to discuss in any detail the "theologies of liberation" that have emerged during the past two decades, but it is important to observe

---

[39] Ibid., pp. 41–42 (my translation).

[40] Ibid., p. 47.

[41] See, e.g., Arthur A. Cohen, *The Tremendum: A Theological Interpretation of the Holocaust* (New York, 1981).

[42] Compare Dietrich Bonhoeffer, *Nachfolge* (1937), 13th ed. (Munich, 1982), p. 22; and see Johann B. Metz, *Zeit der Orden: Zur Mystik und Politik der Nachfolge* (Freiburg im Breisgau, 1978), p. 39, where Metz refers explicitly to Bonhoeffer's distinction between cheap and costly grace.

to what extent they owe their impulse to Bonhoeffer's faith-praxis and to Moltmann's and Metz's retrieval of the political dimension of Christian faith and theology. Indirectly, then, it can be said that these theologies of liberation, which represent a contemporary theological resistance to unjust structures and situations, have grown out of the insights into the failure of Christian theology to resist the Nazi regime.

Although in this article I will focus on examples taken from recent Latin American theology in order to document the wider influence of German political theology more closely, we must also appreciate that there are many more theologies of liberation in this world. I am thinking here also of feminist theologies, ecological theologies, and theologies of cultural liberation.[43] However, all of them are based on the recognition that Christian faith calls for a praxis of transforming this world into a better place. Obviously, this concentration on the right Christian praxis, on "ortho-praxis" over against traditional Christian teaching, "ortho-doxy," points to the dissatisfaction with the traditional overemphasis on orthodoxy and the resulting apolitical nature of much of recent theology.

Gustavo Gutiérrez and Jon Sobrino, to name only two theologians who have advocated and developed a theology of liberation in Latin America, both call for a radically new departure in Christian theology. Following Metz and Moltmann they insist that Christian theology is confronted by concrete situations of human oppression that call for a relocation of theological thought into human history. History, eschatology, hope, the world, and a renewed concept of God as a suffering God are the characteristics also of these creative Latin American appropriations and developments of German political theology.

In terms of the need for a transformed understanding of the concept of God that has been at the root of all the political theologies discussed here, Sobrino formulates his critique of the classical approach to God like this: "Greek thought cannot picture suffering as a divine mode of being because that would imply a contradiction." And he continues: "People in Latin America, however, seem to feel almost automatically what Dietrich Bonhoeffer expressed in intuitive, poetic terms: 'Only a God who suffers can save us.' "[44] Gutiérrez praises Metz for recovering the political dimension of Christian faith, but criticizes him for the lack of the necessary concretization. Offering this latter aspect himself, Gutiérrez analyzes the particular role that faith,

---

[43] In Dorothee Sölle's recent work, *Gott Denken: Einführung in die Theologie* (Stuttgart, 1990), these different aspects of liberation theology are incorporated into a new and comprehensive form of theology.

[44] Jon Sobrino, S. J., *Christology at the Crossroads: A Latin American Approach,* trans. John Drury (London, 1978), pp. 196–97.

gospel, and church have been playing in Latin America and how they usually ended up being on the side of the oppressors.[45] Thus, in Latin America the problem that deprived Christian faith of its political manifestation was not privatization of faith but, rather, the identification of Christian faith with powerful political and economical systems. Thus, the new "political theology" developed by Metz and Moltmann creatively applied and adapted to the Latin American situation must replace the old "political theology" that has been used as an instrument of oppression for centuries in that part of the world.

This critique by Gutiérrez brings home to us the important insight that theology is threatened not only by privatization and marginalization in bourgeois contexts and by overemphasis on theory to the detriment of transforming praxis in intellectual contexts. It is also threatened by the collaboration between throne and altar that found its first manifestation in the Constantinian empire, and that has been advocated in more recent times in Germany by a number of "völkisch gesinnte" thinkers.[46]

"Political theology" is then an ambiguous term that may refer either to the uncritical synthesis of political programs and theological legitimization or to the transformative power of Christian faith-praxis and its inherently critical but constructive reflection on a given power structure. Hitler distanced himself from the former, and during the time of the National Socialist regime German theologians on the whole did not offer the latter.

CONCLUSION

I have tried to trace the emergence and development of a new and critical political theology in response to the failure of much former German theology to provide a theoretical basis for Christian resistance to Nazism. We have seen that the postwar recognition of this theological failure as well as the urgent need to address the suffering of countless people under Hitler's rule led to a new departure in Christian theology in the 1960s. Of course, some theologians have been and still are unmoved by either fact, and continue to do theology as if nothing had happened. But it is important to realize that the failures in theology and society during the Nazi regime have been recognized by some theologians and that by now their thoughts have become influential far beyond Germany. These theologians have been helped in their reflections by the

---

[45] Gustavo Gutiérrez, *Theologie der Befreiung,* mit einem Vorwort von Johann B. Metz, 6th ed. (Munich and Mainz, 1982), p. 214.

[46] See Klaus Scholder, *Die Kirchen und das Dritte Reich,* vol. 2, *Das Jahr der Ernüchterung 1934 Barmen und Rom* (Frankfurt am Main and Berlin, 1988), pp. 19 ff., especially on the influence of Carl Schmitt.

thoughts and examples of people like Bonhoeffer, Niemöller, and countless other Christians whose thoughts and acts of resistance have opened up new alleys of theological reflection and Christian praxis for us today.[47]

One of the lessons of the non/resistance against the Nazi regime has been that a largely spiritual (pneumatological), Barthian understanding of Christian faith is unable to provide the institutional platform needed to identify and fight oppressive political structures and actions from a Christian perspective. At the same time, a predominantly institutional and legal understanding of Christian faith in the tradition of Pacelli is unable to set free the spiritual energy needed by individual Christians to undertake for themselves a responsible assessment of both their faith and the political context in which their faith may require decisive acts of resistance.

In view of theological developments since the 1960s, there is hope that the recognition of the political nature of Christian faith by theologians such as Metz, Moltmann, Sobrino, and Gutiérrez will provide a lasting challenge to all Christians that an active but critical participation in the political processes of this world is the best way of insuring that such dramatic acts of resistance as would have been necessary in the Third Reich will no longer be required in the future.

[47] See James Bentley, *Martin Niemöller* (London, 1984).

Repressing, Remembering, Working Through: German Psychiatry, Psychotherapy, Psychoanalysis, and the "Missed Resistance" in the Third Reich

Geoffrey Cocks
Albion College

In 1949 Alexander Mitscherlich, a lecturer in psychiatry, and Fred Mielke, a medical student, published *Wissenschaft ohne Menschlichkeit* for a research commission formed by the West German Physicians Chambers that documented the recent "doctors' trial" at Nuremberg. The foreword by the members of the working group that sent the commission to Nuremberg observed that of the 90,000 doctors active in wartime Germany, only about 350 had committed medical crimes. This observation was echoed by Mitscherlich and Mielke in the preface, but at the same time they pointed to a larger moral crisis among German doctors as a whole.[1] This book was largely ignored by the medical profession in Germany—one indication of the tensions and disagreements existing among physicians regarding their profession's conduct under Hitler.[2]

Wissenschaft ohne Menschlichkeit includes a chapter on the sterilization and murder of mental patients but, in following the trials, concentrates on bureaucrats and medical experiments rather than on the role of psychiatrists in the so-called T 4 program. Mitscherlich, who with his wife Margarete would become a leading psychoanalytic critic of the postwar German denial of the Nazi past, was himself entangled in the skeins of history and memory regarding his own profession's immediate past.[3] This is evident in the small flier included with *Wissenschaft ohne Menschlichkeit* advertising *Psyche,* a journal for depth psychology founded by Mitscherlich, who now returned to public life. The flier claims that *Psyche* is the only German publication carrying on the tradition of earlier journals that had been forced to cease publication by the Nazis. Yet this version of the *Jahre Null* argument for a new

---

[1] Alexander Mitscherlich and Fred Mielke, *Wissenschaft ohne Menschlichkeit: Medizinische und Eugenische Irrwege unter Diktatur, Burokratie und Krieg* (Heidelberg, 1949), pp. v, 6. Michael Kater, *Doctors under Hitler* (Chapel Hill, N.C., 1989), pp. 12, 267, fixes the number of wartime doctors in Germany at around 79,000.

[2] Robert N. Proctor, *Racial Hygiene: Medicine under the Nazis* (Cambridge, Mass., 1988), p. 309.

[3] Alexander Mitscherlich and Margarete Mitscherlich, *The Inability to Mourn: Principles of Collective Behavior* (1967), trans. Beverley R. Placzek (New York, 1975).

This essay originally appeared in the *Journal of Modern History* 64, suppl. (December 1992).

beginning after 1945 ignores significant developments in depth psychology in Germany between 1933 and 1945, developments that carried over into the postwar period. Although *Psyche,* in the words of its subtitle, was eventually to be transformed from *A Journal for Depth Psychology and Anthropology in Research and Praxis* into one for *Psychoanalysis and Its Applications,* its original aim as described in 1949 was to provide a forum for all schools of *grosse Psychotherapie.* This represented a continuation of the work of the so-called Göring Institute, which, alongside and in line with its stated Nazi goal of establishing a "new German psychotherapy," from 1936 to 1945 attempted to unite the various schools of psychotherapeutic thought. Of the twenty-nine contributors listed in the flier, eight had been members of the Göring Institute, including one who was director of the outpatient clinic and another who was a member of the Nazi party, as well as at least two others who had trained at or otherwise been associated with the institute.

It is within this context of institutional and personal continuities between the postwar Germanies and the Nazi era that an analysis of the phenomenon of "missed resistance" among psychiatrists, psychotherapists, and psychoanalysts must be conducted. This is especially the case with the professions in general, because between 1933 and 1945 a number of professions displayed "a significant degree of functional unity" in defending, advancing, and sacrificing their interests in service to the Nazi regime.[4] Psychiatrists, psychotherapists, and psychoanalysts all to one degree or another sought professional advantage in competition with one another during the Third Reich, an instance of what, in connection with the Holocaust, has been called "the nature of modern sin, the withdrawal of moral concerns from public roles in our lives."[5] As Hans Mommsen rightly observes, there are specific reasons why German elites did not resist Hitler, as much of it having to do with greed, ambition, and power as with obedience, fear, and cowardice.[6] Thus reflections on the "missed resistance" on the part of psychiatrists, psychotherapists, and psychoanalysts have taken place (or not) in the context of a continuum of morally ambiguous professional development as well as that of general German culpability.[7]

---

[4] Geoffrey Cocks, "The Professionalization of Psychotherapy in Germany, 1928–1949," in *German Professions, 1800–1950,* ed. Geoffrey Cocks and Konrad H. Jarausch (New York, 1990), p. 311. See also Jarausch, *The Unfree Professions: German Lawyers, Teachers, and Engineers, 1900–1950* (New York, 1990).

[5] Rainer C. Baum, *The Holocaust and the German Elite* (Totowa, N.J., 1981), p. 266.

[6] Hans Mommsen, "The German Resistance against Hitler and the Restoration of Politics," in this volume.

[7] Rolf Vogt, "Warum sprechen die Deutschen nicht?" *Psyche* 40 (1986): 896–97.

There are three senses in which the term "missed resistance" can be used to illuminate the ways in which German psychiatrists, psychotherapists, and psychoanalysts have avoided as well as confronted the history and memory of the Third Reich. The first sense is that of the missed opportunity for resistance embodied in the accusations of collaboration made by young Germans in the 1960s. They confronted their elders who, during the "economic miracle" of the 1950s, had lied or remained silent about their actions and inactions under nazism. The second sense of missed resistance is that of regret/empathy and longing: regret over and empathy with the conditions that rendered resistance problematic as well as regret over the moral derelictions of their own professional ancestors; and longing for a legacy of resistance as redemption of the past and for moral commitment in the present. The third sense constitutes overlooking the nonheroic tradition of quotidian resistance mixed with compromise and even collaboration. As David Large points out, heroism almost by definition describes actions that are too late; and concentrating on heroism devalues "low-level" civil disobedience that if not preempting evil can mitigate it.[8] This is not to celebrate those many who went along at the expense of those few who did not. There is, as Klemens von Klemperer argues, great importance in the example of an individual resister *(Einzelkämpfer)* like psychoanalyst John Rittmeister.[9] But even Rittmeister's life contains instructive ambiguities in terms of his profession: alongside resistance was, as Rittmeister noted in his prison diary, enthusiasm for much of his work at the Göring Institute.[10] And a post hoc fixation on resistance heroes can substitute a wish-fulfilling "ego-ideal" for historical inquiry, obscuring lines of continuity between past and present. As we shall see, the figure of Rittmeister has been used in just such a way for conscious political purposes by groups of psychotherapists and psychoanalysts in both postwar German states.

Although psychiatrists, psychotherapists, and psychoanalysts shared in the gradual recapturing of memory after 1945—through the repression characteristic of the 1950s, the angry generational confrontations of the 1960s, and the more complicated and thoroughgoing recollections of the 1970s and 1980s—avoidance of and confrontation with the past have taken different forms for each discipline. This is so for two reasons. First, the three disciplines

---

[8] David Clay Large, " 'A Beacon in the German Darkness': The Anti-Nazi Resistance Legacy in West German Politics," in this volume.

[9] Klemens von Klemperer, " 'What Is the Law That Lies behind These Words?' Antigone's Question and the German Resistance against Hitler," in this volume.

[10] "Tagebuchblätter aus dem Gefängnis von Dr. med. John Rittmeister," pp. 3, 4, 15, 19, 23, Nds 721 Acc 69/76 Lüneburg, 10:126–57 (Niedersächsisches Hauptstaatsarchiv, Hanover).

have grown increasingly distinct during the twentieth century, especially since 1933; and, second, the experience of each in the Third Reich differed in crucial respects.

Psychiatrists have displayed an almost seamless repression of the field's activities under Hitler, so much so that instances of genuine resistance as well as collaboration were ignored in the silent assertion of general innocence.[11] Recent research has shown the wide extent to which psychiatrists were involved in the Nazi eugenics program, but in the years immediately following the war only a very few were prosecuted for their roles in this program of involuntary sterilization and murder.[12] Some were even absolved of guilt because German courts ruled that they had acted in the belief that the program was legally constituted.[13] Moreover, a significant demand for medical expertise to rebuild a devastated society occasioned a distinct carryover of medical personnel from the Third Reich into the postwar republics.[14] So even though the reputation of traditional university psychiatry suffered in Germany both during and after the war because of its involvement with the destructive racial policy of the Nazis, many of its representatives, as well as their students, continued on in positions of authority after 1945.

In the case of psychiatrists the continuities were not only personal but conceptual. The psychiatric preoccupation with the hereditary determinants of mental illness was easily exploited by the Nazis. And apart from the authoritarian social and political views commonly held in the German professoriate often linked with this hereditarianism, psychiatrists, like physicians in general, were also heavily influenced by the eugenic thought, social darwinism, and racism endemic to Germany during the late nineteenth and early twentieth centuries.[15] The persistence of this way of thinking into the postwar era is evident in the West German disposition of compensation cases for psychic damage caused by Nazi persecution. A number of these claims were rejected on the basis of psychiatric evaluations that declared that these individuals' difficulties were due to hereditary predisposition *(Anlage)*,

[11] Dirk Blasius, "Psychiatrischer Alltag im Nationalsozialismus," in *Die Reihen fest geschlossen: Beiträge zur Geschichte des Alltags unterm Nationalsozialismus,* ed. Detlev Peukert and Jürgen Reulecke (Wuppertal, 1981), pp. 367–80.

[12] Hans-Walter Schmuhl, *Rassenhygiene, Nationalsozialismus, Euthanasie: Von der Verhütung zur Vernichtung "lebensunwerten Lebens," 1890–1945* (Göttingen, 1987).

[13] Ernst Klee, *"Euthanasie" im NS-Staat: Die "Vernichtung lebensunwerten Lebens"* (Frankfurt am Main, 1985), pp. 384–86.

[14] Kater (n. 1 above), pp. 223–24.

[15] Sheila Faith Weiss, *Race Hygiene and National Efficiency: The Eugenics of Wilhelm Schallmayer* (Berkeley and Los Angeles, 1987).

decisions that produced vigorous dissent from psychoanalysts and psychotherapists.[16]

A systematic confrontation with psychiatry's past did not occur until the 1980s. At first, this critique was part of a larger critical "history of the everyday" *(Alltagsgeschichte)* directed "from below" by students and citizens against the silent bastions of academic and political authority. These campaigns took the form of conferences and the collection, exhibition, and publication of documents, recollections, and studies concerning the activities of individuals, communities, and groups under National Socialism. Some of these concentrated on the medical profession, including psychiatry, and constituted criticism primarily from outside the profession from sociologists, pedagogues, historians, theologians, and the like.[17] And much of this critical work has been neo-Marxist or structuralist in orientation and sees Nazi medicine as a culmination of a Western bourgeois trend toward "social control" and eugenic engineering.

Only recently have members of the psychiatric community begun to question their collective past. And instead of seeking distance between themselves and their compromised predecessors, as was characteristic of the radical confrontation of the late 1960s with "fascism" at home and abroad, these inquiries have focused with some humility on those processes and structures for dealing with the mentally ill that contribute now as then to inhumanity. This does not constitute a facile equation of contemporary society with Nazi Germany but, rather, an attempt to deal with those tendencies toward categorization and evaluation within psychiatry that can stigmatize mental patients as especially disruptive of society and the economy. Klaus Dörner, one of the very few psychiatrists to address the subject relatively early on, later expressed concern that he had only intellectualized the subject rather than confronting it emotionally.[18] Such an emotional confrontation involved for him an effort to work with relatives of mental patients killed by the Nazis who were denied compensation under the Federal Compensation Law. This effort, Dörner says, has brought him face to

[16] Klaus D. Hoppe, "The Emotional Reactions of Psychiatrists When Confronting Survivors of Persecution," *Psychoanalytic Forum* 1 (1966): 187–96.

[17] Gerhard Baader and Ulrich Schultz, eds., *Medizin und Nationalsozialismus: Tabuisierte Vergangenheit—Ungebrochene Tradition?* (Berlin, 1980); Projektgruppe Volk und Gesundheit, ed., *Volk und Gesundheit: Heilen und Vernichten im Nationalsozialismus* (Tübingen, 1982); Kölnische Gesellschaft für Christlich-Jüdische Zusammenarbeit, ed., *Heilen und Vernichten im Nationalsozialismus* (Cologne, 1985). See also Benno Müller-Hill, *Murderous Science: Elimination by Scientific Selection of Jews, Gypsies, and Others, Germany, 1933–1945* (1984), trans. George R. Fraser (Oxford, 1988).

[18] Klaus Dörner, "Nationalsozialismus und Lebensvernichtung," *Vierteljahreshefte für Zeitgeschichte* 15 (1967): 121–52.

face with a continuity of attitude and issue between the Nazi period and the present.[19]

A similar ethic pervades the documentation by a group of young mental health care workers of the asylum at Wittenau in Berlin between 1933 and 1945. The authors ask why they failed during the 1960s to take their teachers to task for their collaboration with the Nazis. The answer, they feel, lies in their own desire to divorce themselves from the horrors of the Nazi era by broadening and thus diluting their criticism into a radical condemnation of society in general and fascism in particular. What they found in scouring the archives at Wittenau was that the procedures and judgments involved in the sterilization and murder of mental patients under Nazi direction blended in rather smoothly with the workings of what up until 1933 had been an institution renowned for its progressive treatment of the mentally ill. This continuity of operation is the reason why documents detailing these measures were found in the archives while documents dealing with Jewish patients had long since disappeared.[20] Investigations and attitudes such as these are in keeping with the second sense of "missed resistance," a regret for failure in the past and the congruent need for commitment in the present.

While psychotherapists and psychoanalysts have not had to confront direct participation in Nazi atrocities, their history displays some disturbing lines of professional continuity extending through the Nazi years. Under the Nazis this meant some specific as well as general violations of professional ethics, but it also fed into a longer-term and morally ambiguous trend toward adjustment of individuals to the demands of society. Agencies of the Nazi regime funded the Göring Institute generously in their mobilization of expertise to assist in rearmament and war. Between 1936 and 1945 a significant number of the men and women who would constitute the postwar psychotherapeutic movement in both German states were members or trainees of Matthias Heinrich Göring's German Institute for Psychological Research and Psychotherapy in Berlin or at its branches in several other cities. It was in this way that those physicians and lay practitioners in Germany who conceived of mental illness principally in psychological rather than physical terms established themselves as competitors to the dominant university psychiatrists. Some of the impetus for the critical examination of the history of German psychotherapy and psychoanalysis stems from concern over the resultant social identity, role, and responsibility of the field, a concern that also often obstructs understanding of the past.

---

[19] Baader and Schultz, eds., pp. 23–24.

[20] Arbeitsgruppe zur Erforschung der Geschichte der Karl-Bonhoeffer-Nervenklinik, ed., *Totgeschwiegen, 1933–1945: Die Geschichte der Karl-Bonhoeffer-Nervenklinik* (Berlin, 1988), p. 151.

Psychotherapists have largely ignored their recent professional past, in part because they were busy first surviving the difficult years after the war and then exploiting their newly professionalized position to meet a growing demand for psychological services. It is also true that time is necessary for historical perspective and that psychotherapists, like psychiatrists and psychoanalysts, are not professional historians, but a distinct unwillingness to deal with the legacy of the Nazi years also marks their treatments of the past. The accepted view in West Germany was that the "political events following 1933 pushed German psychotherapy . . . into the background for a long time."[21] In 1977, on the occasion of the fiftieth anniversary of the founding of the General Medical Society for Psychotherapy, its president observed that the only significance of the psychotherapeutic institute in Nazi Germany was the degree of protection and enforced cooperation it provided for those psychotherapists who had not emigrated.[22] In East Germany an even greater distance was put between postwar psychotherapy and its precedents under German fascism, even though in the socialist republic there was a similar emphasis placed on expert service to the state and a reliance on the short-term methods pioneered in Germany by, among others, J. H. Schultz, deputy director of the Göring Institute.[23] And East German psychotherapists now face the task of confronting a similar association with the late communist regime.

Challenges to this position first came across disciplinary boundaries as a result of the professional competition sharpened and even created under National Socialism.[24] In 1960 the director of the German Society for Psychology responded to charges of Nazi collaboration among psychologists by arguing that psychotherapists had compromised themselves to a much greater degree.[25] This type of counterattack, however, raised defenses and not curiosity or consciousness. As a result, the first study of the history of psychotherapy in Nazi Germany came from abroad in the 1970s.[26] By the 1980s some additional work was being done by historians of medicine at the

---

[21] Walter Theodor Winkler, "The Present Status of Psychotherapy in Germany," in *Progress in Psychotherapy, 1956,* ed. Frieda Fromm-Reichmann and J. L. Moreno (New York, 1956), p. 288.

[22] Walter Theodor Winkler, "50 Jahre AAeGP—ein Rückblick," *Zeitschrift für Psychotherapie und medizinische Psychologie* 27 (1977): 79.

[23] Kurt Höck, *Psychotherapie in der DDR* (n.p., 1979), pp. 7, 14; Dietfried Müller-Hegemann, "Psychotherapy in the German Democratic Republic," in *Psychiatry in the Communist World,* ed. Ari Kiev (New York, 1968), pp. 51–70.

[24] Ulfried Geuter, *Die Professionalisierung der deutschen Psychologie im Nationalsozialismus* (1984), 2d ed. (Frankfurt am Main, 1988).

[25] Albert Wellek, "Deutsche Psychologie und Nationalsozialismus," *Psychologie und Praxis* 4 (1960): 177–82.

[26] Geoffrey Campbell Cocks, "Psyche and Swastika: *Neue deutsche Seelenheilkunde,* 1933–1945" (Ph.D. diss., University of California, Los Angeles, 1975).

University of Leipzig, but its thematic comprehensiveness is limited by a Marxist-Leninist approach emphasizing a top-down nazification of psychotherapy.[27] By this time as well, research in the West had integrated the history of psychotherapy in the Third Reich into the study of professions and professionalization in Germany.[28] This work has had little discernible effect on psychotherapists in Germany, at least partly because the course of their profession's development has scattered them throughout several disciplines and the nature of their practice has oriented them toward issues of application rather than of introspection.

By contrast, psychoanalysts in West Germany (psychoanalysis was officially discouraged in the East) have of late confronted their past. This has to do with the distinct history as well as the distinct nature of psychoanalysis. Two versions of the history of psychoanalysis in Nazi Germany were literally institutionalized in the immediate postwar period. The German Psychoanalytic Society (DPG), which had been founded in 1910 and dissolved in 1938, was reestablished in 1946 but was divided between orthodox Freudians and "neo-analysts" influenced by other schools of psychotherapeutic thought within the Göring Institute. By 1951 the orthodox Freudians had seceded to form the German Psychoanalytic Union (DPV), which that year was recognized by the International Psycho-Analytical Association (IPA). The "official" position of the DPG with regard to psychoanalysis in the Third Reich has been that it had been "saved" by the Freudian members of the Göring Institute.[29] The DPV argued that psychoanalysis had simply been suppressed by the Nazis.[30]

These positions remained unaltered and largely unnoticed until the 1970s when psychoanalytic candidates began questioning this dual orthodoxy. Chief

---

[27] C. Schröder, "Programm und Wirksamkeit der 'Neuen deutschen Seelenkunde,' " in *Medizin unterm Hakenkreuz,* ed. Achim Thom and Genadij Ivanovič Caregorodcev (Berlin, 1989), pp. 283–305.

[28] Geoffrey C. Cocks, "Psychoanalyse, Psychotherapie und Nationalsozialismus," *Psyche* 37 (1983): 1057–1106, *Psychotherapy in the Third Reich: The Göring Institute* (New York, 1985), and "The Professionalization of Psychotherapy in Germany, 1928–1949" (n. 4 above).

[29] Franz Baumeyer, "Zur Geschichte der Psychoanalyse in Deutschland: 60 Jahre Deutsche Psychoanalytische Gesellschaft," *Zeitschrift für psychosomatische Medizin und Psychoanalyse* 17 (1971): 203–40; Rose Spiegel, Gerard Chrzanowski, and Arthur Feiner, "On Psychoanalysis in the Third Reich," *Contemporary Psychoanalysis* 11 (1975): 477–510.

[30] Gerhard Maetze, "Psychoanalyse in Deutschland," in *Die Psychologie des 20. Jahrhunderts: Freud und die Folgen,* ed. Dieter Eicke (Zurich, 1976), pp. 1145–79; Gudrun Zapp, "Psychoanalyse und Nationalsozialismus: Untersuchungen zum Verhältnis Medizin/Psychoanalyse während des Nationalsozialismus" (Inaug. diss., University of Kiel, 1980).

among these was Regine Lockot who in 1985 published a comprehensive critical study of the Göring Institute. By relying on extensive documentary evidence Lockot demonstrated that psychoanalysis was neither merely suppressed nor saved during the Third Reich; rather it was used, compromised, abused, and perverted. On the one hand, Lockot sought to follow what she labeled the *realpolitisch* perspective of the earlier historical work of Cocks and, on the other, to utilize a psychoanalytic point of view to begin the process of what Freud in 1914 called "working through" *(Durcharbeiten)*. Freud had argued that what "distinguishes analytic treatment from any kind of treatment by suggestion" is the process by which the patient works through resistances to an understanding of the repressed content behind neurotic symptoms.[31] This didactic aim is furthered by transference, whereby the patient reexperiences feelings toward parents in the relationship with the analyst, and countertransference, whereby the analyst through the emotions created by the relationship with the patient comes to understand the patient's unconscious. Lockot argues that psychoanalysts in particular must work through the repression of their own past and by means of countertransference come to understand not only their history but themselves as well.[32] The alternative is neurotic repetition of actions in place of self-understanding. Lockot argues that this pattern of behavior was displayed immediately after the war by leading members of the DPG as they struggled with the emotional consequences of a psychoanalytic identity damaged by compromise and collaboration under National Socialism.[33]

It is this psychoanalytic emphasis on repression that in particular characterizes the challenge that young psychoanalysts have raised against their professional elders. All three senses of the missed resistance have been present in this challenge: confrontation, regret/empathy, and a tendency to overlook resistance for Resistance. This challenge manifested itself first at a conference in Bamberg in 1980 and was developed by analysts and nonanalysts in the pages of *Psyche* between 1982 and 1986. Perhaps predictably for a discipline concerned so much with individual cases and characterized organizationally and emotionally by issues of authority between teacher and student, much of

---

[31] Sigmund Freud, "Remembering, Repeating and Working Through (Further Recommendations on the Technique of Psycho-Analysis II)," in *The Standard Edition of the Complete Psychological Works of Sigmund Freud,* ed. and trans. James Strachey (London, 1958), 12:155–56.

[32] Regine Lockot, *Erinnern und Durcharbeiten: Zur Geschichte der Psychoanalyse und Psychotherapie im Nationalsozialismus* (Frankfurt am Main, 1985), pp. 17–38. See also Wolfgang Huber, *Psychoanalyse in Oesterreich seit 1933* (Vienna, 1977).

[33] Regine Lockot, "Wiederholen oder Neubeginn: Skizzen zur Geschichte der 'Deutschen Psychoanalytischen Gesellschaft' von 1945–1950," *Jahrbuch der Psychoanalyse* 22 (1988): 218–35.

the heat (if less of the light) was generated in a controversy over Göring Institute psychoanalyst Carl Müller-Braunschweig.[34] More recently, the Berlin Forum for the History of Psychoanalysis has begun efforts to deposit documents at the Federal Archives in Coblenz pertaining to the history of psychoanalysis in Germany.

The debate within the DPV has overshadowed the discussions within the DPG, such as those held at DPG conferences in West Berlin in 1985 and in Bad Soden in 1989.[35] Young DPV critics see their organization's prior treatment of its past as especially objectionable for two reasons: first, because the notion of the complete suppression of psychoanalysis by the Nazis constitutes silence on the subject; and, second, because collaboration meant forsaking not only the many Jewish colleagues victimized by the Nazi campaign against "Jewish science" but also the ideals embodied in psycho-analytic thought.[36] The DPG, originally displaying the eclecticism in theory and practice that was promoted by the Göring Institute, had been willing to discuss the saving of psychoanalysis but until recently was less willing to examine critically the negative aspects of such salvation. But of late the DPG has been moving away from the neo-Freudian position established chiefly by the Göring Institute's Harald Schultz-Hencke toward the orthodox Freudian tradition represented by the DPV and IPA. This movement has been encouraged by increasing contact among newer members of both groups not divided by traditional rivalries as well as by the growing influence of the DPV both at home and abroad.[37]

Both the DPG and the DPV have attempted to capitalize on the figure of John Rittmeister, the Freudian head of the Göring Institute outpatient clinic

---

[34] Hans-Martin Lohmann, ed., *Psychoanalyse und Nationalsozialismus: Beiträge zur Bearbeitung eines unbewältigten Traumas* (Frankfurt am Main, 1984), pp. 109–36; "Dokumentation des DPV-Vorstands zum Briefwechsel Ehebald/Dahmer" (September, 1984, typescript); Hans Müller-Braunschweig, "Fünfzig Jahre danach: Stellungnahme zu den in PSYCHE 11/1982 zitierten Aeusserungen von Carl-Müller-Braunschweig," *Psyche* 37 (1983): 1140–45; and Ernst Federn, "Weitere Bemerkungen zum Problemkreis 'Psychoanalyse und Politik,' " *Psyche* 39 (1985): 367–74.

[35] Friedrich Beese, "Psychoanalyse in Deutschland: Rückblick und Perspektiven," in *Psychoanalyse der Gegenwart: Eine kritische Bestandsaufnahme 75 Jahre nach der Gründung der Deutschen Psychoanalytischen Gesellschaft*, ed. Gerd Rudolf et al. (Göttingen, 1987), pp. 15–29; Geoffrey Cocks, "Psychoanalyse und Psychotherapie im Dritten Reich," in Rudolf et al., eds., pp. 30–43.

[36] Volker Friedrich, "Psychoanalyse im Nationalsozialismus: Vom Widerspruch zur Gleichschaltung," *Jahrbuch der Psychoanalyse* 20 (1987): 207–33.

[37] Bernd Nitschke, "Psychoanalyse als 'un'-politische Wissenschaft"; and Volker Friedrich, "Die wissenschaftliche und politische Antwort der Psychoanalytiker auf die Herausforderung des Nationalsozialismus und des zweiten Weltkrieges" (papers presented to the International Association for the History of Psychoanalysis, London, July 22, 1990).

who was executed by the Nazis. There is in this a distinct sense of "our Rittmeister." For former colleagues at the Göring Institute it is a matter of innocence by association.[38] For younger members of the DPV he is the counterexample they hold up to their professional elders and from whom they draw inspiration.[39] And Rittmeister's involvement with the communist resistance to Hitler prompted the East German Society for Medical Psychotherapy to create an award in his name in 1979. While Rittmeister is certainly worthy of admiration, concentration on him to the exclusion of other particulars of psychoanalysis and psychotherapy in the Third Reich has been part of the process of denial and repression characteristic of these groups' perceptions of their collective past until recently. Surely it is a relevant irony that some who lived ethically compromised lives as members of the Göring Institute could at the time and later rationalize their behavior because of small acts of courage and compassion while contemporary critics cannot *do* anything either against the Nazis or for their victims except remember for the sake of memory, their contemporaries, and the future. Under such circumstances the figure of a hero provides a certain degree of vicarious satisfaction and emotional nourishment.

German psychoanalysts have thus been somewhat successful in confronting their history. Psychoanalysis, unlike psychiatry or psychotherapy in general, is based on detailed excavation of the past. Their patients have included those whose lives were directly or indirectly affected by the horrors of the Third Reich, even if for a long time the topic was largely taboo in analytic sessions.[40] Moreover, the DPV in particular is the inheritor of an intellectual tradition that is largely Jewish in origin and many of whose practitioners were persecuted by the Nazis. German psychoanalysts were reminded of this in 1977 when, at the Jerusalem meeting of the IPA, a proposal to meet in Berlin was turned down. Yet in 1985 the IPA did meet in Hamburg and devoted a day to discussion of "identification and its vicissitudes in relation to the Nazi phenomenon."[41] In conjunction with the congress a group of young German analysts set up an exhibition on the history of psychoanalysis in Germany highlighting the activities of psychoanalysts at the Göring Institute, a history that they see as still being repressed and not worked through by the West German psychoanalytic

---

[38] Werner Kemper, "John F. Rittmeister zum Gedächtnis," *Zeitschrift für psychosomatische Medizin und Psychoanalyse* 14 (1968): 147–49.

[39] Ludger M. Hermanns, "John F. Rittmeister und C. G. Jung," *Psyche* 36 (1982): 1022–31.

[40] Lutz Rosenkötter, "Schatten der Zeitgeschichte auf psychoanalytischen Behandlungen," *Psyche* 33 (1979): 1024–38.

[41] Edith Kurzweil, "The Freudians Meet in Germany," *Partisan Review* 52 (1985): 337–47. See also Kurzweil, "The (Freudian) Congress of Vienna," *Commentary* 52 (1971): 80–83.

leadership.[42] But although the DPV has been quite willing to benefit from the international success of the Hamburg exhibition, the IPA has not encouraged confrontation with the discipline's German past, preferring at Hamburg as before to concentrate on technical issues of psychoanalytic theory and practice. This neutral "scientific" posture constituted the original response of the IPA to the depredations of nazism in the 1930s.[43]

The Germans make up the second largest national contingent of psychoanalysts in the IPA, behind only the Americans, a position that certainly will be further consolidated through the unification of Germany. But the popularity of psychoanalysis in West Germany is also due to its being "a Jewish heritage in the German language" uncontaminated by the Nazi past that has served, in the eyes of some, to blind the DPV in particular to its compromised past.[44] Moreover, it can be argued that the introspection inherent in psychoanalysis carries a particular appeal for the German Romantic cultural tradition and that such self-absorption can also be a means of avoiding rational confrontation with unpleasant truths. Radical psychoanalysts such as the Siegfried Bernfeld Group see contemporary German conservatism in social, political, environmental, and military affairs reflected in the authoritarian practices of psychoanalytic institutes and an ongoing failure to work through the Nazi past.[45] Moreover, the integration of psychoanalysis into the state health care system has, in the view of many, only aggravated inherent tendencies toward political and social quiescence.[46] And it is anything but clear that Germans in general have laid to rest the legacy of anti-Semitism, particularly with regard to feelings about health and illness.[47]

Like psychiatrists and psychotherapists, psychoanalysts have tended to concentrate on the actions of individuals independent of the broader context

[42] Karen Brecht et al., *"Hier geht das Leben auf eine sehr merkwürdige Weise weiter . . ." Zur Geschichte der Psychoanalyse in Deutschland* (Hamburg, 1985).

[43] Edward Glover, "Report of the Thirteenth International Psycho-Analytical Congress," *International Journal of Psycho-Analysis* 15 (1934): 485–88; Richard F. Sterba, *Reminiscences of a Viennese Psychoanalyst* (Detroit, 1982), p. 163.

[44] Hermann Beland et al., "Podiumsdiskussion: Psychoanalyse unter Hitler—Psychoanalyse heute," *Psyche* 40 (1986): 425; Hans Keilson, "Psychoanalyse und Nationalsozialismus," *Jahrbuch der Psychoanalyse* 25 (1989): 23; and Robert S. Wallerstein, "Psychoanalysis in Nazi Germany: Historical and Psychoanalytic Lessons," *Psychoanalysis and Contemporary Thought* 11 (1988): 360.

[45] Janice Haaken, "The Siegfried Bernfeld Conference: Uncovering the Psychoanalytic Political Unconscious," *American Journal of Psychoanalysis* 50 (1990): 289–304.

[46] Paul Parin, "Warum die Psychoanalytiker so ungern zu brennenden Zeitproblemen Stellung nehmen," *Psyche* 32 (1978): 385–99.

[47] Geoffrey Cocks, "Partners and Pariahs: Jews and Medicine in Modern German Society," *Leo Baeck Institute Yearbook* 36 (1991): 191–205.

of their institutional and professional history, a limitation also manifested in the anecdotal tendencies of *Alltagsgeschichte*. But in the second sense of "missed resistance," that of regret/empathy, for whose exercise the analytic emphasis on intra- and interpersonal psychodynamics is peculiarly suited, German psychoanalysts too have had to deal with the structural continuities in the history of their discipline to, through, and beyond the Third Reich. These continuities raise the disturbing question of the ethical problems inherent in a professionalizing society. For all three disciplines, therefore, there exists the task of working through the present as well as the past.

Resistance as Ongoing Project: Visions of Order, Obligations to Strangers, and Struggles for Civil Society, 1933–1990

Michael Geyer
University of Chicago

In memory of Hermann Geyer (1908–1991)

> All thinking, talking, and organizing in matters of Christian faith must be reborn from prayers and deeds. This transformation has not yet come to an end, and every attempt of turning it into a premature form of institutional aggrandizement will only result in the delay of conversion and chastening.[1]

Dietrich Bonhoeffer's thoughts on the occasion of his nephew's baptism were a bequest. Resistance, he admonished the child and his parents, does not end with rebuilding the institutions destroyed by the National Socialist regime but continues as a process of social and spiritual renewal. The act of resistance during the Nazi regime entails a call not to commemorate but to participate in the reformation of society. Resistance, instead of being the record of past events, thus becomes a defining mark for the ongoing and always contested struggle to carry on a tradition of social action whose moral grounding seems to make it peculiarly German. The eschatological fervor of moral resistance surely remains the exception, but ever since the 1950s it has been an element of German political culture and, at times, a very forceful one at that.[2] Has the successful upheaval against communist regimes completed this project of conversion and brought it to an end? What, if anything, does Bonhoeffer's plea entail in our new *Gründerzeit?*

If the successful mobilization against communist regimes seemed to be a "natural" extension of this tradition in 1990, sentiments have changed drastically in 1991/92. Now, the analogy between the former German Democratic Republic and the Nazi regime has become overwhelming. Implicit in this analogy is the presumption, buttressed by the revelation of the

---

[1] Dietrich Bonhoeffer, *Widerstand und Ergebung: Briefe und Aufzeichnungen* (Munich, 1970), p. 328.

[2] The progression is best described by three authors: Erich Kuby, *Alles im Eimer: Siegt Hitler bei Bonn? Ein politischer Monolog, 1944–1960* (Stuttgart, 1960); Peter Weiss, *Ästhetik des Widerstands,* 3 vols. (Frankfurt, 1977–81); Günter Grass, *Widerstand lernen: Politische Gegenreden* (Darmstadt, 1984).

This essay originally appeared in the *Journal of Modern History* 64, suppl. (December 1992).

Stasi (State Security Service) activities, that the East Germans have failed to resist—to be liberated only now from decades of captivity or conformity. Implicit also is the idea that, somehow, the other and larger part of Germany has managed to overcome its tyrannical past to serve as a fit model for the future. In any case, resistance can now be placed squarely into the past.

There are plenty of reasons to poke holes in these arguments. After all, the eastern Germans have abandoned their government and its institutions and thus have gone through a process of their own liberation which the West Germans never quite did. The western Germans may conveniently confuse the efficient integration into a unified German state with a politics of nation building and thus engage in one of the oldest blunders of unification that has haunted the Second Empire. As the celebrations have died down, Germany as a whole faces a severe bout of xenophobia as one of the first articulations of its unity. Recriminations abound, but these are not issues to be pursued here.

The recent success in bringing down tyrannical regimes has thrown the problem of resistance—and the problem of resistance against the Third Reich in particular—into sharp relief. In all their vacuousness, these regimes did not appear as some alien occupying force but as the despot that "lightly forgive[s] his subjects for not loving him, provided they do not love each other."[3] In the end, the institutions of the state were overthrown very quickly both in 1945 and 1989, despite their massive presence and their infiltration of all aspects of life. But the powers of the state which were embodied in the daily routines and habits of society did not yield so easily—thus rekindling Bonhoeffer's old admonition in a contemporary form. Resistance with the goal of overthrowing tyrannical regimes is but the first step in the ongoing project of bringing together societies that have been rent asunder.

This project did not begin in 1989 but in the cataclysm of the years 1933 to 1945, and it encompasses the whole of German society rather than only that part which was held captive over the last forty years. The challenge is to formulate an understanding of resistance that comes to terms with the institutional as well as the social powers of despotic regimes. This means we must make sense of resistance as the practice of social conversion in the context of the peculiarly antinomic consensus—to distrust each other—that despotism engenders.

Historicizing the Third Reich

"The *Völkerfrühling* [springtime of people] in what is (culturally) central Europe and (politically) eastern Europe, days in which that old continent's

---

[3] Alexis de Tocqueville, *Democracy in America*, ed. J. P. Mayer (New York, 1988), p. 509.

center has been swept by stormy changes and aspires to reemerge as the focus and pacemaker of world events," has added a moment of urgency to revisiting the problem of resistance.[4] It is not, as some fear, that the past would now return, as if nations and continents were doomed to repeat the same course. But the past has undoubtedly gained a new immediacy despite the feeling of central Europeans that they have moved far away from it. The attractions of the past, the desire to return, however, are only one part of the story. The other has to do with the ability to transfer the past from experience and memory into history. This labor of translation has gained an acute currency because the separation between past and present, which was instituted with the Allied victory over the Nazi regime, has now broken down. As the Allied powers withdraw from a divided continent and as the division of Europe fades, the powers of that separation, which effectively relegated the National Socialist experience into history even when and where it was very much alive,[5] have now devolved onto the central European nations.

Working through the present to overcome the effects of the East/West divide thus always also entails working through the past. Together they establish an agenda for resistance scholarship that focuses on the social processes of undoing despotic regimes. This project, in turn, depends on the way in which the Third Reich is placed into the continuities and ruptures of German historiography, that is, on how the Third Reich is historicized. Strategies of historicization, a reassessment of resistance scholarship, and the practice of coping with a newly immediate past in central Europe form an intricate web.

Historians have turned to a historicization of the Third Reich as interpretative strategy to associate events during the years of Nazi rule in Germany and Europe with trends that reach far back into the German and European past.[6] Whether the Third Reich was apogee, dangling end, or betrayal, it was depicted as the consequence of or as the contrast to a previous history. The nature of this history remained as disputed as its connection to the Third Reich

---

[4] Dan Diner, "European Counterimages: Problems of Periodization and Historical Memory," *New German Critique* 53 (Spring/Summer 1991): 162–74, quotation on 164; see also his *Der Krieg der Erinnerungen und die Ordnung der Welt* (Berlin, 1991). The same metaphor was used by Timothy Garton Ash, "Revolution: The Springtime of Two Nations," *New York Review of Books* 26 (June 15, 1989): 3–10.

[5] Michael Geyer and Miriam Hansen, "German-Jewish Memory and National Consciousness," in *Shapes of Memory: The Holocaust and Modern Memory,* ed. Geoffrey Hartman (Oxford, 1993); Michael Geyer, "Looking Back at the International Style: Some Reflections on the Current State of German Historiography," *German Studies Review* 13 (February 1990): 113–27.

[6] Klaus Hildebrand, "Hitlers Ort in der Geschichte des preußisch-deutschen Nationalstaates," *Historische Zeitschrift* 217 (1973): 584–632; Martin Broszat and Saul Friedlander, "A Controversy about the Historicization of National Socialism," *New German Critique* 44 (Spring/Summer 1988): 85–126.

and underwent repeated revisions. As a result, the Third Reich was always seen in relation to the preceding past and in separation from the present. The history of the Third Reich remained—and here conservative and liberal, structuralist and intentionalist historians converged—full of causes, but without any consequence.[7] While continuities of one kind or another were acknowledged, the present remained essentially different and, most of all, outside of history.

The "essential" difference was, in fact, the institution of a divided Europe which was hollowed out for some time and has now broken down. With it, the focus of historicization has begun to shift as well. Niethammer's oral history of the Ruhr, among others, indicated this new trend.[8] He and his collaborators explored the place of the National Socialist experience and of memory in the remaking of postwar society. These were first and tentative steps in an altogether new and different project of historicization of the Third Reich that entails the exploration of its after-history into a present whose undoing we are now experiencing. Too much contemporary history has been prehistory of the Nazi period and too little has been the after-history of the cataclysmic years between the depression and the postwar recovery into the present.[9]

In historicizing what had been the present until a short while ago, the study of the causes of the Third Reich is now superseded by the study of its consequences for national and international society in Europe. The historical or political critique of the remnants of a past age from the vantage point of an invulnerable present gives way to an exploration of "the subject(s) of history" that have shaped mid-twentieth-century Europe. These are the same subjects in the Third Reich as they are in the postwar years, albeit in radically changed (international) political configurations. Who are these subjects and where are they concentrated? This question can be answered only when historians begin to make sense of the Third Reich as a crucial, if vanishing, moment in the

---

[7] Intentionalists and structuralists alike see the National Socialist regime self-destruct: Ian Kershaw, *The Nazi Dictatorship: Problems and Perspectives of Interpretation*, 2d ed. (London, 1989), pp. 131–49.

[8] Lutz Niethammer, ed., *"Die Jahre weiß man nicht, wo man die heute hinsetzen soll": Faschismus-Erfahrungen im Ruhrgebiet* (Berlin, 1983); and *"Hinterher merkt man, daß es richtig war, daß es schiefgegangen ist": Nachkriegs-Erfahrung im Ruhrgebiet* (Berlin, 1983); Lutz Niethammer and Alexander von Plato, eds., *"Wir kriegen jetzt andere Zeiten": Auf der Suche nach der Erfahrung des Volkes in nachfaschistischen Ländern* (Berlin, 1985).

[9] Among the growing number of books which have reversed this trend, see Werner Durth, *Deutsche Architekten: Biographische Verflechtungen, 1900–1970* (Brunswick, 1986); Simon Reich, *The Fruits of Fascism: Postwar Prosperity in Historical Perspective* (Ithaca, N.Y., 1990); H. Bude, *Lebenskonstruktionen sozialer Aufsteiger aus der Flakhelfer-Generation* (Frankfurt, 1987).

making of the postwar European order—an absent and repressed, partially destroyed and partially overcome origin that has left its mark on the whole period and the subjects that shaped it.

If these origins are denied, resistance against the Third Reich will remain misused. The main purpose of resistance studies turns against the practice of resistance in expurgating the mark of origin that was so courageously fought by resisters. The issue here is not misreading the past but misrepresenting the present in misusing resistance history. Resistance studies turn into an effort to block out the lasting effects of the Nazi regime, where resistance during the Third Reich called for vigilance and an ongoing postwar struggle to overcome the practices of the Third Reich. Behind the institutional barrier of the Allied victory, resistance as historiography could come to articulate the separation of the past from a present in societies whose experience proved to be far more continuous than their history.

This is not to deny that resistance history has undergone a process of professionalization. In the decade after the war, the sacrificial monumentalism of official commemorations made resisters into heroes whose actions saved society. Resisters sacrificed their lives so that the present could be set free and an overwhelming memory could be exorcized. The commemoration of resisters separated the past into a discrete province of time—or became, in the more theologically fascinating pieces, the embodiment of transcendence in the modern age.[10] The death of the resisters was the end of the Nazi "period" or, in any case, its spiritual overcoming. Their deaths, rather than their lives, created a fictitious genealogy of the "spirit," a redemption of the many in the present by the precious few in what became "the past"— perceived as a metaphysical clash between good and evil—as a result of their murder.[11]

This totemic use of resistance came under sustained attack. More detailed research revealed an increasingly ambiguous reality of resistance in which affirmation and resistance became inseparably intertwined, and sharply cut taxonomies between resisters and Nazis dissolved. The monumental image of resistance gave way to an exploration of the shifting grounds of cooperation, affirmation, self-defense, rebelliousness, and outright resistance.[12] The sober-

---

[10] Among others, Gerhard Besier and Gerhard Ringshausen, eds., *Bekenntnis, Widerstand, Martyrium: Von Barmen 1934 bis Plötzensee 1944* (Göttingen, 1986).

[11] See, among the earliest examples, Romano Guardini, *Die Waage des Daseins: Rede zum Gedächtnis von Sophie und Hans Scholl, Christoph Probst, Alexander Schmorell, Willi Graf und Professor Dr. Huber* (Tübingen and Stuttgart, 1946).

[12] This development can be traced in the oeuvre of Hans Mommsen, whose ground-breaking work on resistance remains solidly within the domain of political-institutional history; see his "Gesellschaftsbild und Verfassungspläne des deutschen Widerstands," in *Der deutsche Widerstand gegen Hitler,* ed. W. Schmithenner and

ing effects of the uncertain boundaries between resistance and collaboration and the murkiness of attributing unequivocal goals to acts of resistance were quite universal. Institutional actors like "the church," "the military," "the communist movement," or the "working class" were particularly affected by this reassessment and were commonly stripped of their resistance gloriole. Resistance appeared less motivated by a "rebellion of consciousness"[13] than by much more calculated and circumspect considerations that grew as often out of competition and rivalries within the apparatus of the Third Reich as out of deep inner conviction. Historiography replaced mythology.

However, historiographic revisionism did not alter the basic thrust of resistance studies in one crucial respect. One trend of scholarship concentrated on individuals (like the members of the Kreisauer Kreis or the White Rose) to show the circumstances of their resistance; increasingly it focused on the long and solitary struggle that led them into resistance, their courage and moral rectitude.[14] A second and, perhaps, more prevalent school of studies focused on societal groups and subcultures that defended their space through cunning and the tenacity of localisms. Perhaps the single most important controversy focused on the appropriateness of what Martin Broszat had called *Resistenz*, that is, "the many 'small' forms of civil courage that could be expected from every contemporary as opposed to the main stream of fearful adjustment or enthusiastic support for the

---

Hans Buchheim (Cologne, 1966), "Begriff und Problematik des deutschen Widerstands gegen Hitler in der zeitgeschichtlichen Forschung," in *Widerstandsbewegung in Deutschland und in Polen während des Zweiten Weltkrieges* (Brunswick, 1983), "Fritz-Dietlof von der Schulenburg und die preußische Tradition," *Vierteljahrshefte für Zeitgeschichte* 32 (1984): 213–39, and "Der Widerstand gegen Hitler und die deutsche Gesellschaft," in *Der Widerstand gegen den Nationalsozialismus: Die deutsche Gesellschaft und der Widerstand gegen Hitler,* ed. Jürgen Schmädeke and Peter Steinbach (Munich and Zürich, 1985).

[13] *Vollmacht des Gewissens,* 2 vols., ed. Europäische Publikation e.V. (Frankfurt am Main, 1965).

[14] The erosion of a postwar worship of sacrificial resistance initially engendered a new interest in resisters and their aspirations and thought. The shift from group portraits of the *Weiße Rose* to the recovery of the doubts, hesitations, and convictions of individuals indicate this development very well. (See Christiane Moll's essay in this volume.) A similar reassessment is evident even for the conservative resistance, where the near-fundamentalist convictions of a Helmuth James von Moltke have impressed many researchers and have cast even more doubt on the Wilhelmine scheming of military and political notables. The intense deliberations on Dietrich Bonhoeffer are perhaps the best example of this turn. The case of Bonhoeffer also points to an increasingly international concern, less with German resistance as such than with the spiritual and intellectual foundations of resistance—the making of a moral politics and its spiritual foundations.

regime."[15] Both orientations came under sustained scrutiny and led to repeated and controversial efforts to develop new and more appropriate taxonomies for bringing together various resistance activities.[16] But both schools agreed fundamentally in interpreting resistance as a matter of opposition exclusively against a tyrannical state—and as a mark that separated the past from the present.

In these studies, the Nazi regime became a system of "occupation," of an exceptionally cruel *Herrschaft* of the state and its apparatuses pressing down on an otherwise intact and separate, if fraying, community. Here, of course, the German and, for that matter, Austrian revisionists met or tried to associate with the far more compelling, if on the whole no less fictitious, history of the Italian and French resistance movements. Creating distance to the past in commemorating oppositional islands was the key issue in all these enterprises.[17] The main theme became survival and continuity; its prerequisite was to find a "usable past" which was ultimately found in the myth of local integrity and autonomy.[18]

In both schools of historiography, distance was achieved in what is the founding act of history: by collecting individual cases of resistance; separating and segregating them from the rest of society, wherever the regime had not done so with its persecution of what the Nazis considered traitors, offenders, deviants, and malcontents; and in fusing them in a new historical collective— "the resistance movement." The latter denoted a collectivity that was

---

[15] Martin Broszat, "Resistenz und Widerstand: Zwischenbilanz eines Forschungsprojekts," in *Herrschaft und Gesellschaft im Konflikt,* vol. 4 of *Bayern in der NS Zeit,* ed. Martin Broszat, Elke Fröhlich, and Anton Grossmann (Munich and Vienna, 1981), p. 693.

[16] Among others, Richard Löwenthal, "Widerstand im totalen Staat," in *Widerstand und Verweigerung in Deutschland, 1933–1945,* ed. Richard Löwenthal and Patrick von zur Mühlen (Berlin and Bonn, 1984), pp. 11–24; Peter Steinbach, ed., *Widerstand:* (Cologne, 1987); Wilfried Breyvogel, "Resistenz, Widersinn und Opposition: Jugendwiderstand im Nationalsozialismus," in *Piraten, Swings und Junge Garde: Jugendwiderstand im Nationalsozialismus,* ed. Wilfried Breyvogel (Bonn, 1991), pp. 9–16.

[17] The term *Abwehr* (defense of autonomy) is most emphatically used in the interpretation of Catholic resistance. Winfried Becker, "Politische Neuordnung aus der Erfahrung des Widerstands: Katholizismus und Union," in Steinbach, ed., pp. 261–92; Heinz Hürten, "Selbstbehauptung und Widerstand der katholischen Kirche," in Schmädecke and Steinbach, eds. (n. 12 above), pp. 240–53.

[18] This seems to me the core of the Broszat debate with Friedlander (see n. 6 above). I see little difference in this respect between the more conservative and institutional school, on the one hand, and the more liberal and social-history-oriented school, on the other. For the problem of a "usable past," see Charles S. Maier, *The Unmasterable Past: History, Holocaust, and German National Identity* (Cambridge, Mass., 1988).

constituted by historians over and against the variety of resistances against the Nazi regime. In the name of history or, more recently, in the name of plurality, diversity, and justice a collective was created that substituted for the actual absence of solidarity.[19] Resistance as a unified or "integral" activity *(Gesamt-gegnerschaft* [integral resistance])[20] and as a representative activity— facilitating the accommodation of political, cultural, or social difference— only existed as history. Resistance was invested with a quality that emerged, if at all, after the fact, *nachholender Widerstand,* in posthumous acts of overcoming the scatteredness and sheer incongruity of resistance acts, the loneliness of resisters and their families and networks, as well as their mutual hostilities. In short, resistance historiography became the posthumous act of inventing communities, creating fictitious solidarities where the breakdown of solidarity had become and continued to be the insurmountable issue. Resistance became ever more a substitute for the communities that had ceased to cohere and could not be revived.[21] It had become, in theological and historiographical terms, a simulacrum.

In pinpointing the impulse of resistance studies as the making whole in history what had fallen apart in life (and possibly as a consequence of the Nazi regime), we can begin to resituate the problematic of resistance. For the central theme of resistance and resistance historiography can no longer be defined in reference to the rejection of a tyrannical regime as documented in the persecution of the resisters by the regime. There is, instead, a more basic

[19] On the absence of solidarity, see esp. Robert Gellately, "Surveillance and Disobedience: Aspects of Political Policing of Nazi Germany," in *Germans against Nazism: Nonconformity, Opposition and Resistance in the Third Reich,* ed. Francis R. Nicosia and Laurence D. Stokes (New York and Oxford, 1990), pp. 15–36; Timothy W. Mason, "The Third Reich and the German Left: Persecution and Resistance," in *The Challenge of the Third Reich,* ed. Headley Bull (Oxford, 1986); Reinhard Mann, *Protest und Kontrolle im Dritten Reich: Nationalsozialistische Herrschaft im Alltag einer Rheinischen Großstadt* (Frankfurt am Main, 1987).

[20] Peter Steinbach, "Widerstand gegen den Nationalsozialismus: Zur Eröffnung der ständigen Ausstellung 'Widerstand gegen den Nationalsozialismus' in der Gedankstätte Deutscher Widerstand in Berlin," *Nachrichten und Berichte der Universität Passau* 58 (July 1989): 2–8; see also his "Die [*sic*] Widerstand als Thema der politischen Zeitgeschichte: Ordnungsversuche vergangener Wirklichkeit und politischer Reflexionen," in *Bekenntnis, Widerstand, Martyrium: Von Barmen 1934 bis Plötzensee 1944,* ed. Gerhard Besier and Gerhard Ringshausen (Göttingen, 1986), pp. 11–74; and "Wem gehört der Widerstand gegen Hitler?" *Dachauer Hefte* 6 (November 1990): 56–72.

[21] This argument is mainly the result of new research on the working class, but it could be usefully applied to other segments of German society as well. Tilla Siegel, *Leistung und Lohn in der nationalsozialistischen "Ordnung der Arbeit"* (Opladen, 1989); Carola Sachse et al., eds., *Angst, Belohnung, Sucht und Ordnung: Herrschafts-mechanismen im Nationalsozialismus* (Opladen, 1989).

theme for the long waves of resistance, upheaval, and protest: How is solidarity achieved in deeply divided societies and in a Europe that is profoundly disorganized?

To explore this question means first and foremost to inquire into the remaking, even reinvention of oppositional activities in the concrete historical situation of the 1930s and 1940s. Resistance as radical oppositional activity aimed at the overthrow of unjust rule had, of course, a long bourgeois, religious, and socialist tradition. But if some of these traditions survived the onslaught of the Gestapo, albeit in a much reduced form, they were unable to cope with shifting oppositional moods and the rise of new subjects of resistance. They were most of all incapable of coming to grips with a basic popular affirmation of the Nazi regime, which could go hand in hand with a puzzling popular insistence, in opposition to Nazi institutions, on depoliticized partial publics.[22] The simultaneity of affirmation and distance, an altogether new but from now on recurring experience, indicated that the act of resistance was not just wrested from the overwhelming power of the regime but also from habits of oppositional behavior that no longer worked.

To elaborate the problematic of solidarity, second, means to explore the reinvention of solidarities. For again, there were well-established languages of collectivity, but none of them remained unscathed. In fact, the deep crisis of these collective identifications—of liberalism, communism, and nationalism in the nineteenth-century tradition—was one of the key difficulties in mobilizing resistance. In the end, new languages of collectivity emerged. National identification—often formulated in a curious reversal of Nazi ideologemes as a strategy of distantiation from occupiers and collaborators (a wartime as much as a postwar project)—was one crucial medium of reconciliation. Europeanization as the discovery and, indeed, invention of a common humanistic heritage against the brutal regime of exploitation imposed by the Nazis was a second, if more tentative agenda. Above all, there was and is yet another form of reconciliation that so far has received only scant attention. It is the recognition that human bonds include the radically other—Jews as much as those who had formed ethnic underclasses or were labeled "asocial." For it is human solidarity above all which National Socialist politics attacked, threatened, and destroyed. Of all the identifications, the bond to the radically other was unquestionably the most difficult to mobilize; it is also the most difficult to remember and the first to be forgotten.

If we redefine the central theme of resistance as the problem of how to create solidarity, the terror of Nazism is not diminished but put into its historical

---

[22] Detlev Peukert, *Inside Nazi Germany: Conformity, Opposition and Racism in Everyday Life* (New Haven, Conn., and London, 1987), esp. pp. 145 ff. Still the best account of this tension is Günter Grass, *The Tin Drum* (New York, 1990).

place as the crucible for the formation of a new Europe. Resistance is not synthesized into a historical object but becomes an ongoing and continuing struggle, in various articulations, to ascertain bonds of collectivity and to find a language of communicating them. To study the difficulty of putting together what had been rent asunder by the Nazi regime, of reconceiving human bonds, and of restoring a sense of polity is the charge of resistance studies which do not efface the mark of violence on postwar societies. Such efforts take up Bonhoeffer's bequest in that they become the scholarly reflection of ongoing processes of creating, in a slower and more piecemeal but also more deliberate process than either the totemic or the redemptive postwar historiography suggests, new solidarities, post-Holocaust publics *(Öffentlichkeiten)* on a national and European level.

The challenge then consists in reinterpreting resistance against the Third Reich within a context that reaches from the 1930s to the 1980s and 1990s. In this forward-extended context the unsuccessful oppositions both in the Third Reich and in occupied Europe turn into a first, death-defying deed in a much longer history or histories. Resistance in the Third Reich leads into a long series of oppositional practices that have run up against the social, political, and cultural formations—on national and international scales—that germinated in the wake of the world economic crisis in Europe. Resistance against the Third Reich will always hold a special place in the articulation of oppositional movements during this age. But its place is not outside of European history and its time does not end in 1945; it is part of a history that begins in the 1930s rather than ending there.

Thinking resistance against unjust rule and inhumanity thus entwines the drama of existential decisions to challenge the powers of tyrannical rule with that most general of all political problems, faced by every generation anew, of how to constitute social and political order. In focusing on the former, the study of resistance has always had the pathos of history on its side, even when it concentrated on everyday expressions. Yet it is the latter, the significance of resistance for the constitution of civil order, that emerges as the main and common concern.

The Subjects of Resistance

Professional historiography had always known that resistance had to be wrested from the powerful definition which the regime's persecution imposed on its enemies. However, as laudable as the recovery of all acts of resistance may be, an approach in which everyone—from members of the Jewish underground, military and bourgeois notables, to communists and youth gangs—is summarily integrated overlooks that the subjects of resistance are unequal and that their acts are radically dissimilar. As important as the recovery of persecution records is, such accounts say little about the subject positions of the persecuted. We need, instead, an understanding of resistance that makes resistance into a distinguishable practice that transcends both Nazi and professional historiographic definitions.

Resistance historiography is rather curious in this respect. It surely does not lack careful reconstructions of the social origins or the milieu of resisters. But looking at communities that harbored resisters through the lens of Gestapo records, historians tend to freeze these communities in their relation to resisters and to resistance. They appear as working-class, peasant, or aristocratic milieus as if those milieus were something fixed and steady. Moreover, historians have come to divide up their labor so as to study one particular milieu (of Protestant ministers, youth gangs, intellectuals) as if societies were all parceled up into autonomous micro-communities. On this basis we learn a great deal about resistance activities and about resisters, but it is virtually impossible to comprehend anything about the place of resistance in the remaking of European society. Resistance studies cannot make sense of expressions of self-will as opposed to resistance beyond noisy debates over definitional issues. More important, they are unable to assess the very real differences among resistance activities, which depend on the subject positions of the resisters. Both problems indicate a thorough lack of understanding of the transformation of European societies in this period of upheaval.

Even a casual reading of records reveals how profoundly unstable communities and groups had become by the 1940s. We consistently read about communities in upheaval and transition, voluntary or forced migration, the mixing together of groups and ethnicities, and the very unclear separation of resistance and collaboration. This is as true for French resistance as it is true for Penzberg, the Bavarian mining town, or the famous Infantry Regiment No. 9, home of some of the main military resisters. Such observations suggest that a trigonometric history with its two fixed points of Gestapo records and milieu studies misses out on exactly the key to resistance—the struggle for the reformation of a nascent society in the midst of massive social upheaval. This is what we learn in turn from the diligent counterintelligence of the SOPADE or from the occasional observations of priests and ministers.[23] They report on the threat to and the collapse of traditions of solidarity and resistance as well as the weakening of autonomy as a result—not so much due to the attractions of National Socialism but to the power of mobility and privilege. The rise of a new and privileged society in the midst of the wreckage of the war disrupted traditional milieus and created opportunities for collaboration—but ultimately also shaped new modes of resistance.

[23] *Deutschland-Berichte der Sozialdemokratischen Partei Deutschlands (SOPADE), 1934–1940* (Salzhausen, 1980) are an invaluable source in this regard.

The most telling test for an interpretation of this transformation is the assessment of youth resistance. While one would not want to mistake the self-will of individuals and groups or the style of the *Swings* or *Zazous* for resistance, they surely account for something.[24] Similarly, the notorious run-ins between the Hitler Youth and various kinds of youth gangs all over the Reich cannot be called resistance, but they were effective in curtailing the reach of the Hitler Youth. At issue was a struggle over the control and terrain of an emergent leisure culture—the alternative to state-organized, institutional leisure activity or privatized desire organized as public consumption. In many ways, this conflagration within the Third Reich was but the continuation of the older Weimar Republic tensions between institutional cultures (of socialists and Catholics) and commodity cultures (film palaces); it functioned as a transition point to the subsequent postwar upheaval.[25] These struggles pitted the National Socialist institutions of youth culture not just against families and cultural institutions but also against the emergent partial publics of a young generation.[26]

These struggles were shaped by a wide range of opinions and orientations. Some participants wanted to preserve a precious past, some dreamed of a utopian future, and some simply wanted to have their fun and games, which included beating up on the Hitler Youth. Resistance this was not, but it was corrosive in terms of all efforts to control and coordinate a nascent consumer culture, not just private life in a tradition-bound culture, as is often argued. The point here is that resistance must be seen against the background of a highly mobile and reasonably privileged society which was in the process of working out new kinds of identities with and against the Nazi state and its institutions, with and against the occupiers. The tyrannical regime is, in other words, not the sole focus of activities (as a foreshortened vision of so much of professional history would like it) but the space within which struggles over identity and difference of various kinds took place. The National Socialist regime attempted to master and to control these struggles, and it was a terroristic force in this process. But it was never the sole reason why these contentions existed in the first place.

[24] Arno Klönne, "Jugendprotest und Jugendopposition: Von der HJ-Erziehung zum Cliquenwesen der Kriegszeit," in Broszat, Fröhlich, and Grossmann, eds. (n. 15 above), 4:527–620; and Breyvogel, ed. (n. 16 above) provide comprehensive surveys.

[25] Detlev Peukert, "Die 'Halbstarken': Protestverhalten von Arbeiterjugendlichen zwischen Wilhelminischem Reich und Ära Adenauer," *Zeitschrift für Pädagogik* 30 (1984): 533–48.

[26] Detlev Peukert, "Edelweißpiraten, Meuten, Swing: Jugendsubkulturen im Dritten Reich," in *Sozialgeschichte der Freizeit: Untersuchungen zum Wandel der Alltagskultur in Deutschland,* ed. Gerhard Huck (Wuppertal, 1980), pp. 307–27.

If we consider the Third Reich as a highly charged and extremely violent moment in the reforging of German society, it is no longer farfetched to argue that activities (such as gatherings of youth gangs of all kinds) which were not meant to overthrow or even to oppose the Third Reich had inadvertent consequences that undermined the regime and its policies in a far more effective manner than many, if not most, acts of actual resistance—at least as far as Germany is concerned. More generally, any unequivocal definition of resistance tends to exclude a whole array of activities that effectively countered the purpose of the regime without ever breaking with it; at the same time, any loose definition of resistance takes away from the sharp edge of the decision to sacrifice one's life in order to overthrow unjust and inhuman rule.[27] But both activities—formation of partial publics and resistance to create counter-publics—have to be seen side by side.

The radical opposite of youth gangs is not German resistance (although resisters' readiness to give their lives to overthrow the regime sets them apart) but the forced mobilization of those who had no escape. Only the juxtaposition of German oppositional practices with those of the subaltern begins to make sense of the location of German or, for that matter, Austrian resistance and of the European resistance movements at large. Nowhere do we encounter the limits of a pluralizing resistance historiography more acutely than in the effort to integrate Jewish resistance under the common denominator of resistance in any meaningful fashion. The problematic of Jewish resistance, itself a thorny and hotly debated issue,[28] makes instantly evident the powers of differentiation that the Nazi regime imposed on the process of social transformation. The deliberations of Jewish groups and of local Jewish communities and their wavering between affirmation, disbelief, and resistance may have superficial and formal similarities with other debates over complic-

---

[27] While this debate is directed against the notion of popular dissent as "resistance," it seems, at this point of the debate, to apply far more to the problem of Catholic resistance. The latter is one of the few remaining areas where "ducking under," institutional defense of autonomy, altruism, resistance as overthrow of the regime, and postwar rise of the CDU/CSU are casually fused. See Klaus Gotto and Konrad Repgen, eds., *Die Katholiken und das Dritte Reich* (Mainz, 1983). A useful corrective are the papers of Alfred Delp, *Gesammelte Schriften,* ed. Roman Bleistein, 4 vols. (Frankfurt, 1982–84).

[28] See generally on German-Jewish resistance, Arnold Paucker, "Jewish Resistance in Germany: The Facts and the Problems" (Gedenkstätte Deutscher Widerstand, Berlin, 1992, mimeographed). In lieu of the extensive references to eastern European resistance, see the plea for the necessity of Jewish resistance as a starting point for thinking about the Holocaust: Emil Fackenheim, *The Jewish Return into History: Reflections in the Age of Auschwitz and a New Jerusalem* (New York, 1978), and *To Mend the World* (New York, 1982).

ity, compliance, or resistance, but the Jewish subject-positions in occupied Europe were so radically opposite from those of any other resister that any all-embracing notion of resistance is facile.

German and Austrian resistance as well as the resistance from most parts of occupied Europe (as opposed to many other forms of rebellion and opposition) was crucially predicated on the conscious, if often spontaneous, choice of death over life in order to oppose the inhuman practice of the Nazi regime. The reverse is the case for Jews in occupied Europe: they did not have a choice over death but only a marginal choice of survival in escaping the regime. We glimpse here an inverted world in which many decisions made by resisters appeared to be similar, to be sure, but in which the grounds and consequences of decisions were exactly opposite. For Jews there were no rules of the game, no spaces of autonomy, no voice that mattered, no partial community with the persecutor. Hence, for Jews, every act of establishing ties among themselves was resistance, as has been argued by a powerful strand of historiography. For it is the effort of constituting in transcripts, hidden from the persecutors, what is denied to them: community.[29] To make public this act of community building was ipso facto insurrection, an articulation of autonomy, the struggle with a deadly enemy over the right to existence.

The Jewish turn to resistance was much more starkly articulated partly because of the terror of annihilation and partly because of the long history of oppression; however, there is an element in it that sheds light on a condition of all resistance. Jews asserting difference and identity had a chance of survival only if they left behind communal traditions of affirmation as they had been passed on from one generation to the next. Assertion of identity became active resistance by breaking away from traditional communities. The inward concentration on community was not only the result of a violently imposed segregation but was also a precondition for annihilation. Resistance within Jewish communities required breaking out of existing milieus into emigration, into hiding, or into armed resistance.

Because of its extreme nature, the case of Jewish resistance helps us see as basic the dual bind that haunts most other forms of resistance—and that includes organized resistance movements in occupied Europe. "Resistance" as it is commonly understood was the opposition of all those who did or could, in principle, find a place in the regime's newly emerging social order in Germany and Austria as well as in occupied countries.[30] Resistance thus

---

[29] This is the main thrust of the postcolonial debate on resistance. James C. Scott, *Domination and the Arts of Resistance: Hidden Transcripts* (New Haven, Conn., and London, 1990). It is worth noting that the kind of resistance which European resistance history addresses has come under sustained attack in the "subaltern studies."

[30] Czesław Madajczyk, *Faszyzm i okupacje, 1938–1945: Wykonywanie okupacji przez państwa Osi w Europie,* 2 vols. (Poznań, 1983–84).

reverberated with the deadly divides that segregated and divided European societies. What we know as resistance was the resistance of those who had a chance of collaboration. While their margins of maneuver varied greatly because of the extreme inequality of a nascent European society, this does not alter the basic paradox. Resistance emerged from some kind of integration and involvement in the machinations of the regime.

There is perhaps one exception if we consider areas liberated by partisans. But even if these areas were supplied from the outside and even if they managed to maintain tenuous control over a region, they were never sovereign, autonomous islands in the sea of occupation. They formed an "underground" beneath a society that was tied into the nexus of the occupation regime. The Soviet suspicion of guerrillas, while clearly laced with Stalinist paranoia, is not entirely unwarranted.[31] Liberated areas were necessarily involved in a double game of involvement and resistance. But note first that resistance involved negotiations in varying degrees, even in the most brutalized areas like eastern Poland or the Krajina (literally: border) between Serbia and Croatia. The reality of resistance, be it in Berlin or in the Krajina, is one of turning involvement into refusal as opposed to participation.

Such refusal, in turn, required deliberately stepping out of existing communities and milieus. "Ducking under" to weather the storm, "beating the system" was a common solution to coping with the Nazis, but it was the blueprint for collaboration rather than the mainspring of resistance.[32] Reliance on traditional forms of protest proved to be outright disastrous, as the many histories of communist resistance attest.[33] Resistance flourished only in as much as it was capable of change, of adopting and inventing new practices of opposition. This was not just a condition of the relentless terror of the regime but of the changing nature of society and its struggle over order and normality.

Resistance, then, entails the deliberate decision to step out of existing "communities" in order to challenge the regime. This decision to resist was made against a moving background, as it were, and against gradations of involvement in the everyday life of a tyrannical regime. It was made against all forms of accommodation that declared as normal what was outrageous and exceptional. Simple withdrawal or a neutral stance were not possible under the conditions of the Nazi regime. However, this omnibus definition is too broad

---

[31] John A. Armstrong, *Soviet Partisans in World War II* (Madison, Wis., 1964); Jorgen Haestrup, *Europe Ablaze: An Analysis of the History of the European Resistance Movement, 1939–1945* (Odense, 1978).

[32] Jill Stephenson, "War and Society in Württemberg, 1939–1945: Beating the System," *German Studies Review* 8 (1985): 89–101.

[33] Detlev Peukert, *Die KPD im Widerstand: Verfolgung und Untergrundarbeit an Rhein und Ruhr* (Wuppertal, 1980).

to make any sense. But what is the difference between resistance and a grievance or a discontent? The answer is not, as is often argued, the intent to overthrow the regime. Instead it is the opposition against the violence of the regime wherever and whenever it occurred. Hence, neither village communities that withdrew nor youth gangs that opposed the Hitler Youth fit the description, although they were undoubtedly corrosive elements that undermined Nazi and fascist efforts to control public and private life. Effective it may have been, resistance it was not. To refuse involvement in the violence of the regime, to oppose the societies that tolerated it or thrived on it, and to destroy the powers that enforced it—this was and is resistance.

The Obligation to Strangers

What does it mean to reject a society that underwrites opportunities of collaboration? How can scholarship elucidate the nature of nascent counterpublics?

As long as historians use an "occupation model" in order to explain resistance—that is, the presumption of some residual free space or essence that remains intrinsically outside of domination like the institution of the church, a particular milieu, or an immutable sense of class or nation—resistance studies will never find an answer. This notion of resistance has always already externalized the "enemy" (Bonhoeffer), set them apart in the elsewhere of institutions, occupying forces, or Germans at large. It deflects the Nazi rule into a problem of the state apparatus. However, the Nazi regime lived off its ability to instrumentalize enmity time and again in various local contexts. It fed on the European proliferation of exclusions and genocides which pivoted around the state-organized annihilation of European Jewry and the concomitant, if always incomplete, formation of a racist core society. Inasmuch as the Nazi regime was successful both in Germany and as a German-Austrian regime occupying Europe, it hooked onto social, political, ethnic, and gender formations under duress and exploited cleavages to turn them into civil wars. Tyrannical power did not reside with the state and its coercive agencies alone but was embodied in all social transactions—in the exercise of everyday routines and the self-evident acceptance of their meaning.[34]

Only the individual and collective counterassertion of a responsibility for one's neighbor undid the violence of linkage that held the Third Reich together. Resistance against the Third Reich thus entailed, crucially, the

---

[34] On the routinization of terror in everyday life, see Heide Gerstenberger and Dorothea Schmidt, eds., *Normalität oder Normalisierung: Geschichtswerkstätten und Faschismusanalyse* (Münster, 1987); and esp. Robert Gellately, *The Gestapo and German Society: Enforcing Racial Policy, 1933–1945* (Oxford, 1990).

recognition of human bonds with the "other." For it was the rejection of the possibility of human solidarity with strangers—the critical as well as moral presupposition of civil society—that the National Socialist regime made into the foundation for its existence.[35] We might want to call this politics of human solidarity a "moral politics," countering the divisive politics of the Nazi *Gemeinschaft*. It is here that we find a reconsideration of the moral impulse of resistance—clearly not as the call of conscience, but as the working through of the modes of affirmation demanded and imposed by an inhuman regime to create the moral choices of resistance. None of these choices were unambiguous, and all of them required a deliberate conversion—an act that many anti-Nazis, among them the most successful postwar politicians, chose not to undergo. Resisters differed from other anti-Nazis in their commitment to convert state and society.

These moral dimensions of resistance are difficult to grasp as long as society is considered a natural preserve of normalcy outside of and separate from Nazi crimes. As long as the Nazis were "the evil up there" (and this was, indeed, the way they were commonly talked about),[36] resistance could be easily understood as a process of regaining one's sense in grasping or, as the case may be, holding onto basic values and transcendental truths. In this fashion, resistance is reduced to a moment of recognition of what had always been there: the transcendence of human conscience, the universalism of human rights, or the transcendental normativism of Law or Beauty.[37] Unlike social historians, who sought their referent in the autonomy of the milieu, moral historians have tended to seek theirs in a metaphysics of norms and values and their institutional facilitators: the church(es), the state, and the academy or, alternatively, the party.[38]

---

[35] Allan Wolfe, *Whose Keeper? Social Science and Moral Obligation* (Berkeley and Los Angeles, 1989); Zygmunt Bauman, *Modernity and the Holocaust* (Ithaca, N.Y., 1990).

[36] Ian Kershaw, *Popular Opinion and Political Dissent in the Third Reich* (Oxford, 1983).

[37] On the legal dimensions of this issue, see Heinrich Oberreuter, "Widerstandsrecht als Aspekt politischer Kultur," in Steinbach, ed. (n. 16 above), pp. 293–310. The relevance of this argument in the present is immediately evident, if we consider the trial and conviction of two East German border guards, in which the presiding judge ruled that "not everything that is legal is right," arguing further "at the end of the 20th century . . . no one has the right to ignore his conscience when it comes to killing people on behalf of the power structure," and sentencing the two on counts of the violation of "a basic human right," i.e., to emigrate. Stephen Kinzer, "2 East German Guards Convicted of Killing Man as He Fled to West," *New York Times* (January 21, 1992), sec. A.

[38] The withdrawal of the German educated bourgeoisie from public responsibility is nowhere more evident than in the absence both of academic resistance and the lack of plausible suggestions for rebuilding moral education. An exception is Friedrich Meinecke, *The German Catastrophe: The Social and Historical Influence Which Led*

In many ways, the insistence on the articulation of transcendental values—as opposed to a historical-situational ethic—is the perfect conservative parallel to liberal historiography's insistence on dissent as resistance. These historians argue not for moral action but for *doxa*—be it that of the church and its revelation in resistance; that of the communist resistance, reasserting the vanguard position of the party; or that of civil institutions, whether raison d'état or human rights.[39] Their vision of order runs counter to a situational notion of resistance. Instead, it aims at institutional closure of social/moral action.

It is doubtful if this approach could even explain the calculated single-issue protestations of the representatives of moral institutions like the Bekennende Kirche or the Catholic hierarchy, even if the latter were motivated by insistence on the Bible or, respectively, canonic law. Like so many other institutions, the churches were involved in a sharp competition over a share of state power. They were disadvantaged, to be sure: their freedom of action was curtailed, and, in response, they engaged in sharp counterattacks. But this meant that they were playing the game of competition, on unequal terrain, which pushed and pulled the Nazi regime in many directions and gave it its polymorphous shape. Like the nascent consumer culture, this competitive jostling of bishops and prelates may have done more to corrode the regime-centered organization of society than actual resistance, but it did not overcome the National Socialist state.

Some of the best-known Catholic, Protestant, and military resisters were unequivocal in denouncing this kind of "resistance." Resistance did not spring from these moral institutions but from their failure to uphold a sense of obligation. Resistance materialized from the rejection of everyday routines that led to the implicit or explicit formulation of a moral praxis. Moral consciousness emerged as a result of social action rather than preceding it. Rather than being a moment of revelation of eternal truth, resistance emerged as situational ethic—not as an assertion of what had always been right, but as a query of what ought to be right under changing circumstances. The point here is twofold: first, an inquiry into the motivation for resistance emphasizes the authority of social actors rather than that of transcendental institutions; second, it explores the struggle of regaining moral judgment.[40]

---

to the *Rise and Ruin of Hitler and Germany* (Cambridge, 1950) and his plea for Goethe communities.

[39] The most interesting case is the raison d'état as a *doxa* that has nearly vanished from the debate, even if it was one of the central issues during the 1940s and 1950s. See Gerhard Ritter, *Die Dämonie der Macht: Betrachtungen über Geschichte und Wesen des Machtstaates im politischen Denken der Neuzeit*, 6th ed. (Munich, 1948).

[40] Obviously, this interpretation is open to a position such as the one by Guardini (n. 11 above) who did not speak of the authority of the church, as conservative historians have come to argue, but of the revelation of God's grace in the decision for martyrdom by individuals.

The act of re-creating social bonds that had been sundered by the Nazi regime entailed first and foremost the active, personal decision of stepping out of the entangling and compromising environment of a racist and genocidal regime. This act was at once a most intimate and a socially conditioned process. It entailed a moment of personal recognition about one's place in the operation of the regime which led individuals beyond the routines of participation. It applied to the general staff officer who began to reflect upon, question, and reject the functionality of his work as much as to the nurse who had second thoughts about the sterilization of some of her patients or about euthanasia, not to mention the soldier who refused orders. The rescue of Jews or other persecuted individuals, escape aid at the borders, or acts of kindness to forced laborers were also among these activities. They all involved risks, often the risk of life, but their criminalization by the regime only underlined the main point. They countered directly and immediately the inhuman practices of the regime. Had tens of thousands in Germany or in occupied countries engaged in such acts, it would have made a different society. It is this resistance that undid, in everyday life, what the Nazi regime erected.[41]

This primary resistance was manifold and disconnected. But it was rarely what a melodramatic impulse would like it to be: innocence finally facing up to the brutal reality of the Nazi regime. On the contrary, the very same workers who helped forced laborers had often colluded with the institution of a new ethnic underclass. Professionals like military officers had managed to create the situation with which they broke. Armed resisters had collaborated before they joined resistance movements. The commonality of these actions consisted in reversing and undoing what had been socially instituted in the first place. It was a reactive process of forging human bonds that the Nazi society had severed. Resistance as altruism challenged the processes of functionalization and of a division of labor that systematically displaced the civic reciprocity of social action.[42] Such acts of resistance entailed the re-creation of a linkage between action and its social consequences, the constitution of a social horizon that negated the "violence of linkage" created by the regime.[43]

---

[41] Nechama Tec, *When Light Pierced the Darkness: Christian Rescue of Jews in Nazi-occupied Poland* (New York, 1986). Samuel Oliner and Pearl Oliner, *The Altruistic Personality: Rescuers of Jews in Nazi Europe* (New York and London, 1988). References are also in Deborah Dwork, *Children with a Star: Jewish Youth in Nazi Europe* (New York and London, 1991); and Ulrich Herbert, *Fremdarbeiter: Politik und Praxis des "Ausländer-Einsatzes" in der Kriegswirtschaft des Dritten Reiches* (Berlin and Bonn, 1985).

[42] See the theoretical argument in Bauman; and the narrative interpretation of Peukert, *Inside Nazi Germany* (n. 22 above).

[43] Oskar Negt and Alexander Kluge, *Geschichte und Eigensinn* (Frankfurt am Main, 1981), pp. 777 ff. Jacques Semelin, *Unarmed against Hitler: Civilian Resistance in Europe, 1939–1945* (Westport, Conn., 1993).

A skeptical postwar generation argued that these moral actions were few and far between. There is surely truth to this. Resistance remained an exception throughout the Third Reich. But it is worth considering possible distortions as a result of historiography's vision of order. First of all, there is the record of all those who stood accused and were imprisoned or killed, if not shot on the spot as often happened late in the war. It indicates that a considerable number of people countered the regime and paid for it with their lives. Thus, the soldiers who deserted or shot themselves in the foot or malingered are so conveniently forgotten because they rejected a society and its norms which survived the war.[44] Second, there are those who did not conform and got away with it, most likely because their superiors did not want to create trouble. The most notorious cases of this kind have come from *Einsatzgruppen* and security divisions, but similar cases appear virtually everywhere. The fact that these people got away with their refusal is perhaps less noteworthy than the fact that they did not come out with their story after the war.[45] Third, historians may have followed the Gestapo in looking at the wrong people, because both expected resistance to emanate from traditional institutions in traditional forms—the collective actions of the working class or the churches—only to discover that these were not the sites from which resistance came. To take but one example, there are extremely few studies on women at work and at home. While such studies do not at all indicate that women as a gender resisted,[46] they suggest a remarkable rebelliousness on the shop floor that had previously only been attributed to male workers as well as a public stubbornness that was usually reserved for male parishioners.[47]

This points to more than a casual oversight. For one thing, historians followed the logic of the Gestapo, which expected and persecuted classic modern forms of mass protest, secret organization, and expressions of discontent. For another, they modeled their notion of resistance after the self-interpretation of resistance organizations. These, in turn, recycled national resistance mythologies. As a result, whole nations came to believe in canonic examples for resistance—a parade of historical masks that had little

[44] Franz W. Seidler, *Prostitution, Homosexualität, Selbstverstümmelung: Probleme der deutschen Sanitätsführung, 1939–1945* (Neckargemünd, 1977).

[45] Helmut Krausnick and Hans-Heinrich Wilhelm, *Die Einsatzgruppen der SIPO und des SD, 1938–1942* (Stuttgart, 1978); Christopher Browning, *Ordinary Men: Reserve Police Battalion 101 and the Final Solution in Poland* (New York, 1992).

[46] Claudia Koonz, *Mothers in the Fatherland: Women, the Family, and Nazi Politics* (New York, 1987), shows quite visibly her disappointment.

[47] Annemarie Troeger, "Die Planung des Rationalisierungsproletariats: Zur Entwicklung der geschlechterspezifischen Arbeitsteilung und des weiblichen Arbeitsmarktes im Nationalsozialismus," in *Frauen in der Geschichte*, ed. Anette Kuhn and Jörn Rüsen (Düsseldorf, 1982), 2:245–98.

to do with what actually happened in the resistance against the Third Reich. The Home Army was modeled on the national insurrection movements in Poland, the *résistance* on the Jacobin ideal of the revolution in France, and the German resistance either on the mass organization of the working class and Catholics or on the idealistic individualism of literature in Germany. But this is exactly what resistance against the Third Reich was not, because the institutions for such resistance were smashed and their main protagonists drawn into the National Socialist mobilization of society.

The memory of the refusal to participate in the making of this new society, the sheer spirit of negation, or the acceptance of the obligation for others—this resistance was hidden after the war. It was never a mass phenomenon by any count, but the disavowal of the few indicates their defeat. But resistance it was. It emerged from new sites and mobilized new groups of people that had not previously been active in oppositional movements or had been active in very different capacities. Resistance against the Third Reich was, indeed, a "new beginning."

The history of resistance as an ongoing process entails the study of individual and collective choices and decisions. In these explorations, the monumental dimensions of a moralizing resistance history are abandoned to give way to an investigation of the struggles of individuals and whole groups to stem the violence that holds societies together. What emerges here is something akin to a moral history for the twentieth century. This is not a history of disciplining individuals into civil society, but it is a history of the social, political, and cultural efforts to establish bonds between people in a world in which "community" was no longer a given resource, but the supreme challenge.

THE SUBJECT OF HISTORY

All kinds of people did resist, but not quite the way historians envisioned it. The disjuncture between action and historical representation results from an implied sense of order that runs counter to the moral politics of resistance. Social historians were drawn to the defense of "classic modern" milieus, classes, and autonomies, as if this innocence of origins was the only means to save people from complicity.[48] They did not look for the discrepancies and fissures that resulted from the multiple rearrangements of German society, nor really for new forms, new sites, and new groups of people to enter the arena of oppositional organization. Political historians, in turn, remained wedded to institutions of authority and their defense, as if only this authoritative

[48] On the "classic modern," see Detlev Peukert, *Max Webers Diagnose der Moderne* (Göttingen, 1989), and his newly translated *The Weimar Republic* (London, 1991).

grounding of resistance turned social action into a moral one. They neither looked for the break-up of moral codes in a competitive, racist society nor for situationally motivated action, emanating from mundane working and living environments. The historians' vision remained glued to turn-of-the-century forms and fictions of oppositions and rebellions.

In part, these nostalgic visions of order were the result of the substitution effect of much resistance research. Resistance studies in Germany were never just an academic matter. Like few other topics, resistance studies offered moral education by nonresisters for nonresisters. As such they initially provided legitimation for the East and West German states as well as their hegemonic institutions, the church(es), the military, and *the* party, respectively. Official commemorations, such as that of July 20, 1944, are a good indication of this particular state control of memory.[49]

However, more important was the fact that this vision of order formed one aspect of the *imaginaire* of the new "subjects of history"—the societies that emerged from the war to rearrange themselves politically, within the confines of an increasingly divided Europe, as the dominant core of Europe. They rose with daunting consequence from the transnational reformation of a cluster of privileged European societies sustaining and sustained by renovated capitalist economies; those economies surfaced from the world economic crisis of the 1930s and the cauldron of war in both Germany and Austria as well as in central regions of occupied Europe. To insist on this joint trajectory is surely not to confuse the histories of the occupied with that of the occupiers. But it is to point to the difference between the subject of history and the subjects of resistance, between those who competed and those who refused. And it is to remind us of the divide between both the subject and the subjects on the one hand and the subalterns on the other who, if they were not annihilated or expelled from Europe, had no subjectivity, no voice, no choice, no history at

[49] The contrast with Austria is striking in this regard. Resistance research in Austria was largely a matter of former resisters, exemplified by the work of the Widerstandsarchiv in Vienna. It was memory work that was set against an incorporated politics that denied the past. As a result, resistance research remained very much an issue for outsiders and was taken up, not simply to chronicle those who had resisted or those who had been their murderers between 1938 and 1945, let alone to erect monuments for sacrifice in the service of an institutional idea, but to confront Austrian society with the fact that there had been resistance and collaboration in the first place. France provides yet another articulation of resistance memory. There, resistance became a moral monopoly of intellectuals in the postwar years. They turned their notion of resistance as existential choice against the state and its political-administrative elites and, indeed, against politics in the defense of the universally victimized and oppressed. This monopoly began to crack at exactly the moment in the 1970s when resistance became a public concern in Germany.

all. (Their memory, which could neither be annihilated nor transferred into history, is a different matter.)

At stake here is not simply the fact that after the war most everyone claimed to be a resister and, eventually, everyone came to be a victim as well. Whole nations claimed the mantle of resistance, whereas only a few acted and they did so remarkable late. This Orwellian double-speak is pervasive; it is widely believed but easy to see through. However, the challenge lies beyond the critique of individual or collective myths. For these myths hide another truth—not necessarily of collaboration but of the relentless transformation of Europe under the Nazi regime. The myth of resistance hides the violent transformation of Europe and its victims. It hides the institutions of social, ethnic, and racial divisions that were to shape postwar Europe. Resistance myths are so deceitful not because they claim something that was not but because they silence a process that did occur and continued into the postwar years: the remaking of European society. They hide the trace of violence that clings to postwar societies.

This is to suggest that defining resistance as opposition to the Nazi regime (with the intent to overthrow the regime) is not a very useful way to make sense of resistance. As much as resistance was directed against the powers of a tyrannical state, its object was the society which embodied that state and which survived. Resistance forms the counterpoint to an altogether overwhelming process of "institutional" social transformation that shaped mid-twentieth-century Europe. In turning against the Nazi regime, resisters called for the renovation of society and the deliberate reconstitution of its social bodies in a process of healing. Overthrowing the Nazi regime was only the first step in a process of social conversion.

Hence, efforts to rethink the place of European resistance need to take into account two historical configurations. First, they have to situate resistance in the remaking of the order of European nation-states and, within this international context, of citizenship and state power. Second, they have to take into account the spatial organization of Europe into core and peripheral societies. In this context, the difference between primarily agricultural regions (from Poland to Macedonia, southern Italy and Spain) and the formation of Fordist (mass production and mass consumption) societies (along the Po, Rhone, Loire, and Rhine—what has casually been named "Lotharingia") weigh in heavily. In all this, the Nazi regime played a pivotal role. It acted as the vanishing catalyst for an unequal and deeply divided European society that emerged from the cauldron of the 1930s and 1940s.

The role and place of these European core societies between the Po and the Rhine has confounded contemporary historiography for some time. Protest movements in the past two decades have labeled them "fascist" which they clearly are not.[50] And yet, it is equally unconvincing to argue that these societies somehow only sprang up after 1943, 1944/45, or 1949 in the wake of the defeat of the Nazi regime. Instead, they were part of the Third Reich and its occupation regime. They were implicated in the regime's crimes, yet they outlived the regime with extraordinary ease and impunity. The absence of resistance from key sectors of European economy and society is indeed notorious, and yet these sectors slipped away from the Nazi regime as if they were just changing their skins.[51] They ultimately provided the forces that destroyed the remnants of the National Socialist regime to build new institutions.

Even if we limit ourselves to Germany, this process was anything but a homogeneous development. In fact, the only homogeneity these societies produced was fictitious—including the fictions of Resistance as an authoritative, institutional, or pluralizing form of opposition against the Nazi regime. The success of these societies in overcoming the remnants of the Nazi state consisted in their relentless fracturing of homogeneity and the dissolution of state-controlled publics into competing and partial ones—until the Nazi elements had themselves shrunk into one microcosm among many. As such

---

[50] This debate formed the background for a far-reaching shift in the reception of resistance. During the 1970s resistance studies shifted from an audience of university professors and notables to a (young) mass audience in search of enlightenment about the past, and from the celebratory style of official commemorations to media-driven events. With the increasingly public and even civic nature of the concern with resistance during the 1970s and 1980s came new forms of scholarly exploration and information. Historical exhibitions, TV docudramas, and the like became the new outlet for satisfying civic curiosity. These novel forms of research and dissemination were driven by an expansive and affluent, university-educated intellectual class that spoke for large segments of the postwar generation in both Germanies and appropriated the resistance against the Nazi regime in coming to terms, and more often in coming to blows, with their parents. The search for alternative identities was undoubtedly a prevalent theme. But even there it is useful to distinguish between a prevalent consumption of history (as a way of incorporating and, quite manifestly, undoing the past) that became a predilection of so many Germans in the 1980s and the roughly simultaneous, activist uses of a new and expansive notion of resistance. This call for civil disobedience, nonconformity or "resistance" reached its high point in the New Social Movements. Past and present were intrinsically linked and hopelessly conflated. Resistance studies became part of that mass phenomenon of the 1980s in which the recovery of memory and, particularly, of the memory of victims of the National Socialist regime ran over messily into a sense of victimization and a good deal of breast beating. Note, however, that the revolution took place elsewhere.

[51] Peter Hayes, *Industry and Ideology: IG Farben in the Nazi Era* (Cambridge and New York, 1987); Ludolf Herbst, *Der totale Krieg und die Ordnung der Wirtschaft: Die Kriegswirtschaft im Spannungsfeld von Politik, Ideologie und Propaganda, 1933–1945* (Stuttgart, 1982).

the newly miniaturized Nazi society survived to burst forth occasionally in moments of crisis and reorientation as, for example, in the mid-1960s.

The rupturing of National Socialist institutionalized publics, in turn, was more than an incidental response to the Nazi regime—the consequence of Nazi polymorphousness or simply the chaos of war. It was rather one moment, and a crucial one at that, in the "structural transformation of the public sphere"[52] that originated from the competing organization of totalizing publics of Catholics, socialists, and nationalists since the turn of the century and the fracturing of these organized social spheres.[53] In view of the military defeat of the Third Reich the dissolution of the nationalist/National Socialist public was perhaps least effective and most delayed because its dissolution never became an issue of open contestation. This was due to the absence of resistance and the complicity of the Resistance Myth in the violent transformation of Europe that had made the postwar societies. The Nazi regime had been destroyed, but its traces were everywhere. The nationalist public really only broke apart in conjunction with the fraying of one of its grand competitors in the 1960s and 1970s: the Catholic-Christian effort to organize a national public. The last to follow was the socialist-communist public in 1989—and not surprisingly this collapse was pushed by resisters but executed through the wholesale disbanding of any and every public into a world as seen by Kaspar Hauser, in which "everyman [is] for himself and god against all." In 1990 as in 1945, it was not resisters but pragmatic politicians who began to build new institutions; it was the opportunism of consumption that dissolved the remnants of despotic regimes.

But did they create a more civil society? Did they make the effort to recreate the social, familial, ethnic, political, and human ties that were sundered by tyrannical rule which was at the origin of all postwar societies? Did they admit "difference and differentiation within one's own boundaries"?[54] Only thus could be countered the most noxious impact of National

[52] The reference to Jürgen Habermas, *The Structural Transformation of the Public Sphere: An Inquiry into a Category of Bourgeois Society* (Cambridge, Mass., 1989) can only be ironic because my argument is that the twentieth century has its own publics and that they are at the very center of contestation. See now Jean L. Cohen and Andrew Arato, *Civil Society and Political Theory* (Cambridge, Mass., and London, 1992) for a not entirely convincing, because too presentist, argument that suffers from the obfuscation of the historical conjuncture of the 1930s and 1940s as the crucial turning point in the constitution of publics.

[53] Michael Geyer, "Krieg, Staat und Nationalismus im Deutschland des 20. Jahrhunderts," in *Deutschland und Europa: Kontinuität und Bruch: Gedenkschrift für A. Hillgruber,* ed. Jost Dülffer et al. (Berlin, 1990), pp. 250–72.

[54] Miriam Hansen, "Unstable Mixtures, Dilated Spheres: Negt's and Kluge's *Public Sphere and Experience,* Twenty Years Later," *Public Culture* 5, no. 2 (1993): 179–212.

Socialism: the self-evident process of exclusions that separated and segregated European society.

As long as there is doubt about the latter there will be resistance; this resistance will find inspiration in the practice of opposition against the Third Reich, however insignificant the latter may have been. Resistance against the Third Reich has become the crucible for the oppositional task that marks the age: how to create civil society from the ruins of organized and totalizing publics, how to shape relations that are bounded and yet acknowledge the humanity of others, and how to articulate identities while acknowledging difference.[55] This is the bequest that Bonhoeffer passed on to a new generation in 1944. It has lost none of its urgency after 1989.

[55] Andreas Huyssen, "After the Wall: The Failure of German Intellectuals," *New German Critique* 52 (Winter 1991): 109–43.

Index